ONLINE DELIBERATION

CSLI Lecture Notes Number 182

ONLINE DELIBERATION
Design, Research, and Practice

Edited by
Todd Davies and
Seeta Peña Gangadharan

CSLI
PUBLICATIONS
Center for the Study of
Language and Information
STANFORD, CALIFORNIA

Printed in the United States
13 12 11 10 09   1 2 3 4 5

Library of Congress Cataloging-in-Publication Data

Online deliberation: design, research and practice /
by Todd Davies and Seeta Peña Gangadharan

p.   cm. – (CSLI lecture notes ; no. 182)

Includes bibliographical references and index.

ISBN-13: 978-1-57586-554-6 (pbk. : alk. paper)
ISBN-10:   1-57586-554-8 (pbk. : alk. paper)

1. Deliberative democracy–Online chat groups 2. Deliberative democracy–Electronic
discussion groups 3. Political participation–Online chat groups 4. Political
participation–Electronic discussion groups 5. Internet–Political aspects.
I. Davies, Todd, 1961- II. Gangadharan, Seeta Peña, 1974- III. Title. IV. Series.

JF799.O55 2010
323'.04202854693 –dc22

2009031800

CIP

∞ The acid-free paper used in this book meets the minimum requirements of the
American National Standard for Information Sciences—Permanence of Paper for
Printed Library Materials, ANSI Z39.48 -1984.

CSLI was founded in 1983 by researchers from Stanford University, SRI International, and
Xerox PARC to further the research and development of integrated theories of language,
information, and computation. CSLI headquarters and CSLI Publications are located on the
campus of Stanford University.

CSLI Publications reports new developments in the study of language, information, and
computation. Please visit our web site at
http://cslipublications.stanford.edu/
for comments on this and other titles, as well as for changes
and corrections by the authors, editors, and publisher.

Contents

Part II   Online Dialogue in the Wild

Part III   Online Public Consultation

Part IV   Online Deliberation in Organizations

Part V   Online Facilitation

Part VI   Design of Deliberation Tools

Contributors

SAMEER AHUJA: Department of Computer Science, Virginia Tech, Blacksburg, VA 24061, USA.
safall07@vt.edu

ADAM BLISS: Bellevue, WA, USA.
abliss@gmail.com

ROBERT CAVALIER: Department of Philosophy, Carnegie Mellon University, Pittsburgh, PA 15213-3890, USA.
rc2z@andrew.cmu.edu

ALEX COCHRAN: Intuit Inc., 190 Jefferson Drive, Menlo Park, CA, 94025, USA
acochran@stanfordalumni.org

MARK COOPER: 504 Highgate Terrace, Silver Spring, MD, USA.
MarkCooper@aol.com

DANA DAHLSTROM: Department of Computer Science and Engineering, University of California San Diego, La Jolla, CA 92093-0114, USA.
dana@cs.ucsd.edu

MICHAEL DALE: Wikimedia Foundation, 39 Stillman Street, San Francisco, CA 94107, USA.
dale@ucsc.edu

TODD DAVIES: Symbolic Systems Program, Stanford University, Stanford, CA 94305-2150, USA.
davies@csli.stanford.edu

MARILYN DAVIS: UCSC-Extension, 10420 Bubb Road, Cupertino, CA 95014, USA.
marilyn@deliberate.com

MATTHEW W. EASTERDAY: Human-Computer Interaction Institute, School of Computer Science, Carnegie Mellon University, Pittsburgh, PA 15213-3891, USA.
mwe@andrew.cmu.edu

JONATHAN EFFRAT: Google Inc., 1600 Amphitheatre Parkway, Mountain View, CA 94043, USA.
jje@cs.stanford.edu

DANYEL FISHER: Microsoft Research Redmond, One Microsoft Way, Redmond, WA 98052, USA.
danyelf@microsoft.com

JAMES S. FISHKIN: Center for Deliberative Democracy, Department of Communication, Stanford University, Stanford, CA 94305-2050, USA.
jfishkin@stanford.edu

DAVID FONO: 27 Heathdale Road, Toronto, ON M6C 1M7, Canada.
fono@mobilefono.com

SEETA PEÑA GANGADHARAN: Department of Communication, Stanford University, Stanford, CA 94305-2050.
whoa@stanford.edu

MARALEE HARRELL: Department of Philosophy, Carnegie Mellon University, Pittsburgh, PA 15213, USA.
mharrell@cmu.edu

JORDAN S. KANAREK: frog design, 660 Third St., San Francisco, CA 94107, USA.
jordansimonkanarek@gmail.com

ANDREA KAVANAUGH: Department of Computer Science, Virginia Tech, Blacksburg, VA 24060, USA.
kavan@vt.edu

JOHN KELLY: 365 West 123rd Street, New York, NY 10027, USA.
kjw1@columbia.edu

EUN-MEE KIM: Department of Communication, Yonsei University, Seoul, Korea.
milthop@googlemail.com

MISO KIM: 4716 Ellsworth Avenue Room 806, Pittsburgh, PA 15213, USA.
misok@andrew.cmu.edu

DOMINIQUE KREZIAK: Institut de Recherche en Gestion et Économie, Université de Savoie, 74944 Annecy, France.
dominique.kreziak@univ-savoie.fr

GILLY LESHED: Information Science, Cornell University, Ithaca, NY 14850-4623, USA.
gl87@cornell.edu

AZI LEV-ON: Department of Political Science, Stanford University, Stanford, CA 94305-6044, USA.
azilevon@gmail.com

ARTHUR LUPIA: Department of Political Science, University of Michigan, Ann Arbor, MI 48109-1045, USA.
lupia@isr.umich.edu

BERNARD MANIN: Department of Politics, New York University, New York, NY 10012, USA.
bm20@nyu.edu

HÉLÈNE MICHEL: Groupe ESC Chambéry, Savoie Technolac, 73381 Le Bourget du Lac Cedex, France.
H.MICHEL@esc-chambery.fr

BENJAMIN NEWMAN: Mozilla Foundation, 650 Castro Street, Suite 300, Mountain View, CA 94041-2021, USA.
benjamin@cs.stanford.edu

BRENDAN O'CONNOR: Language Technologies Institute, Carnegie Mellon University, Pittsburgh, PA 15213-3891, USA.
brenocon@gmail.com

TOMAS OHLIN: Ministry of Integration and Gender Equality-Democracy Unit, SE-10333 Stockholm, Sweden.
tomas@telo.se

ANDREW PARKER: Union Square Ventures, 915 Broadway, Suite 1408, New York, NY 10010-7143, USA.
andrew.parker@gmail.com

MANUEL PÉREZ-QUIÑONES: Department of Computer Science, Virginia Tech, Blacksburg, VA 24061, USA.
mperezqu@vt.edu

JACKIE PHAHLAMOHLAKA: Council for Scientific and Industrial Research, Pretoria 0001, South Africa.
jphahlamohlaka@csir.co.za

MARK E. PHAIR: Bellevue, WA, USA.
mphair@gmail.com

RAYMOND J. PINGREE: School of Communication, Ohio State University, Columbus, OH 43210-1339, USA.
pingree.2@osu.edu

VINCENT PRICE: Annenberg School for Communication, University of Pennsylvania, Philadelphia, PA 19104, USA.
vprice@asc.upenn.edu

KEVIN S. RAMSEY: Department of Geography, University of Washington, Seattle, WA 98195-3550, USA.
kramsey@u.washington.edu

KATE RAYNES-GOLDIE: Department of Internet Studies, Curtin University of Technology, Perth, Western Australia.
kate@k4t3.org

JUNE WOONG RHEE: Department of Communication, Seoul National University, Seoul, Korea.
june.w.rhee@gmail.com

ELISABETH RICHARD: Public Works and Government Services Canada, 4900 Yong Street, Toronto, ON M2N 6A6, Canada.
elisabeth.richard@pwgsc.gc.ca

GUNNAR RISTROPH: 1703 Johnson Way, Round Rock, TX 78681, USA.
gristroph@gmail.com

WARREN SACK: Film and Digital Media Department, University of California, Santa Cruz, CA 95064, USA.
wsack@ucsc.edu

DAVID SCHLOSBERG: Department of Politics and International Affairs, Northern Arizona University, Flagstaff, AZ 86011-5036, USA.
David.Schlosberg@nau.edu

DOUGLAS SCHULER: The Evergreen State College, Olympia, WA 98505-0002, USA.
douglas@cpsr.org

PETER M. SHANE: Moritz College of Law, Ohio State University, Columbus, OH 43210-1391, USA.
Shane.29@osu.edu

BAYLE SHANKS: Computational Neurobiology Graduate Program, University of California, La Jolla, CA 92093, USA.
bshanks@ucsd.edu

STUART SHULMAN: Department of Political Science, University of Massachusetts-Amherst, Amherst, MA 01003, USA.
stu@polsci.umass.edu

MARC SMITH: Telligent Research, 2617 Hallmark Drive, Belmont, CA 94002, USA.
marc.smith.email@gmail.com

AARON TAM: Acumen, LLC, 500 Airport Boulevard, Suite 365, Burlingame, CA 94010, USA.
aarontam@stanfordalumni.org

MATTHIAS TRÉNEL: Zebralog-Cross Media Dialogues, 10115 Berlin, Germany.
trenel@zebralog.de

HOSSANA TWINOMURINZI: Department of Informatics, University of Pretoria, Pretoria 0002, South Africa.
twinoh@gmail.com

MATTHEW W. WILSON: Department of Geography, Ball State University, Muncie, IN 47306, USA.
mwwilson@bsu.edu

SCOTT WRIGHT: School of Political, Social, and International Studies, University of East Anglia, Norwich NR4 7TJ, United Kingdom.
Scott.Wright@uea.ac.uk

ZACHARY SAM ZAISS: 705 East Republican Street #502, Seattle, WA 98102, USA.
zaiss@alumni.cmu.edu

STEVE ZAVESTOSKI: Department of Sociology, University of San Francisco, San Francisco, CA 94117, USA.
smzavestoski@usfca.edu

Preface

The present volume, *Online Deliberation: Design, Research, and Practice*, grew out of the Second Conference on Online Deliberation: Design, Research, and Practice (OD2005/DIAC-2005), which was held at Stanford University May 20-22, 2005. After the conference, participants were offered the opportunity to submit draft manuscripts for publication. Beth Simone Noveck assisted in the selection, and we secured an agreement with CSLI Publications to publish the book simultaneously in print and in a free version online. Seeta Gangadharan joined the project as a coeditor in 2008, and contributed a concluding chapter.

In the age of the Internet, and especially in a field tied to evolving technology, it would be difficult to justify the time required to carefully edit a book whose purpose was to capture the latest technology. Instead, we sought to put together a collection that will have lasting value, capturing some of the most important lessons learned during the formative years of this field. The result, we hope, is a volume that will serve as a useful record and guide to the development of the field as we move forward in the years to come.

There are several people we would like to thank: Beth Noveck for her help in the early stages of this project, Dikran Karagueuzian of CSLI Publications for his friendly helpfulness and patience, Robert Cavalier and Peter Shane for helping to organize the Stanford conference, Socoro Relova and Natalie Mendoza for providing staff support, Jim Fishkin for providing help and advice in organizing the conference and since, Fiorella De Cindio and Jerry Feldman for reviewing and vetting the manuscript, and all of the authors for sticking with this project through publication. We are most grateful.

–Todd Davies and Seeta Peña Gangadharan, Stanford, August 29, 2009

Online Deliberation: Design, Research, and Practice.
Todd Davies and Seeta Peña Gangadharan (eds.).
Copyright © 2009, CSLI Publications.

Introduction

The Blossoming Field of Online Deliberation

TODD DAVIES

> E-democracy may be the 21st century's most seductive idea. Imagine technology and democracy uniting to overcome distance and time, bringing participation, deliberation, and choice to citizens at the time and place of their choosing. Goodbye, then to 'attack ads' and single-issue politics — and to dimpled chads. E-democracy will return the political agenda to citizens. Or so the dream goes. —Keith Culver (2003)

1 Why 'Online Deliberation'?

The present decade has seen a blossoming of software tools, research projects, and everyday practice that can loosely be characterized under the heading of 'online deliberation'. A community has formed around this concept, and has met in international conferences, workshops, and special interest group sessions. The present volume, which grew out of the Second Conference on Online Deliberation in 2005, is an edited collection of research, experience, and insights that I, along with Beth Noveck (who helped select the papers) and Seeta Gangadharan (the coeditor of this volume), felt should be preserved and organized as a record of that conference and as a snapshot of the field during its early years. The chapters of this book do not include all of the work that has come to define the field, but several of the prominent early advocates of 'online deliberation' are represented here, along with a few of their critics.

Online Deliberation: Design, Research, and Practice.
Todd Davies and Seeta Peña Gangadharan (eds.).

Copyright © 2009, CSLI Publications.

1

The online deliberation community was born of both frustrations and possibilities. Some of these are touched on in the quotation above from Keith Culver. In large-scale 'democracies', for example, the complexity and reach of political decisions appears to be overwhelming the capacity of most citizens to make well-informed voting choices and to have an acceptable level of influence on governments. Even at much smaller scales— neighborhoods and organizations for example—the pace of contemporary life in industrialized societies, and the globalized forces of control that seem to dictate much of life around the world, can leave one feeling alienated from decisions that affect one's life. In these circumstances, the Internet in particular has seemed to many of us to be a potential antidote. The 20th Century saw a massive centralization of power over flows of information, through one-way mass media such as radio and television. The Internet, by contrast, is a two-way, many-to-many medium with the potential, now arguably being realized, to open communication to almost everyone in a medium that is not centrally controlled and that is flexible enough to facilitate citizen action (Rheingold 1999; Shane 2004).

Whether the Internet will continue to be maintained and developed as an open medium conducive to democracy is an important question, and is far from settled.[1] Online deliberation advocates generally rely on the vision of a communication network that is relatively unencumbered for deliberative activity, but many now realize that topics such as Internet governance and communication law and policy have profound implications for the dream of e-democracy. Another crucial issue is the ongoing existence of 'digital divides'—inequalities of access and capacity that reflect and can exacerbate social and economic inequity between individuals, groups, and polities (Norris 2001; Riley 2007). Again, the online deliberation field has become identified with some assumptions about the future course of such divides, namely that they can be overcome sufficiently so that online deliberation does not amplify inequalities. But this too must be watched and acted upon by online deliberation advocates.

The focus of this book is not the Internet, society, and politics generally, but rather work that is especially related to online deliberation tools and their use. 'Deliberation' denotes 'thoughtful, careful, or lengthy consideration' by individuals, and 'formal discussion and debate' in groups (Collins English Dictionary 1979). We are therefore primarily interested in online communication that is reasoned, purposeful, and interactive, but the power and predominance of other influences on political decisions (e.g. mass me-

---

[1] For some different possible futures, see Benkler (2006), Lessig (2004), and Zittrain (2008).

dia, appeals to emotion and authority, and snap judgments) obviously make them relevant to the prospects for deliberative e-democracy.[2]

The term 'online' is difficult to define precisely, but could be read to include any electronic communication medium that augments our usual abilities to see or hear information separated from us in time or space and to communicate with other people, and that does so on demand. In addition to the Internet, this would include telephone and teleconferencing systems, broadcasting, and electronic tools for presenting information in face-to-face meetings.

A focus on *deliberation*, as opposed to the many other forms of communications that occur online and that bear on democracy (e.g. social networking, Internet campaigning), reflects another set of frustrations and possibilities. The possibility comes from the flexibility of information and communication technology, which appears to make deliberation online possible and even, possibly, superior to offline deliberation in cases where information access, time demands, and other constraints limit deliberation's potential face-to-face. But the frustration is that deliberative activity of the kind defined above has been slow to gain traction on the Internet relative to communication that is more geared toward entertainment and toward personal rather than collective needs.

Deliberation online turns out to be a hard problem. Perhaps because it runs against the grain of how people naturally spend time online (and offline), or because deliberative democracy has not been high on the agenda for people designing tools for profit or personal gain, or because it is a more complex task that requires more technology than the early Internet made available, the dream that technology can facilitate a more deliberative society has been at best slow to be realized. The challenges, though, appear exciting for many. Hence the field, and this book.

2 Out of Many Communities

A common question underlies the work represented in this book: Can online tools be designed and used in ways that significantly enhance the quality of our discussion and decision making? But there are many communities and individuals who have been addressing this question, often without awareness of each other. As a first cut, we might classify efforts as primarily concerned with one or more of the following endeavors:

- *design* — the creation of online tools for deliberation;

---

[2] This paragraph is slightly adapted from the call for participation distributed prior to OD2005.

- *research*—studying the effects of online tools for deliberation via theories, observations, or experiments; and
- *practice*—using online tools as a participant in or facilitator of deliberative activity.

Although there is much overlap between them, these endeavors tend to draw people from different communities, with different sets of goals. Design typically involves software developers, user interface and human-computer interaction specialists, and a growing set of people interested in both deliberation and tool creation. Research is spread across various disciplines, including communication, information science, political science, computer science, sociology, psychology, organizational behavior and management science, philosophy, and public policy, and takes place in universities, corporate laboratories, nongovernmental organizations, and government agencies. The practice of online deliberation can of course involve anyone with the necessary access and skills to use available tools, but is especially common among politically active citizens and those whose work involves deliberation online, including online facilitators and dialogue and deliberation professionals.

Each of the fields mentioned above has a large and growing body of artifacts and literature relating to online deliberation. In the call for participation for OD2005, we noted:

> Human-computer interaction approaches emanating from computer science tend to emphasize tool design and the use of networked computing by teams of problem solvers,[3] while more theoretical work in computer science has focused on designs for secure voting systems.[4] Political communication researchers, on the other hand, tend to study the effects of Web access or messaging software on civic engagement or voting among citizens outside of their work environments.[5] Social choice theorists have developed powerful aggregation procedures that are now feasible given the storage and computing capacity of the Internet.[6] Meanwhile, there is a great deal being done and written by practitioners outside of academia that is changing how people work and dialogue together online.[7]

---

[3] See, e.g., the proceedings of the Computer Supported Cooperative Work (CSCW) conferences and the CRIWG—International Workshop on Groupware series.

[4] See Helger Lipmaa's electronic voting links. Available at http://web.archive.org/web/20050407054759/http://www.tcs.hut.fi/~helger/crypto/link/protocols/voting.html (last accessed January 24, 2009)

[5] See for example the online journals *IT & Society* (especially Price and Capella (2002)) and *Journal of Computer Mediated Communication*.

[6] See Casella, Gelman, and Palfrey (2003) and Shah (2003).

[7] See Rheingold (2002) and Allen (2004).

The challenge in creating a field for those involved in online deliberation is to identify, bring together, and organize the many strands of work that bear on this topic. Doing so has many potential benefits. When our work is fragmented and we are isolated from those who could influence us, we are much less likely to take advantage of what has been learned by others. Efforts are duplicated, and we may fail to see which problems have already been solved, which ones we may contribute to solving, and which ones have proven intractable after much work. Bringing communities together under these circumstances helps facilitate communication and organization needed for the field to progress, fostering relationships, collaboration, and institutional infrastructure that includes funding, professional recognition, and stable venues for sharing.

Recognizing the potential impact of bringing people together from these different communities related to online deliberation and electronic democracy, several initiatives with this aim have appeared in the last six years. From academia, U.S. efforts were spearheaded by Peter Shane, Peter Muhlberger, and Robert Cavalier at Carnegie Mellon University. With funding from the Hewlett Foundation, Shane and Muhlberger organized the 'Prospects for Electronic Democracy' conference in September 2002, which resulted in an edited volume that included several chapters focused on online deliberation specifically (Shane 2004). A National Science Foundation grant funded Cavalier, Muhlberger, and Shane to organize the first conference on online deliberation, titled 'Developing and Using Online Tools for Deliberative Democracy' at Carnegie Mellon in June 2003. This has been followed by online deliberation conferences at Stanford in May 2005 and Berkeley in June 2008 (Foster and Schuler 2008).

Other organizations aimed at bringing together dialogue and deliberation practitioners with academic researchers have also sponsored working groups, documentation of practice, and meetings related to online deliberation. These organizations include the Deliberative Democracy Consortium and its online working group (the ODDC), the National Coalition on Dialogue and Deliberation (NCDD), the Canadian Community for Dialogue and Deliberation (C2D2), the International Association for Public Participation (IAP2), the Online Community Research Network (OCRN), and various initiatives associated with e-democracy pioneer Steven Clift (Publicus.net).

In Europe, online deliberation has been a topic within several initiatives, including the Towards Electronic Democracy (TED) program of the European Science Foundation, the Council of Europe's Ad-hoc Committee on E-Democracy (CAHDE), DEMO-net—the eParticipation Network of Excellence (funded by the European Commission), the eParticipation Trans-

European Network for Democratic Renewal & Citizen Engagement (funded by eTEN), and the recently formed Pan-European e-Participation Network (PEP-NET).

The above paragraphs illustrate the confusing and evolving landscape of terms and acronyms revolving around online deliberation: e-democracy, e-participation, online community, and so on. A definitive catalogue would be foolish to attempt, and would in any case be out of date in short order. Many of the more common terms (including 'online deliberation' itself) have entries on Wikipedia, and others can be found easily on the Web, with links that form an association network. Situations like this impel us toward synthesis—discovering what is common in the work of many communities and individuals, and toward the discovery of gaps between goal and achievement, where no one seems to have an answer yet. It also calls for attempts to identify what has been learned that will have lasting value. Developing a field to the point where it easily generates this kind of synthesis and analysis takes a long time. The early conferences on online deliberation and related concepts have initiated this process.

3   Organizing Questions

At OD2008 in Berkeley, James Fishkin said that one of the most important potential outcomes of bringing together people working in online deliberation is that it helps us clarify what are the organizing questions that define the field. These questions should help guide us in our future work, and a common recognition of them helps to tell us when progress has been made. What follows is one attempt to list and organize such questions.

We can begin by noting several sources of variety in the online deliberation community, a multiplicity of...

- *disciplines*—design, research, practice, and the various academic fields mentioned above;
- *institutional settings*—governments, formal and informal organizations, unorganized citizens, schools, businesses, and consultative forums that bring two or more of these together;
- *modalities*—speech, text, images, video, and immersive virtual environments;
- *technologies*—the Web, Usenet, IRC, email lists, message boards, wikis, blogs, cell phones, land lines, teleconferencing systems, smart rooms, low- or no-tech communication, etc.;
- *use contexts*—home, office, transit, etc.;
- *designs*—interfaces, facilitation structures, system features, etc.;
- *goals*—planning, law making, conflict resolution, commerce, learning, citizen action; and, of course,

- *populations*—ages, ethnicities, genders, etc.

A useful way to classify questions involves the distinction (Baron 2008) between the *normative* (how things should be ideally), the *descriptive* (how things are empirically), and the *prescriptive* (how we can change things for the better given real constraints). Each of the above sources of variety in online deliberation suggests normative, descriptive, and prescriptive questions.

We might imagine a matrix of these questions based on combinations of the above categories. Normatively, each source of variety can be translated as a 'Which is best?' question, especially when specifying a context. We might ask, for example, whether communication by voice or by text is preferable for some type of deliberation based on *a priori* criteria, such as the ability of the modality itself to convey complex information, assuming users are fully competent at speaking, listening, writing, and reading. As we let go of the ideal and focus on systems and people as they are, questions become more descriptive: Do real populations of deliberators achieve more with voice or text? Prescriptively, we can ask questions like: How can we design or facilitate text- (or voice-) based deliberation so that a target population will get the most out of the experience?

Throughout this space of possibilities, here is one progression of question types that illustrates how design, research, and practice can inform each other:[8]

What problems arise in practice and/or theory? This type of question can arise at any point in work on online deliberation, but seems especially likely to be informed by the experience of those who practice it in settings with real stakes, or whose work in the field is motivated by problems people face. A Deliberative Polling® practitioner (Fishkin 2009) might, for example, find that audiences are skeptical about the robustness of a polling result. How much can we rely on the poll to tell us what would happen if another group of pollers, using different materials and perhaps a different deliberation method and at a different time, had conducted the poll instead? This can also be noted as a theoretical objection by someone who has looked at the method and results of deliberative polls. Identifying the problem is a contribution to the field, albeit one that may leave us without a solution.

What techniques can be applied to solve a problem? When a problem is the starting point, one can try to develop a solution. If we take the robustness problem in Deliberative Polling, for example, a solution might involve a new technique that would appear, *a priori*, to reduce the sensitivity of poll

---

[8] The discussion below refers to Deliberative Polling in order to illustrate the progression of organizing questions. This is not meant to imply that Deliberative Polling is definitive of the field or to exclude other approaches to online deliberation.

results to the details of a deliberation exercise. A designer might put together a procedure for selecting reading materials and argue that the new procedure is more neutral than the one used previously. Since face-to-face Deliberative Polls are expensive and difficult to replicate, online deliberation appears more suited to experimental tests of robustness. A researcher might design an experiment to test reliability across different populations of poll facilitators and poll takers, choosing different sets of informative materials, presented in different ways, and so on, while of course being careful to distinguish their own innovations from the techniques that are approved under the trademark name of Deliberative Polling.

What measures should be applied to evaluating a technique? Designing a technique can itself be a contribution to the field, but for the OD community to judge whether the technique is valuable, we may need to agree on a set of measures. A common problem in evaluating deliberation, for example, is how we should measure its quality. If we think about techniques for enhancing the robustness of a Deliberative Poll, there are various ways that robustness can be measured. The developer of a technique might survey participants and ask them to express their confidence that the poll was fairly conducted. A full-blown test of reliability across conditions might require more data than is available (for example if each participant reports only their opinion at the beginning and end of a poll), so an experimenter might test for significant differences between group averages and argue that the statistical power of the test is sufficiently high. The questions here can become narrowly technical, but can also be highly philosophical.

What effects does a given technique have on an agreed measure? The development of techniques and measures can be just the starting point for future work. Once a measure is established as valid for some type of question, many people can apply it. Designers can evaluate their designs against others using the measure. Practitioners can adopt techniques and measures and do applied research. And, of course, learning about effects can influence future designs, research studies, and practice. If a technique for enhancing robustness were to be incorporated into online Deliberative Polling, for example, a researcher could compare it to some other technique of online deliberation on a standard measure, and report the effect of the variation. The field advances as it builds on previous work.

What principles emerge from testing for an effect in multiple studies? The highly multivariate nature of the online deliberation space means that any finding is likely to require testing in other environments, for replication, validation, or refinement. A pattern of finding similar effects (or a lack of effects) for a given type of comparison (e.g. offline versus online) can at some point imply a discovered principle, which is usually the product of many members of the community. For a principle to achieve wide acceptance, it will require validation in practice as well as in prototypes and laboratories. At the same time, principles that guide practice should be studied carefully by researchers. Clinical psychotherapy provides examples of how techniques and principles evolved toward wide acceptance among practitioners but found weak or no support when subjected to careful empirical tests (Dawes, Faust, and Meehl 1989).

The above approach to defining some organizing questions for the field of online deliberation might appear to be overly quantitative and analytical. It advocates carving up the space of possibilities into dimensions and asking questions that have quantifiable, generalizable answers. A more holistic or qualitative approach might sometimes be called for, however. I do not mean to suggest that case studies, impressionistic sharing of experience, intuitive arguments, and the like should not have a place in the field. Indeed, the vast space of possible tool and deliberation process designs seems to justify such approaches in the early stages of the field, and many of the chapters in this book (and published elsewhere) reflect that. In suggesting the types of questions discussed above as appropriate for the field, I am merely trying to say how online deliberation as a community of practice is most likely to make progress as it evolves. If the experience of other interdisciplinary enterprises is any guide, we are, I think, likely to get more systematic and rigorous in our approach, and in the standards that are applied to new work. I hope that, as this happens, we reserve space for the creative, the anecdotal, and the holistic, and that we will remain open to new vistas in our blossoming field.

4   An Overview of the Book

The book is organized into six parts, each of which is an attempt to group contributions under a unifying question. This is obviously an oversimplification, as the authors are all addressing multiple questions that may only sometimes overlap. As a record of the early work in online deliberation, however, these groupings appear to reflect distinct communities within the field.

The previous section of this Introduction was an attempt to define the field of online deliberation more comprehensively and long-term. The actual contributions in this book represent a snapshot of how this space has been explored in the coalescing of the field. What follows is a brief overview, designed as a guide to the rest of the book rather than a summary of each chapter.

Part I: Prospects for Online Civic Engagement

The unifying question for the first part of the book is: *Do online dialogue and online information about political issues have significant potential to improve the quality of citizens' political participation and judgments?*

All of the chapters in this part of the book focus on structured online deliberation exercises and what they can teach us about the future of democracy. The term 'online deliberation' really originated with this type of work among political communication researchers and political scientists, growing out of the 'deliberative democracy' movement in political theory and the face-to-face Deliberative Polls pioneered by James Fishkin.

James S. Fishkin opens the book with a chapter titled 'Virtual Public Consultation: Prospects for Internet Deliberative Democracy'. He reviews the theoretical and historical rationale for Deliberative Polling, and describes the results of recent online Deliberative Polls conducted using a voice interface. The online version produces results 'broadly similar' to the face-to-face 'deliberative weekend', but the effects appear more modest for an equivalent period of time. Still, the greater convenience and flexibility, and lower cost, of online deliberation are cited as reasons for optimism that this technique can be extended to longer periods and more issues with beneficial results for the quality of political judgment. **Vincent Price**'s chapter, 'Citizens Deliberating Online: Theory and Some Evidence' reports on the results of two extended studies of participants invited to attend online text deliberations about a Presidential election and health care policy, respectively. In addition to finding a positive relationship between participation in these sessions and political engagement, Price's results suggest that text-based chatrooms may produce more equal participation levels across individuals than does face-to-face discussion, and, also interestingly, that those holding minority views in a text chat session are if anything more likely than average to contribute to the discussion. These results are intriguing and may be related to the modality of communication (text). The contrasting modalities in Fishkin's and Price's studies invite further investigation.

Arthur Lupia emerges as both a supporter and skeptic of online deliberation's potential to extend citizen engagement in 'Can Online Deliberation Improve Politics? Scientific Foundations for Success'. Lupia argues that online deliberation is promising as a way to enhance civic education, but that its researchers and practitioners should pay more attention to psychological research elucidating people's cognitive limitations. He also argues that deliberation's effectiveness can only be measured when it is compared with the effects of information in the absence of deliberation. **Robert Cavalier with Miso Kim and Zachary Sam Zaiss** report on a series of structured online deliberation exercises in 'Deliberative Democracy, Online

Discussion and Project PICOLA (Public Informed Citizen Online Assembly)'. They used a multimedia environment in which participants conversed in audio with video-based moderators, and they found no significant differences on measured dependent variables between this approach and face-to-face deliberations similarly structured.

Part II: Online Dialogue in the Wild

Unifying question: *What patterns characterize political discourse online that has emerged outside of structured deliberation exercises?*

The four chapters in this part all focus on online discussion as it occurs naturally online, *viz* not as a result of invited participation in an online deliberation experiment. The authors draw lessons for how people interact politically online, and what factors are likely to affect deliberative behavior. One of the core issues in studying Internet dialogue is whether the Internet promotes discussion and information seeking primarily within like-minded communities, so that Internet users are less likely to be exposed to information and opinions at odds with their own views. This hypothesis was put forward by Cass Sunstein (2001)[9], and is addressed by three of the chapters in this part of the book.

In 'Friends, Foes, and Fringe: Norms and Structure in Political Discussion Networks', **John Kelly, Danyel Fisher, and Marc Smith** report on patterns of authorship in politically-oriented Usenet newsgroups. They find that, contrary to Sunstein's hypothesis, political newsgroups tend to be ideologically diverse, and that most post authors are more likely to engage with those who oppose than with those who agree with them. They find, however, that authors fall into different categories, with some engaging only the like-minded and others representing fringe viewpoints that isolate them within the group. **Warren Sack, John Kelly, and Michael Dale** develop a metric for the deliberativeness of Usenet discussion threads in 'Searching the Net for Differences of Opinion'. Referring again to Sunstein, who worried that 'The Daily Me' predicted by Negroponte (1995) would filter out viewpoints opposed to that of a given Internet user, Sack et al. write that they aim to create a 'Daily Not Me'—automatically finding diverse opinions through techniques like those they describe in their chapter.

Whereas both of the preceding chapters focus on Usenet, a pre-Web forum technology in which users gather more by topic than by ideological affiliation, **Azi Lev-On and Bernard Manin** examine the Sunsteinian debate over whether the Internet promotes homophily (like-minded clustering) in the context of the modern Web. They find a mixed picture, with the Web

---

[9] See Sunstein (2006) for a later, more nuanced perspective by the same author.

having some features that lead to homogeneity and others that lead to (unintended) exposure to opposing views. People do tend to filter out opposing content when they are easily able to do so, suggesting that as tools such as custom RSS readers become more commonplace, fewer users will encounter opposing views. **Sameer Ahuja, Manuel Pérez-Quiñones, and Andrea Kavanaugh** explore how a website might make it easier for users to find and discuss locally relevant content in 'Rethinking Local Conversations on the Web'. They describe a system they are designing called 'Colloki' that replicates many of the features of Web 2.0 in a community-based website.

Part III: Online Public Consultation

Unifying question: *How are online tools being used for official public input into government policies, and how could such processes be made more effective?*

The five chapters in this part of the book explore the record and potential of online tools used by governments to obtain input from citizens on matters of policy. Governments around the world have been creating ways to consult their citizenry online, and research that has looked at this has generally asked how effective such systems are (or could be) in improving citizen involvement in government decisions.

In 'Deliberation in E-Rulemaking? The Problem of Mass Participation', **David Schlosberg, Steve Zavestoski, and Stuart Shulman** report failing to find significant differences in the deliberativeness of electronic versus paper form commenters providing input on environmental regulations. They detect a potential in current U.S. Government commenting sites that they argue is underappreciated by environmental advocacy groups: that they facilitate individual comments that are more likely to affect policy than are form letter comments of the kind often promoted by organizations mobilizing their constituencies. **Peter M. Shane** takes a critical look at the U.S.'s e-rulemaking process in 'Turning GOLD into EPG: Lessons from Low-Tech Democratic Experimentalism for Electronic Rulemaking and Other Ventures in Cyberdemocracy'. Shane considers the potential for online public consultation to transform the way government works now into 'empowered participatory governance' or 'EPG' (Fung and Wright 2003). Dismissing technology barriers as a limiting factor for online participation in government decisions, Shane analyzes the barriers of inertia to both EPG and a more meaningful form of online public consultation than that currently practiced by the U.S. Federal Government, and concludes that locally based efforts will be needed to push the Federal Government into a more participatory model.

Hélène Michel and Dominique Kreziak's chapter, 'Baudrillard and the Virtual Cow: Simulation Games and Citizen Participation', describes an online simulation game called 'Vacheland' that was developed by a regional government in France to facilitate learning and communication about agriculture. Based on the game's lack of effect on users' attitudes, Michel and Kreziak express skepticism over the potential of simulation games to engage citizens more productively in policy areas outside their immediate experience. Along the way, they distinguish 'e-administration', 'e-government', and 'e-governance' as being about government for, of, and by the people, respectively. In another chapter, **Hossana Twinomurinzi and Jackie Phahlamohlaka** report on a preliminary study in 'Using Web Based Group Support Systems to Enhance Procedural Fairness in Administrative Decision Making in South Africa', with both positive and negative early findings. Their chapter illustrates the movement toward Web-based tools for citizen input in governments all over the world. Finally, one of the early advocates of online democracy going back to the early 1970s—**Tomas Ohlin**—describes a combined face-to-face and online public consultation in 'Citizen Participation Is Critical: An Example from Sweden'. Elderly citizens of a Stockholm suburb took part in large numbers and enthusiastically in a prioritizing exercise for city planning.

Part IV: Online Deliberation in Organizations

Unifying question: *What online tools and processes of deliberative decision making are being, or could be, used within organizations?*

The five chapters in this part describe different types of organizations' use of online tools for internal deliberation. This institutional setting contrasts with consultation between governments and citizens, and also with citizen-citizen dialogue. Themes of this work include how both governmental and nongovernmental organizations can function most effectively online, and how online tools change the nature of the organization itself.

Elisabeth Richard's chapter is titled 'Online Deliberation in the Government of Canada: Organizing the Back Office'. Canada has been an early adopter of online public consultation. Richard describes the set of government employee roles that have evolved to handle online interactions with the public, with the implication that these new ways of serving the public are significantly altering the structure of government in Canada, raising the profile of some tasks (e.g. facilitation) while lessening others (e.g. expertise). In 'Political Action and Organization Building: An Internet-Based Engagement Model', **Mark Cooper** explores the consequences of online engagement with members in politically-oriented, membership NGOs. He characterizes effective Internet-based organizing as a very challenging process that requires continual reporting of results and updating of the organization's goals, in ways that respond to members' goals and political circumstances.

In 'Wiki Collaboration Within Political Parties: Benefits and Challenges', **Kate Raynes-Goldie and David Fono** study the Green Party of Canada's use of a wiki for its Living Platform. Their interviews provide an early look at how wikis affect deliberation. The wiki presented a technical barrier for users early on, it sometimes failed to facilitate dialogue, and its flexibility allowed content to be created that might reflect negatively on the party. On the other hand, it promoted the refinement of the platform rather than mere dialogue about the platform, and provided an outlet for members to express themselves, which members seemed able to do once they learned how. **Gunnar Ristroph** provides another case study in 'Debian's Democracy'. While the citizens of this democracy (open source software developers) are among the most technically literate people in the world, the long-term stability of Debian's online governance model provides an existence proof that asynchronous discussion via email lists can suffice for maintaining a fairly complicated set of internal rules in a constitutional document. Finally, **Dana Dahlstrom and Bayle Shanks** discuss 'Software Support for Face-to-Face Parliamentary Procedure'. They describe a system that allows an organization to keep track of a meeting under *Robert's Rules of Order*, and report the results of preliminary trials with a student government.

Part V: Online Facilitation

Unifying question: *How do the different ways of structuring and facilitating online deliberation affect its quality and quantity?*

This part features six chapters, focusing on the facilitation of deliberation forums and asking what effects different structures have on the amount and quality of participation, and on the longer-term consequences of a deliberation. Issues that arise in this area include whether and how moderators affect discussion, and the effects of variables such as anonymity, reward systems, and the composition of the deliberating group.

The chapter by **June Woong Rhee and Eun-mee Kim**, 'Deliberation on the Net: Lessons from a Field Experiment', explores many of the empirical issues related to structural and regulative variables. In an online experiment with voters during the 2004 Korean General Election, Rhee and Kim found several effects when they varied social identity cues (present versus anonymous), the presence or absence of a moderator, and reinforcement (a points system versus no system). Among their findings: moderation decreased message postings, anonymity produced more engagement, and the points system seemed to have positive effects. **Scott Wright** then discusses

'The Role of the Moderator: Problems and Possibilities for Government-Run Online Discussion Forums'. He points out that moderation can take many different forms. Building on earlier work, Wright analyzes the models of moderation employed in two online forums in Great Britain, and argues that censorship (message filtering) and facilitation should be separated into different roles, with message deletion, where necessary, done by an independent body following openly available rules. **Gilly Leshed**'s chapter, 'Silencing the Clatter: Removing Anonymity from a Corporate Online Community', describes a natural experiment in which the management of a company eliminated anonymous participation by workers in the firm's internal online community, following a series of postings that were deemed inappropriate. Mirroring Rhee and Kim's results, Leshed reports that removing anonymity in this setting significantly decreased both the number of postings and the amount of dialogue that occurred.

In 'Facilitation and Inclusive Deliberation', **Matthias Trénel** analyzes a field experiment conducted in an online forum for discussing the future of New York's World Trade Center site. Groups were given either 'advanced' or 'basic' facilitation, with the former type involving professional facilitators who took a more active role in steering and summarizing discussions. Nonwhite (especially) and women residents were less likely to register for the discussions, but advanced facilitation appeared to boost participation for both groups relative to the basic condition, indicating that a more active approach might draw out underrepresented participants once they are part of the process. In 'Rethinking the Informed Participant: Precautions and Recommendations for the Design of Online Deliberation', **Kevin S. Ramsey and Matthew W. Wilson** offer a critique of online consultation practices, using the example of maps as forms of data that are inherently political. They recommend interventions to enhance participants' ability to think critically about the information presented during a deliberation. Finally, **Mark E. Phair and Adam Bliss**'s 'Perlnomic: Rule Making and Enforcement in Digital Shared Spaces' describes the online game that they implemented. Players in Perlnomic vote on rule changes that are embodied in software code. The code awards points to those who make successful proposals, and this too is subject to debate. Perlnomic embodies a vision of online governance in which facilitation is done automatically, and Lawrence Lessig's famous phrase 'Code is law' becomes more true than ever (Lessig 1999).

Part VI: Design of Deliberation Tools

Unifying question: *What are online deliberation tools, and what principles should guide their design?*

The last part of the book focuses on software tools designed to support online deliberation and decision making. Six chapters describe tools designed for various uses and settings. Design is exciting because it offers a chance to implement and test our assumptions about what will lead to good deliberation. At the same time, it carries both responsibilities for the designer and risks for users. A lurking danger as we move toward e-democracy is the potential for *technocracy*—rule by those with technical skills, and by technology itself. Online deliberation system designers should be humble, open, and willing to work with people who are not programmers or designers. At the same time, their designs should reflect knowledge about end users' needs and likely behaviors. Work in this area typically draws on theory, research data, and practical experience, ideally from many sources, and explores how multiple goals and constraints can be satisfied in a unified design. A common feature of design papers in this area is the 'lessons learned' section. This reflects the trial-and-error character of designing for a complex task set, and is likely to be with us for some time.

The chapter entitled 'An Online Environment for Democratic Deliberation: Motivations, Principles, and Design' by **Todd Davies, Brendan O'Connor, Alex Cochran, Jonathan J. Effrat, Benjamin Newman, and Aaron Tam** recounts work by students and myself on the early versions of our tool: Deme (which rhymes with 'team'). We try to ground the design of this Web-based groupware in the needs of geographical communities such as East Palo Alto, California, where we did consulting research for the city's private nonprofit Community Network. Our design aims to satisfy four criteria: supporting the group, comprehensive support for deliberation-related tasks, maximizing desired participation, and maintaining high quality deliberation. Early experience with Deme led, among other conclusions, to the view that Web-based forums are generally more engaging for group members if they are integrated with email for both posting and notifying. **Douglas Schuler** describes another tool in 'Online Civic Deliberation with E-Liberate'. His system, also developed with students, was an early online implementation of *Robert's Rules of Order*. Parliamentary procedure is central to formal deliberation in the United States, so an online implementation seems like a natural place to start in developing a deliberation tool. Schuler argues that groupware designers should respect the accumulated wisdom embodied in *Robert's Rules* and should modify the rules only when they prove deficient. He reports that this perspective is at odds with that of many developers who prefer to start from scratch, but does note several features of the online environment that might justify deviations from parliamentary procedure. In 'Parliament: A Module for Parliamentary Procedure Software', **Bayle Shanks and Dana Dahlstrom** follow up on their contribution to Part IV with a detailed description of their software module implementing *Robert's Rules*. The module can be used in a variety of settings, including face-to-face deliberation and online meetings. A key feature of the module is its rule specification language, which allows the rules to be individually modified to match a given group's process needs.

In 'Decision Structure: A New Approach to Three Problems in Deliberation', **Raymond J. Pingree** describes a design for an Issue Congress, based on his Decision-Structured Deliberation (DSD) model (Pingree 2006). Pingree's design rethinks several assumptions about online deliberation software in order to address problems of scale, cognitive capacity, and imposed organization. He proposes more flexible and modular structures for organizing and labeling messages, and argues that an online environment has the potential to solve age-old problems of democracy. **Matthew W. Easterday, Jordan S. Kanarek, and Maralee Harrell**'s chapter, 'Design Requirements of Argument Mapping Software for Teaching Deliberation', focuses on tools for teaching argumentation skills. They analyze several existing tools according to six criteria: correct representation of argument structures, flexible construction, visual control, automation of extraneous tasks, multiple covisible diagrams, and cross platform compatibility. Finding other tools lacking on one or more of the criteria, they describe their own system, iLogos, and show how it meets all six criteria. Finally, **Marilyn Davis** describes 'Email-Embedded Voting with eVote/Clerk'. This system allows an email list to be used for voting. A way to make decisions seems crucial to online deliberation, and this system essentially converts an email list into a tool for decision making. The system makes it possible to trace how someone voted, which is at odds with the secret ballot. Davis argues that this is necessary, however, to ensure election integrity.

Epilogue, Appendix, and the Book Website

The book concludes with an epilogue, 'Understanding Diversity in the Field of Online Deliberation', by my coeditor **Seeta Peña Gangadharan**, drawing some lessons from the early years of research in this field and pointing toward the future. The Appendix lists online deliberation projects and applications. Any such list is obviously incomplete, but the book's website at Online-Deliberation.net will feature reader-driven updates of the list, with live links, together with the full text of the book.

References

Allen, C. 2004. *Tracing the Evolution of Social Software*. Available at http://www.lifewithalacrity.com/2004/10/tracing_the_evo.html (last accessed December 23, 2008)

Baron, J. 2008. *Thinking and Deciding*. 4th ed. Cambridge, UK: Cambridge University Press.

Benkler, Y. 2006. *The Wealth of Networks: How Social Production Transforms Markets and Freedom*. New Haven: Yale University Press.

Casella, A., A. Gelman, and T. R. Palfrey. 2006. An Experimental Study of Storable Votes. *Games and Economic Behavior* 57(1): 123-154.

Culver, K. 2004. The Future of E-Democracy. *OpenDemocracy.net*. November 13, 2004. Available at http://www.opendemocracy.net/null-edemocracy/article_1586.jsp (last accessed January 18, 2009)

Dawes, R. M., D. Faust, and P. E. Meehl. 1989. Clinical Versus Actuarial Judgment. *Science* 243(4899): 1668-1674.

Fishkin, J. 2009. Virtual Public Consultation: Prospects for Internet Deliberative Democracy. *Online Deliberation: Design, Research, and Practice*, eds. T. Davies and S. P. Gangadharan, 23-35. Stanford, CA: CSLI Publications.

Foster, D. and D. Schuler, eds. 2008. *Tools for Participation: Collaboration, Deliberation, and Decision Support (Berkeley, June 26-29)*. Stanford, CA: Computer Professionals for Social Responsibility.

Fung, A. and E. O. Wright. 2003. Thinking About Empowered Participatory Governance. *Deepening Democracy: Institutional Innovations in Empowered Participatory Governance*, eds. A. Fung and E. O. Wright, 3-42. New York: Routledge.

Lessig, L. 1999. *Code and Other Laws of Cyberspace*. New York: Basic Books.

Lessig, L. 2004. *Free Culture: How Big Media Uses Technology and the Law to Lock Down Culture and Control Creativity*. New York: Penguin Press.

Negroponte, N. 1995. *Being Digital*. New York: Knopf.

Norris, P. 2001. *Digital Divide: Civic Engagement, Information Poverty, And The Internet Worldwide*. Cambridge, UK: Cambridge University Press.

Pingree, R.J. 2006. Decision Structure and the Problem of Scale in Deliberation. *Communication Theory* 16: 198-222.

Price, V. and J. N. Capella. 2002. Online Deliberation and its Influence: The Electronic Dialogue Project in Campaign 2000. *IT & Society* 1(1). Available at http://www.stanford.edu/group/siqss/itandsociety/v01i01/v01i01a20.pdf (last accessed December 23, 2008)

Rheingold, H. 1999. *The New Interactivism: A Manifesto for the Information Age*. Available at http://www.voxcap.com/content/misc/interactivism.pdf (last accessed December 23, 2008)

Rheingold, H. 2002. *Smart Mobs: The Next Social Revolution*. New York: Basic Books.

Riley, D. 2007. America: The Growing Digital Divide. *TechCrunch*. May 6. Available at http://www.techcrunch.com/2007/05/06/america-the-growing-digital-divide/ (last accessed December 23, 2008)

Shah, R. 2003. Statistical Mappings of Social Choice Rules. M.S. Thesis, Stanford University. Available at http://www.stanford.edu/~davies/Shah_thesis.pdf (last accessed December 23, 2008)

Shane, P. M., ed. 2004. *Democracy Online: The Prospects for Political Renewal Through the Internet*. New York: Routledge.

Sunstein, C. 2001. *Republic.com*. Princeton: Princeton University Press.

Sunstein, C. 2006. *Infotopia: How Many Minds Produce Knowledge*. Oxford: Oxford University Press.

Zittrain, J. 2008. *The Future of the Internet and How to Stop It*. New Haven: Yale University Press.

Part I
Prospects for Online Civic Engagement

1

Virtual Public Consultation: Prospects for Internet Deliberative Democracy

JAMES S. FISHKIN

1 Introduction

Innovations in the technology of communication easily affect the possibility and feasibility of different methods of public consultation. To consult the public, we must somehow communicate with it, or allow it to communicate with itself. How this is done can affect both who is consulted and the kinds of opinions that are solicited.

Let us posit two fundamental democratic values for public consultation. The history of democratic practice and reform is a history enmeshed in visions that more greatly emphasize one or another of these values. I will term these two values 'deliberation', on the one hand and 'political equality' on the other. For our purposes here, we can simplify with some working definitions. By *deliberation* I mean the thoughtful weighing of policy or political alternatives on their merits, in a context that facilitates access to good information. By *political equality* I mean the attributes of a decision process whereby the preferences of each member are counted as having the same weight. When some portion of the population is consulted about the views of the rest, political equality implies representativeness. Deliberation is

Online Deliberation: Design, Research, and Practice.
Todd Davies and Seeta Peña Gangadharan (eds.).
Copyright © 2009, CSLI Publications.

about the development of preferences, and political equality is about how those preferences weigh in the decision process.[1]

This conflict has a long history. For example, in the debate over the founding of the United States, the Federalists emphasized deliberation (representatives were to 'refine and enlarge the public views') while the Antifederalists were, among the disparate values they emphasized, more interested in political equality. The Antifederalists embraced a 'mirror' notion of representation in which representatives should be exact replicas of the people as they are. They were concerned about the elite character of the Federalists' proposed deliberative institutions, institutions that might be dominated by the rich and educated. In opposing the Constitution they asked: Where will there be a farmer or blacksmith in the senate if it is going to be so small and selective? Ideally, as in their advocacy of a referendum in Rhode Island, decisions should be taken to the people themselves so that all their votes could be counted. And if decisions could not be taken by the people directly, they should be taken by people who were exactly like the entire people in microcosm. The Federalists opposed this notion (see Hamilton in *Federalist*, no. 35). Indeed their notion of refining public opinion involved refining the views of the public through deliberation as well as refining via the choice of representatives, selecting only the most competent, most virtuous and most qualified.

We can capsulize the debate by saying that the Federalists wanted *reflective* public opinion (refined by representatives) while the Antifederalists wanted *reflected* public opinion (provided by a mirror). The aspiration to somehow get both has played a key role in efforts to improve public consultation, both formal and informal. As we will see below, it is possible that the Internet may make such an aspiration more feasible than it has been previously.

2 Empowering the Public

In the two centuries since the debate over the American founding, the general direction of democratic reform has been to emphasize political equality over deliberation. We have brought power to the people through increasingly direct forms of consultation, without worrying too much about whether or not we have given the people much incentive to think about the power they are asked to exercise. We choose senators directly rather than

---

[1] For some more detailed reflections on the definition of these two values, see Fishkin (1991), chapter four. Of course these are not the only values that are implicated by efforts for democratic reform. The book discusses two others as well, participation and non-tyranny (avoiding tyranny of the majority).

through state legislatures, we have mass primaries for candidate selection, we have referenda in many states, and we constantly assess the pulse of the public via the public opinion poll. Yet, all these efforts serving political equality have given greater emphasis to mass opinion that is seldom deliberative. The mass public is typically uninformed and disengaged.[2] As Anthony Downs hypothesized, it can plausibly be considered 'rationally ignorant'. Each person having but a single vote can see that his or her vote (or opinion) will not make much difference to any public decisions, so it may not be worth a lot of time and effort to make oneself more informed (Downs 1957).[3]

Consider the moment of triumph for the public opinion poll. When George Gallup reflected on his successful use of the poll in the United States presidential election of 1936, he argued that it provided the basis for a serious democratic reform—one that would bring the democracy of the New England town meeting to the large-scale nation state. The poll is obviously an embodiment of political equality in that it offers a statistical microcosm of the entire electorate, and one in which each person's preferences count equally. More surprisingly, Gallup also thought its use would contribute to deliberation. Newspapers and radio would send out the views of competing policy makers. The public would talk over the issues and send back its considered judgments via the poll. It would be 'as if the nation is literally in one great room' (Gallup 1939). The difficulty is that the room was so big, no one was listening with the care that Gallup imagined for the town meeting.[4] Downsian arguments about the rationality of investing in political knowledge may come into play when small-scale political notions are applied to the large-scale nation state. The poll may help achieve political equality, but for uninformed and disengaged preferences. Later we will turn to different institutional designs, to achieve the 'whole country in one room' in a different way.

Note that Gallup's aspiration was to achieve political equality combined with the public's considered judgments or its more deliberative preferences. In effect, he hoped to combine reflective and reflected preferences. However, he achieved political equality in the representation of mostly uninformed and disengaged opinions. That achievement was greatly facilitated over time with some technical advances. Interviews were initially conducted face-to-face with quota samples. With the development of the tele-

---

[2] For an overview, see Carpini and Keeter (1996).

[3] For some thoughtful reflections on this argument, see Hardin (2003).

[4] The town meeting is not always what Gallup imagined. See Frank Bryan for the argument that participation and attention to the issues in the town meeting are inversely related to the size of the town (Bryan 2004).

phone and the invention of random digit dialing, it became practical to conduct polling without face-to-face interviewing, greatly lowering the costs for ever more continuously checking what Gallup called 'the pulse of democracy' (Gallup and Rae 1940).

3   Experimenting with Deliberation

As we look to other methods for combining political equality with deliberation, a key question will be whether or not the Internet will serve, as did the telephone before it, to lower the cost and increase the frequency of efforts to combine these two key values. Deliberative Polling® was developed explicitly to do so, to combine political equality with deliberation.[5] It is meant to include everyone (via random sampling) under conditions where the public can think. Deliberative Polling attempts to employ social science to uncover what deliberative public opinion would be on an issue by conducting a quasi-experiment, and then it inserts those deliberative conclusions into the actual public dialogue, or, in some cases, the actual policy process.

Deliberative Polling begins with a concern about the defects likely to be found in ordinary public opinion—the incentives for rational ignorance applying to the mass public and the tendency for sample surveys to turn up nonattitudes or phantom opinions (as well as 'top of the head' opinions that approach being nonattitudes) on many public questions. At best, ordinary polls offer a snapshot of public opinion as it is, even when the public has little information, attention or interest in the issue. Deliberative Polling, by contrast, is meant to offer a representation of what the public would think about an issue under good conditions. Every aspect of the process is designed to facilitate informed and balanced discussion.

Consider the face-to-face version. After taking an initial survey, participants are invited for a weekend of face-to-face deliberation. They are given carefully balanced and vetted briefing materials to provide an initial basis for dialogue. They are randomly assigned to small groups for discussions with trained moderators, and encouraged to ask questions arising from the small group discussions to competing experts and politicians in larger plenary sessions. The moderators attempt to establish an atmosphere in which participants listen to each other and no one is permitted to dominate the discussion. At the end of the weekend, participants take the same confidential questionnaire as on first contact and the resulting judgments in the final questionnaire are usually broadcast along with edited proceedings of the

---

[5] Deliberative Polling® is a trademark of James S. Fishkin. Any fees from the trademark are used to support research at the Stanford Center for Deliberative Democracy (http://cdd.stanford.edu, last accessed November 1, 2008).

discussions throughout the weekend.[6] The weekend microcosm tends to be highly representative, both attitudinally and demographically, both of the entire baseline survey and of census data about the population. In every case thus far, there have also been a number of large and statistically significant changes of opinion over the weekend. Considered judgments are often different from top of the head attitudes solicited by conventional polls. Looking at the full panoply of Deliberative Polls (which have been held on many different kinds of issues), we believe that perhaps two thirds of the opinion items change significantly following deliberation.

But what do the results represent? Our respondents are able to overcome the incentives for rational ignorance normally applying to the mass public. Instead of one vote in millions, they have, in effect, one vote in a few hundred in the weekend sample, and one voice in fifteen or so in the small group discussions. The weekend is organized in order to make credible the claim that their voice matters. They overcome apathy, disconnection, inattention, and initial lack of information. Participants from all social locations change in the deliberation. From knowing that someone is educated or not, economically advantaged or not, one cannot predict change in the deliberations. We do know, however, from knowledge items, that becoming informed on the issues predicts change on the policy attitudes. In that sense, deliberative public opinion is both informed and representative. As a result, it is also, almost inevitably, counterfactual. The public will rarely, if ever, be motivated to become as informed and engaged as our weekend microcosms.

If a counterfactual situation is morally relevant, why not do a serious social science experiment—rather than merely engage in informal inference or armchair empiricism—to determine what the appropriate counterfactual might look like? And if that counterfactual situation is both discoverable and normatively relevant, why not then let the rest of the world know about it? Just as Rawls's original position can be thought of as having a kind of recommending force, the counterfactual representation of public opinion identified by the Deliberative Poll also recommends to the rest of the population some conclusions that they ought to take seriously. They ought to take the conclusions seriously because the process represents everyone under conditions where they could think more carefully.

The idea may seem unusual in that it melds normative theory with an empirical agenda—to use social science to create quasi-experiments that will uncover deliberative public opinion. But most social science experiments are aimed at creating a counterfactual—the effect of the treatment

---

[6] For an overview, see Fishkin (1997). For more detailed analysis, see Luskin, Fishkin, and Jowell (2002).

condition. In this effort to fuse normative and empirical research agendas, the trick is to identify a treatment condition that embodies the appropriate normative relevance.

Two general questions can be raised about all research designs—questions of internal and external validity.[7] Sample surveys are relatively high on external validity. When they are done well, we can be fairly confident about generalizing the results to larger populations. By contrast, most social science experiments done in laboratory settings are high in internal validity: we can be fairly confident that the apparent effects are, indeed, the result of the experimental treatments. However, experiments done with college students, for example, lack external validity if the aim is to find out something about the general population.

If a social science experiment were to have relatively high internal validity, where we could be confident that the effects resulted from the normatively desirable treatment, and if it were also to have relatively high external validity where we could be confident about its generalizability to the entire citizen population, then the combination of those two properties would permit us to generalize the consequences of the normatively desirable property to the entire citizenry. We could be confident in the picture of a counterfactual public reaching its conclusions under normatively desirable conditions. In other words, if an experiment with deliberation were high on internal validity, then we could be confident that the conclusions were the result of deliberation (and related factors such as information). And if such an experiment were high on external validity then we could be confident about generalizing it to the relevant public of, say, all eligible voters. Only with both kinds of validity would the quasi-experiment called Deliberative Polling have any claim to represent the considered judgments of the people.

4 Online Deliberation

We have completed several full-scale Deliberative Polling projects on the Internet. The first, culminating in January 2002, was parallel to a national face-to-face Deliberative Poll on American foreign policy. The second took place during the presidential primary season in early 2004. The third was completed during the 2004 presidential election, while the last, as noted below, used a more cost effective methodology.

In the first three projects, a national random sample recruited by Knowledge Networks deliberated each week in moderated small group discussions. Computers were provided to those who did not have them. Microphones were provided to all participants so that the discussions could take

---

[7] See Campbell and Stanley (1963).

place using voice rather than text. Special software was employed that allows the small group participants to keep track of who is talking and who wishes to talk next. The discussions proceeded for an hour or an hour and fifteen minutes each week with carefully balanced briefing materials. During discussions, the participants identified key questions that they wished competing experts to answer. Our media partner, MacNeil/Lehrer Productions (including the Online Newshour with Jim Lehrer) provided the competing expert answers and distributed them to the participants in between the weekly discussions. After several weeks of these discussions, the participants took the same survey as at the beginning. Meanwhile, a separate control group that did not deliberate took the same questionnaire at the beginning and end of the process.

In the foreign policy Deliberative Poll, the results online were broadly similar to the face-to-face results. Respondents came to take more responsibility for world problems, preferring increases in foreign aid, more resources devoted to AIDS in Africa and world hunger, and more multilateral cooperation on military matters. These responses were plausibly connected to large increases in information (as measured by separate information questions). In the Presidential primary deliberative poll, the respondents also showed large increases in knowledge, both about policies and about particular candidate positions. In contrast to the control group, the issues played a major part in respondents' candidate preferences. In the control group, the evaluation of candidate traits dwarfed all other factors, while in the deliberative treatment group, policy issues became very important as well.

Eventually, Deliberative Polling on the Internet promises great advantages in terms of cost and in terms of flexibility in the time required of participants. National Deliberative Polls require the logistics of national transportation, hotels, and food. Two face-to-face Deliberative Polls have even had official airlines (American Airlines for the National Issues Convention in Austin, Texas, and Ansett for Australia Deliberates). Face-to-face Deliberative Polls also require that respondents give up an entire weekend for the deliberations as well as for travel to them. While we have used funds to ameliorate practical difficulties (paying for child care and even in one case providing a researcher to milk a respondent's cows during her absence), it is obvious that we lose some respondents because of the demands we place on them. Internet-based Deliberative Polls offer the promise of greater convenience and continuing dialogue.

As access to the Internet approaches the near universality of the telephone, and the digital divide (eventually) disappears, the Internet may well succeed in lowering the costs of deliberative public consultation with scientific samples just as the telephone lowered the cost of conventional polling. However, for the foreseeable future, the digital divide poses a serious problem, one that substantially raises the cost, and hence challenges the feasibility, of Deliberative Polling online.

The fourth Internet-based project, a collaboration with Polimetrix and with MacNeil/Lehrer Productions, points to an interim solution. Polimetrix uses a matching methodology to reverse engineer a national random sample from a one million plus national panel that is already online. Instead of starting with random digit dialing and having to live with low response rates, it constructs a sample in reverse from a large panel that has been constructed without any clue to what they might be asked about. On a host of demographic criteria, the process of sample construction attempts to mirror what a random sample taken from either census data or from voter lists, would look like.[8]

Sample selection in this process occurs in two stages. First, a true random sample is selected from the U.S. population, called the 'target sample'. For this study, the target sample was from the American Community Study, conducted by the U.S. Bureau of the Census. In the second stage, the closest matching respondent in the Polimetrix panel to each member of the target sample was found. 'Closeness' was measured by the respondent's demographic characteristics, including age, race, gender, education, marital status, and income.

Of course, perfectly realized random sampling would be preferable, but because of all the people who are difficult to reach and who refuse to participate when they are reached, perfectly realized random sampling is not a practical alternative. In the meantime, to the extent that such samples can plausibly represent the entire electorate, and not just those on the advantaged half of the digital divide, then the matching strategy offers a more cost effective alternative than starting with random digit dialing.

In any case, the key aims of the projects we are launching with Polimetrix depend more on internal validity than random selection. With a pre and post control group that is carefully matched to the participant sample, we can assess the effects of deliberation on opinion change without worrying about whether the changes are coming from the media and the wider world or from the treatment in the experiment. The degree of representativeness provided by sample matching provides more than adequate external validity.

To the extent that matching technology does approximate a good random sample of the entire electorate and to the extent that the treatment (de-

---

[8] For a detailed description with results, see http://cdd.stanford.edu/polls/btp/2005/onlinebtp/index.html (last accessed August 30, 2008).

liberation) produces the changes, there is a case to be made that the result combines external and internal validity. It is a public consultation that combines political equality (it is a representation of what political equality would produce, reverse engineered), and it embodies, by the end, the public's considered judgments. In that sense, it puts the whole country in one (virtual) room, under conditions where it can think for an extended period— a period of weeks so far, but perhaps eventually months.

Thus far, it is clear that the online version of Deliberative Polling is a more modest treatment than the one we produce face-to-face. Instead of the intensity of a deliberative weekend that totally immerses participants, hourly discussions take place in home environments. In between the sessions, the participants are subject to all their normal habits, news sources and conversation partners. These factors probably dampen the effects. However, online DPs have the potential to be extended longer. The face-to-face DP is limited to the duration of a long weekend. But online, the process could, in theory and with sufficient incentives, extend for months rather than just weeks. Perhaps the resulting treatment, if sufficiently extended, may eventually surpass the face-to-face process. One can only answer this question through further empirical work.

5   Strategies of Public Consultation

Deliberative Polling, like conventional polling, occurs at the intersection of social science and public consultation. But there are many efforts to consult the public that do not take such care either with political equality or with deliberation. Some practices are not representative and some do not solicit anything like informed and considered judgments. To fix thought, consider just these four simple possibilities:

	Unrepresentative	Representative
Nondeliberative	1	2
Deliberative	3	4

A great deal of public consultation now takes place on the Internet but most of it is in category 1. It is neither deliberative nor representative. The easiest way to consult the public, one might think, is just to ask them. But self-selected, top of the head consultations do not provide a microcosm of the public, and do not represent considered judgments.

Category 1 is exemplified by what Norman Bradburn of the University of Chicago has called the SLOP. We see it daily on media websites, such as CNN's which solicits a 'quick vote' from self selected samples on an ever changing array of topics. In the days of radio, the term SLOP referred to 'self-selected listener opinion poll'. Radio call-in shows would commonly ask for responses by telephone to some topic. Now the SLOPs have spread throughout the Internet. Media organizations like to solicit active involvement from the owners of eyeballs, and SLOPs accomplish this effectively. To be clear, SLOP respondents are not selected by scientific random sampling as in public opinion polls. The respondents instead select themselves. They are predominantly those who feel more intensely or are especially motivated. Sometimes, they are organized. The SLOP, it is thought, gets 'grassroots' opinion. However, in the parlance of American lobbyists, sometimes the response is something more organized and synthetic—the impression of grassroots that is really 'astroturf'.

A good example of the dangers of SLOPs came with the world consultation that Time magazine organized about the 'person of the century'. Time asked for votes in several categories, including greatest thinker, greatest statesman, greatest entertainer, greatest captain of industry. Strangely, one person got by far the most votes in every category, and it turned out to the same person. Who was this person who towered above all rivals in every category? Ataturk. The people of Turkey organized to vote, by post card, on the Internet, and by fax, and produced millions more votes, as a matter of national pride, than the rest of the world could muster for any candidate, just through individual, unorganized voting (Morris et al. 1997). More recently, SLOPs showed that Alan Keyes was a leading presidential candidate, because he had an organized and intense following that was willing to mobilize to vote over and over online. Without scientific sampling, but while still representing a tiny fraction of the population, SLOPs are open to capture.

Category 2 is of course represented by the conventional public opinion poll. Now with Internet technology, it is moving online. Some efforts employing mere post hoc weighting from self-selected samples have only suspect claims to representativeness. But other efforts, such as those of Knowledge Networks and Polimetrix, attack the problem of representativeness in more credible ways. In the Knowledge Networks case, the strategy is to begin with random sampling. In the Polimetrix case, the strategy is to reverse engineer the panel that would have resulted from good random sampling. In both cases, there is room for continuing empirical investigation as to how successful these efforts may be.[9]

But as we noted in our earlier discussion of Deliberative Polling, conventional polling, whether undertaken online, on the phone, or face-to-face, may achieve representativeness when done well, but will do nothing, despite Gallup's initial aspirations, for deliberation. Polls will tend to reflect

---

[9] In the Knowledge Networks case, see Chang and Krosnick (2003).

the public's top of the head impressions of sound bites and headlines. The views represented by polls are crippled, as we noted, by 'rational ignorance'.

A second difficulty is that the views reported by polls on complex political or policy matters are often crippled by a second factor—the tendency to report opinions that are not only based on little thought or reflection, but that may not exist at all. Phantom opinions or 'nonattitudes' are reported by polls because respondents almost never wish to admit that they do not know, even when offered elaborate opportunities for saying so.

Building on the classic work of Phil Converse of the University of Michigan, George Bishop and his colleagues at the University of Cincinnati dramatized this issue with their study of attitudes towards the so-called 'Public Affairs Act of 1975'. Large percentages of the public offered an opinion even though the act was fictional. The Washington Post more recently celebrated the twentieth 'unanniversary' of the nonexistent 'Public Affairs Act of 1975' by asking respondents about its 'repeal'. The sample was split, with half being told that President Clinton wanted to repeal the act and half being told that the 'Republican Congress' wanted its repeal. While such responses were based on a minimal amount of information (or misinformation provided to the participants, since the act did not exist in the first place), the information base was really just a response to a cue about who was for the proposal and who was against it.[10]

It is possible to have serious deliberation on the Internet but without representativeness. Self-selected forums can exchange information and come to grips with trade-offs. There is, however, a serious empirical question about the extent to which such efforts will be distorted by unrepresentativeness. When I do not hear opposing views or just commune with those with whom I already agree, I am less able to deliberate. I may engage in what Cass Sunstein (2001) calls 'enclave deliberation'—the reasoning together of the like minded. Sometimes enclave deliberation produces more extreme views (as in movements either to the far right or far left) and sometimes it lays the basis for important and constructive social movements that define a new center (consider the civil rights movement and the environmental movement). But whenever only the likeminded discuss a topic, the opportunity to weigh, and really take seriously, counterarguments and discrepant information has been limited. Ultimately, representativeness and deliberation can facilitate each other—if only we achieve the appropriate institutional designs.

---

[10] For a good overview of this work by George Bishop and the replication by the Washington Post under the direction of Richard Morin, see Bishop (2004).

The Deliberative Poll, filling out category 4, is one attempt to do this. Madison began with representatives refining and enlarging the public views. But to leave deliberation in the hands of representatives alone has been viewed as elitist and undemocratic. In a host of ways, we have brought power to the people, while we have, at the same time, ignored the conditions that might facilitate the public thinking about the power we would have them exercise. The Deliberative Poll is not the only such effort.[11] But we believe that by attempting to combine social science with public consultation, it offers prospects for realizing these two values on an ever improving basis—both to achieve representativeness and to fine tune the process of deliberation. If the online version manages to achieve cost effectiveness for national consultations, then it may finally result in Gallup's aspiration to put the whole country in one (virtual) room—but under conditions that aspire to adapt the town meeting to a national scale. Cost effectiveness is not just a matter of practicality. It is also necessary if episodic experiments are also to become a continuing part of democratic practice.

We have only begun to assess the implications of virtual democracy, and some of them, such as the proliferation of SLOPs and the communing of the like minded, may not be constructive. But if we think of democratic practice as a problem of institutional design, then new technologies allow us to experiment with improvements. Perhaps, eventually, we will be able to periodically take the 'pulse of democracy' in a more deliberative manner.

References

Bishop, G. 2004. *The Illusion of Public Opinion: Fact and Artifact in American Public Opinion*. Lanham, MD: Rowman and Littlefield.

Bryan, F. M. 2004. *Real Democracy: The New England Town Meeting and How It Works*. Chicago: University of Chicago Press.

Campbell, D. and J. Stanley. 1963. *Experimental and Quasi-Experimental Designs for Research*. Chicago: Rand-McNally.

Carpini, M. D. and S. Keeter. 1996. *What the American Public Knows and Why It Matters*. New Haven: Yale.

Chang, L. C. and J. A. Krosnick. 2003. *RDD Telephone vs. Internet Survey Methodology: Comparing Sample Representativeness and Response Quality*. Unpublished Paper, Ohio State University.

Downs, A. 1957. *An Economic Theory of Democracy*. New York: Harper and Row.

Fishkin, J. S. 1991. *Democracy and Deliberation: New Directions for Democratic Reform*. New Haven: Yale.

---

[11] See Gastil and Levine (2005) for an overview of many efforts to realize deliberative democracy.

Fishkin, J. S. 1997. *The Voice of the People: Public Opinion and Democracy*. Expanded Paperback Edition. New Haven: Yale University Press.

Gallup, G. 1939. *Public Opinion in a Democracy*. Princeton: The Stafford Little Lectures.

Gallup, G. and S. F. Rae. 1940. *The Pulse of Democracy*. New York: Simon and Schuster.

Gastil, J. and P. Levine, eds. 2005. *The Deliberative Democracy Handbook*. San Francisco: Jossey Bass.

Hardin, R. 2003. Street-Level Epistemology and Democratic Participation. *Debating Deliberative Democracy*, eds. J. S. Fishkin and P. Laslett, 163-181. Oxford: Basil Blackwell.

Luskin, R. C., J. Fishkin, and R. Jowell. 2002. Considered Opinions: Deliberative Polling in Britain. *British Journal of Political Science* 32: 455-87.

Morris, C., M. Tran, and A. Bellos. 1997. Is This the Man of the Century? *The Guardian* (October 30, 1997): 1.

Sunstein, C. R. 2001. *Republic.com*. Princeton: Princeton University Press.

2

Citizens Deliberating Online: Theory and Some Evidence

VINCENT PRICE

1 Introduction

The capacities of ordinary citizens to engage in successful political give-and-take, and thus to participate in meaningful deliberative democracy, have been debated for some time. Even those espousing great faith in the deliberative citizen, however, have expressed doubts about the suitability of online, text-based exchanges for meaningful and constructive political discussion. Some argue that the impersonal nature of computerized communication renders it poorly suited to developing meaningful relationships, encourages uncivil discourse, facilitates diffusion of unverified information, and ultimately serves to polarize opinions rather than support finding common ground.

This chapter reviews theory and available evidence bearing on the functional utility of online 'discussion' for political deliberation, arguing that characteristics of computer-mediated exchanges (namely reduced social cues, relative anonymity of participants, and reliance on text-based exchanges lacking nonverbal, facial, and vocal cues) may, under the right conditions, facilitate open exchanges of controversial political ideas. Thus, far from compromising the benefits of face-to-face group meetings, computer mediated communication may prove especially useful for deliberative work.

Online Deliberation: Design, Research, and Practice.
Todd Davies and Seeta Peña Gangadharan (eds.).
Copyright © 2009, CSLI Publications.

Data from two, year-long panel experiments in online political discussion are considered in light of these propositions.[1] One experiment involved the creation of sixty groups of representative American citizens who engaged in monthly discussions leading up to the 2000 presidential campaign. The second studied eighty groups of citizens meeting several times to debate issues related to health care reform in 2004 and 2005. Both projects gathered extensive survey data from participants, including those in control groups who did not engage in any online deliberation, and recorded the full text of all group discussions for analysis. Main findings largely confirm the value of online deliberation and paint a broadly optimistic portrait of the deliberative citizen online.

2   The Deliberative Citizen

Democratic theory is of at least two minds about the capacities of ordinary people for rational self-governance. Many express suspicions about the ability of typical citizens to comprehend and decide complicated public issues, and thus doubt the value of mass participation in policy making. Lippmann (1922), for example, finding a number of fundamental inadequacies in both the press and the public, argued for a form of elite, technocratic rule relying on political leaders and technical experts to determine policy and then to organize public opinion for the press. By contrast, other theorists place far more faith in the ability of citizens to deliberate public issues and render sensible judgments about policies. In rebutting Lippmann, for instance, Dewey (1927) argued that modern democracies were threatened less by incompetent citizens than by communication systems that did not adequately serve them. With improvements in the means of public discussion, he argued, the ends of true participatory democracy were attainable. People are indeed capable, he proposed, though conditions had not permitted them to realize their potential.

The former, dim view of citizen capacities appears to square reasonably well with much survey research over the past several decades, which documents wide swaths of indifference and political ignorance in the American public (Neuman 1986). A significant number of opinions given in response to public opinion surveys—indeed, by some estimates perhaps as many as a third—may be 'top of the head' responses, given rather thoughtlessly and loosely rooted, if at all, in knowledge of the issues at stake (Graber 1982).

[1] This research is supported by grants from The Pew Charitable Trusts, the Annenberg Public Policy Center of the University of Pennsylvania, and the National Science Foundation (Grant EIA-0306801) to Vincent Price and Joseph N. Cappella. Views expressed are those of the author alone and do not necessarily reflect those of the sponsoring agencies.

As an input to policy making, mass opinion is thus commonly discounted, in favor or more informed and presumably rational elite opinion. This is not to say that public opinion is accorded no value by such accounts. Rather, it is considered a legitimate input to policy making only in a highly circumscribed and indirect fashion, through periodic elections to accept or reject political leaders, and not as a more direct means of deciding policy (Schumpeter 1942; Sartori 1962). Barber (1984) has termed this 'weak' democracy. Like others, he argues that a disparaging view of the public underlies the dominant 'liberal rationalist' model of democratic government. Citizens are seen as largely ignorant and intolerant, with highly unstable and untrustworthy opinions (Dryzek and Berejikian 1993: 48).

A burgeoning number of political scientists and policy researchers, however, challenge the liberal rationalist model, arguing that despite claims of being democratic in character, it renders government incapable of adequately reflecting popular interests. They propose instead various forms of 'strong' democracy built upon direct, participatory, and deliberative engagement of ordinary citizens in ongoing policy formation (Macpherson 1977; Barber 1984; Dryzek 1990; Warren 1992; Mathews 1994). While proposals vary widely in how best to achieve such strong democracy, they rest on a common set of propositions: political autonomy grows out of collective engagement in political discussion, and if people were better engaged in discursive politics, they would be transformed as citizens. People 'would become more public-spirited, more knowledgeable, more attentive to the interests of others, and more probing of their own interests' (Warren 1992: 8).

The Call for Citizen Deliberation

Echoing Dewey's (1927) call for improvements in the methods of public communication and debate, participatory democratic theorists submit that the mass media have transformed politics into a kind of spectator sport. Audiences simply consume political views disseminated by elites through the mass media, rather than function as autonomous, deliberating bodies. The *public,* which should rightly be a sovereign, reasoning collective, has been displaced by disconnected *masses* assembled around political spectacle (Mills 1956; Habermas 1989; Ginsberg 1986; Fishkin 1991). Opinion polls and popular referenda only amplify shallow mass opinion formed without any meaningful public debate, producing a mere echo chamber for elite debate.

Arguing against the inevitability of these conditions, participatory theorists argue advance an agenda to engage the electorate, rebuild lost social capital, and reform the press. While proposed remedies for treating the ailing body politic are myriad (see Price and Neijens 1997, 1998), most emphasize citizen deliberation and identify in it a number of powerful benefits. Discussion theoretically allows citizens to air their disagreements, creates opportunities to reconsider initial, unreflective impulses, and ideally fosters understanding of alternative perspectives and viewpoints (Arendt 1958; Habermas 1989, 1984; Gutmann and Thompson 1996). It is also thought to promote tolerance and understanding between groups with divergent interests, foster mutual respect and trust, lead to a heightened sense of one's role within a political community, and stimulate further civic engagement (Barber 1984; Bohman 1996; Dryzek 2000). The central normative proposition is communitarian in spirit. 'When citizens or their representatives disagree morally, they should continue to reason together to reach mutually acceptable decisions' (Guttman and Thompson 1996: 1).

Calls have been increasingly issued on these grounds for engaging ordinary citizens in structured political deliberations (Fishkin 1991, 1995) and for including lay citizens in technical policy deliberations (Fischer 1990, 1993; deLeon 1995). In many such proposals, citizens are selected at random, given incentives to engage in collaborative, face-to-face sessions with their peers, and invited to expert briefings and question-and-answer sessions (Dienel 1978; Renn et al. 1984, 1993; Fishkin 1991, 1995). A large number of other kindred efforts—citizen issue forums, citizen juries, consensus conferences, and the like—has been mounted as well.

Doubts about the Deliberative Turn

Deliberative theory has garnered many advocates and become popular among reform-minded practitioners, but it has attracted critics as well (Sanders 1997; Hibbing and Theiss-Morse 2002). Bases for criticism are both theoretical an empirical in nature.

First, the argument that group discussion improves the quality of opinion can be questioned in light of much of the research on group decision making. Group discussion has, after all, been known to produce opinion polarization, shifts in new and risky directions, and other undesired outcomes (Brown 2000). It entails social pressures that can lead to reticence on the part of those holding minority opinions, contributing to 'political correctness' or 'spirals of silence' that distort the communication of true preferences (Noelle-Neuman 1984).

Second, it may well be doubted whether the core attributes of high-quality deliberation—'egalitarian, reciprocal, reasonable, open-minded exchange' (Mendelberg 2002: 153)—are reasonably attainable in practice. While the goal of deliberative theory is to embrace all views and empower the disenfranchised, Sanders (1997) argues that deliberative encounters likely do just the opposite, discouraging participation by those who lack social or political status (e.g., women or ethnic minorities) or deliberative ability (e.g., the less well educated), thus only further empowering high-status, educated participants. The purportedly egalitarian nature of deliberation cannot be assured merely by invitation. It must be demonstrated in practice by vocal participation and equitably distributed. Also open to question is the degree to which citizen deliberation will be reciprocal, reasonable, and open-minded. People may exchange views, and in some sense argue, without giving reasons for their views. Or, if reasons are given, they may simply be ignored rather than given a response.

Third, the vital role accorded to disagreement in deliberative theory may be misplaced. People may well find it uncomfortable to disagree, particularly those uncertain of their views, and take political disagreement personally (Mansbridge 1983; Pin 1985; Schudson 1997; Eliasoph 1998). They may avoid confrontation and hence real debate. Or, if citizens do air disagreements, the result may prove to be increased animosities rather than mutual respect and trust. Even if disagreement does induce greater political tolerance, it might as well induce ambivalence, and thus come at the expense of political action (Mutz 2002). For reasons such as these, Hibbing and Theiss-Morse (2002) posit that many citizens do not want, and would likely resist rather than embrace, direct involvement in policy making through public discussion.

With the growth of deliberative programs, some of these propositions have been subjected to empirical scrutiny (Fishkin and Luskin 1999; Price and Cappella 2002). Still, available evidence has been limited and mixed, so the effects of such deliberative exercises, along with clear understanding of the causes of any effects obtained, is presently difficult to determine (Price and Neijens 1997; Delli Carpini, Cook, and Jacobs 2003; Ryfe 2005). Several studies, particularly those by Fishkin and colleagues involving 'deliberative polls', indicate that citizens learn from their discussions and sometimes arrive at positions that would not have been registered by conventional means such as a public opinion poll. However, most research has tended toward simple input-output models of deliberation effects and has not tested, for example, whether the content and structure of actual citizen discussions follows normative assumptions, or whether exposure to disagreement from political opponents indeed has the beneficial effects postulated.[2]

---

[2] Survey-based studies, relying on self-reports of perceived disagreement in political conversations, indicate mixed effects. Perceived disagreement predicts greater awareness of reasons supporting opposing opinions (Price, Nir, and Cappella 2002; Mutz 2002) but may also predict lower, not higher, rates of political participation (Mutz 2002). Laboratory experiments

3 The Online Setting

The Internet and World Wide Web have been greeted by some as cause for optimism about a revitalized public sphere (Poster 1999; Becker and Slaton 2000; Papacharissi 2004). While growing at a fairly rapid rate, however, political 'conversation' online remains a rare phenomenon. According to a Pew Research Center study (2005), about 10% of those responding to a national survey reported taking part in online discussions about the 2004 U.S. presidential election. Nevertheless, Internet technologies have considerable appeal to adherents of deliberative theory and practice, in that they permit group interactions among geographically dispersed and diverse participants, potentially bringing far greater reach, reduced cost, and increased representation to exercises in deliberative democracy.

At the same time, some analysts have questioned whether electronic, text-based interactions are well suited to fruitful political deliberation. Fishkin (2000) argues, for example, that text-based Internet discussions are likely too superficial to sustain sound political deliberation.[3] Putnam (2000) also remains skeptical of the Internet's capacities for generating social capital, in part because 'computer-mediated communication networks tend to be sparse and unbounded', encouraging 'easy-in, easy out' and 'drive-by' relationships rather than the close acquaintance promoted by face-to-face contact (177). Computer-mediated communication is often framed as an impersonal phenomenon that de-individuates participants, rendering it poorly suited to getting to know others, instead encouraging uncivil discourse and group-based stereotyping (see Kiesler, Siegel, and McGuire 1984; Rice 1993). Sunstein (2001) warns that the Internet, far from encouraging reasonable dialogue over shared issues, merely encourages 'enclave' communication among very like-minded citizens, circulating unfounded and often false information, polarizing and intensifying opinions, and contributing to widening gaps between those on opposite sides of public issues. Even if designers of online deliberative programs were able to counter such tendencies, they would still contend with the so-called 'digital divide': structural inequities in access to computing equipment, familiarity with its use, liter-

---

do sometimes directly engage research subjects in discussion, for instance, in business decision making or juries. However, analyses have not focused on the tenets of deliberative theory, and moreover, the experimental settings often bear little resemblance to citizen discussion as normally understood.

[3] Fishkin has since experimented with voice technologies, eschewing the usual text-based 'chat' formats characteristic of most online group discussions. Iyengar, Luskin, and Fishkin (2003) report that voice-only deliberations (akin to conference calls) produce information gains and opinion changes roughly comparable to those found in face-to-face deliberative polls.

acy, and typing ability. The prospects for successful political deliberation online, then, remain unclear.

With each of these potential liabilities, though, come potential benefits. The quasi-anonymity and text-based nature of electronic group discussion, for instance, might actually reduce patterns of social dominance. Studies demonstrate that online discussions are generally much more egalitarian than face-to-face encounters, with reduced patterns of individual dominance and increased contributions by low-status participants (Dubrovsky, Kiesler, and Sethna 1991; Rice 1993; Walther 1995; Hollingshead 1996). Task-oriented groups generate more unique ideas working in computer-mediated settings than when face-to-face (Gallupe, DeSanctis, and Dickson 1988; Dennis 1996). Group decision making experiments generally indicate that online discussions, relative to face-to-face group meetings, generate more open exchanges of ideas (Rains 2005), suggesting considerable utility for deliberative work.

Moreover, recent studies suggest that the computer may not be the 'impersonal' medium it is commonly made out to be and that, in fact, people find it useful in forming relationships (Walther 1992). Experimental comparisons show that computer-mediated discussions produce more questions, greater self-disclosure, more intimate and direct questions, and fewer peripheral exchanges than face-to-face encounters (Tidwell and Walther 2002). Other research similarly suggests that people find the lack of physical presence and reduction in social cues to be useful rather than limiting. Bargh, McKenna, and Fitzsimmons (2002) find that their experimental participants feel better able to reveal their 'true selves' online than in person. Meanwhile, Stromer-Galley (2003) found a number of people reporting that they felt better able to discuss political disagreements over the Internet than face-to-face, because it felt to them more comfortable and less dangerous. Finally, online encounters may assist people in formulating their thoughts, by requiring greater economy of expression and the conversion of inchoate ideas into text and by permitting statements to be reviewed and edited prior to posting.

Political discussion online surely differs in fundamental ways from that carried out face to face. Its distinctive features, however, may well prove to help rather than hinder the core attributes of sound deliberation. The reduction in social cues, by restricting the projection of social status, may produce less deferential behavior and so undercut status hierarchies. The ability to input 'statements' simultaneously may assist the sharing of ideas, while anonymity should reduce inhibitions and anxieties about expressing one's honest views, particularly when they are likely to be unpopular.

4 Two Empirical Forays

While by no means resolving these many issues, data from several field experiments help shed important light on the nature of online deliberation. Unique in their design and scale, these two studies, *Electronic Dialogue* and *Healthcare Dialogue*, provide unusual empirical leverage on debates over the utility of text-based, electronic group interactions for political discussion. Importantly, neither project aimed at replicating 'typical' Internet discussion. Instead, they pursued an experimental logic: what *would* occur if we were to bring a representative sample of Americans online to discuss politics, or to debate public policy? The results begin to address fundamental questions concerning the putative value of citizen deliberation and, in particular, of airing opposing points of view.

Our review will out of necessity be brief, intended to provide an overview rather than a thorough presentation of findings. After sketching the outlines of each study, we consider evidence bearing on five basic questions. Who attends such discussions? Who talks? How can we characterize the discussions vis-à-vis normative ideals? How do the discussions influence, if at all, knowledge and opinion? And what of their transformative potential: Can we discern any impact on civic attitudes or subsequent engagement?

The *Electronic Dialogue* Project

The *Electronic Dialogue* project was a year-long panel study conducted during the 2000 U.S. presidential election. It involved a multi-wave, multigroup panel design, lasting roughly one year. All data gathering was conducted over the World Wide Web. The core of project consisted of sixty groups of citizens who engaged in a series of monthly, real-time electronic discussions about issues facing the country and the unfolding presidential campaign.

Sample

Unlike many Web-based studies, the project did not rely upon a convenience sample of Internet users. Instead, respondents came from a random sample of U.S. citizens age eighteen and older drawn from a nationally representative panel of survey respondents maintained by Knowledge Networks, Inc. of Menlo Park, California.[4]

---

[4] The Knowledge Networks panel includes a large number of households (in the tens of thousands) that were selected through RDD (random digit dialing) methods and agreed to accept free WebTV equipment and service in exchange for completing periodic surveys on line.

Details of the sampling are presented in Price and Cappella (2002). Briefly, a random sample was drawn from the Knowledge Networks panel for recruitment to the year-long project. Just over half (51%) agreed to participate, and the great majority of those consenting (84%) subsequently completed the project's two baseline surveys in February and March 2000. Comparisons of the obtained baseline sample (N = 1684) with a separate random-digit dialing telephone survey and with U.S. Census data indicated that the *Electronic Dialogue* sample was broadly representative, though it tended to slightly over-represent males and to under-represent those with less than a high-school education, nonwhites, and those with weak interest in politics.

Design

All baseline respondents were randomly assigned to one of three groups. Those in the *discussion* group (N = 915) were invited to attend eight online group deliberations, roughly once a month, beginning in April and continuing through December. Members of this group, regardless of whether they attended discussions or not, were also asked to complete a series of surveys, one preceding and one following each discussion event. Participants assigned to the *survey-only control* group (N = 139) were also asked to complete all the surveys, although they were never invited to attend any online group meetings. The remaining participants were assigned to a *project pre/post only* condition: they were asked to complete only the baseline surveys and, one year later, the final end-of-project surveys.

Anticipating far less than perfect attendance, sixty groups were formed with roughly sixteen invitees per group, in order to produce groups of five to ten participants at each round of discussions. Because of the theoretical interest in the impact of disagreement, three experimental group conditions were created using baseline data: *homogeneously liberal* groups (N = 20); *homogeneously conservative* groups (N = 20); and *heterogeneous* groups with members from across the political spectrum (N = 20). Participants maintained group assignments over the full course of the study.

Discussion groups met live, in real-time, with membership straddling several time zones. Participants logged on to their 'discussion rooms' at pre-arranged times, using their Web TV devices, television sets, and infrared keyboards. All discussions were moderated by project assistants working out of the Annenberg School at the University of Pennsylvania, and were carefully coordinated and scripted to maintain consistency across groups. Discussions were not intended to be formally deliberative exercises. Instead, group members were simply invited to discuss a number of topics, including which issues ought to be the focus of the campaign, a variety of candidate policy proposals (e.g., in areas of education, crime and public safety, taxes, and foreign affairs), the candidates' qualifications, campaign advertising, and the role of the media. In all, nine rounds of meetings were held. The full text of all discussions, including time stamps for each comment posted, was automatically recorded.

All respondents to the initial baseline (those invited to discussions, the survey-only control group, and the project pre/post-only group) were contacted again for end-of-project surveys in January and February 2001. Fifty-five percent completed the first survey, and 56% completed the second.

The *Healthcare Dialogue* Project

The *Healthcare Dialogue* project shared many of the features of the 2000 campaign study but focused instead on formal policy deliberations about a complex issue: health care reform. It also created online discussions involving health-care policy elites in addition to ordinary citizens. Project objectives included: (1) examining online deliberation as a means of maximizing public influence in policy making, (2) studying the interaction of policy elites and ordinary citizens in online discussions, and (3) testing hypotheses related to group composition and the quality of deliberations and outcomes.

Sample

The project again drew upon the Knowledge Networks panel but employed a stratified sampling strategy, such that the final baseline sample (N = 2497) represented both a general population sample of adult citizens, age 18 or older (N = 2183), as well as a purposive sample of health care policy elites with special experience, knowledge, and influence in the domain of health care policy and reform (N = 314). The general population sample was further stratified into members of 'issue publics' who are highly attentive to and knowledgeable about health care issues (N = 804) and ordinary citizens (N = 1379). Comparisons of the obtained baseline general population sample to a random-digit dialing telephone sample and to U.S. Census data indicated that the samples were broadly comparable, although project participants were somewhat more likely to be middle aged and to follow politics more frequently.

Design

A subset of the baseline panel (262 health care policy elites, 461 issue-public members, 768 ordinary citizens) was randomly assigned within strata to participate in a series of four moderated online group discussions, including pre- and post-discussion surveys, which were conducted over the course of the year. Participants were further randomly assigned to participate in a group that was homogeneous within strata (either elite-only, issue-public-only, or general-citizen-only) or mixed across the three strata. Discussion groups were again scripted to ensure consistency across groups, and short briefing materials were made available prior to each online meeting. The full text of all discussions, including time stamps for each comment, was automatically recorded.

Because baseline surveys indicated broad agreement that the most pressing problems facing the health care system included the rising costs of health insurance, the large number of uninsured Americans and the rising costs of prescription drugs, these issues were the focus of the online deliberations. Eighty groups (8 homogeneous elite, 12 homogeneous issue-public, 20 homogeneous general citizen, and 40 heterogeneous across strata) met twice in the fall of 2004 to discuss insurance-related issues. A total of 614 project participants (123 elites, 206 issue-public members, and 285 general citizens) attended at least one of the two discussions. The subset of 614 fall discussion attendees was then reassigned to 50 new groups for another round of two discussions in the spring of 2005, focusing on prescription drugs. In this second round, a random half of the participants remained in homogeneous or heterogeneous groups as before, while half were switched (from homogeneous to heterogeneous groups, or vice versa).

Following the four discussion waves—in September and November 2004 and in February and April 2005, with each consisting of a brief pre-discussion survey followed by an hour-long online chat and then another brief post-discussion survey—an end-of-project survey was conducted in August 2005 (completed by roughly three-quarters of all baseline respondents).

5 The Evidence to Date

Taken together, these two studies provide observations of close to 800 online group discussions involving more than 1200 different participants, most of whom attended three or four group meetings over several months. With extensive survey data (nineteen survey waves in the 2000 project and ten in the 2004-2005 project), full transcripts of the online interactions, and carefully designed experimental comparisons, we are in a good position to evaluate who attends such discussions, the nature of citizens' online behavior, and the influence of the discussions on knowledge, opinions, and attitudes.

Who Attends?

Rates of participation in the online discussions generally ranged from about 30% to 40% of those invited, producing groups averaging around a half-dozen persons each. In both projects, comparisons of attendees to nonattendees found no significant differences in gender, region of the country, or political leanings. However, people who showed up for the electronic discussions were, again in both projects, significantly more likely to be white than those who did not (about a 3% to 4% difference), significantly older (by about 3 years on average), and better educated.

Importantly, data from both projects indicate that attendees were significantly higher than nonattendees in their levels of interpersonal trust, regular 'offline' political discussion, political participation, and community engagement. Overall, the experience of both projects strongly supports the view that 'social capital' goes hand in hand with deliberative participation (Putnam 2000). Trusting people who are engaged in their communities— even when their activities are not expressly political in nature—were more likely to attend. Those who attended the electronic conversations also scored significantly higher than nonattendees on scales measuring political knowledge and interest in public affairs, and in the *Healthcare Dialogue* project were also significantly more knowledgeable about health related policy issues and more confident in health care institutions. Multiple regressions consistently show that the most powerful predictor of attendance is 'argument repertoire', a count of the reasons a respondent gives in support of his or her opinion on an issue, along with reasons why other people might disagree (which has proved to be a validated and reliable measure of opinion quality) (Cappella, Price, and Nir 2002).

Two overall conclusions can be drawn from these analyses. First, robust and predictable differences between project attendees and nonattendees emerge, although most such differences are relatively small in magnitude. The best multivariate models, even those employing as many as thirty predictors, account for only small proportions of variance in participation— less than 20% in *Electronic Dialogue* and less than 10% in *Healthcare Dialogue*. Most of the variability in attendance among invitees, then, appears to be random rather than systematic. Notwithstanding concerns about the difficulty of overcoming the digital divide, both projects managed to assemble samples of discussion participants which, while over-representing engaged and knowledgeable citizens, were as a group highly diverse and broadly representative of the general population.

Second, many of the phenomena thought to stem from engagement in deliberation—trust in other citizens, knowledge, the ability to understand reasons on both sides of issues, civic participation—are also predictors of attendance. Any attempt to gauge the impact of deliberation on attitudes, knowledge, or subsequent engagement, then, must carefully account for this fact.

Who Talks?

Bringing a diverse and representative sample of citizens together for discussion is a necessary but by no means sufficient condition for democratic deliberation. We turn, then, to a consideration of what transpired online. How engaged were participants? How egalitarian were the exchanges?

Participants in both projects contributed on average several hundred words per discussion. For example, discounting informal 'small talk' at the beginning and end of each discussion and focusing only on the main deliberations, we found that participants in the *Healthcare Dialogue* project averaged just over 300 words per person. Importantly, 'talking' in the online groups tended to be distributed very evenly across participants, with variance across group members typically reaching about 80% of its maximum value (Undem 2001). Not surprisingly, average words per person declined as groups increased in size.

Multiple regressions predicting individual word counts indicate that older participants—though more likely than younger people to attend discussions—contributed significantly fewer words. In the 2000 campaign study, women contributed significantly more words, but no significant gender differences emerged in the health care deliberations. Typing skills have a discernable though not large effect. The most notable pattern, overall, is the tendency of more politically involved and more knowledgeable participants to enter more words into the discussions: education, political participation, political knowledge, and especially argument repertoire had positive effects on the amount of 'speaking'. Thus, in the *Healthcare Dialogue* deliberations, policy elites contributed significantly more words than even members of the health care issue public, who in turn contributed significantly more words than ordinary citizens who are less interested in and knowledgeable about the issues.

Despite such predictable biases in favor of more knowledgeable participants, these are small relative to what one might expect from the literature on face-to-face groups. Over all, the word count evidence suggests that the exchanges were quite equitable (Undem 2001). Neither project offered any indication that those holding minority views are reticent in the online group environment. Indeed, those whose issue preferences are furthest from other group members, if anything, tend to contribute *more* rather than fewer words.

The Nature of Citizen Discussion

Deliberation is more than a mere exchange of words. It should be reciprocal, reasonable, and open-minded. As noted above, people may exchange
views without giving reasons, or they may ignore rather than respond to
contrary views. However, both qualitative and quantitative analyses of transcripts indicate that the citizen discussions, while not especially sophisticated in policy terms, were nonetheless substantive and responsive. This is
true even of the *Electronic Dialogue* discussions, which were framed only
as talk about candidates and the issues, not as any sort of formal deliberation (see Price, Nir, and Cappella 2005; Price and David 2005).

People freely and frankly exchanged opinions. In the 2000 campaign
discussions, for example, people expressed on average fifteen statements of
opinion, pro or con, with reference to the issues discussed. Moreover, they
explained their views. Close to 40% of all these opinion statements were
coupled with one or more arguments to bolster a position (Price and David
2005). Almost all groups, even those that were homogeneously liberal or
conservative, produced a reasonable balance of both pro and con arguments
on most issues. Opinion expression and argumentation both tended to be
equitably distributed: once word counts are controlled for, only strength of
opinion showed much relationship to the number of arguments made (Price
and David 2005). Analysis of transcripts and survey responses in both projects suggest that views expressed were diverse, and perceived as such by
group members.

Participants had little or no trouble adapting the text format to their discussion aims, and there are many indications that people felt positively
about their online experience (Price and Cappella 2002, 2006). Large majorities in both projects reported that the discussion experience was interesting and enjoyable. Liking of the experience was uniform across liberal, conservative, and mixed groups in the 2000 study, while in the health care deliberations, even though policy elites expressed slightly less positive reactions than other citizens, a substantial majority of elites reported liking the
experience. *Healthcare Dialogue* groups, which concluded their deliberations by voting on priorities for health care policy, expressed high levels of
satisfaction with their final choices (Price and Cappella 2006). The vast
majority of attendees said that they think 'the potential of this technology
for good political discussions' is either 'good' or 'excellent' (Price and Cappella 2002).

Perhaps most important, adverse reactions to disagreement were not
much in evidence. To the contrary, exposure to opposing views appears if
anything to be an attraction of the online encounters. Open-ended survey
questions invited *Electronic Dialogue* participants to identify what they

liked and disliked about the experience. Almost half of all coded 'likes' referred to hearing others' views, interacting with people from different parts of the country, or learning how much they agreed or disagreed with other citizens. By comparison, just over 12% singled out the chance to express their views (Undem 2001). Aspects of the discussions that were disliked were fewer in number, and most commonly had to do, not with the substance of personal interactions at all, but instead with technical issues such as logging in or keeping up with scrolled comments on screen.

Impact on Knowledge and Opinion

Analyzing the impact of deliberation is complicated by the fact that, as noted earlier, the best *predictors* of attendance proved to be precisely those variables usually cast as theoretical *outcomes*. While this can be interpreted as partly confirming the reciprocal relationship between deliberation and good citizenship, it must be taken into account when attempting to gauge the effect of deliberation on attitudes and knowledge. Toward this end, using dozens of measures available from our extensive baseline surveys, we calculated an estimate of each person's *propensity to attend* and controlled for this propensity score to remove the effects of potential confounding variables (Rosenbaum and Rubin 1983; D'Agostino 1998). Propensity scoring succeeds in balancing almost all differences between attendees as a group and their counterparts who did not attend. Particularly when coupled with separate statistical controls for baseline levels of target outcomes and any variables that may remain imbalanced, it enables fair experimental comparisons to test hypothesized deliberation effects (see Price, Goldthwaite, and Cappella 2002; Price et al. 2006).

Analyses of this sort support several general conclusions bearing on putative increases in opinion quality resulting from deliberation. First, while there are some gains in objective knowledge (e.g., knowing that George W. Bush supported government-funded private school vouchers in the 2000 campaign) (Price and Cappella 2002), gains in issue-knowledge are modest at best. On the other hand, deliberation does appear to produce significant gains in 'argument repertoires'—the range of arguments people hold both in support of and *against* their favored positions. Online discussion attendance significantly and positively predicted scores on this argument repertoire measure, controlling for argument repertoire assessed on the baseline survey and for propensity to attend the discussions (Cappella, Price, and Nir 2002).

Second, aside from any influence it may have on the direction of public opinion, deliberation increases levels of opinion holding. Thus, for example, attendance in the *Healthcare Dialogue* discussions significantly predicted fewer 'don't know' responses to a range of policy-opinion questions, again controlling for baseline opinion holding and propensity to attend (Price et al. 2006).

Third, shifts in policy preferences induced by deliberation are usually readily interpretable and appear to reflect the tenor of group argumentation. Although on many topics aggregate levels of support or opposition for the policies discussed remained unchanged, when group-level opinion did shift, the data suggest generally rational movements in keeping with the pattern of group argumentation (Price and Cappella 2002). In discussing federal funding for character education or school vouchers, for instance, *Electronic Dialogue* groups tended to produce more opposing than supportive arguments and thus became on average less enthusiastic about such funding.

Deliberation-induced changes in preferences also seem to reflect movement toward more informed and politically sophisticated positions. Price et al. (2006) found that, after controls for propensity to attend, preferences at baseline, and other background characteristics, *Healthcare Dialogue* attendees were less likely than nonattendees to support tax based reforms and were more supportive than nonattendees of government programming and regulations as a means to cut heath care costs. Importantly, these differences between participants and nonparticipants parallel those between policy elites and general citizens at baseline. Thus, the impact of deliberation was to move citizens in the direction of elite opinion (even though, since such movements occurred to a greater degree in groups *without* elite members, they were not apparently the mere product of elite persuasion).

Impact on Citizen Engagement

Finally, what of the transformative potential of online deliberation? Although the estimated effects on civic engagement are small in size, results are consistent across a number of different indicators and across both projects. Online discussion attendees, relative to nonattendees with comparable propensities to participate, score significantly higher in end-of-project social trust, community engagement, and political participation. For example, participants in the *Electronic Dialogue* discussion reported voting in the 2000 presidential election at significantly higher rates than their counterparts who did not attend, even after extensive controls (Price and Cappella 2002; Price, Goldthwaite, and Cappella 2002). While the 2000 project did not find similar increases in personal political efficacy, the later *Healthcare Dialogue* project did, along with increases in self-reported engagement in health policy related activities such as working for advocacy groups, attending meetings, or donating money to a group pursing health care reform

(Feldman and Freres 2006). Thus, the sorts of social and political capital that contribute to participation in online deliberations (see Section 5, 'Who Attends?' above) are themselves *products* of discussion as well, lending support to claims that social capital and deliberative behavior are mutually reinforcing.

Analyses based on coded transcripts find almost no evidence that observed gains in social trust or in electoral and community participation were mitigated by encountering disagreement (Price et al. 2005). Estimated effects of *Electronic Dialogue* participation on post-project community engagement were slightly larger for those who encountered more supportive group members, but there were nonetheless significant, positive effects of discussion even for those who met with substantial disagreement in their groups. No moderating effect of disagreement was found in connection with either voting or post-project social trust. Thus, although some survey studies using self-reports of perceived disagreement have suggested that face-to-face political opposition can lead to ambivalence and withdrawal (Mutz 2002), here we find little to suggest that online disagreement disengages.

6 Taking Stock

As noted earlier, these research findings of themselves do not resolve the many issues raised by critics of deliberative democracy, nor by those adherents of deliberative theory who have questioned the utility of text-based 'chat'-type modes of computer-mediated communication for productive deliberation. Lacking reasonable experimental comparisons to face-to-face deliberations, we cannot say which if any of our observations are the unique product of the online environment itself. Thus, although we might suspect that participants' openness and tolerance of disagreement resulted from the diminished social cues and relative anonymity afforded by text-based exchanges, such propositions must remain speculative.

Similarly, in the absence of comparisons to other online deliberation programs, or to typical Web-based discussions as they now occur naturally, we cannot say how much our findings stem from the particular manner in which these discussions were designed and undertaken (e.g., under the auspices of university researchers with the sponsorship of respected nonpartisan and governmental agencies). We make no effort to generalize to other online settings.

Still, these experiments in 'online democracy' do begin to address systematically questions concerning the putative value of online deliberation. Randomly selected citizens adapted readily and well to the online environment. They produced reasonably coherent political discussions, showed willingness to debate and engage their opponents, responded favorably to their online experiences, developed opinions and grasped arguments for and against those views, and came away a bit more trusting and civically engaged than comparable nonparticipants. Though broad stroke, the picture emerging from these analyses of citizens deliberating online shows them, if not quite meeting all the lofty ideals of deliberative theory, certainly coming closer than might have been expected.

References

Arendt, H. 1958. *The Human Condition*. Chicago: University of Chicago Press.

Barber, B. 1984. *Strong Democracy: Participatory Politics for a New Age*. Berkeley: University of California Press.

Bargh, J. A., K. Y. A. McKenna, and G. M. Fitzsimmons. 2002. Can You See the Real me? Activation and Expression of the 'True Self' on the Internet. *Journal of Social Issues* 58: 33-48.

Becker, T. and C. D. Slaton. 2000. *The Future of Teledemocracy*. Wesport, CT: Praeger.

Bohman, J. 1996. *Public Deliberation: Pluralism, Complexity, and Democracy*. Cambridge, MA: MIT Press.

Brown, R. 2000. *Group Processes: Dynamics Within and Between Groups*. Oxford: Blackwell Publishers.

Cappella, J. N., V. Price, and L. Nir. 2002. Argument Repertoire as a Reliable and Valid Measure of Opinion Quality: Electronic Dialogue in Campaign 2000. *Political Communication* 19: 73-93.

D'Agostino, R. B. 1998. Tutorial in Biostatistics: Propensity Scoring Methods for Bias Reduction in the Comparison of a Treatment to a Non-randomized Control Group. *Statistics in Medicine* 17: 2265-2281.

deLeon, P. 1995. Democratic Values and the Policy Sciences. *American Journal of Political Science* 39: 886-905.

Delli Carpini, M. X., F. L. Cook, and L. R. Jacobs. 2003. Public Deliberation, Discursive Participation, and Citizen Engagement: A Review of the Empirical Literature. *Annual Review of Political Science* 7: 315-344.

Dennis, A. R. 1996. Information Exchange and Use in Group Decision Making: You Can Lead a Group to Information, But You Can't Make It Think. *MIS Quarterly* 20: 433-457.

Dewey, J. 1927. *The Public and Its Problems*. New York: Holt, Rinehart & Winston.

Dienel, P. C. 1978. *Die planungszelle: Eine Alternative zur Establishment-Demokratie. Dur Bürger Plant seine Umwelt*. Opladen: Westdeutscher Verlag.

Dryzek, J. S. 1990. *Discursive Democracy: Politics, Policy, and Political Science*. New York: Cambridge University Press.

Dryzek, J. S. and J. Berejikian. 1993. Reconstructive Democratic Theory. *American Political Science Review* 87: 48-60.

Dubrovsky, V. J., S. Kiesler, and B. N. Sethna. 1991. The Equalization Phenomenon: Status Effects in Computer-Mediated and Face-to-face Decision Making Groups. *Human-Computer Interaction* 6: 119-146.

Eliasoph, N. 1998. *Avoiding Politics*. Cambridge: Cambridge University Press.

Feldman, L. and D. Freres. 2006. *Efficacy, Trust, and Engagement Analyses*. Unpublished report of the *Healthcare Dialogue* project. Annenberg School, University of Pennsylvania.

Fischer, F. 1990. *Technocracy and the Politics of Expertise*. Newbury Park, CA: Sage Publications.

Fischer, F. 1993. Citizen Participation and the Democratization of Policy Expertise: From Theoretic Inquiry to Practical Cases. *Policy Sciences* 26: 165-88.

Fishkin, J. S. 1991. *Democracy and Deliberation: New Directions for Democratic Reform*. New Haven: Yale University Press.

Fishkin, J. S. 1995. *The Voice of the People: Public Opinion and Democracy*. New Haven, CT: Yale University Press.

Fishkin, J. S. 2000. *Virtual Democratic Possibilities: Prospects for Internet Democracy*. Paper presented at the conference on Internet, Democracy and Public Goods, Belo Horizonte, Brazil, November 2000.

Fishkin, J. S. and R. C. Luskin. 1999. Bringing Deliberation to the Democratic Dialogue. *The Poll with a Human Face: The National Issues Convention Experiment in Political Communication*, eds. M. McCombs and A. Reynolds, 3-38. Mahwah, NJ: Lawrence Erlbaum.

Gallupe, R. B., G. DeSantis, and G. W. Dickson. 1998. Computer-Based Support for Problem Finding: An Experimental Investigation. *MIS Quarterly* 12: 277-296.

Ginsberg, B. 1986. *The Captive Public: How Mass Opinion Promotes State Power*. New York: Basic Books.

Graber, D. A. 1982. The Impact of Media Research on Public Opinion Studies. *Mass Communication Review Yearbook*, eds. D. C. Whitney, E. Wartella, and S. Windahl, 555-564. Newbury Park, CA: Sage.

Gutmann, A. and D. Thompson. 1996. *Democracy and Disagreement*. Cambridge, MA: Harvard University Press.

Habermas, J. 1984. *The Theory of Communicative Action—Volume 1*, trans. T. McCarthy. Boston: Beacon.

Habermas, J. 1989. *The Structural Transformation of the Public Sphere: An Inquiry into a Category of Bourgeois Society*, trans. T. Burger. Cambridge, MA: MIT Press.

Hibbing, J. R. and E. Theiss-Morse. 2002. *Stealth Democracy: American's Beliefs about How Government Should Work*. Cambridge, UK: Cambridge University Press.

Hollingshead, A. B. 1996. Information Suppression and Status Persistence in Group Decision Making: The Effects of Communication Media. *Human Communication Research* 23: 193-219.

Iyengar, S., R. C. Luskin, and J. S. Fishkin. 2003. *Facilitating Informed Opinion: Evidence from Face-to-face and On-line Deliberative Polls*. Paper presented at the annual meeting of the American Political Science Association, Philadelphia, September 2003.

Kiesler, S., J. Siegel, and T. McGuire. 1984. Social Psychological Aspects of Computer-Mediated Communication. *American Psychologist* 39: 1123-1134.

Lippmann, W. 1922. *Public Opinion*. New York: Harcourt Brace Jovanovich.

Macpherson, C. B. 1977. *The Life and Times of Liberal Democracy*. Oxford: Oxford University Press.

Mansbridge, J. J. 1983. *Beyond Adversary Democracy*. Chicago: University of Chicago Press.

Mathews, D. 1994. *Politics for People: Finding a Responsible Public Voice*. Chicago: University of Chicago Press.

Mendelberg, T. 2002. The Deliberative Citizen: Theory and Evidence. *Research in Micropolitics* 6: 151-193.

Mills, C. W. 1956. *The Power Elite*. Oxford, UK: Oxford University Press.

Mutz, D. 2002. The Consequences of Cross-Cutting Networks for Political Participation. *American Journal of Political Science* 46: 838-855.

Neuman, W. R. 1986. *The Paradox of Mass Politics: Knowledge and Opinion in the American Electorate*. Cambridge, MA: Harvard University Press.

Noelle-Neumann, E. 1984. *The Spiral of Silence: Public Opinion—Our Social Skin*. Chicago: University of Chicago Press.

Papacharissi, Z. 2004. Democracy Online: Civility, Politeness, and the Democratic Potential of Online Political Discussion groups. *New Media and Society* 6: 259-284.

Pew Research Center. 2005. *Trends 2005*. Washington, DC: Pew Research Center.

Pin, E. J. 1985. *Pleasure of Your Company: A Social-Psychological Analysis of Modern Sociability*. New York: Praeger.

Poster, M. 1999. The Net as a Public Sphere. *Communication in History: Technology, Culture, Society* (3rd Edition), eds. D. J. Crowley and P. Heyer, 335. New York: Longman.

Price, V. and J. N. Cappella. 2002. Online Deliberation and Its Influence: The Electronic Dialogue Project in Campaign 2000. *IT and Society* 1: 303-328. Available at http://www.stanford.edu/group/siqss/itandsociety/ (last accessed August 30, 2008)

Price, V. and J. N. Cappella. 2006. *Bringing an Informed Public Into Policy Debates Through Online Deliberation: The Case of Health Care Reform*. Paper present at the National Conference on Digital Government Research, Digital Government Research Center, San Diego, CA, May 21-24, 2006.

Price, V. and C. David. 2005. *Talking about Elections: A Study of Patterns in Citizen Deliberation Online*. Paper presented at the annual meeting of the International Communication Association, New York, May 2005.

Price, V., L. Feldman, D. Freres, W. Zhang, and J. N. Cappella. 2006. *Informing Public Opinion About Health Care Reform Through Online Deliberation*. Paper presented at the annual meeting of the International Communication Association, Dresden, Germany, June 19, 2006.

Price, V. and P. Neijens. 1997. Opinion Quality in Public Opinion Research. *International Journal of Public Opinion Research* 9: 336-360.

Price, V. and P. Neijens. 1998. Deliberative Polls: Toward Improved Measures of 'Informed' Public Opinion? *International Journal of Public Opinion Research* 10: 145-176.

Price, V., D. Goldthwaite, and J. N. Cappella. 2002. *Civic Engagement, Social Trust, and Online Deliberation*. Paper presented at the annual meeting of the American Association for Public Opinion Research, St. Pete Beach, Florida, May 2002.

Price, V., D. Goldthwaite-Young, J. N. Cappella, and A. Romantan. 2006. *Online Political Discussion, Civic Engagement, and Social Trust*. Unpublished manuscript, Annenberg School, University of Pennsylvania.

Price, V., L. Nir, and J. Cappella. 2002. Does Disagreement Contribute to More Deliberative Opinion? *Political Communication* 19: 95-112.

Price, V., L. Nir, and J. Cappella. 2005. Framing Public Discussion of Gay Civil Unions. *Public Opinion Quarterly* 69: 179-212.

Putnam, R. D. 2000. *Bowling Alone: The Collapse and Revival of American Community*. New York: Simon and Schuster.

Rains, S. A. 2005. Leveling the Organizational Playing field—Virtually. *Communication Research* 32: 193-234.

Renn, O., H. U. Stegelmann, G. Albrecht, U. Kotte, and H. P. Peters. 1984. An Empirical Investigation of Citizens' Preferences Among Four Energy Alternatives. *Technological Forecasting and Social Change* 26: 11-46.

Renn, O., T. Webber, H. Rakel, P. Dienel, and B. Johnson. 1993. Public Participation in Decision Making: A Three-Step Procedure. *Policy Sciences* 26: 189-214.

Rice, R. E. 1993. Media Appropriateness: Using Social Presence Theory to Compare Traditional and New Organizational Media. *Human Communication Research* 19: 451-484.

Rosenbaum, P. R. and D. B. Rubin. 1983. The Central Role of the Propensity Score in Observational Studies for Causal Effects. *Biometrika* 70: 41-55.

Ryfe, D. M. 2005. Does Deliberative Democracy Work? *Annual Review of Political Science* 8: 49-71.

Sanders, L. M. 1997. Against Deliberation. *Political Theory* 25: 347-376.

Sartori, G. 1962. *Democratic Theory*. 2nd Edition. Detroit, MI: Wayne State University Press.

Schudson, M. 1997. Why Conversation Is Not the Soul of Democracy. *Critical Studies in Mass Communication* 14: 297-309.

Schumpeter, J. A. 1942. *Capitalism, Socialism and Democracy*. New York: Harper and Brothers.

Stromer-Galley, J. 2003. Diversity of Political Conversation on the Internet: Users' Perspectives. *Journal of Computer-Mediated Communication* 8(3). Available at http://jcmc.indiana.edu/vol8/issue3/stromergalley.html (last accessed August 30, 2008)

Sunstein, C. 2001. *Republic.com*. Princeton, NJ: Princeton University Press.

Tidwell, L. and J. B. Walther. 2002. Computer-Mediated Communication Effects on Disclosure, Impressions, and Interpersonal Evaluations: Getting to Know One Another a Bit at a Time. *Human Communication Research* 28: 317-348.

Undem, T. 2001. *Factors Affecting Discussion Quality: The Effects of Group Size, Gender, and Political Heterogeneity in Online Discussion Groups*. Unpublished master's thesis, University of Pennsylvania, Philadelphia.

Walther, J. B. 1992. Interpersonal Effects in Computer-mediated Interaction. *Western Journal of Communication* 57: 381-398.

Walther, J. B. 1995. Relational Aspects of Computer-mediated Communication: Experimental Observations Over Time. *Organization Science* 6: 186-203.

Warren, M. 1992. Democratic Theory and Self-Transformation. *American Political Science Review* 86: 8-23.

3

Can Online Deliberation Improve Politics? Scientific Foundations for Success

ARTHUR LUPIA

1 Introduction

Interest in deliberative democracy grows. Its appeal is understandable. Deliberation, with its emphasis on distributed speech rights and information exchange, has the potential to increase the quality and quantity of political interest and participation (Habermas 1996).

While the benefits of deliberative democracy are easy to imagine, they can be hard to achieve. Like any form of civic education, the success of a deliberative endeavor depends on choices made by its designers. For a deliberative endeavor to increase participation, or affect how a target audience thinks about an important political matter, its informational content must, at a minimum,

- attract the audience's attention and hold it for a non-trivial amount of time,
- affect the audience's memories in particular ways (not any change will do), and
- cause them to retain subsequent beliefs—or choose different behaviors—than they would have had without deliberation (Lupia 2002).

Online Deliberation: Design, Research, and Practice.
Todd Davies and Seeta Peña Gangadharan (eds.).
Copyright © 2009, CSLI Publications.

A problem for the deliberative democracy movement lies in its tendency to ignore these requirements. Consider, for example, deliberation practitioners who have rushed into grand attempts to demonstrate the effectiveness of deliberative democracy (see Fishkin and Ackerman 2005). They base their designs, and claims about the likely impact of their endeavors, on folk theories about information, communication, and choice. They proceed as if decades of scientifically validated evidence about human thinking and learning do not apply. Henceforth, I refer to such scholars collectively as deliberation practitioners.[1]

The claims that many deliberation practitioners make about what citizens will pay attention to, what parts of a conversation or presentation citizens will remember, and the conditions under which people will find relevant the kinds of information that deliberative democrats favor are incorrect. These errors are problematic for those who contribute their time, money, or energy to deliberative endeavors, because when deliberative strategies are based on such claims (or the unstated presumption that deliberation participants will simply learn what a practitioner wants them to learn), the consequences can include indifference (by driving people further from political participation), socially unproductive feelings about others (by adding to or reinforcing false beliefs or unjustified stereotypes), and lower competence at key democratic tasks (by highlighting false or biased information). More likely, it can be inconsequential (ignored by the target audience or completely forgotten soon after the deliberative gathering). Even the most basic of findings about human thinking and learning from fields such as psychology, the neurosciences, sociology, and political science are sufficient to convert the grand claims of deliberation's most vocal practitioners into empty promises.

Online deliberation, the focus of this book, is promising because of its ability to bring people together for the purpose of information exchange without the difficulties caused by physical distances between participants. Can practitioners in this field succeed where others have failed? I argue that it can. The blueprint for success involves a commitment to consider objective and scientifically validated evidence about the conditions under which bringing people together in a deliberative setting can produce specific kinds of cognitive and behavioral changes.

This essay describes practices that people interested in making online deliberation succeed should follow. First, I offer a brief discussion about how to evaluate the success of a deliberative democratic exercise. Next, I continue by describing a set of *necessary conditions for deliberative suc-*

---

[1] Professor Habermas, to the best of my knowledge, has not rushed into such endeavors and would not be included in this group.

cess. These conditions apply basic scientific findings about attention, memory, and learning to the question of when deliberation can change participants' beliefs and/or behaviors. Throughout the essay, discussions of measurement and the conditions for learning are unified by a commitment to objectivity, replicability, and transparency—hallmarks of the scientific method. Practitioners and scholars who make such commitments are more likely to realize online deliberation's substantial potential. As is also true in the domain of shareware, people who follow such practices are in a better position to provide credible advice to others who wish develop effective deliberative utilities, and to contribute to important ongoing conversations about the conditions under which deliberation is effective.

2 Measuring Success

To speak about necessary conditions for successful online deliberation requires a way to measure success. Since people pursue deliberative strategies for different reasons, an identical metric will not work for everyone. To keep this essay brief, I will focus on one kind of metric, pertinent to task-specific competence, that many people find useful.

Many deliberative strategies are put forward to increase a civically relevant form of competence (e.g., a citizen's ability to accomplish well-defined tasks in her role as voter, juror, or legislator). The task in question can include voting, speaking, or participating as one would if they possessed certain kinds of information. In such cases, the measure of success should capture the extent to which online deliberation increases the targeted skills.

If deliberation is to increase a civic competence, it must cause specific kinds of changes in how participants think about targeted aspects of politics—not any change will do. Suppose, for example, that we can define a 'competent vote' as the one that a person would cast if she knew where a specific set of candidates stood with respect to a well-defined list of major policy debates. For deliberation to *increase* a voter's competence, she must not be voting competently initially. Deliberating must *cause* her to do so.

To measure success in such cases, we need reliable data on how the voter would have behaved absent deliberation as well as data on how she would have behaved if she had the information listed above, so that we can compare those estimates to what actually happened during the deliberative setting. If we have only data on how she would have behaved absent deliberation, we can document that deliberation induced behavioral change but not necessarily whether the change constitutes an increase in competence. The task of accumulating such data is achievable, but it is not always easy. Difficulties inherent in measuring what a voter would have chosen if she were better informed set traps into which practitioners regularly fall.

Many people simply presume that if others were more informed, they would see the world as they—the practitioners—do.[2] They then proceed as if the voter's competence should be measured by the extent to which the voter, after deliberating, reaches the practitioners' preferred types of conclusions. But when the presumption is incorrect (e.g., 'what is good for the participants is not the same as what is good for the practitioners' or 'the information that practitioners presume relevant has less or no relevance to the practitioners'), then deliberation that leads people to mimic the practitioners can stifle—or even reduce—competence. Such possibilities raise questions about the value of deliberative democracy, such as that voiced by Posner (2005):

> I think that what motivates deliberative democrats is not a love of democracy or a faith in the people, but a desire to change specific political outcomes, which they believe they could do through argument, if only anyone could be persuaded to listen...I sense a power grab by the articulate class whose comparative advantage is—deliberation (42).

To parry such critiques of deliberative endeavors, it is helpful to offer not only concrete evidence about what behaviors constitute competent performance in advance of the deliberation but also to be very direct about who such increased competence is supposed to benefit. With such evidence, claims about the success, failure, and value of a deliberative endeavor can be more effectively and objectively evaluated.[3]

3 Necessary Conditions for Deliberative Success

Once designers of a deliberative enterprise agree on what they want to accomplish and how to measure it, the question becomes, when can online deliberation increase the desired competence? Designers can choose to answer this question effectively or ineffectively. An effective answer can begin with just a few scientifically validated findings about how people think

---

[2] See Hewstone and Fincham (1996) for a general and accessible discussion of this topic. See Lupia (2006) for a discussion that focuses on questions of voter competence.

[3] Others simply presume that any change in opinion that follows a deliberative endeavor must be evidence of increased civic competence or social value. There are two problems with such claims. First, if the opinion changes cannot be tied strongly and directly to changes in a person's ability to accomplish concrete and socially valuable tasks, then the extent to which they constitute evidence of increased civic competence is questionable, at best. Second when such data are offered as evidence of the value of deliberation to participants, it is question begging. Without a transparent and objective way to determine the kinds of opinion changes that are of value, such changes cannot be easily distinguished from the kinds of opinion change (following exposure to thirty-second advertisements or political cartoons), than many deliberation practitioners abhor.

and learn from others. Many deliberation practitioners do not take this step. Instead, they describe deliberation as if it is a place where ideas travel from one mind to another unadulterated—as if listeners interpret ideas exactly as speakers intend to convey them. *This is incorrect.*

In human communication, all but the simplest utterances and stimuli are parsed. People pay attention to only a tiny fraction of the information available to them, and they can later recall only a tiny fraction of the things to which they paid attention (see Kandel et al. 1995). To keep this essay brief, I will attempt to draw your attention to a short set of necessary conditions for deliberative success that follow directly from basic attributes of the process by which information is parsed. Lupia (2002, 2005a, 2000b) offers a more detailed treatment of this topic.

The Battle for Attention/Working Memory

Working memory is the aspect of cognitive function that regulates and processes our conscious thought at any given moment. Its capacity is very limited. Regardless of how hard we try, we can pay attention to relatively few things at any one time (Baddeley and Hitch 1974; Kandel et al. 1995). As a result, we must ignore almost everything around us.

To get our attention, an utterance made during the course of deliberation must fend off competitors such as a person's preoccupation with certain prior or future events, the simultaneous actions or utterances of others, and even the color of the wallpaper. So, for online deliberation to increase competence, the key is not simply putting people in a place where others speak. It is putting them in situations where they want to pay attention to information that will help them acquire the kinds of competence that motivated the deliberative enterprise in the first place.

I was reminded of the challenges of gaining attention during the conference from whence this book emanated. The conference organizers were considerate enough to ensure that everyone had Internet access in the main conference room. I chose to sit in the back of the auditorium during some of the sessions. From there, I verified that many people who, from the stage, may have appeared to be attentive to the lecture were, instead, checking email and surfing the Web.

This outcome should not be at all surprising. In everyday conversations, we vary in the extent to which we pay attention to what others are saying. Many scientific studies document and verify a range of cognitive and contextual factors that lead to substantial variations in the parts of conversations to which we attend (see Kitayama and Burnstein 1988). At the same time, an important social skill that we gain is to feign interest in a conversation even though our thoughts have drifted elsewhere. We learn to take in key words and to nod at appropriate times even though we are focusing most of our mental energies elsewhere. Sitting behind a room full of laptops only verifies the cognitive multitasking in which we all regularly engage.

The challenge posed for online deliberation is that even if a person is online, their attention can wander. It can wander off the screen to other topics, or it can wander to any of the billions of colorful diversions that the Internet offers. For an online deliberative attempt to succeed at increasing a participant's competence, it must be structured in a way that allows the endeavor to win the battle of attention for a period of time sufficient to accept and process the focal content. Simply 'being there' is not enough. As Lupia and Philpot (2005) demonstrate in experiments on how variations in the content and design of news websites affect participants' subsequent interest in politics, the structure of an online deliberation website must give participants an incentive to engage—an incentive strong enough to defeat participants' urges to attend to other stimuli when parts of the deliberation are of less than immediate relevance to participants.

The Battle for Elaboration/Long-Term Memory[4]

Other research reveals deep problems in grand claims about deliberation's transformative effects. In short, participants in a deliberative democracy session are going to remember precious little of what happened during the session. And the small fragments of the session that they retain may be quite different from what designers anticipated or practitioners led them to believe.

Even if a piece of information is attended to (wins a spot in short-term memory), it can only increase competence if it is processed in a particular way that leaves a unique cognitive legacy in long-term memory, or LTM. If it is not processed in these ways, it is—from a cognitive perspective—gone forever. LTM depends on chemical reactions within and across specialized cells in the brain, with a particular reliance on each neural connection's 'long-term potentiation', or LTP (Churchland and Sejnowski 1992; Kandel, et al. 1995; Schacter 2001). LTP corresponds to the probability of remembering something, and what we usually call learning involves changing LTP. The physical embodiment of learning that smoking is highly correlated with lung cancer, for example, is a change in LTP that makes you more likely to associate pain and death with smoking.

Two facts are important here for understanding the impacts of deliberation. First, if a speaker's attempt to increase another person's competence does not lead to a change in that person's long-term memory, then the attempt does not increase competence. Second, not every change in

---

[4] The content of this section is drawn primarily from the critique of Fishkin and Ackerman (2005) in Lupia (2005b).

LTP/LTM is sufficient to increase competence—the change must be significant enough to help someone accomplish a task that she could not do before.

These facts imply that it is hard to get participants in a deliberative setting to walk away from deliberation remembering what practitioners might want them to remember. To see why, think about the most important events in your life: your marriage, the birth of a child, times spent with your best friends, personal accomplishments, and depressing disappointments. Chances are that most of these events took place over a series of hours or days. How much do you remember about them? Even if you focus with all of your might, you can probably generate only a few seconds of distinct memories, tiny fragments of these critical events. Recall from long-term memory is not like bringing up an old document on your computer—which comes back exactly the way you saved it. There is significant forgetting.

Deliberation practitioners who ignore how citizens think about politics are often surprised to learn about how little they can control what participants will remember. 'The better argument', a construct that deliberative practitioners have used to characterize what participants will recall from a deliberative setting, can easily be crowded out in LTM by something else such as an outrageous statement or gossip conveyed between sessions. To scientists who have worked in laboratories, conducted experiments on thinking or learning, or rigorously engaged the evidence and logic of such literatures, the facts about cognition listed above are core elements of their common knowledge. The same should be true for deliberation practitioners. But it is not.

The competition among stimuli for a place in the working memory of any conscious human is fierce and ever present. Once a stimulus enters working memory, subsequent effort must be devoted towards processing it if the stimulus is to leave a cognitive legacy in LTM. Stimuli that are novel and of immediate relevance are privileged in such competitions (see Kandel et al. 1995). For deliberation scholars and designers, the implication of these attributes of attention and memory is that success requires a relationship between the goals of the deliberative enterprise and the desires of participants. Regardless of how important deliberation designers or scholars perceive their own activities or worldviews to be, deliberative presentations will 'fall on deaf ears' if they ignore, or discount as unenlightened, the desires or worldviews of participants.

4 An Alternate View

Deliberation, in either its online or conventional guise, is a form of civic education. In this and other writings, I have argued that such endeavors can more effectively and efficiently achieve civic-oriented objectives if they embrace, rather than run from, the underlying science of thinking and learning. I conclude this essay by offering a parallel argument from a different set of references—the social marketing literature. Social marketing is defined as: 'the application of commercial marketing technologies to the analysis, planning, execution, and evaluation of programs designed to influence the voluntary behavior of target audiences in order to improve their personal welfare and that of their society' (Andreasen 1995: 7).

Andreasen (1995) offers a simple way of distinguishing civically oriented informational efforts that fail from those that succeed in their efforts. He distinguishes effective from ineffective social marketers in several ways. Five of these ways are as follows.

1. Effective: 'The organization's mission is seen as bringing about behavior change by meeting the target market's needs and wants'.

Ineffective: 'The organization's mission is seen as inherently good'.

2. Effective: The customer is seen as someone with unique perceptions, needs, and wants to which the marketer must adapt. 'The assumption is made that customers have very good reasons for what they are doing'.

Ineffective: Customers are the problem. Here, the customer (or in the case of deliberation, citizens) are 'seen as the source of the problem. The customer is seen as deficient in one of two ways.

Ignorance. Because the social marketer knows what a good idea it is to practice safe sex or put campfires out carefully, he or she assumes that the reason other people don't do this is that they simply do not know how desirable the marketer's favorite behavior is. Customers who are not complying are just too ignorant of the virtues of the proposed action'.

Lack of Motivation. Every once in a while, social marketers who are convinced that customer ignorance is the main source of their lack of success are confronted by research data showing that customers are not all as ignorant as the marketers thought. They then turn to their backup explanation: the real problem must be a character flaw'.

3. Ineffective: 'Marketing research has a limited role'. 'Formative research (before the campaign gets underway) is typically limited to finding out the extent of consumer ignorance or apathy...But they do not look at what customers want, what they actually do, or what is keeping them from acting'.

Effective: Marketing research is vital. '[I]n evaluating overall program, good social marketers look to long-run behavioral impact and not to such potentially transient factors as information learned or attitudes changed...[to] give some assurance that there will be effects lasting well-beyond the limited span of the social marketing program'.

4. Ineffective: 'Customers are treated as a mass'. Organizers 'tend not to see the need for segmenting consumers into meaningful subgroups...They tend to treat customers as a mass, saying things like 'We want to reach everyone with our program', or to divide their customers into two of three elementary segments (men and women, urban and rural, young and old) and treat them essentially all alike with 'the one best approach'.

Effective: Customers are grouped in segments.

5. Ineffective: 'Competition is ignored'. Organizers 'seldom really get inside the heads of their target consumers... Now, if you mention this to [an organizer], the response will probably be something like 'Well the competition is the consumer's ignorance and lack of motivation'. But this attitude both misses the point and is patronizing to consumers. Target consumers in most behavior-change situations have very good reasons for maintaining the behavior patterns they have held—often for a lifetime. As experience has shown, a great many of these behavior patterns are not the result of ignorance but of conscious choice'.

Effective: Competition is seen to be everywhere and never ending.

Items one through three above parallel my earlier discussion of measurement. The items stress the importance of being objective and transparent about the purpose of a deliberative endeavor—particularly when it comes to distinguishing deliberation participants' best interests from a deliberation practitioner's (possibly self-centered view) of how the world should be. When rationalizing why people do not now engage in the particular form of deliberation that a particular practitioner prefers, broad—and untested— claims about the public's ignorance or lack of information are offered. Citizens are often portrayed in such appeals as simple-minded, not because the practitioner has conducted any research on what people want but because the potential audience has made different choices about how they use their time. Good intentions can become demagoguery if deliberation practitioners fail to take participants' concerns seriously.

Items four and five speak to the conditions under which deliberation can succeed. It reminds us that people pay attention to and remember different things. Therefore, a deliberative endeavor is more likely to succeed if it recognizes the challenges of winning the battles for participants' attention and memory—in particular the conditions for success stated above along with an understanding of how easy (or difficult) such conditions are to satisfy for particular individuals or groups. If deliberation practitioners are not discussing, or deliberation designers are not thinking about the conditions under which certain kinds of people will pay attention to, and be influenced by, certain kinds of presentations. That is, if they are claiming that deliberation would be good for everyone without a mention of the conditions, this is a sign that the practitioners are either unaware of—or have chosen to ignore—the underlying science of human thinking and learning. As utopian wordplay, such grand and universal claims can be quite stimulating. As a foundation for the actual practice of deliberation, they have the unstable properties of quicksand.[5]

5 Conclusion

The Internet makes possible kinds and quantities of communication and coordination that are unprecedented in human history. Through these portals people can learn about others in exciting new ways. The Internet domain has great untapped potential for transforming social life. Yet how and when such transformations will occur is governed, in part, by forces of nature, including basic properties of human cognition and perception—and in particular their implications for attention and memory.

For decades, a wide range of scholars has built a base of scientifically validated claims about human learning. The most effective among them have constructed evaluations of their research projects in a clear and transparent manner and have been vigilant in remaining open to credible third-party evaluations of their projects' performance. Deliberation scholars have been inconsistent, at best, in following these practices. The field of online deliberation can improve by better by using science's findings and evaluative practices as foundations of their own efforts. The promise of online deliberation is more likely to be achieved if its practitioners commit to transparency, replicability, and objectivity as the foundations of their endeavors.

References

Andreasen, A. R. 1995. *Marketing Social Change: Changing Behavior to Promote Health, Social Development, and the Environment.* San Francisco: Jossey-Bass Publishers.

Baddeley, A. D. and G. J. Hitch. 1974. Working Memory. *Recent Advances in Learning and Motivation, Volume 8*, ed. G. H. Bowker, 47-90. New York: Academic Press.

Churchland, P. S. and T. J. Sejnowski. 1992. *The Computational Brain.* Cambridge, MA: MIT Press.

---

[5] Dickson, Hafer, and Landa (2006) provide another recent example of research that distinguishes goals of deliberation practitioners from the conditions under which they can be achieved. The authors integrate insights from cognitive science, formal logic, and clever experiments to demonstrate that participants with different political ideologies will affect participants' willingness to speak and willingness (and ability) to attend to what others say. The results further document the often unexpected outcomes that deliberative democracy can produce and reinforce the importance of understanding deliberation's scientific foundations.

Dickson, E. S., C. Hafer, and D. Landa. 2006. *Cognition and Strategy: A Deliberation Experiment*. Working Papers 0016. New York: New York University, Center for Experimental Social Science.

Fishkin, J. S. and B. A. Ackerman. 2005. *Deliberation Day*. New Haven: Yale University Press.

Habermas, J. 1996. *Between Facts and Norms: Contributions to a Discourse Theory of Law and Democracy*. Cambridge, MA: MIT Press.

Hewstone, M. and F. Fincham. 1996. Attribution Theory and Research: Basic Issues and Applications. *Introduction to Social Psychology*, eds. M. Hewstone, W. Stroebe, and G. M. Stephenson, 167-204. Oxford: Blackwell.

Kandel, E. R., J. H. Schwartz, and T. M. Jessell. 1995. *Essentials of Neural Science and Behavior*. Norwalk, CT: Appleton and Lange.

Kitayama, S. and E. Burnstein. 1988. Automaticity in Conversations: A Reexamination of the Mindlessness Hypothesis. *Journal of Personality and Social Psychology* 54(2): 219-224.

Lupia, A. 2002. Deliberation Disconnected: What it Takes to Improve Civic Competence. *Law and Contemporary Problems* 65: 133-150.

Lupia, A. 2005a. Necessary Conditions for Increasing Civic Competence. A chapter of the book manuscript *Questioning Our Competence: Science versus Elitism in the Quest to Make Better Citizens*. Available at http://www.umich.edu/~lupia (last accessed September 26, 2008)

Lupia, A. 2005b. The Wrong Tack (Can Deliberation Day Increase Civic Competence?). *Legal Affairs* 3(1): 43-45.

Lupia, A. 2006. How Elitism Undermines the Study of Voter Competence. *Critical Review* 18(1-3): 217-232.

Lupia, A. and T. S. Philpot. 2005. Views from Inside the 'Net: How Websites Affect Young Adults' Political Interest. *The Journal of Politics* 67(4): 1122-1142.

Posner, R. 2005. Smooth Sailing: Democracy Doesn't Need Deliberation Day. *Legal Affairs* 3(1): 41-42.

Schacter, D. L. 2001. *The Seven Sins of Memory: How the Mind Forgets and Remembers*. Boston: Houghton-Mifflin.

4

Deliberative Democracy, Online Discussion, and Project PICOLA (Public Informed Citizen Online Assembly)

ROBERT CAVALIER WITH MISO KIM AND ZACHARY SAM ZAISS

1 Introduction

Basic to deliberative democracy is an *inclusive conversation* that is *informed and well structured.* All the better if there are ways to capture the *results* of the dialogue and present these to stakeholders in such a way as to *influence* policy and other sorts of practical outcomes. To implement this kind of environment online is the goal of what could be called 'deliberative e-democracy' (Flew 2005).

In 2001, Robert Cavalier, Peter Muhlberger, and Peter Shane used a National Science Foundation (NSF) grant to develop software tools to support this kind of online deliberation and to do basic social science research on the phenomenon of political deliberation. The project, completed in the summer of 2005, and entitled 'Developing and Testing A High Telepresence Virtual Agora for Broad Citizen Participation: A Multi-Trait, Multi-Method Investigation', had three aims: (1) develop software that will support an online environment conducive to effective citizen deliberation on public policy issues, (2) use that software to explore the dynamics and outcomes of online deliberation, as well as the comparison between online

Online Deliberation: Design, Research, and Practice.
Todd Davies and Seeta Peña Gangadharan (eds.).
Copyright © 2009, CSLI Publications.

and face-to-face deliberation, and (3) offer a framework for analyzing the legal policy making processes of government agencies. Cavalier's participation focused mainly on discussions of interface design, Peter Muhlberger was the chief social science researcher, and Peter Shane's interests focused on issues relating to the policy making processes of government agencies.

The software developed for this project made it possible for us to stage a two-phase experiment in online citizen deliberation. Phase One, in July, 2004, involved a highly controlled comparison of real-time online and face-to-face deliberation. Phase Two, from September, 2004 through March, 2005, involved citizens in a combination of real-time online meetings and asynchronous deliberations to identify (1) critical issues facing the Pittsburgh school system, (2) a promising policy approach to addressing those issues, and (3) a strategy for implementing the citizens' preferred policy approach. We were able to perform this experiment with a genuinely representative sample of Pittsburghers, including many with little or no computer or online experience prior to our study. Although data analysis remains preliminary, it appears that there was no difference between the Phase I computer-mediated and face-to-face discussions in terms of the attitudes of the participants changing as a result of their engaging in discussion. Both groups tended to end with participants forming a strong consensus on the issues, always in the direction of the expert opinion. Discussants in both conditions reported higher levels of critical thinking, confidence, and empowerment than did our control group, which read about the issue under discussion, but did not participate in deliberations. Further, participants ascribed a very high degree of legitimacy to the collective outcome of their deliberations.[1]

This was one of the largest university-based social science studies of a random sample of citizens (N = 571). The research showed that *audio-based conversations with video-based moderators* (using deliberative practices such as turn-taking, etc.) showed no significant difference from face-to-face deliberations following the same practices. The significance of this outcome is far reaching: well designed and carefully implemented online tools for deliberation can be used alone or in conjunction with face-to-face deliberations to deliver useful results to decision makers.

---

[1] A website, The Virtual Agora Project, contains all the studies and research relating to this NSF Grant (http://www.virtualagora.org/, last accessed November 1, 2008).

2 Augmenting Deliberative Democracy with Online Tools: Project PICOLA

Project PICOLA[2] (Public Informed Citizen Online Assembly) evolved as a parallel development project designed specifically to model the protocols of Fishkin's Deliberative Poll® (Fishkin 1995). A front-end interface tied together software for both synchronous and asynchronous discussions as well as tools for registration and survey taking.[3] Because PICOLA, like the Virtual Agora, was based on a complex programming environment that combined both commercial and open software tools, we were not able to sustain it past its initial five-year cycle.[4] However, the successful use of the prototype has led us to conclude that the design of PICOLA constitutes a paradigm for these kinds of online tools. It stands as a 'regulatory ideal' for high telepresence, integrated deliberative e-democracy.[5]

PICOLA delivered a multimedia environment designed for enabling online structured dialogue. At the highest level, it embeds in its design the notion of 'computers as theatre', first described by Laurel (1993). By redescribing the relation of user to screen along the lines of Aristotle's *Poetics*, Laurel argues that the user must be brought *into* the drama of the program and not seen merely as someone outside the screen in need of guidance. This approach is now apparent in the design of video games, where users can be transformed into a 'skier' or 'medieval knight'. In a similar manner, a user enters PICOLA in such a way as to be transformed into a 'citizen' engaged in a community conversation. If we are successful in this, we can make the computer disappear and replace it with a virtual public sphere (Laurel 1993; see also Murray 1997; Cavalier 2005c).

---

[2] The term and acronym 'PICOLA' was coined by Peter Shane. Development of PICOLA occurred at Carnegie Mellon's Center for the Advancement of Applied Ethics and Political Philosophy. See also Cavalier (2005a, 2005b).

[3] See http://caae.phil.cmu.edu/picola/ (last accessed September 26, 2008).

[4] This is a cautionary note: While customized software based on open source and commercial tools is an enticing concept, the truth is that such programs often require a $60,000/year programmer to maintain them. And it is all too common to find such environments orphaned once the programmer moves on.

[5] Commercial products such as Polimetrix's *Vox Populi* (http://www.polimetrix.com/services/products.html, last accessed November 1, 2008) and Adobe's Connect are tools useful for the kinds of discussion environments envisioned by PICOLA. But a full-bodied implementation of the PICOLA design remains to be developed.

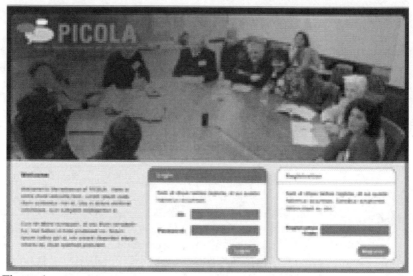

Figure 1.

In line with many virtual environments, PICOLA has a standard login or registration area, as well as the capability for administrators to add announcements and other information to help orient the participants' understanding of a particular event. Its login area also has a place for picture taking. This allows the program to capture an image of the participant, reduce it to a 'picon' and place it next to the person's name in the synchronous roundtable discussion area. It is remarkable how a simplified image of a person lends itself to a sense of presence so important to the 'virtual experience' of another human being.

But to create a virtual public sphere where the participant truly feels immersed as a citizen in PICOLA's virtual environment, it was also necessary to gain an in-depth understanding of the environment that exists for the typical face-to-face experience. This task was an important part of a year-long study in human computer interaction.[6]

PICOLA includes an *education phase* where participants can learn about the issue through readings in an online reading room with customizable content, a *discussion phase* where participants join together as citizens

---

[6] The study employed four analysis methods: contextual inquiry and design, heuristic evaluation, cognitive walkthrough, and think aloud interviews. The investigators were Alex Darrow, Peter Jones, Jessica Smith, Greg Vassallo, and Sam Zaiss. Elements of this study have been incorporated into the design of PICOLA.

to discuss the issue at hand and develop questions to ask an expert panel, and a *reflection phase* where participants can think about the issues further, continue discussions in the asynchronous forum, and take a survey to express their opinions on the topic. The resulting program, 'deliberative by design,' delivers and supports an online conversation that is *informed, structured,* and *documented.*

Unlike a face-to-face deliberative experience, which follows a linear process, PICOLA needs to be accessible at any time and anywhere.[7] Thus the interface first brings participants to the 'My PICOLA' page after logging in, where they can view announcements for their discussion group, review readings that they previously marked as meaningful or important, and check for new postings in the asynchronous forum.

Participants can jump to a particular document or forum topic within the 'My PICOLA' page, or they can navigate to those pages using the tabbed browsing available at the top of the page. In this way, participants are able to freely browse the PICOLA environment, restricted only by scheduled events (such as a synchronous discussion), which would naturally be available at their scheduled times.

We chose readings and recent forum postings to be called out on the 'My PICOLA' page in order to encourage participants to peruse those pages early and often. In so doing, we hope to ground participants in the topic via the 'Reading Room' and, if appropriate, to encourage early discussions and camaraderie in the 'Asynchronous Forum'.

While these aspects of PICOLA do much to draw participants in as citizens, it is in the 'Synchronous Discussion' area that participants become fully immersed in the virtual public sphere. We arrived at this immersive environment by studying how these types of discussions happen in real life. Naturally, some positive aspects need to be maintained, such as: (1) enabling people to carry on brief, side conversations with one another (supported by the 'Text Chat'), (2) allowing for immediate, nonverbal responses to various points (supported by the inclusion of emoticons for each participant), and (3) having one focal point where important issues and questions for the expert panel can be displayed (supported by the moderator's 'Whiteboard'). On the other hand, we included a speaking queue to add a level of order to the conversation (and to prevent one person from monopolizing the discussion or interrupting other participants continuously). We also have a

---

[7] For optimal use, certain bandwidths are recommended (T1 or DSL). These requirements are driven by certain design features. While we remain concerned with the digital divide, we decided to aim for the future. This is also one reason we chose Libraries as recommended host sites for PICOLA. Furthermore, the penetration of WiFi in both urban and rural areas will ameliorate some of these concerns.

clock feature to indicate a certain upper limit to each participant's 'turn at the microphone' (while this is variable, two or three minutes seem to work well).

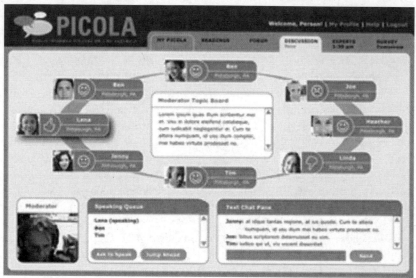

Figure 2.

After observing the 'Expert Panel' (or an archive of one), participants are able to continue the discussion synchronously in a second 'Discussion' or asynchronously in the 'Forum'. Expert opinions, if delivered in the form of education and not rhetorical debate, have an important role to fulfill, as certain discussions can generate inaccurate information that requires a 'reality check' from time to time. In the asynchronous area of the 'Expert Panel', further discussion and clarification by the experts themselves can assist in the overall quality of the discussion. Last, but not least, the 'Survey' feature contains standard social science formats for measuring opinions and is designed to elicit the reasons behind the opinions as well as the intensity of those opinions.

An 'Administration Console' should allow for customization of the materials as well as management of registration, forums, and survey. Influenced by an interest in the social science aspect of deliberation, information on users would be tracked, and the live synchronous conversations could be retrieved and displayed.

3   Mobile PICOLA

With mobile technologies, yet another 'public sphere' is emerging. It is our hope that this democratic mobile movement can also be made deliberative and hence stronger in its use and impact. To see how this might come into being, we explored the integration of PICOLA functionality into cell phone/PDA devices (Mobile PICOLA). How people will eventually use the tools that we prototyped for Mobile PICOLA can only be guessed at, but the advantages of these features could already be seen in our beta-tests.[8]

Figure 3.

The audio-based synchronous roundtable in PICOLA has been the best example of high telepresence in this project. Once people enter the roundta-

---

[8] Miso Kim was lead designer. Her work was inspired by Howard Rheingold (2002).

ble, making all the necessary adjustments to their sound and headset components, an effortless conversation ensues. But people are not always at their computers when we are ready to start. They need to check the current set up (e.g., 'has the audio control panel been left on mute by the previous user?'), and they often need us to reschedule. Cell phone or personal digital assistant (PDA) devices may be able to close the gap between user and machine. The advantages of cell phone-PDA devices include *mobility* (anytime, any place), *identity* (cell phones are customized by each individual user and are part of their apparel, so to speak), and *accessibility* (I can join a PICOLA roundtable even as I walk across campus). These advantages can break down the barriers to the use of PICOLA-like environments, and they can do so in a way that will enhance its impact *qualitatively*.

4 PICOLA-lite

After the backend for PICOLA could no longer be maintained, we developed an html-based 'lite' version that used a single, customizable interface. This tied together different programs like Adobe Connect for synchronous conversations, Microsoft SharePoint for an asynchronous discussion board, and SurveyMonkey for polling.

A version of PICOLA-lite was used as a way to augment the face-to-face forum. We found that it is important to give participants an extra five days to 'continue the conversation'. This allows people to add new points that they may have considered after the event, and its very availability prevents people from feeling frustrated that they did not get a chance to follow up (even if they do not use that opportunity). We also experimented with what we called 'Alumni Assemblies'.[9] In this case, PICOLA-lite was the only way to bring such a dispersed group together.

5 Concluding Remarks: The Importance of Institutional Infrastructure

The various uses and settings for PICOLA highlight the importance of context in the use of online tools as well as the need for varying degrees of institutional support. Indeed, just as a child may need a whole village to grow successfully, software needs an organizational infrastructure to be used successfully.

---

[9] Jim Fishkin first mentioned this idea as a good way to build 'social capital' amongst college alumni. See http://caae.phil.cmu.edu/picola/public_art/ (last accessed September 26, 2008) for a sample PICOLA-lite Campus Conversation.

Throughout all these applications of deliberative democracy—face-to-face and online—the tasks of representing issues, getting good samples, creating the conditions for well-structured conversations, and conducting useful surveys are enormous. The required time and personnel are daunting. In short, the task of *doing democracy*, of making democracy stronger, is incredibly hard. But in today's world, we have no other choice. And it is our hope that well-designed forums, augmented by well-designed online tools, will help in some way to bring about these needed changes.

References

Cavalier, R. 2005a. *Project PICOLA*. Paper presented at the Second Conference on Online Deliberation: Design, Research, and Practice, Stanford, CA, May 20, 2005.

Cavalier, R. 2005b. *PICOLA and On-Line Deliberative Polling*. Paper presented at Building Democracy through Online Citizen Deliberation, Ohio State University—Moritz College of Law, Columbus, November 18, 2005.

Cavalier, R. 2005c. The Poetics of Simulation: An Analysis of Programs in Ethics and Conflict Resolution. *Virtual Decisions: Digital Simulations for Teaching Reasoning in the Social Sciences and Humanities*, ed. S. Cohen, 115-36. New York: Lawrence Erlbaum.

Fishkin, J. 1995. *The Voice of the People*. New Haven: Yale University Press.

Flew, T. 2005. *From e-Government to Online Deliberative Democracy*. Presented at the Oxford Internet Institute Summer Doctoral Program, Chinese Academy of Social Sciences, Beijing. July 11, 2005.

Laurel, B. 1993. *Computers as Theatre*. Reading, MA: Addison-Wesley Publishing, Co.

Murray, J. H. 1997. *Hamlet on the Holodeck: The Future of Narrative in Cyberspace*. New York: Free Press.

Rheingold, H. 2002. *Smart Mobs: The Next Social Revolution*. Basic Books.

Part II
Online Dialogue in the Wild

5

Friends, Foes, and Fringe: Norms and Structure in Political Discussion Networks

JOHN KELLY, DANYEL FISHER, AND MARC SMITH

1 Introduction

The Internet offers numerous modes of online discussion, with many different forms of control. Some empower one person to control agenda and content. Blogs are perhaps the most extreme version of this, in which one person contributes most of the content and can censor, delete or disallow feedback from others. Moderated discussion groups offer a less extreme version of such control, in which discussants are expected to carry on the majority of the discourse. Still other forums allow collaborative, group controls. Slashdot is a premiere example, in which users deploy randomly assigned rating points to grade particular comments up or down, making them more or less visible to subsequent readers (Lampe 2004). If we envision a continuum of control, from the dictatorial blog on the one hand, through the constitutional monarchy of moderated discussion, to the kind of Athenian democracy (power being randomly assigned to 'citizens' for short durations) of Slashdot, the extreme anarchic pole is perhaps best represented by Usenet (Pfafenberger 2003).

Except in the case of a relatively few moderated discussions, Usenet offers no overt forms of control to any participant. At most, one author can add disfavored others to their 'killfile' and thus turn a deaf ear toward them

Online Deliberation: Design, Research, and Practice.
Todd Davies and Seeta Peña Gangadharan (eds.).
Copyright © 2009, CSLI Publications.

But they cannot diminish any other author's access to the forum, and their only real power is to choose people to engage with, by deciding which posts to reply to. And yet, despite the 'anarchy' of Usenet, its newsgroups feature stable, measurable structural characteristics. Somehow, order is maintained. Most interestingly, these regular structures vary greatly according to the social purpose of the newsgroup. For instance, a technical newsgroup, populated mainly with questions from the befuddled many and answers by the expert few, has a very different network profile from a support group, in which many regulars send welcoming messages to newcomers and there are broadly distributed exchanges of advice and emotional solidarity (Turner, Smith, Fisher, and Welser 2005).

Political newsgroups have their own distinctive network characteristics, and offer an interesting lesson in how regular structural features emerge from individual-level choices (Fisher, Smith, and Welser 2006). Despite persuasive speculation (Sunstein 2001) and the tentative findings of some early Internet research efforts (Wilhelm 1999), online political discussions need not necessarily become echo chambers of the like-minded. The tendency to political homophily clearly exists in blogs (Adamic and Glance 2005) and seems to appear as well in more controlled environments featuring gatekeepers of one sort or another, but the kind of open, anarchic discussions found on Usenet have quite the opposite tendency. We have previously found that debate, not agreement or reinforcement, is the dominant activity in political groups (Kelly, Fisher, and Smith 2005).

Consider the implications of a genre of discourse based around debate rather than information-sharing, emotional support, social coordination, or some other purpose. Clearly, the latter sorts of groups feature rather decisive boundary maintenance. In a technical newsgroup about Unix (for instance), someone offering a recipe for meatloaf would probably be ignored. Likewise someone posing as a Unix expert but offering fallacious advice would soon be identified as a charlatan (Donath 1999), and likewise ignored. In a cancer support group, an author attacking the attitudes of other authors and offering detailed disputations of their posts would be denounced and subsequently ignored by the community. In most newsgroups, antagonism and perceived wrongfulness are a ticket to rapid ostracism through the collective silence of the core author population. 'Newbies' are admonished not to 'feed the trolls'—that is, participants new to the community are asked by seasoned members not to respond to blatantly provocative posts.

By contrast, it would at first blush seem like political newsgroups have no need of such boundary maintenance. As we found previously, the great majority of authors (let us call them *fighters*) preferentially respond to messages from those on the other side; they respond to opponents more often than their allies. A second, smaller group of authors (we can call them *friendlies*) direct their attention to allies and refuse to engage opponents, despite the fact that they are routinely ignored by the former and harangued by the latter. Because their opponents do not reciprocate their discursive predilections by ignoring them, the *friendlies* are just as central to a political newsgroup's core discussion network as the much more numerous *fighters*. In a political newsgroup, posters cannot be left alone by the opposing cluster even if they try. Indeed, it would seem that the only way to opt out of the fight is by opting out of posting to the newsgroup altogether.

The boundaries of the group are illustrated by a third type of author, even more rare, who tries not to be ignored, and nevertheless usually is. This type of author—the 'fringe'—helps show how boundary maintenance is at work in political newsgroups as well.

We discovered this type of author serendipitously, while looking at ego network diagrams of core political newsgroup authors. In the following section, we will take a look at some of these network diagrams and see how they illustrate the link between authors' microlevel choices about whom to talk to, and macrolevel structure of the discussion network. We also see boundary maintenance at work in an environment where most 'enemies' are *good*, in the sense of being in demand, but how some exceed the bounds of appropriate opposition.

2   Political Discussion Networks

The current paper builds on the same data as our previous research (Kelly, Fisher, and Smith 2005), which contains a detailed account of the base data collection and analysis. In brief, core authors were identified from eight political newsgroups during November 2003. Microsoft Research's Netscan tool was used to capture a wide range of data on author behavior and thread structure and to extract network data on core author behavior. A *core author* is one who was among the twenty to forty most frequent (in terms of days active) contributors to the newsgroup during that month. A corpus of threaded political discussions was assembled containing hundreds of posts by all core authors. These were coded for evidence of political attitudes and for aspects of discursive behavior. Authors were clustered according to political attitudes, with only a small few found to be unclassifiable.

In the previous work, we showed that political newsgroups were found to have some distinctive features:

- Almost all participants can be meaningfully assigned to distinct ideological or issue position clusters, depending on the particular newsgroup, for instance *left* and *right,* or *pro-choice* and *pro-life.*

- Most newsgroups are bipolar or organized around two dominant opposing clusters. In principle, some newsgroups could be multi-polar: one of the eight studied in the previous work appeared to be centered around three dominant sides.
- Replies to posts—and thus newsgroup interaction—are over-whelmingly across ideological or issue clusters, not within them.
- Most authors choose to reply to messages by their opponents over their allies and respond to far more messages on average from in-dividual opponents than to individual allies. Further, Fisher, Smith, and Welser (2006) argue that political group members prefer to re-spond to people who are well embedded in the conversation over new members.
- Those rare authors who prefer to reply to allies are themselves nevertheless disproportionately responded to by opponents. Be-cause of these authors, 'in-links' (i.e. responses to an author by others) are very highly predictive of that author's political position, much more so than their 'out-links' (i.e. whom they choose to re-spond to).
- There are tendencies toward balance in political newsgroups, in the following two patterns:
    - o Groups focused on a range of issues and featuring clusters best described as *ideological* (left/right, lib-eral/conservative, socialist/capitalist, etc.) are generally balanced in both the populations of regular authors be-longing to each cluster, and in the amount of message traffic generated by each cluster.
    - o Groups focused on a single contentious issue, like abor-tion or Middle East politics, are generally unbalanced in the population of authors belonging to each *issue-position* cluster. Yet the minority authors post more messages on average, and the message traffic generated by the clusters is thus significantly more balanced than the author popu-lations.

As we will see in detail, these political and discursive tendencies yield a network structure in which an author population of discursive opponents, though politically clustered into two (or potentially more) distinct groups, are tightly bound in a central discussion core by dense bonds of replies that tie opponents to one another more tightly than allies.

This does not mean that authors do not reply periodically to people who agree with them. We can show this visually by looking at a network dia-gram of the core authors' reply structure. If a node is a core author, and a network tie is considered to be a single reply, the core author population is so densely connected as to form almost a complete graph, i.e. a network is which all nodes are directly connected (Figure 1). To see the structure more clearly we must raise the number of replies that constitute a link, filtering out weaker bonds (Figure 2). Figures 1 and 2 show linked discussion cores from the newsgroup *alt.politics.bush*.

In those figures, nodes representing the core authors are laid out in a circle; authors who share a political position are placed near each other: liberals near other liberals (circles); conservatives near other conservatives

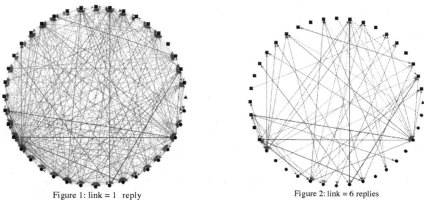

Figure 1: link = 1 reply Figure 2: link = 6 replies

(squares). Edges with arrows connect replies: an author 'points to' another author by replying; more replies get a thicker edge. Figure 1 shows that virtually all authors have replied to each other at some point or another, while Figure 2 shows that the dominant portion of replies falls across groups. The cross-cluster pattern of replies is very clear when the threshold of replies that define a link is increased.

3 Author Behavior and Network Position

Differences among types of political authors arise from their discursive behavior, and can be seen in (1) their choices about whom to reply to, (2) decisions by network members to reply to them, and (3) their position in the network structure arising from *a* and *b* (in combination with the same relationships among other actors in the network). In Figure 3, we can see microlevel features of author behavior for an exemplar of each of the tree types and the network's response. In these figures, too, authors from the two dominant political clusters are represented by squares and circles. Minor players—not in the core—are drawn as smaller gray shapes.

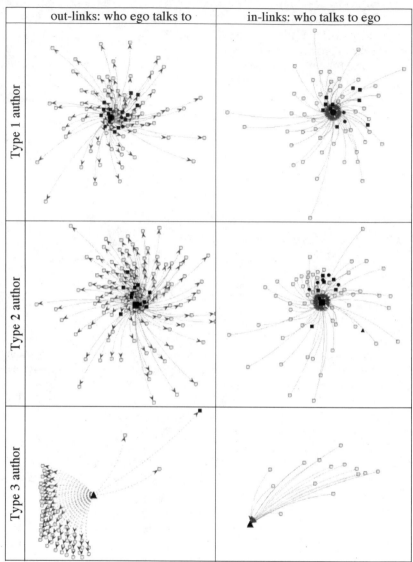

Figure 3: author choices and network response

A *fighter* (type 1 author) preferentially responds to opponents (out-links) and is likewise responded to mainly by opponents (in-links), with only partial reciprocation from friends. The *friendly* (type 2 author) responds only to friends, most of who do not reciprocate, and is responded to by a number of opponents anyway.

The *fringe* author exists at the edge of acceptable discourse within the group. Remember that the *fringe* author only shows up in the analysis because he (this author self-identifies as male) is a regular contributor to the newsgroup, posting messages to it nearly every day. The *fringe* author's views are extreme and do not fall into the newsgroup's dominant ideological clusters (and so is coded as a triangle). This *fringe* author is a provocateur, posting a great number of initiating posts rather than replies. Many of the replies that he posts are 'cross-posts': he replies to a message in a different group and adds this group to the conversation. (Cross-posts are symbolized with dotted lines.) The author's reply to a message by a core author (coded with a square) is ignored, and the only responses from the mainstream newsgroup population come from new and/or infrequent participants ('newbies', coded light gray).

If we now turn from microlevel reply behavior to network structure, certain implications of that behavior are clear. The network diagrams of Figure 4, like Figure 3, use a so-called 'physics model': nodes repel from ones they are not linked to and try to be a fixed distance from ones that they are linked to. Roughly, 'close' suggests 'likely to be connected', while 'far' suggests 'less likely to be connected'. In these egocentric diagrams, focusing on the neighbors around a single, larger node, we can see that both *fighters* and *friendlies* are well-enmeshed in the discussion core. In fact, it is impossible to tell the difference between the two based on overall network position, because the replies to their messages are so dense. In contrast, the *fringe* author sticks out like a sore thumb. An author whose views are not seen as worthy of rebuttal or response by core authors is, figuratively, expelled from the network. Here we see boundary maintenance at work.

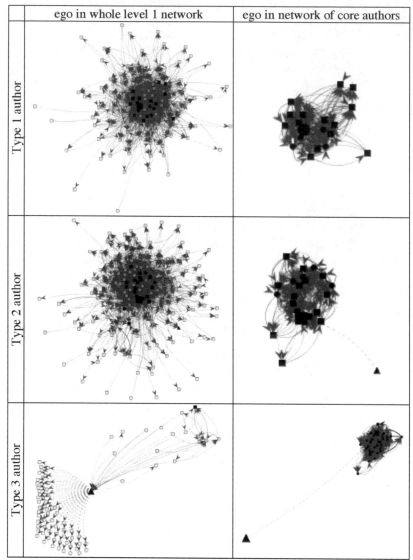

Figure 4: network position by author type

Group members use the one tool available to them, then, to maintain the boundary of 'acceptable dialogue': they ignore this fringe author, giving him little satisfaction of triggering a broader discussion. Even in an arena dedicated to opposition—where every issue is contentious—the group manifests tacit accord on what issues and ideas are not worth discussing, and leaves them behind.

4 Conclusion

Our example *fringe* author is just one instance of the type. We have observed other fringe authors in different newsgroups, also far from the mainstream of debate. Their ego networks are similarly distinctive: they are isolated, garnering few responses from the active core of the newsgroup. Some of them attempt to reply more to core authors, some of them generate more or fewer seed posts, but all of them are relegated to the network periphery by the lack of demand for their ideas. What is very important to recognize, and very interesting, is that they are not marginalized because their ideas are uncomfortable, contentious, or, simply, disagreed with by others.

Keep in mind that most interaction, in fact the soul of interaction, in political newsgroups is strong, often vehement, disagreement between opponents. One finds Marxists sparring with Libertarians, liberal Democrats battling conservative Republicans, 'pro-life' opponents of abortion calling 'pro-choice' authors 'murderers', Israeli citizens arguing with Arab nationalists. In Usenet political newsgroups, one finds people with strong and often irreconcilable views fighting each other in extended chains of argumentation. Sometimes it is emotional, with name calling of the worst sort. Sometimes it is highly rational, with detailed point-by-point rebuttals of quoted sentences and paragraphs. Usenet authors seek out those with whom they disagree and expend enormous energy arguing with them. But the authors we here call *fringe* usually can't get the time of day.

This behavior is noticeably different from that described by Baker (2001). Baker describes an amiable group, fans of a popular television show, that try to work over a period of several months to understand and change the behavior of an egregious 'troll'. The group repeatedly engages the troll, responding to his posts and discussing his ideas, attempting to change his mind. Nowhere does Baker document a notion of ignoring the troll.

The reason for this requires further investigation no doubt, but is interesting to ponder. How might trolls and *fringe* authors be alike and how different? In some ways, the *fringe* authors behave like trolls, for instance posting incendiary messages and cross-posting their responses to messages into lots of other newsgroups. In other ways, including motivation, they may differ. Trolls often seem to be out to inflame other participants for the sake of being troublesome or disruptive, often appearing disingenuous or inauthentic to an experienced reader. By contrast, *fringe* authors in political groups usually seem quite sincere in their adherence to fanatical views. So, are *fringe* authors a type of troll? Or are both simply cases of bad citizens in the discursive community? Or are they very different types of actor altogether? In terms of behavior and motivation, and also network response, we should look more closely at *fringe* authors in relation to the more well-studied troll.

The *fringe* authors we have encountered are exactly the ones one would hope to find marginalized in a political discussion network. They are the sort who quote the 'Protocols of the Elders of Zion' and offer genetic justifications for racial discrimination. Their views are not ignored because they are considered objectionable or extreme; indeed, extremity is often incorporated into the discussion. They are ignored because their ideas are not considered even mildly relevant to any debate that anyone, on whichever side of whichever spectrum, wants to have. They are not even worthy of rebuttal.

What people participating in political discourse care to discuss, as well as the particular attitudes they have about any given topic, are meaningfully related to the structure of concerns and attitudes in the larger political society to which they belong. In that larger society there are well-established political issues, frames and philosophies. To be involved in democratic life is to be engaged with these. People sometimes fear the Internet as a political discussion medium. On one hand it is accused of promoting smug, ideologically insular echo chambers, and on the other, it is said to hand the keys of the castle to Nazis, violent anarchists, and other assorted ideological bogeymen. But we should take heart from the findings of this study. In anarchic (in terms of rules of governance, not political philosophy) online political discourse networks, there is active boundary maintenance, informed by group norms held even among those who disagree strongly with one another about the topics under discussion. An author must be interesting to be engaged by others. The discourse network is shaped, and maintained, by *demand*, not *supply*. An implication of this is clear. What threatens democratic online political discourse and invites the worst sort of extremity is not the presence of radical voices, but the absence of reasoned ones.

References

Adamic, L. and N. Glance. 2005. *The Political Blogosphere and the 2004 U.S. Election: Divided They Blog.* Paper presented at LinkKDD-2005, Chicago, Illinois, August 21, 2005.

Agrawal, R., S. Rajagopalan, R. Srikant, and Y. Xu. 2003. *Mining Newsgroups Using Networks Arising from Social Behavior.* Paper presented at WWW2003, Budapest, Hungary, May 20-24, 2003.

Baker, P. 2001. Moral Panic and Alternative Identity Construction in Usenet. *Journal of Computer-Mediated Communication* 7(1). Available at http://jcmc.indiana.edu/vol7/issue1/baker.html (last accessed August 31, 2008)

Donath, J. S. 1999. Identity and deception in the virtual community. *Communities in Cyberspace*, eds. P. Kollock and M. Smith, 29-59. London: Routledge.

Fisher, D., M. Smith, and H. Welser. 2006. *You Are Who You Talk To: Detecting Roles in Usenet Newsgroups*. Paper presented at the Hawai'i International Conference on Systems Science, Kauai, Hawaii, January 4-7, 2006.

Kelly, J., D. Fisher, and M. Smith. 2005. *Debate, Division, and Diversity: Political Discourse Networks in Usenet Newsgroups*. Available at http://www.coi.columbia.edu/pdf/kelly_fisher_smith_ddd.pdf (last accessed August 31, 2008)

Lampe, C. and P. Resnick. 2004. Slash(dot) and Burn: Distributed Moderation in a Large Online Conversation Space. *Proceedings of ACM CHI 2004 Conference on Human Factors in Computing Systems, Vienna, Austria, April 24-29, 2004*, eds. E. Dykstra-Erickson and M. Tscheligi, 543-550.

Pfafenberger, B. 2003. A Standing Wave in the Web of Our Communications: Usenet and the Socio-Technical Construction of Cyberspace Values. *From Usenet to CoWebs: Interacting with Social Information Spaces*, eds. C. Lueg and D. Fisher, 20-43. London: Springer.

Sunstein, C. R. 2001. *Republic.com*. Princeton, NJ: Princeton University Press.

Turner, T., M. Smith, D. Fisher, and H. Welser. 2005. Picturing Usenet: Mapping Computer-Mediated Collective Action. *Journal of Computer-Mediated Communication* 10(4): Article 7. Available at http://jcmc.indiana.edu/vol10/issue4/turner.html (last accessed August 31, 2008)

Wilhelm, A. 1999. Virtual Sounding Boards: How deliberative is online political discussion. *Digital Democracy: Discourse and Decision Making in the Information Age*, eds. B. N. Hague and B. Loader, 154-178. New York: Routledge.

6

Searching the Net for Differences of Opinion

WARREN SACK, JOHN KELLY, AND MICHAEL DALE

1 Introduction

Political theorists, at least since John Stuart Mill in his book *On Liberty* (1859), have asserted that exposure to conflicting viewpoints is beneficial for democracy. Through exposure to political viewpoints contrary to their own, citizens are said to gain political tolerance and an understanding of opposing rationales. Recent empirical work has confirmed these assertions (Fishkin 1992; Mutz 2002). However, there is no clear means by which a citizen can find opposing opinions. Factors such as the consolidation of media ownership (Bagdikian 2004), neighborhood segregation (by, for example, race, and class), lack of weak ties in personal and cross-community-oriented social networks (Putnam 2000; Granovetter 1973), proliferation of ideologically exclusive weblogs and radio and television talk shows, and recent technological developments that allow the 'filtering' of Internet-distributed news (Sunstein 2001), all make it difficult for individual citizens to find significantly different opinions. Contrary to Negroponte (1995), we posit the development of a software technology to facilitate the construction of a 'Daily Not Me', a sort of 'search engine' that, when given a topic (e.g., 'abortion'), will return a range of diverse opinions about the topic (e.g., 'pro-choice' and 'pro-life').

In this chapter, we present some preliminary results towards this long-term goal. Our work bootstraps recent, prior work in which one of the

Online Deliberation: Design, Research, and Practice.
Todd Davies and Seeta Peña Gangadharan (eds.).
Copyright © 2009, CSLI Publications.

co-authors used qualitative content analysis to characterize the political leanings of 120 prolific Usenet newsgroup authors (Kelly 2004). Software was developed to automatically download, from a Usenet newsgroup archive, tens of thousands of discussion threads containing over one million individual messages. Within these threads of discussion, we were able to find several thousand 'mixed exchanges' in which known discussants (i.e., two or more discussants identified by Kelly) of differing political opinion exchanged messages. We have performed an empirical analysis of the structural characteristics (e.g., size, branching factor) of the discussion threads surrounding these mixed exchanges. Our goal is to identify a set of computable, search heuristics that might be employed in a 'Daily Not Me' technology for finding opposing, political viewpoints as expressed in the archives of online discussion groups.

We understand this work to be complementary to the work of Fishkin (1991) and others who have created new environments and situations where deliberative discussion can take place. We hypothesize that in vast, online discussion spaces—like the space of Usenet newsgroups—there must exist places, or at least moments, when deliberative discussion already takes place 'in the wild'. We envision a search engine that, when given a topic, will find likely threads of discussion where opposing opinions are being or have been expressed. In this chapter, we report on our initial efforts to implement the first preprocessing step of such a search engine. We need to identify one or more quick and relatively accurate heuristics that can be used to comb through a large database of newsgroup or weblog postings to identify likely places of political exchange. The output of the mechanisms we describe here will be the input to further processing steps of the search engine that perform a detailed analysis of the contents of the messages. In short, the heuristics described here are 'triage' techniques intended to narrow down which message threads should be given more detailed analyses.

First, we give an overview of the newsgroup messages we have examined and briefly describe the results of a previous study by one of the co-authors upon which we rely for the present work (Kelly 2004). Second, we describe a set of independent variables associated with the discussion threads. Our dependent variable concerns whether or not liberals and conservatives exchanged messages in a discussion thread. We seek a heuristic in which some combination of easily measured, independent variables can be used to predict the likelihood that a thread contains an exchange of views between at least one liberal discussion participant and one conservative discussant. Third, we present such a thread categorization heuristic as a simple discriminant function. We further simplify this function by eliminating some of the independent variables that are closely correlated with others. Finally, we present our conclusions and briefly discuss future work.

2 Messages, Discussion Threads, and Newsgroups

Kelly (2004) read several thousand posts made to six Usenet newsgroups: (1) alt.fan.noam-chomsky, (2) alt.politics.bush, (3) alt.politics.democrats.d, (4) alt.politics.economics, (5) talk.abortion, and (6) talk.politics.mideast. All of these newsgroups are public, online discussions archived on thousands of newsgroup (NNTP) servers throughout the Internet. Kelly was able to identify about twenty high-frequency posters from each of the six newsgroups. Extensive study of the messages posted by these 119 frequent participants led to the articulation of a set of political categories and the identification of the political category associated with 97 of the 119 posters. The political point of view of 22 of the posters was uncharacterizable.

We will not review Kelly's results in this chapter but rather explain how we have incorporated a simplified version of some of his results into the present study. While Kelly identified twelve different political positions occupied by newsgroup participants, we have (perhaps too insensitively) coerced these twelve positions into just three categories: left, right, and unrecognized. Thus, each of the participants studied by Kelly has been labeled as unrecognizable or political left or right.

Recall that a discussion thread is constituted from an initial message, all of the replies to the initial message, all of the replies to these replies, etc. Our aim has been to study the structure of those discussion threads in which at least one known person of the left exchanged a message with at least one known person of the right. We call an exchange of messages between posters of opposing political positions a 'mixed exchange'. We are interested in threads that contain one or more mixed exchanges because they are potentially deliberative exchanges. We hope to be able to formulate heuristics to automatically detect threads that are likely to contain a mixed exchange.

Because Kelly made known to us the political position of 119 frequent Usenet newsgroup posters, it was a straightforward task to download another set of threads—from the same time period—that contain messages posted by one or more of the these known participants. We downloaded over one million messages from an NNTP server but chose to focus on a subset of about sixteen hundred (1664 out of 25,590) discussion threads in which at least two messages were posted to the thread and in which at least two-thirds (66%) of the messages posted in the threads were posted by one or more of our known participants. A total of 13,156 messages were posted to these 1664 discussion threads.

3   Variables: On the Structure of Discussion Threads

From a graph theoretic perspective, discussion threads are trees because when one hits the 'reply' button in an email program, one is replying to one and only one previous message.

We can therefore define a set of variables that characterize the size and shape of the discussion threads:

M: the number of messages posted to a thread;

L: the number of leaves in a thread tree (leaves are messages that received no replies);

P: the number of people who posted a message to a thread;

maxMp: the maximum number of messages posted by one person to a thread;

maxD: the maximum depth from the root of the tree (i.e., the initial post) to one of the leaves of the thread tree;

meanD: the mean depth from the root to the leaves of the tree;

maxB: the maximum branching factor in the tree (corresponding to the message in the thread with the greatest number of replies);

meanB: the mean branching factor in the tree;

meanMp: the mean number of messages posted by a person participating in the thread; and,

meanT: the mean amount of time (in seconds) between messages posted to the thread.

In addition we assigned a score to each thread, where a score of '1' indicates a mixed exchanged (as defined above): a person of the left replied to a message from a person of the right or vice versa. A score of '0' indicates that no such exchange happened in the thread. Scores of greater than one occurred when more than one mixed exchange occurred. We calculated a Spearman's r correlation between each of our independent variables and the score. A linear regression model works quite well for threads with 25 or fewer messages (correlation 0.72). But, the linear model does not seem to fit as well for threads of size larger than 25 messages. Examination of the correlation for this subset of threads ($25 \leq M$) shows it to be weaker (correlation = 0.48).

It is unfortunate that the correlation between M and a thread's score is weak for large discussion threads, because we need a model that will work for large threads as well as for relatively small threads. Large threads are of interest because they are more likely than small threads to contain a deliberatively elaborated point of view. While small threads containing one or more long messages might contain a detailed explanation of someone's point of view, it is only through an extended back-and-forth with an interlocutor that the strengths and weaknesses of a point of view can be unpacked and explored in detail. So, we assume that long threads are more likely to be representative of some sort of deliberative exchange than short, small threads.

Second, recall that our immediate goal is to find a set of quick and computationally inexpensive heuristics for predicting if a thread is likely to contain a mixed exchange and thus for determining if more computational resources should be devoted to analyzing the thread in detail. A linear model (like this correlation) would roughly predict that we should look at all of the large threads and none of the small ones. However, simply because they contain a large number of messages, large threads are computationally expensive to analyze in detail. If we can eliminate even some of the large threads, then we are likely to save many computational resources in the subsequent phases of analysis. Consequently, we desire a model that works for small and large threads but especially for large threads.

4   A Thread Categorization Model: Search Heuristics

To create a model that will work for small and large discussion threads, we first simplify the problem. Rather than attempting to predict the number of mixed exchanges in a thread, we will be satisfied with sorting threads into one of two categories: (1) those containing mixed exchanges; and, (2) those containing no mixed exchanges. Consequently, the problem we now face is this: Can a categorization function (i.e., a *discriminant function*) be designed such that, given a thread, when it is greater than zero it is more likely that the thread contains one or more mixed exchanges, and, when it is zero or less than zero, it is more likely that the thread does not contain a mixed exchange?

This can be formalized as follows. Associated with each thread is a vector of independent variables, as detailed in the first part of this chapter (M, L, P, maxMp, maxD, meanD, maxB, meanB, meanMp, meanT). We are exploring 1664 discussion threads, thus we can order the thread trees from 1 to 1664. For a given thread tree j, in this order, we will denote the vector of independent variables simply as v_j. Since we are examining thread trees in which participants provided a political position known to us in 66% of the messages posted, each of these threads has an associated score. However, we are restricting our interest to the distinction between those threads with scores greater than zero (score > 0) versus those threads with scores of zero (score = 0).

Using the associated vectors and scores for our 1664 threads, we estimate the following two sets of conditional probabilities:

$$P(\mathbf{v}_j|score=0) = \prod_{k=1..12} p(\mathbf{v}_k|score=0); \text{ and,}$$
$$P(\mathbf{v}_j|score>0) = \prod_{k=1..12} p(\mathbf{v}_k|score>0).$$

Thanks to Bayes formula, we can convert the estimated prior probabilities (i.e., in which we know the score) into posterior probabilities (in which we want to predict the score). So, our estimated discriminant function is this:

$$g(\mathbf{v}_j) = P(score>0|\mathbf{v}_j) - P(score=0|\mathbf{v}_j)$$
where if $g(\mathbf{v}_j) \geq 0$ then the score is more likely to be positive; else the score more likely to be zero.

But this estimated discriminant function cannot be applied to discussion threads outside our original set of 1664 thread trees unless the unseen discussion thread has a vector associated with it that exactly matches the vector of some tree in our original set of trees. We, rather crudely, address this problem by dividing the values for each variable into equally populated quartiles that we call small, medium, large and extra large. For instance, the quartile divisions for M, the number of messages in the thread trees are small ($M < 3$); medium ($M = 3$); large ($3 < M < 6$); and, extra large ($M \geq 6$). This allows one to see, for example, that if a thread has an extra large number of messages, then it is more likely to have a positive score (i.e., more like to contain one or more mixed exchanges) than to have a score of zero.

Given these definitions and this simplification of values into quartiles a discriminant function can be calculated and then tested against the same 1664 thread trees to get some idea of how accurate it might be. Using all variables in the function, we find that it predicts the correct category (either score = 0 or score > 0) for 1156 out of the 1664 thread trees (accuracy of 69%). But, since we are searching for threads likely to contain a mixed exchange, the power of the model is better measured according to the usual criteria of information retrieval where recall denotes the completeness of the retrieval and precision denotes the purity of the retrieval.[1] Using Kelly's

---

[1] 'Consider an example information request I (of a test reference collection) and its set R of relevant documents. Let |R| be the number of documents in this set. Assume that a given retrieval strategy (which is being evaluated) processes the information request I and generates a document answer set A. Let |A| be the number of documents in this set. Further, let |R$_a$| be the number of documents in the intersection of the sets R and A. ... The recall and precision measures are defined as follows. Recall is the fraction of the relevant documents (the set R) which

(2004) analysis we know that 660 of the threads had a positive score, and 1004 had a score of zero. The model miscategorized 508 threads out of which 122 of them were miscategorized as having a mixed exchange (when their actual score was zero), and 386 of them were mistakenly assigned a score of zero. Consequently, the results for this model (with all the variables) are: precision = 69% and recall = 42%.

As is always the case in information retrieval tasks, there is a tradeoff that must be made between precision and recall (Buckland and Gey 1994). In our case, a low—but nonzero—recall rate is fine because discussion threads are not a scarce commodity. For example, Google Groups (http://groups.google.com/) has hundreds of millions of newsgroup messages indexed. We would, however, like a precision score that is as high as possible so that fewer threads without mixed exchanges are given further scrutiny.

We can refine this estimated discriminant function by first simplifying it. Our initial discriminant function—which includes all the variables—is based on the assumption that each of the variables which describe the size and shape of the thread trees, is independent from all of the other variables. This is clearly not the case. For example, the mean depth of the tree (meanD) is likely to be correlated with maximum depth (maxD) and the number of messages in the tree (M); and, such is the case: $r(\text{meanD},\text{maxD}) = 0.97$; $r(\text{meanD},\text{M}) = 0.93$. So, a refined discriminant function need not contain all of the variables.

Our simplified, discriminant function contains three almost independent variables: maxB, meanMp, and maxMp/M (i.e., the maximum number of messages posted by one person to a thread divided by the number of messages posted to a thread). This function of three parameters, g(maxMp/M, maxB, meanMp), accurately categorizes 68% of the threads with precision of 75% and recall of 29%.

When maxMp/M is extra large, mixed exchanges are unlikely. Intuitively one can understand the logic of this: when maxMp/M is large one participant has posted many more messages than the other participants in the thread. Thus, the thread is dominated by one voice and more likely to be monological rather than dialogical in nature.

When maxB is small, the score for the thread is more likely to be zero. This too is relatively intuitive: threads containing at least one message that received a lot of replies are more likely to incorporate many engaged discussants than threads containing only messages with few replies.

---

has been retrieved; i.e., Recall = |R$_a$| / |R|. Precision is the fraction of the retrieved documents (the set A) which is relevant; i.e., Precision − |R$_a$| / |A|' (Baeza-Yates and Ribeiro Neto 1999: 75).

Finally, we are interested in threads in which meanMp is relatively large as this is an indication that several people are contributing substantially to the discussion.

5   Verification of the Model

A set of one hundred discussion threads was randomly selected from the same six newsgroups. To approximate the size distribution of our original collection of 1664 threads, 25 threads with 2 messages, 25 threads with 3 messages, 25 threads with 4 or 5 messages, and 25 threads with 6 or more messages were selected. Each of the authors of this chapter independently read and tagged the threads as either containing or not containing a mixed exchange. Our purpose was to verify our discriminant function on a manually tagged corpus of discussion threads.

It is noteworthy that even the three of us did not always agree on which threads did or did not contain a mixed exchange. All three of us were in agreement only 58% of the time. To test our model we used a majority vote: if two of us agreed that a mixed exchange had taken place in the thread, then the thread was marked as having a mixed exchange. This difficulty in manual tagging indicates a much deeper problem: can even a well educated, interested, and motivated person recognize a deliberative discussion when he or she sees one? While we would like the computer to recognize such an exchange, it is not clear what criteria people use to recognize such an exchange.

For discussion threads containing six or more messages the refined discriminant function (of only three variables) performed with 71% recall and 94% precision.

6   Conclusions, Discussion, and Future Work

The approach demonstrated in this work, to attempt to automatically identify mixed, possibly deliberative, exchange in discussion threads by examining the thread trees' structures—their topologies and morphologies—might strike some as quixotic. Or, perhaps, at least as quixotic as the enterprise of Chomskyan linguistics in its attempts to tell us something about language and the human mind by closely reading syntax trees. Nevertheless, even outside of Chomskyan linguistics, there is a long history of employing structural characteristics in order to define and distinguish social (e.g., social network analysis) and cultural or literary genres or discourses (Propp 1928).

For the purposes of this project we are tactical—not committed— structuralists. Our work essentially boils down to this: if one wants to find a mixed—potentially deliberative—exchange in a large set of Usenet newsgroup threads, look for those threads in which (a) no one person dominates the discussion, (b) everyone participating in the thread has posted at least a couple of messages, and (c) there is at least one message with multiple replies. This chapter details our search for this heuristic and presents the heuristic in a more precise form, as what one in the discipline of pattern classification might call a 'discriminant function' (Duda et al. 2001).

In future work, we plan to extend these simplest of models for identifying discussion threads containing mixed (political) exchanges to include a set of linguistic and social network criteria—criteria that we have already implemented in computational form in the Conversation Map system (Sack 2001). This, we hope, will bring us closer to achieving our long-term goal to implement a search engine that, when given a topic, will find likely threads of discussion where opposing opinions have been expressed.

Acknowledgements

This work has been supported by Award #0416353 ('An Interface and Search Engine for Deliberation') from the National Science Foundation, Directorate for Computer and Information Science and Engineering; and by National Science Foundation Award #IIS-0441999. Any opinions, findings and conclusions or recommendations expressed in this chapter are those of the authors and do not necessarily reflect those of the National Science Foundation.

References

Baeza-Yates, R. and B. Ribeiro-Neto. 1999. *Modern Information Retrieval*. New York: Addison-Wesley.

Bagdikian, B. 2004. *The New Media Monopoly*. Boston: Beacon Press.

Buckland, M. K. and F. Gey. 1994. The Relationship between Recall and Precision, *Journal of the American Society for Information Science* 45(1): 12-19.

Duda, R. O., P. E. Hart, and D. G. Stork. 2001. *Pattern Classification*. New York: Wiley.

Fishkin, J. S. 1991. *Democracy and Deliberation: New Directions for Democratic Reform*. New Haven: Yale University Press.

Fishkin, J. S. 1992. Beyond Teledemocracy: 'America on the Line'. *The Responsive Community* 2(3): 13-19.

Granovetter, M. 1973. The Strength of Weak Ties. *American Journal of Sociology* 78: 1360-1380.

Kelly, J. 2004. *Community and Selectivity in Unstructured, Online, Political Discourse*. Paper presented at Internet Research 5.0 (Association of Internet Researchers), Sussex, September 2004.

Mill, J. S. 1993. *On Liberty*. New York: Bantam.

Mutz, D. C. 2002. Cross-cutting Social Networks: Testing Democratic Theory in Practice. *American Political Science Review* 96(1): 111-126.

Negroponte, N. 1995. *Being Digital*. New York: Knopf.

Propp, V. 1928(1968). *Morphology of the Folktale*. Austin, TX: University of Texas Press.

Putnam, R. D. 2000. *Bowling Alone: The Collapse and Revival of American Community*. New York: Simon & Schuster.

Sack, W. 2001. Conversation Map: An Interface for Very Large-Scale Conversations. *Journal of Management Information Systems* 17(3): 73-92.

Sunstein, C. R. 2001. *Republic.com*. Princeton, NJ: Princeton University Press.

7

Happy Accidents: Deliberation and Online Exposure to Opposing Views

AZI LEV-ON AND BERNARD MANIN

1 Introduction

In this chapter, we consider the deliberative potential of Internet communication. We first draw a distinction between diverse and opposing views, arguing that the deliberative potential of Internet communication turns on exposing users to opposing, not just diverse views. We then ask if online experiences facilitate exposure to opposing views. Using recent empirical findings, we argue that Internet communication is a 'mixed blessing' for deliberation, as it generates both unintentional exposure to opposing views, as well as 'drivers' that channel users away from opposing views.

2 Distinguishing Opposing from Diverse Views

Proper deliberation extends beyond the mere consideration of reasons for actions. It also requires considering reasons against the contemplated actions. Considering, and weighing, pros and cons distinguishes deliberation from other forms of reasoning.[1] We say that we deliberate, individually or

---

[1] This understanding of deliberation is in keeping with a long philosophical tradition. For example, Aristotle (*Rhetoric*, I, 2): 'Deliberation [*sumbouleuein*] consists in arguing for or against something'; and Hobbes (*De Cive*, XIII, 16): 'Deliberation is nothing else but a weighing, as it were in scales, the conveniencies, and inconveniencies of the fact we are attempting'.

Online Deliberation: Design, Research, and Practice.
Todd Davies and Seeta Peña Gangadharan (eds.).

collectively, when we use reason in a distinctive way.[2] We deliberate about a given course of action when we suspect that there might be reasons against it as well as reasons for it. If we did not think that there might be, at least potentially, reasons for not doing X alongside reasons for doing it, we would use reason in a different way. We would seek to establish that X is the right course of action by supplying compelling arguments for it. We would not be concerned about potential counterarguments, nor would we actively seek them.

In this section, we wish to emphasize the distinction between diverse and opposing views.[3] A long tradition in liberal theory has been praising the benefits of diverse and opposing views for adequate deliberation. It has often been argued that a necessary and sufficient condition for the benefits of deliberation to materialize is that participants in discussion hold diverse views and articulate a variety of perspectives. That tradition ranges from Mill, to Popper, to Sunstein, to many others.

The problem with this line of thinking is that 'diversity of views' and 'opposing views' get treated as roughly interchangeable notions. It is our contention that these notions are not interchangeable. While both opposing and diverse opinions may be needed for adequate deliberation, diversity of opinions alone is insufficient for adequate deliberation.

Elsewhere, Manin (2004) has elaborated on the reasons why even agents coming from a variety of perspectives would likely fail to search for and articulate arguments against a given measure, once a reasonably good argument for it has been advanced. For example, the costs of information search may lead people to use 'satisficing' heuristics and stop the search for reasons once a good argument has been found. Others may not wish to be seen as opponents of a measure that arguably promotes a common goal. Yet others may surrender to conformity pressures. As a result few, if any, arguments pointing to the potential downsides of a proposed measure may be

---

[2] The duality between internal and external modes of deliberation is evident in a recent *Oxford English Dictionary* definition which includes two sub-definitions: 1. 'The action of deliberating, or weighing a thing in the mind; careful consideration with a view to decision'. 2. 'The consideration and discussion of the reasons for and against a measure by a number of councilors (e.g. in a legislative assembly)'. Goodin (2005: 171) argues that the 'micro-work' of deliberation occurs primarily due to 'internal' cognitive processes, and re-frames deliberation as 'less a matter of making people "conversationally present" and more [as] a matter of making them "imaginatively present" in the minds of deliberators. Note that in spite of the epistemic priority of "internal" over "external" deliberation, the collective aspect of deliberation is a useful means to set the introspective process in motion, as it generates present and insistent "others" pressing their claims upon deliberants' (Goodin 2005: 183). But whether collective or not, deliberation would imply consideration of reasons for as well as against courses of action.

[3] This section is based on earlier work by Manin (2004).

heard in deliberative settings even if members of the deliberating body hold diverse views, and the set of arguments will be lopsided.

Two further points lend additional weight to our claim that diversity of views *per se* is insufficient for adequate deliberation. These two points, regarding cognitive processes and selection effects, are especially relevant to our discussion below about exposure to opposing views online.

Social and cognitive psychological research shows that people do not process information in a neutral and unbiased manner but instead tend to misperceive and misinterpret evidence that is counter to their prior beliefs. Not only do people strive to reconcile the new information with their prior beliefs, they are also prone to interpreting the new evidence, especially if it is ambiguous, as lending additional support to such prior beliefs. This phenomenon is known as *biased assimilation*. Even if decision makers are exposed to a variety of arguments about a given view, they can still fail to consider properly, on their merits, those arguments that run counter to their prior beliefs. There is, however, some experimental evidence that the most effective way of countering the effects of such biases is to give greater salience to information that runs counter to prior beliefs (Lord, Lepper, and Preston 1984).

Most importantly, and most relevant to the Internet, is the possibility that mere diversity of views may result in the generation of enclaves of like-minded people. A robust finding from a large body of research on social and political behavior is that when choice is available, agents prefer to interact and organize with, and receive information from like-minded others, a phenomena known as *homophily* (Huckfeldt and Sprague 1995; McPherson, Smith-Lovin, and Cook 2001; Mutz 2006). Below we show that this tendency is manifest in a variety of spheres online.

When diversity of views is combined with freedom of speech and association, and especially with enhanced abilities to locate like-minded others and filter out opposing views, the result may be enclaves of like-minded people talking to one another, even in a context of a wide multiplicity of views. In the light of trends such as residential segregation, fragmentation of the media, and narrowcasting, the consequences of segmentation seem to be of prime concern from a deliberative standpoint.

The deliberative potential of a given environment or medium should be assessed by looking at the probability that agents will be confronted with opposing views and will give them due consideration. Thus in seeking to estimate the deliberative potential of Internet communication, we should focus on the probability that users will be exposed to opposing views online and on the probability that such exposure will trigger the distinct deliberative mode of reasoning 'within' individuals.

3 Generating Exposure to Opposing Views

Heterogeneous backgrounds and opinions do not necessarily entail the articulation of arguments both for and against particular courses of action. It is the *opposition* of views and reasons that is necessary for deliberation, not just their diversity. Diversity of views may fail to bring opposing views into contact.

But exposing agents to opposing views during deliberation entails a number of challenges. First, typically there are substantial opportunity costs for the deliberating agents, as deliberation takes time and cognitive resources that may be devoted to other issues, more aligned with the deliberants' interests and concerns. Hence, debates on issues of public concern may have to be actively promoted.

Second, debates with an *adversarial* character need 'enhanced' promotion and organization, since they require participants to face conflict and generate talk across cleavages. Research shows, however, that people tend to *avoid* the psychic discomfort of involvement in contentious discussions. Whereas learned scripts largely regulate recurring interactions with others, a cognitive shift occurs when others challenge one's views or when one feels the need to challenge others' views (Ryfe 2005). Such a cognitive shift disrupts individual reasoning routines and generates anxiety. People are therefore reluctant to experience it and try to avoid it in their daily lives (Ryfe 2005; Marcus, Neuman, and Mackuen 2000; see also Eliasoph 1998).

As a result, people tend to carefully select their conversation partners. Research indeed shows that offline political talk occurs mostly among friends, family, and like-minded others (see Huckfeldt and Sprague 1995; Kim, Wyatt, and Katz 1999; Conover, Searing, and Crewe 2002). Even the voluntary associations that people choose to join become rather homogenous ideologically (Theiss-Morse and Hibbing 2005).

One therefore cannot expect adversarial debates to arise spontaneously in a diverse society with freedom of speech. Public deliberation is a complex public good whose facilitation has to overcome a number of obstacles (opportunity costs, generating cross-cleavage communication, overcoming conflict avoidance) and requires extensive organizational work. When organizational costs are borne by interested parties, the hazard is that they may skew the deliberation to favor their interests (Przeworski 1998), for example by manipulating agendas, argument pools, and procedures. Presenting 'devil's advocate' arguments may be especially challenging if the organizers of deliberation feel that allowing them may have adverse consequences.

In discussing the possibilities of exposing agents to opposing views online, one should steer away from simplistic arguments that directly link, for example, abundance of information to familiarity with opposing views

(Bimber 1998; Delli Carpini and Keeter 2002). When information is abundant but attention is scarce, agents use selection strategies and short-cuts or even choose to remain uninformed. The logic of 'rational ignorance' still prevails even if, as Lippmann (1993) nicely put it, 'by some development of the radio every man could see and hear all that was happening everywhere, if publicity, in other words, became absolute' (33-34). Scale and accessibility are insufficient to account for the deliberative possibilities of Internet communication. The *effective* possibility of exposure to opposing views is also determined by such factors as the organization of content and links, and the ideological makeup of deliberative spheres online.

The literature on online deliberation focuses on facilitated settings. Organizing such forms of deliberation online is substantially less expensive than offline. Participants can deliberate from the comfort of their homes, without necessarily limiting themselves to very specific times and places. It is also significantly less expensive to create a representative sample of a decision making body online (due to reduction of coordination costs, transportation costs, and so on). Offline, when organizers aim at achieving a representative sample of a geographically dispersed population, they must bring participants to a common physical location at a specific time, which can be extremely expensive (Iyengar, Luskin, and Fishkin 2003). Even more expensive to organize are offline longitudinal deliberations, which require multiple sessions separated by long intervals of time.

Experiments in online deliberation have produced encouraging results such as lack of polarization and radicalization, knowledge gains, more considered opinions, satisfaction from the deliberative process, and enhanced feelings of efficacy (Price and Cappella 2002; Iyengar, Fishkin, and Luskin 2003; Muhlberger 2005). Such experiments point to the continuing promise of utilizing the Internet to support facilitated deliberative arenas to discuss the problems of heterogeneous publics (see also Price 2003).

Such deliberative moments of interactive exchange among members of heterogeneous groups are rare, because they are still relatively expensive to organize, require cross-cleavage communication, and interrupt regular reasoning habits. We concentrate instead on the large number of interactions that users engage in each day. We argue that these online experiences both limit exposure to opposing views *and* generate unintended contact with such views. We therefore refer to two sets of factors: 'drivers of homogeneity' and 'drivers of opposition', respectively.[4] In the following two sections we analyze them using a broad brush.

---

[4] Stromer-Galley (2002) argues that research on the deliberative potential of the Internet oscillates between perspectives emphasizing 'diversity' and 'homophily' (Stromer-Galley

4 Drivers of Homogeneity

Internet communication enhances abilities to locate a variety of communication partners, to acquire information from a multiplicity of sources, and to 'surf' between websites that present diverse and opposing views. These abilities can be utilized in different ways; some users can choose to communicate with and receive information from agents with opposing views, some can choose to communicate with and receive information from those who are like-minded, and others can choose to randomize. However, a robust finding is that the enhanced possibilities for *intentional* exposure online primarily lead to exposure to like-minded others.

To study the consequences of selective exposure, it would be useful to look at some empirical research. Especially telling is research that deduces 'macro-regularities' and patterns from the accumulated 'micro-behaviors' of large numbers of users. The consequences of homophily are manifest in a variety of settings online: the Internet is used for forming clubs of like-minded people, receiving information primarily from like-minded others, and creating homogenous hyperlinked spaces. Let us review these three 'drivers of homogeneity' in some detail.

Associations and Normative Pressures

The Web allows agents to create homogenous clubs of the like-minded. Of prime concern are the segregating effects of virtual groups. In a 2001 Pew survey, 84% of Internet users indicated that they contacted a virtual group, and 79% of them identified at least one group with which they maintained regular online contact. It should be noted, however, that politics is not a main reason for association: only 22% reported that they contacted a 'political' virtual group (Horrigan and Rainie 2001: 4). We will come back to this point later.

Survey work shows that agents join virtual communities for a variety of reasons, but primarily to obtain relevant information at low costs (Horrigan and Rainie 2001; Ridings and Gefen 2004). When a large number of agents join for such reasons, the group is essentially composed of members who choose to communicate with others with whom they share hobbies, lifestyles, professional interest, or health or other concerns.

Unlike in more 'traditional' offline communities, exiting Internet-based communities is usually very easy. When members feel their voices are not heard, they may prefer low-cost exit over voice or loyalty, leaving the community and establishing a new subcommunity that is better oriented to

---

2002). In light of the earlier discussion, we think that the labels 'opposition' and 'homogeneity' better capture the distinctions that really matter for deliberation.

their interests and concerns. When such a dynamic occurs, it tends to eliminate not just diversity of views, but opposing views in particular.

Research on the social and cognitive effects of computer mediated communication (CMC) shows that, perhaps counter-intuitively, under some conditions CMC can lead to enhanced normative pressures and generate a sort of 'panoptic power' (Spears and Lea 1994). CMC environments (particularly text- and audio-based) disable a range of contextual cues (e.g. social, visual), but often some group-level social cues remain intact and are the only cues available for virtual group members. In such conditions, group membership becomes *situationally salient*. When a CMC environment is characterized by a salient sense of group membership, the lack of other cues leads to stronger influence of social norms on behavior and to compliance with the situational norms (Postmes, Spears, and Lea 1998). Spears and Lea (1994) argue that in such CMC environments, the over-reliance on minimal cues to 'cognitively compensate' for the absence of other cues can lead to in-group favoritism, stereotyping, and disapproval of out-groups.

This line of research is very relevant to virtual communities, where members are aware of their common group membership but may be otherwise anonymous to one another. Under such conditions, discussion can become highly normative, leading to suppression of opposing views and radicalization (Sunstein 2001).

Collaborative Filtering and Popular Feedback Loops

By choosing a group, agents select whom to communicate with, about a topic they commonly find worth pursuing, thus sorting themselves into clubs. Such clubs can function as efficient information aggregators and can facilitate organizing for collective action, including for otherwise latent causes.[5] But they can also function as information filters at the price of suppressing opposing views.

Many virtual associations enable 'collaborative filtering' or allowing group members to collaboratively prioritize the information they are exposed to. For example, members can rate contributions and contributors; their votes can be tallied and weighted to decide the rating of contributions. Automated mechanisms can then edit community Web pages and present items according to their ratings. Popular content thus becomes more visible than unpopular content. This practice of a popular feedback loop has its

---

5 This is true, for example, for widely dispersed interests, or for groups whose members may not be interested in exposing themselves to anyone other than to similarly-situated others, or for groups of individuals who can find it difficult to locate similarly situated others offline (Lev-On and Hardin 2007).

advantages, as it minimizes information search costs and enables a short-cut to relevant information.

At its best, when collaborative filtering is based on the force of the better argument/article, the ability to prioritize content based on discussion and evaluations publicly provided by many self-selected 'experts' seems very promising. However, at its worst, collaborative filtering can generate a high-tech version of majority tyranny, amplifying popular opinions and muting opposing views. Even if an occasional thought-provoking but non-conforming view is expressed, it can be effectively shunned because of its non-conforming character and in spite of its argumentative value. As a result, for example, members of progressive-leaning groups not only talk primarily amongst themselves but also efficiently screen out opposing views expressed by thoughtful conservatives, and vice versa (see Lampe 2005). When applied in such ways, collaborative filtering can render opposing views literally invisible.

Ideologically Homogeneous Hyperlinked Spaces

A third 'driver of homogeneity' is apparent in the multiplicity of homophilic hyperlinked ideological spaces online, in which surfers are effectively channeled to similar views and away from opposing views.

Let us start with the World Wide Web. Research suggests that Web links follow homophilic patterns. Hindman, Tsioutsiouliklis, and Johnson (2003) analyzed the link structure of political issues on the Web, particularly focusing on themes such as abortion, gun control, and capital punishment. They found clusters of opposing views in each of these categories. The authors also found that each cluster was regulated by power laws, such that a small number of sites inside each cluster emerge as focal sites, while the majority of sites receive a negligible number of inbound links. These focal sites help to organize the conversation inside ideological clusters. The consequence is that linking patterns spontaneously generate, for instance, not just a small number of focal sites addressing abortion but also a small number of focal pro-life and pro-choice sites, with little inter-linking between them.

Research shows that the same homophilic link structure is evident on the blogosphere as well. Adamic and Glance (2005) studied the linking patterns of political bloggers. They found that the blogosphere is composed of tightly connected clusters of liberal and conservative blogs, with very few links between clusters; the great majority of links are internal to either the liberal or the conservative blog clusters (Adamic and Glance 2005; Ackland 2005). The authors also found that political blog clusters focus on news articles that support their political views.

The macro-outcome of segmentation (with its adverse consequences for exposure to opposing views) results from the linking micro-practices of authors. We can think of links between websites as constituting a form of conversation, where links manifest recognition of the importance of the linked sites and their 'legitimacy' as interlocutors. The linking choices of authors direct surfers to potential conversation partners (see Herring et al. 2005). The implication of the homophilic structure of these linked spaces is that surfers are likely to come across sites (or blogs) with similar ideological affinities, effectively filtering out sites with opposite views from public deliberation.[6]

5   Drivers of Opposition

The phenomena described above demonstrate that a diversity of views is entirely consistent with the formation and persistence of enclaves of like-minded agents. More importantly, they also demonstrate that *intentional choices drive out opposing views*. Some agents may appreciate and enjoy conversing with others with diverse and opposing views (Stromer-Galley 2002). But we should not assume that users, as a general rule, actively look for opposing views. Empirical studies seem to show that users prefer to organize with and get their information from like-minded others, when given the opportunity to do so.

This fact, however, suggests another possibility. If users' choices hinder exposure to opposing views, such exposure might still happen *unintentionally* or even *against users' intention*. We should therefore ask whether Internet communication holds the potential for unintended encounters with opposing views. If this were the case, the Internet would qualify as a deliberative medium for a quality that it is not usually praised for.

In the following sections we argue that such is indeed the case: alongside the enhanced abilities to filter out opposing views, Internet communi-

---

[6] Research on exposure to opposing views in newsgroups is more encouraging from a deliberative standpoint (note that this genre is much less popular than the Web, particularly for political involvement (Kohut 2004; Madden and Rainie 2003). Kelly, Smith, and Fisher (2005) use social network analysis to reveal the structure of relationships among key participants in eight political USENET newsgroups. The authors find high rates of interactive dialog among opposing views, even in groups that are prima facie suspected to be highly partisan, such as alt.politics.republican. However, earlier work on newsgroups, which used simpler methods, identified high doses of homophily. Wilhelm (2000) who studied patterns of interaction in ten political newsgroups, argued that conversation is extremely partisan; 70% of the messages were classified as homophilic, expressing support for a dominant position or a popular political figure. Davis (1999), who found similar patterns in a study of three political newsgroups, argues that newsgroups function as forums of reinforcement.

cation also facilitates 'happy accidents', i.e. *unintended* exposure to opposing views. We investigate the factors driving such exposures.

We focus on three factors: the creation of a variety of settings for cross-cleavage communication; reduced cognitive pressures to express opposing views in such settings; and imperfect abilities to tailor one's communicative environment online.[7]

Cross-Cleavage Communication

We claimed above that generating cross-cleavage political communication is a complex public good. Offline, sites of exposure to opposing views and especially interactive discussion with people with opposite opinions are rare. Others have argued that the leading candidates to generate such cross-cleavage exposure are the mass media (Mutz and Martin 2001) and the workplace (Mutz and Mondak 2006; Mutz 2006). Our proposition is that Internet communication generates a variety of sites that are a welcome addition to such spheres. We focus on online magazines and nonpolitical virtual communities to demonstrate this point.

Currently, the most popular news sources online are the websites of 'traditional' general interest media outlets (such as the BBC, CNN, and the New York Times), supplemented by additional news portals (like Yahoo News or Google News) and focal political blogs (Rainie, Cornfield, and Horrigan 2005). Such websites include not only news stories but also enhanced 'talk-back' features which enable readers to interactively respond to articles and comments made by others and to post links to stories published elsewhere. Such sites not only attract general readership but also enable critical discussions among readers. Such sites seem to support and enhance the role of the mass media as an agent of cross-cleavage exposure (Mutz and Martin 2001) and seem conducive to encounters with opposing views.

Nonpolitical virtual communities are additional candidates for generating cross-cleavage political communication. As stated before, survey work (Horrigan and Rainie 2001: 4) shows that only 22% of the people who contacted virtual groups, contacted 'political' virtual communities. Thus, self-described 'nonpolitical' communities seem to be much more prevalent than 'political' ones.

---

7 Another source of 'deliberative optimism' comes from survey work. For example, Stromer-Galley (2002) conducted sixty-nine in-depth interviews in three deliberation spaces (USENET newsgroups, Yahoo message boards, and Yahoo chat spaces) and found that users 'appreciate and enjoy the diversity of people and opinions'. In another survey, Horrigan, Garrett, and Resnick (2004) found that Internet use is correlated with familiarity with more arguments for and against the position of a candidate for president on key campaign issues; participants reported that they do not limit information seeking to sites which support their political views (see also Rainie, Cornfield, and Horrigan 2005).

Lampe (2005) examined the characteristics of political conversation in one of the most popular communities, Slashdot. Although functioning as a community for computer hobbyists and professionals (famously providing 'news for nerds'), Slashdot became a vivid deliberative forum prior to the 2004 presidential elections in the United States.

Lampe shows that before the elections, more and more political stories were posted to the community portal. Political stories not only received significantly more comments than stories on other topics, but the comments were much more contentious. Commentators on political stories also received significantly more ratings than commentators on other stories, and there were significantly higher inter-moderator disagreements about the value of comments, suggesting that 'moderators are using selection bias to judge comment values' (Lampe 2005: 21).

Such nonpolitical virtual communities, just as online news magazines, attract large crowds across political cleavages. Some of them evolve to become focal sites for large-scale cross-cleavage communication among people who did not join for ideological reasons. The combination of political heterogeneity, scale, and interactivity contributes to the rise of such new intermediaries for exposure to opposing views.

Reduced Cognitive Pressures

Earlier we claimed that two key problems in the organization of deliberation are overcoming self-selection and conflict avoidance. In the previous section we suggested that a variety of novel and supplementary intermediaries for cross-cleavage exposure are created online, relaxing the selection problem. Now we wish to show that in such settings (and a variety of other online settings), it is also easier to overcome the psychic discomfort that is typically generated by exposure to opposing views.

Why is self-expression easier online, particularly when the communication channel is poor (text- or even audio-based)? Research on the social effects of computer mediated communication suggests that it should be understood as an 'amplifier or magnifier of social psychological and communication phenomena' (Walther 1997: 360). Earlier we noted that when CMC environments disable contextual cues but group membership is situationally salient, the result can be stronger influence of situational norms on behaviors. However, when no cues are available and group membership is not salient, the opposite effect occurs: the total absence of cues generates a reduced sense of social presence, reduced awareness of the social environment, and consequently reduced concerns for social approbation, decreased awareness of, and adherence to social norms, and reduced opportunities for social control and regulation.

When the communication medium is poor, the cognitive discomforts associated with disagreement is reduced. It then becomes easier to express nonconforming or opposing views, and to engage in debates. Obviously the expression of dissonant views by some translates into exposure to such views by others. The consequences can vary; in some contexts CMC can encourage antinormative and disinhibited behaviors such as 'flaming'. At other times, it can also support the expression of nonconformist views and brainstorming (see Walther 1996; McKenna and Seidman 2005; Postmes, Spears, and Lea 1998).

Imperfect Tailoring and Chance Encounters

We saw earlier that the homophilic structure of Web links can channel users away from opposing views. If hyperlinked spaces were not only homophilic but also 'hermetically sealed' surfers would be perfectly locked in them and there would be few possibilities for chance exposures to opposing views. However, a third factor leading to exposure to opposing views is the *inability* to perfectly tailor exposure to political information online.

Since the link structure of the Web is not created by a 'social planner', but linking decisions are made instead by individual authors, there is always the possibility that sites will include links to opposing views. The ease of following these links makes opposing views more immediate and accessible. Even when people surf the Web looking for information to reinforce their prior beliefs, they can at times be routed to or stumble upon opposing views. Even if such cases are not common, when they do occur opposing views are just a click away, unlike access to opposing views offline.

Search engines demonstrate the imperfect opportunities to tailor one's communicative environment.[8] Search engines are popular starting points for information searches; on any given day, fifty-six of those online use them (Fallows 2005). Like the websites of traditional media outlets, they attract substantial amounts of traffic and consistently top the lists of popular websites.

An interesting feature of search engines, not often noted by commentators, is that users cannot perfectly tailor the ideological affiliation of the sites towards which they are channeled. For example, users who champion capitalism or globalization and want to learn more about these topics can be channeled to anti-capitalist or anti-globalization sites, respectively.

Elsewhere, Lev-On (2008) points out that such 'tailoring failures' are caused by certain aspects of the process of retrieving information through search engines. First, currently there is no comprehensive and reliable network of keywords that properly describe the content of Web documents (a

---

[8] This section is based on Lev-On (2008).

semantic Web.) Such an absence makes it difficult not just to retrieve information relevant to a query but also to discriminate between content based on ideological leanings.

Second, the interface of search engines is essentially textual, which mutes the richness of natural language and provides limited interactivity between the searcher and the engine that searches for him (compared to the much richer interaction between a searcher and a human who is asked to do a similar search). This disables a fine-grained understanding of the intentions behind a formal query and limits the relevance of responses to users' queries.

A third and last obstacle to 'perfect search' involves the way in which users formulate and articulate their queries. A number of studies on information seeking online reveal that users compose very short queries, rarely use advanced searching options, view a very small number of documents per query, and almost never view more than one page of results (see Spink and Jansen 2004; Machill et al. 2004). Spelling mistakes and nongrammatical formulations are frequent. Such information seeking patterns limit searchers' ability to retrieve information tailored to their views. When agents use search engines to locate information that reinforces their views, they can be directed to sites that present information and arguments opposing their views.

6   (Provisional) Conclusions

We began by arguing that deliberation consists in the seeking and weighing of pros and cons concerning a given proposition or course of action. We emphasized the importance of exposure to opposing views. The deliberative potential of online environments thus seems to be based on their effective capabilities to confront agents with opposing views, even against their will, and to generate due consideration of such views.

Our analysis suggests that the Internet is a mixed blessing for deliberation. On one hand, people find it much easier to organize with and receive information from like-minded others. The homophilic link structure of the most traveled Web spaces can further channel agents away from opposing views.

But 'drivers of opposition' mitigate the effects of these 'drivers of homogeneity'. Perfectly tailoring one's communicative environment is not all that easy. Furthermore, there are extended opportunities online for communication across political cleavages, as well as reduced cognitive pressures to express opposing views.

What are we to make of all this? The arguments presented here suggest that the deliberative potential of an online space depends on the drivers, whether of homogeneity or of opposition, that dominate in a particular context.

It seems too early to formulate a comprehensive theory of deliberation online. Some of the technologies involved in online communication are still changing at a fairly rapid pace. Access to the medium is spreading, with many people still learning how to use it. Usage patterns are probably not stabilized yet. Finally, research on some of relevant dimensions of exposure to opposing views online is still in its infancy. Nonetheless, we wish to advance a couple of limited and provisional claims.

When users efficiently choose their communicative environment, they tend to build echo chambers. Tailoring one's online communicative environment is certainly feasible, but it is also costly. It requires time, energy, and skills, which many users do not possess and which are costly to acquire. It seems reasonable to surmise that not all users are equally prepared to incur such costs. In all likelihood many will content themselves with imperfect tailoring, thereby increasing their chances of encountering opposing views. Thus the costs of tailoring one's communicative environment limit intentionality in communication.

Another factor limiting the intentional search for like-minded communication partners is that like-mindedness is typically not an all-encompassing feature. Users may be of like mind on one issue or in a given domain while holding opposing views on other issues or in other areas. People are bundles of characteristics. Similarity along one dimension does not necessarily carry similarity on another. This is especially relevant for online communication. Dissimilarities on other dimensions are potential sources of opposing views, and thereby of deliberation, on topics other than that which brought users in contact.

The critical role of intentionality in driving out opposing views suggests one last point concerning political opinions. It seems reasonable to infer that when agents are interested in political issues and are sufficiently motivated to incur the costs of tailoring their communicative environment—or of learning how to do so—the drivers of homogeneity become dominant. For such agents, and more broadly for users highly committed to a given cause, the Internet offers the opportunity to build their own effective echo chamber, therefore not enhancing, and even possibly impairing, their deliberative capabilities.

However, for the many agents who do not care much about politics, are incapable of manipulating their communicative environment, or are unwilling to put up with the cost of doing so, the mechanisms of segregation may not be efficient enough, and the drivers for opposition can become more dominant. Most likely, online communication enhances the deliberative opportunities for such agents.

These conclusions are highly provisional. To better understand the possibilities of exposure to opposing views online, we need more empirical research. For example, we need to know more about the implications of preferential attachment as expressed by the ideological composition of Web-based discursive genres (such as virtual communities and newsgroups.) We need to know more about the occurrences and characteristics of cross-cleavage communication in various Internet-based spheres, like Web-based magazines and virtual communities. We also need to know more about, for example, the effects of collaborative filtering and the patterns of political information seeking online. Such research is necessary to understand if, where and how the promises of improved public deliberation online will become realities.

References

Ackland, R. 2005. Mapping the US Political Blogosphere: Are Conservative Bloggers More Prominent? Available at http://voson.anu.edu.au/papers/polblogs.pdf (last accessed September 20, 2008)

Adamic, L. and N. Glance. 2005. The Political Blogosphere and the 2004 U.S. Election: Divided They Blog. Available at http://www.blogpulse.com /papers/2005/AdamicGlanceBlogWWW.pdf (last accessed September 20, 2008)

Aristotle. 2004. *Rhetoric*, trans. W. Rhys Roberts. New York: Dover.

Bimber, B. 1998. The Internet and Political Transformation: Populism, Community and Accelerated Pluralism. *Polity* 31:133-160.

Conover, P. J., D. D. Searing, and I. M. Crewe. 2002. The Deliberative Potential of Political Discussion. *British Journal of Political Science* 32: 21-62.

Davis, R. 1999. *The Web of Politics*. New York: Oxford University Press.

Delli Carpini, M. X. and S. Keeter. 2002. The Internet and An Informed Citizenry. *The civic web: Online politics and democratic values*, eds. D. Anderson and M. Cornfield, 129-156. Lanham, MD: Rowman and Littlefield.

Eliasoph, N. 1998. *Avoiding Politics: How Americans Produce Apathy in Everyday Life*. New York: Cambridge University Press.

Fallows, D. 2005. Search Engine Users: Internet Searchers Are Confident, Satisfied and Trusting—But They Are Also Unaware and Naïve. Available at http://www.pewInternet.org/pdfs/PIP_Searchengine_users.pdf (last accessed September 20, 2008)

Goodin, R. E. 2005. *Reflective Democracy*. New York: Oxford University Press.

Herring, S. C., I. Kouper, J. C. Paolillo, L. A. Scheidt, M. Tyworth, P. Welsch, E. Wright, and N. Yu. 2005. Conversations in the Blogosphere: An Analysis 'From the Bottom Up'. *Proceedings of the Thirty-Eighth Hawai'i International Conference on System Sciences (HICSS-38)*. Los Alamitos: IEEE Press.

Hindman, M., K. Tsioutsiouliklis, and J. A. Johnson. 2003. Googlearchy: How a Few Heavily-Linked Sites Dominate Politics Online. Available at http://www.coi.columbia.edu/pdf/kelly_fisher_smith_ddd.pdf (last accessed September 20, 2008)

Hobbes, T. 1998. *De Cive*. New York: Cambridge University Press.

Horrigan, J. B., and L. Rainie. 2001. *Online Communities: Networks that Nurture Long-Distance Relationships and Local Ties*. Pew Internet & American Life Project. Available at http://www.pewInternet.org/pdfs/PIP_Communities_Report.pdf (last accessed September 20, 2008)

Horrigan, J., K. Garrett, and P. Resnick. 2004. The Internet and Democratic Debate. Pew Internet and American Life Project. Available at http://www.pewInternet.org/pdfs/PIP_Political_Info_Report.pdf (last accessed September 20, 2008)

Huckfeldt, R. and J. Sprague. 1995. *Citizens, Politics, and Social Communication*. New York: Cambridge University Press.

Iyengar, S., R. Luskin, and J. Fishkin. 2003. Facilitating Informed Public Opinion: Evidence from Face-to-Face and On-line Deliberative Polls. Available at http://pcl.stanford.edu/common/docs/research/iyengar/2003/facilitating.pdf (last accessed September 20, 2008)

Kelly, J., D. Fisher, and M. Smith. 2005. *Debate, Division, and Diversity: Political Discourse Networks in Usenet Newsgroups*. Available at http://www.coi.columbia.edu/pdf/kelly_fisher_smith_ddd.pdf (last accessed August 31, 2008)

Kim, J., R. O. Wyatt, and E. Katz. 1999. News, Talk, Opinion, Participation: The Part Played by Conversation in Deliberative Democracy. *Political Communication* 16: 361-385.

Kohut, A. 2004. Cable and Internet Loom Large in Fragmented Political News Universe. Pew Internet & American Life Project. Available at http://www.pewInternet.org/pdfs/PIP_Political_Info_Jan04.pdf (last accessed September 20, 2008)

Lampe, C. A. C. 2005. *Talking Politics on the Side: Political Conversation on Slashdot*. Paper presented at the Second Conference on Online Deliberation: Design, Research, and Practice, Stanford, CA, May 22, 2005.

Lev-On, A. and R. Hardin. 2007. Internet-Based Collaborations and their Political Significance. *Journal of Information Technology and Politics* 4(2): 5-27.

Lev-On, A. 2008. The Democratizing Effects of Search Engine use: On Chance Exposures and Organizational Hubs. *Web Search: Interdisciplinary Perspectives*, eds. A. Spink and M. Zimmer, 135-150. New York: Springer.

Lippmann, W. 1993. *The Phantom Public*. New Brunswick, NJ: Transaction Publishers.

Lord, C. G., M. R. Lepper, and E., Preston. 1984. Considering the Opposite: A Corrective Strategy for Social Judgment. *Journal of Personality and Social Psychology* 47: 1231-1343.

Machill, M., C. Neuberger, W. Schweiger, and W. Wirth. 2004. Navigating the Internet: A Study of German-Language Search Engines. *European Journal of Communication* 19: 321-347.

Madden, M. and L. Rainie. 2003. America's Online Pursuits: The Changing Picture of Who's Online and What They Do. Pew Internet & American Life Project. Available at http://www.pewInternet.org/PPF/r/106/report_display.asp (last accessed September 20, 2008)

Manin, B. 2004. Délibération et Discussion. *Revue Suisse de Science Politique* 10: 180-192.

Marcus, G. E., W. R. Neuman, and M. MacKuen. 2000. *Affective Intelligence and Political Judgment*. Chicago: University of Chicago Press.

McKenna, K. Y. A. and G. Seidman. 2005. You, Me, and We: Interpersonal Processes in Electronic Groups. *The Social Net: Human Behavior in Cyberspace*, ed. Yair Amichai-Hamburger, 191-217. New York: Oxford University Press.

McPherson, M., L. Smith-Lovin, and J. Cook. 2001. Birds of a Feather: Homophily in Social Networks. *Annual Review of Sociology* 27: 415-444.

Muhlberger, P. 2005. The Virtual Agora Project: A Research Design for Studying Democratic Deliberation. *Journal of Public Deliberation* 1(1), Article 5. Available at http://services.bepress.com/jpd/vol1/iss1/art5 (last accessed September 20, 2008)

Mutz, D. C. 2006. *Hearing the Other Side: Deliberative versus Participatory Democracy.* New York: Cambridge University Press.

Mutz, D. C. and P. S. Martin. 2001. Facilitating Communication Across Lines of Political Difference: The Role of Mass Media. *American Political Science Review* 95: 97-114.

Mutz, D. C. and J. J. Mondak. 2006. The Workplace as a Context for Cross-Cutting Political Discourse. *Journal of Politics* 68: 140-155.

Postmes, T., R. Spears, and M. Lea. 1998. Breaching or Building Social Boundaries? SIDE-Effects of Computer-Mediated Communication. *Communication Research* 25: 689-715.

Price, V. and J. N. Cappella. 2002. Online Deliberation and its Influence: The Electronic Dialogue Project in Campaign 2000. *Information Technology and Society* 1: 303-328.

Price, V. 2003. *New Technologies and the Nature of Democratic Discourse: Inquiries and Issues*. Paper presented to the preconference at the annual meeting of the International Communication Association, San Diego, CA, May 23, 2003.

Przeworski, A. 1998. Deliberation and Ideological Domination. *Deliberative Democracy*, ed. J. Elster, 140-160. New York: Cambridge University Press.

Rainie, L., M. Cornfield, and J. Horrigan. 2005. The Internet and Campaign 2004. Pew Internet & American Life Project. Available at http://www.pewInternet.org/pdfs/PIP_2004_Campaign.pdf (last accessed September 20, 2008)

Ridings, C. M. and D. Gefen. 2004. Virtual Community Attraction: Why People Hang Out Online. *Journal of Computer Mediated Communication* 10(1): Article 4. Available at http://jcmc.indiana.edu/vol10/issue1/ridings_gefen.html (last accessed September 20, 2008)

Ryfe, D. 2005. Does Deliberative Democracy Work? *Annual Review of Political Science* 8: 49-71.

Spears, R. and M. Lea. 1994. Panacea or Panopticon? The Hidden Power in Computer-Mediated Communication. *Communication Research* 21: 427-459.

Spink, A. and B. J. Jansen. 2004. A Study of Web Search Trends. *Webology: An International Electronic Journal* 1(2): Article 4. Available at http://jcmc.indiana.edu/vol10/issue1/ridings_gefen.html (last accessed September 20, 2008)

Stromer-Galley, J. 2002. Diversity and Political Conversations on the Internet: Users' Perspectives. *Journal of Computer Mediated Communication* 8(3): Article 6. Available at http://jcmc.indiana.edu/vol8/issue3/index.html (last accessed September 20, 2008)

Sunstein, C. R. 2001. *Republic.com*. Princeton, NJ: Princeton University Press.

Theiss-Morse, E. and J. R. Hibbing. 2005. Citizenship and Civic Engagement. *Annual Review of Political Science* 8: 227-249.

Walther, J. B. 1996. Computer-Mediated Communication: Impersonal, Interpersonal, and Hyperpersonal Interaction. *Communication Research* 23: 3-43.

Walther, J. B. 1997. Group and Interpersonal Effects in International Computer-Mediated Collaboration. *Human Communication Research* 23: 342-360.

Wilhelm, A. G. 2000. *Democracy in the Digital Age: Challenges to Political Life in Cyberspace*. New York: Routledge.

8

Rethinking Local Conversations on the Web

SAMEER AHUJA, MANUEL PÉREZ-QUIÑONES, AND ANDREA
KAVANAUGH

1 Introduction

Local voluntary groups are crucial to creating awareness and drawing average citizens into dialogue about their communities (Putnam 2000; Verba
and Nie 1972). These groups act as intermediaries between the individual
and the government (Verba et al. 1995). But many voluntary organizations
face challenges of leadership burnout and limited resources. There is growing evidence that information and communication technology aids in resolution of these problems and increases participation among the members of
these organizations (Kavanaugh et al. 2007).

While the mainstream Web has seen explosive growth of social software systems in the past few years, local online deliberation systems are
still using the traditional discussion forums and email listservs. Online deliberation systems for small groups have unique design challenges that
separate them from mainstream systems. Hence mainstream social software
systems do not translate very well to the local environment. However, we
believe that there is tremendous potential in using technology, in the form
of social software and information aggregation tools, to help facilitate citizen-to-citizen and citizen-to-government interactions.

Online Deliberation: Design, Research, and Practice.
Todd Davies and Seeta Peña Gangadharan (eds.).
Copyright © 2009, CSLI Publications.

In this chapter, we argue that current social software is not a good fit for local conversations. We then describe a design for Colloki, an online 'local conversation hub' that we are designing in close collaboration with several civic organizations in Blacksburg, Virginia, such as the grassroots organization, Citizens First, and the community computer network known as the Blacksburg Electronic Village, which represents the Web presence of many local community groups.[1] This design aims to utilize features and patterns of social software (Web 2.0) in a local setting to provide what we believe is a more effective local conversation medium.

2 Social Software and Web 2.0

Social software can loosely be defined as software that enables people to rendezvous, connect or collaborate through computer-mediated communication. This type of software has existed for years in the forms of listservs, forums, newsgroups, and other online systems. Recently, however, blogs (Tepper 2003), Really Simple Syndication (RSS) feeds, tagging systems, collaborative filters, and other technologies and features collectively referred to as Web 2.0 have made social software very popular, particularly among young computer users. A recent Pew Internet & American Life Project found that 55% of all American youth (ages twelve to seventeen) use some form of social networking site (Lenhart 2007).

Social software today goes beyond email and forums in that it allows social networks to be formed among people who already have something in common. For email and forums, users must know each other's email address or where to find a forum with a particular topic. Social software, on the other hand, is organized around a particular activity or topic, such as photo sharing. Users often find value in putting their information in a social system. But the biggest value comes from the social network and the 'sum of the parts' effect that comes from many people crossing paths online.

One of the most intriguing features of most social software systems is the tagging of resources by the members of the community. We are just beginning to understand how this tagging works, its implications, and its possible uses (Furnas 2006; Marlow et al. 2006). Marlow and colleagues (2006) have proposed a taxonomy that offers two classifications for social networking systems which support tagging. The first refers to user incentives. All social systems have user provided content. Users must have an incentive to contribute information to the site. The incentive can be organizational, such as saving a URL in del.icio.us so that it can be found at a later time, or social, such as uploading pictures to Flickr to share with

---

[1] See http://citizensfirstforblacksburg.org (last accessed November 1, 2008) and http://bev.net (last accessed November 1, 2008).

time, or social, such as uploading pictures to Flickr to share with others. In other instances, providing content serves a role of attracting attention, for example uploading video files to YouTube. In addition, social software systems provide ways for users to organize their content in a flexible manner, using folksonomy to minimize predefined categories and structures (Veres 2006).

The second classification focuses on system design and attributes, including connections, commenting capability, and syndication. Social systems find 'connections' between users based on the system's organizational scheme. Finding these connections might not be the primary goal of these systems, but it is nonetheless a feature (boyd and Ellison 2007; Lampe et al. 2006). In general, social software exploits weak ties for added functionality and benefits—or what Marlow et al. (2006) calls 'social connectivity'. Social systems also provide commenting features that allow some form of community discussion. The discussion, however, varies, from polite social commentary to product reviews to debate. Finally, most social systems provide some form of syndication, permitting the user to 'subscribe' to a particular stream of information as it becomes available. Some successful social systems also provide a developer 'application programming interface' or API that allows others to build extended services, including importer/exporter tools, offline viewers, editors, and visualizations.

3 Social Software and Local Conversations

Often finding local news sources and local online discussions is difficult. First, news agencies devote fewer and fewer resources to local issues. Second, online deliberation at the local level often occurs in particular groups, deterring broad citizen participation. Third, conventional social software systems (e.g., Digg, Slashdot, and similar sites) work in part due to the large number of people participating and are not as effective when the social network is small.

In addition, for local participation, the number of participants will always be low when compared to national opportunities for discussion, as only people with local concerns would be participating. Automated solutions and aggregators are not sensitive enough to pick up material that is truly relevant. Either the service is too simplistic, doing mostly 'surface' checks (e.g., matching 'Blacksburg' to identify local news), or it requires specialized programming to do 'smart' aggregation.

A solution is needed that: (1) does not depend on thousands of users participating in the social networking sites, (2) does not depend on automated ways of identifying relevant information, (3) provides support for opinion leaders, politically active citizens, and lurkers, and (4) makes use of

Web 2.0 concepts (content syndication, tagging, user-provided content, and organization).

4 Colloki

Our goals for Colloki are to support local discussion and information discovery. Colloki is a replicable social networking system that aggregates news and local information in such a way that it becomes the 'hub' of local deliberation. The goal of aggregating information is to have a combination of automated plus human provided content. In addition, the Colloki site will include blogs, citizen commenting, links to town and county information, links to other relevant online information, aggregation of new feeds, and other online mechanisms to support citizen-to-citizen interaction. In the remainder of the paper, we present the design of Colloki as it stands at the time of this writing. We have developed this design using low fidelity paper prototypes (Snyder 2003). These prototypes provide a visual understanding of the concepts being discussed and help us gather feedback on our design from local citizens before we commit resources to building the system.

User Contributed Content: Citizen Opinions

The design of Colloki allows multiple ways for users to express their opinions. For example, opinions can be typed text, video postings, or even audio postings. We will support doing so from mobile devices as well.

Opinions are organized in sections of interest called 'Hot Topics' (see figure below). Hot topics are usually a small number of significant issues that a local community is facing, such as 'Upcoming Town Elections', 'Revisions to Comprehensive Plan', and 'Downtown Revitalization'. Community leaders have a significant role in defining these sections. We are organizing Colloki in a manner similar to the organizational logic of local civic groups who put a community leader in charge of an issue or issues that concerns them.

Browsing one of these topics is like browsing a subsection of the newspaper. Each section will have a different type of content depending on how it is defined and used by participating citizens.

With collaboration from the local town government, officials could use appropriate tags for communications and town council agendas so that information is automatically classified into the appropriate section of Colloki. Our aggregator will pick up content from local town and community group websites and listservs, and automatically classify it in Colloki.

User Contributed Content: Local Deliberation

Beyond the top level organization around 'Hot Topics', all online participants are allowed to comment on each other's contributions, in a manner similar to blog comments. This supports discussion and deliberation by citizens as a response to the postings of community leaders. We will develop an easy cross-referencing system, allowing people to link their comments to other stories/comments within the site.

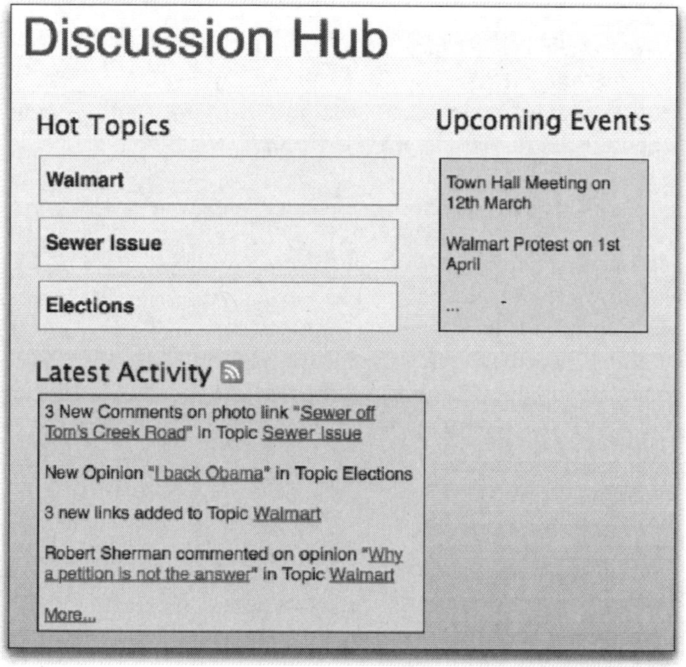

Figure 1. Opinions are organized in sections of interest called 'Hot Topics'

5   Reuse

Colloki is being designed with reuse in mind. The software would be built on open systems and would be available as an open source project when complete. Other local communities across the world would be able to host the software on their own servers or build over it. Colloki is being designed to use technology platforms that are easily available and economically viable.

6   Conclusion and Future Work

Our work on Colloki has just begun. We have designed the prototype and expect to have it in operation soon. We work closely in the Blacksburg and New River Valley areas with several civic organizations committed to helping us in the design and evaluation. Colloki is a part of our vision for the Virtual Town Square (Kavanaugh et al. forthcoming), a central online space for local information from government and citizen sources and for conversations between government and citizen entities around topics of local interest.

The main challenges we face include making the system easy to use and getting people to use it regularly. By collaborating with local civic organizations and local town government staff and officials, we hope to have the initial support to get this service off the ground.

7 Acknowledgements

We would like to express our gratitude to our colleagues, Byoung Joon Kim and Candida Tauro who contributed to earlier versions of this paper. We would like to thank William Sanders, John Tedesco, and Dave Britt for their extended collaboration. We are grateful for support from the National Science Foundation Digital Government Program (IIS-0429274) that supported underlying research and development of ideas described in this paper.

References

boyd, d. m. and N. B. Ellison 2007. Social Network Sites: Definition, History, and Scholarship. *Journal of Computer-Mediated Communication* 13(1): Article 11. Available at http://jcmc.indiana.edu/vol13/issue1/boyd.ellison.html (last accessed August 18, 2008)

Furnas, G. W., C. Fake, L. von Ahn, J. Schachter, S. Golder, K. Fox, M. Davis, C. Marlow, and M. Naaman. 2006. Why Do Tagging System Work? *CHI 2006 Extended Abstracts on Human Factors in Computing Systems (Montreal, Canada, April 22-27)*, 36-39. New York: ACM.

Kavanaugh, A., M. Pérez-Quiñones, J. Tedesco, and W. Sanders. forthcoming. Toward a Virtual Town Square in the Era of Web 2.0. *Handbook of Internet Research*, eds. J. Hunsinger, L. Klastrup, and M. Allen. Surrey, UK: Springer.

Kavanaugh, A., T. T. Zin, M. B. Rosson, J. M. Carroll, J. Schmitz, and B. J. Kim. 2007. Local Groups Online: Political Learning and Participation. *Journal of Computer Supported Cooperative Work* 16(September): 375-395.

Lampe, C., N. Ellison, and C. Steinfield. 2006. A Face(book) in the Crowd: Social Searching vs. Social Browsing. *Proceedings of the 2006 20th Anniversary Conference on Computer Supported Cooperative Work (Banff, Alberta, Canada, November 4-8)*, 167-170. New York: ACM Press.

Lenhart, A. and M. Madden. 2007. *Social Networking Websites and Teens: An Overview*. Washington, DC: Pew Internet & American Life Project. Available at http://www.pewinternet.org/ppf/r/198/report_display.asp (last accessed November 1, 2008)

Marlow, C., M. Naaman, d. boyd, and M. Davis. 2006. HT06, Tagging Paper, Taxonomy, Flickr, Academic Article, to Read. *Proceedings of the Seventeenth Conference on Hypertext and Hypermedia (Odense, Denmark, August 22-25)*, 31-40. New York: ACM.

Putnam, R. 2000. *Bowling Alone: The Collapse and Revival of American Community*. New York: Simon and Schuster.

Snyder, C. 2003. *Paper Prototyping: The Fast and Easy Way to Design and Refine User Interfaces*. San Francisco: Morgan Kaufmann, Elsevier Science.

Tepper, M. 2003. The Rise of Social Software. *netWorker* 7(3): 18-23.

Verba, S. and N. H. Nie. 1972. *Participation in America: Political Democracy and Social Equality*. New York: Harper & Row.

Verba, S., K. Schlozman, and H. Brady. 1995. *Voice and Equality: Civic Voluntarism in American Politics*. Cambridge, MA: Harvard University Press.

Veres, C. 2006. The Language of Folksonomies: What Tags Reveal About User Classification. *Natural Language Processing and Information Systems* 3999(2006): 58-69.

Part III
Online Public Consultation

9

Deliberation in E-Rulemaking? The Problem of Mass Participation

DAVID SCHLOSBERG, STEVE ZAVESTOSKI, AND STUART SHULMAN

1 Introduction

The United States federal government has, over the past decade, facilitated the electronic submission of citizen comments during federal regulatory rulemaking comment periods.[1] In response, citizens of many stripes, but particularly environmentalists, are taking advantage of newly developed Web-based tools for generating large numbers of public comments. The confluence of these two trends has altered the rulemaking environment. Government agencies take comments on rules via their websites. Mass-mailed postcards initiated by interest groups, familiar from past activism, have been modestly enhanced as customizable e-form letters.[2] This type of Internet-enabled participation will likely become the dominant form of mass political communication between average citizens and decision makers in controversial rulemakings.

---

[1] The federal eRulemaking Initiative (http://www.regulations.gov/eRuleMaking.cfm, last accessed November 20, 2008) is one of twenty-four e-Government efforts at the federal level (http://www.whitehouse.gov/omb/egov/l, last accessed November 20, 2008). On the progress of the President's Management Agenda to date, see GAO 2004.

[2] This strategy is often initiated by expensive for-profit intermediaries. See http://www.getactive.com/ or http://capitoladvantage.com/ (both last accessed November 20, 2008) for examples of firms that sell e-advocacy services.

Online Deliberation: Design, Research, and Practice.
Todd Davies and Seeta Peña Gangadharan (eds.).
Copyright © 2009, CSLI Publications.

As a result of these and other trends, a growing research community is looking closely at electronic rulemaking as a possible area for online political deliberation.[3] This fledgling interdisciplinary research is generally long on theory, hopes, and predictions while too often short on empirical data. In this chapter, we discuss an attempt to collect such data, a survey of 1553 participants in regulatory public comment processes.

Our initial research question asked whether new electronic forms of participation introduce a degree of public deliberation absent in the traditional mailing or faxing of letters that dominated pre-Internet era public comment periods (Schlosberg, Shulman, and Zavestoski 2005; Shulman et al. 2003). Contrary to much research and development in this field, we did not seek to develop new forms of online interaction that optimize deliberative behavior. Rather, we set out to evaluate the deliberative nature of existing forms of electronic citizen participation. We also examine differences between those who submitted original letters and those who submitted a version of a mass-mailed form letter.

Overall, our survey failed to reveal evidence of deliberative differences between electronic and paper commenters, but we did find some support for the possibility that the comment process induces deliberative behaviors. We also discovered that some fundamental attitudinal differences exist between citizens who submit original comments and those who submit mass-mailed letters. Form letters, obviously, are less deliberative than original comments. These mass-mailed comments contribute to aggregative, rather than deliberative, democracy. The differences between these writers exist not just in terms of their self-described deliberative practices but also in terms of their overall trust in government and feelings of efficacy as participants in the rulemaking process. Stated bluntly, participants in form letter campaigns, whether using paper or the Internet, behave in a way that is more simplistic and cynical, and less inclined to deliberative behavior, whereas the writers of original comments report personal practices that embody many of the characteristics of deliberative democracy. The two obvious questions raised here are: (1) why is this the case, and (2) how can Internet-based participation in rulemaking become more deliberative and effective? This chapter begins with a discussion of our survey and findings and concludes with some reflections on those key questions.

---

[3] On electronic rulemaking, see Shulman et al. (2003), Shulman (2004a), Coglianese (2003, 2004), Lubbers (2002). On online political deliberation, see Beierle (2004), Schlosberg and Dryzek (2002), Shane (2004), Zavestoski and Shulman (2002).

2   Democracy, Online Deliberation, and E-Rulemaking

Public participation and citizen deliberation continue to be hallmarks of democratic theory. As Dryzek (2001) notes, 'the essence of democracy itself is now widely taken to be deliberation' (1). Our central aim in this project is to evaluate the move to Web-based public participation in rulemaking against various criteria established by theorists of deliberative democracy. For example, one of the basic concepts in the field is that deliberation is reflective rather than simply reactive (Bohman 1996; Dahlbergh 2001; Janssen and Kies 2004). We assume reflection is based on collecting diverse information and forming an understanding of various positions on an issue. A second central concept in deliberative theory is that such engagement with other positions will bring recognition of others in the process (Young 2000; Froomkin 2004; Witschge 2004). Participants in democratic deliberation ideally listen to others, treat them with respect, and make an effort to understand them. Third, deliberative theory examines the relation between discourse and the transformation of individual preferences (Bohman 1996; Dryzek 2000; Habermas 1996). The ideal of deliberation is that of communication which actually changes the preferences of participants as they engage the positions of others. Citizen efficacy and the perceived authenticity of the process are also central to deliberative democracy, as deliberation is offered as a more authentic form of political participation (Barber 1984).

Our questionnaire included items intended to measure each of these dimensions of deliberation. While we do not claim to cover the full range of concerns of every deliberative theorist, our measures capture the concepts central to recent developments in democratic theory and provide a reasonable proxy for deliberative activity.

Citizen access to rulemaking information is quite different from what it was when the Administrative Procedure Act (APA) was passed in the U.S. The framers of the APA could not have imagined the ways that new media and tools using information and communications technologies (ICTs) would create a complex and teeming digital landscape with such democratic and deliberative potential.[4] The once reasonably straightforward processes of democratic participation found in the classic works of political science such as those written by Dahl (1961) or Truman (1960) are now largely anti-

---

[4] We should not, however, ignore the important point of the very real digital divide. A recent report from the American Political Science Association Task Force on Inequality and American Democracy stated 'the Internet may "activate the active" and widen disparities between participants and the politically disengaged by making it easier for the already politically engaged to gain political information' (2004: 69).

quated in the age of blogs, podcasts, listservs, mass email campaigns, and a proliferating array of Web services.

Research into the practice and potential of online deliberation covers a broad array of activities. One of the problems with this research is that there are so many avenues for such participation—websites, Usenet bulletin boards, chats, blogs, podcasts—making it difficult to systematically track and measure the impact of online deliberation. As Froomkin (2003) notes, 'the Internet can be seen as a giant electronic talkfest, a medium that is discourse-mad' (777).

We focus, however, on just one particular element in that 'talkfest': public participation in regulatory rulemaking. The development of rulemaking technologies appears to embody a democratic direction. Many agencies now use open electronic dockets, which allow citizens to review and comment on the rules proposed by agencies, supporting documentation, and comments of other citizens. In an early benchmark case of mass deliberation online, personnel managing the National Organic Program rulemaking at the United States Department of Agriculture (USDA) allowed citizens to read comments as they were posted, whether they came via fax, paper, or online (Shulman 2003).

Second, electronic rulemaking systems are highly structured, hence quite different from other Web-based discourse that is one-way, isolated, or homogenous. Sunstein (2001) argues that the Web enables people to pay attention to other like-minded people and ignore those who are unlike them or disagree with their positions on issues. The Web, for Sunstein, diminishes exposure to heterogeneity and is far from the ideal of an authentic public forum. Yet, the argument here is that the structure of e-rulemaking, in particular the open docket system, enables citizens to engage the positions of others, including those with whom they disagree. The open docket architecture of e-rulemaking may mitigate some of the anti-deliberative dangers engendered by the Web.

Other reasons to examine rulemaking are more specifically political. For example, on environmental issues, the big political battles have moved out of the legislative arena and into the realm of regulatory rulemaking. 'Perhaps the most significant administrative law development during the last two decades', notes Jeffrey Lubbers (1998), 'has been the increased presidential involvement in federal agency rulemaking' (19). While one of the reasons for this move has certainly been to try to avoid controversy, recent administration decisions and proposals have drawn considerable attention to the rulemaking process itself, in turn increasing the likelihood of large numbers of public comments.[5]

Rulemaking also goes somewhere; it gets implemented. Simply put, the process frequently leads to actual changes of agency-enforced rules. Here, a focus on rulemaking differs from other examinations of Web-based discourse. A common critique of online deliberative polling, cyberjuries, or Web-based policy discussions is that the deliberative work often produces few if any tangible or pragmatic results. People spend time and energy working toward consensus, only to see it ignored or rejected politically. This problem of implementation deficit can deplete citizen energy devoted to discourse. Rulemaking requires agencies to respond to substantive public comments. It may be the only form of online deliberation that regularly ends in government policy implementation.

3 Why Environmental Rules?

Environmental rules, especially over the last few years, have been highly controversial, attracting large numbers of comments (Zavestoski et al. 2006). More comments potentially could mean more discourse and increasingly diverse participants. We also sought to ensure a chance for deliberation, which meant restricting ourselves to rules in which the lead agency posted citizen comments to its website so that visitors could see the comments of others. Both the Environmental Protection Agency (EPA) and Department of Transportation (DOT) implemented such 'open docket' systems.

Much of the environmental politics literature claims high levels of democratic involvement in environmental policy making. 'One of the most distinctive features of modern U.S. environmental protection policy', writes Andrews (1999), is the 'broad right of access to the regulatory process, which extends not only to affected businesses but to citizens advocating environmental protection' (240). Paehlke (1989) argues that the environmental arena has led all others in its scope and extent of innovations in public participation, including public inquiries, right-to-know legislation, alternative dispute resolution, advisory committees, and policy dialogues. Hence, a leading edge of democratic public participation in the U.S. is in the environmental field, and this seems to have continued into Web-based participation processes.

---

[5] See Goldstein and Cohen (2004), the first of a series of three *Washington Post* articles on recent regulatory politics; see also Brinkley (2004).

Given our interest in controversial environmental regulations that elicited large numbers of public comments, we settled on the following cases (with the colloquial designations shown in bold):

1) EPA's advanced notice of proposed rulemaking on the Clean Water Act regulatory definition of the 'Waters of the United States' **(Waters)**[6]

2) EPA's proposed National Emissions Standards for Hazardous Air Pollutants **(Mercury)**[7]

3) DOT's advanced notice of proposed rulemaking on the Corporate Average Fuel Economy Standards **(CAFE)**[8].

The proposed Waters rule was to clarify, and limit, the federal jurisdiction over so-called 'isolated' wetlands. Whereas development lobbies saw the prospect of a Bush administration rulemaking as an opportunity to free up considerable chunks of land that had been protected for thirty years, environmentalists feared the potential rollback of federal regulatory powers would undermine core principles articulated in the landmark 1972 Clean Water Act. Ultimately, after extensive criticism and approximately 133,000 public comments, the EPA dropped the proposal.[9] The EPA claimed that the proposed Mercury rulemaking represented the largest air pollution reductions of any kind not specifically mandated by Congress, yet the vast majority of the nearly 500,000 public comments tended to disagree. After the comment process, the EPA issued a final controversial rule on March 15, 2005, and was met with promises of lawsuits by a number of states and nongovernmental actors. The CAFE rulemaking focused on reforming the automobile fuel economy standards program to address the continuing criticism related to energy security, traffic safety, economic practicability, and the definition of the separate category for light trucks. The process received 66,786 public comments.

4 The Survey Results

Submitted comments become part of the public record, so we were able to rely on relatively open access to the comment sets on each rule in order to contact individual citizen commenters.[10] Respondents were asked a range

---

[6] See *Federal Register* Vol 68, No. 10 pp. 1991-1998.

[7] Ibid. Vol. 69, No. 20 pp. 4652-4752.

[8] Ibid. Vol. 68, No. 248, pp. 74908-74931.

[9] See http://snipurl.com/dace (last accessed November 20, 2008).

[10] Comments either contained phone numbers or address information used in a reverse phone number look-up (http://www.whitepages.com/, last accessed November 20, 2008). We

of questions about their commenting behavior, including the number of times that they had commented on rules, how much information they obtained before commenting, how they typically submit a comment, the reasons that they commented, and whether they refer to other citizens' comments and, if so, the effect this has on their comments.[11] Respondents were also asked whether they thought their comments were reviewed by a government employee and whether they heard about, and were satisfied with, the final agency decision. Specific questions were also asked about the use of agency websites, including the frequency of visits, type of information accessed, whether they used these websites to submit a comment, and their general perceptions of the effect Federal agency websites have on commenting. Finally, respondents were asked if they believe submitting comments individually or as a group has the ability to change the outcome of the final rule.

Differences Between Paper and Electronic Commenters

Our survey of commenters on recent rulemakings brought us to three important conclusions about e-rulemaking and the potential of online deliberation in this area. First, electronic commenters do not appear to be any more deliberatively engaged than paper commenters. Second, despite failing to find that electronic commenters are more deliberative, we observed greater levels of self-reported deliberative activity across all types of commenters than expected. A surprisingly large number of respondents reported that they read other individuals' comments, acquire increased understanding of other people's positions as a result and even occasionally change their own positions. Third, rather than significant differences between electronic and paper commenters, the main differences we found were between individuals who submitted original comments and those who posted form letters.

The main goal of the survey was to look for differences between those who submitted comments on paper, either through postal mail or fax, and those who submitted comments electronically, through agency Web-based forms, interest group websites, or email. The survey suggests that those differences simply do not exist. This may be due to the fact that many submitters of original paper comments also use the Internet and Web-based

---

obtained phone numbers for more than 60% of the names and addresses entered. The survey was completed by 1553 respondents between the dates of August 30 and November 24, 2004. This represented a cooperation rate of 48%, with a margin of error of +/- 2.5%.

[11] While we are discussing 'citizen' commenters, we should make clear that a small percentage of our respondents were involved in the rulemaking process in roles other than private citizen. Of those surveyed, 86.4% reported that they generally commented as private citizen, 7.1% as a paid employee, 3.4% as an unpaid volunteer, and 3.2% as something else (though mostly as a representative of an interest group).

agency dockets extensively. While there is a distinction between the medium citizens use to *comment*, all types of commenters used electronic means to *gather* information in the commenting process. As for the lack of discursive indicators by electronic commenters, while technology makes commenting easier than before, it may also encourage the rapid submission of comments, which is antithetical to more thoughtful and carefully reasoned arguments.

The Prevalence of Deliberative Indicators

While differences between electronic and paper commenters are practically nonexistent, there are indicators that all types of commenters practice or benefit from certain types of deliberative activity. We found four significant indicators of such deliberative discourse: the frequency with which commenters seek out a variety of information, the tendency to review other citizens' comments, gaining an understanding of the positions of others, and changing one's own position after being exposed to the arguments of others.

First, the use of information in developing a public comment is quite high. Overall, commenters, regardless of medium, are information-seekers. Forty-five percent said they get a lot of information, while those that write original paper comments claim the most, at nearly 51%. Over 71% of those surveyed said that they referred to the arguments, studies, statements, or positions of agencies or independent organizations before submitting a comment. Again, those who submitted original paper comments were at the top with nearly 77%. Agency websites are important sources of information for commenters. Half of those surveyed said they used these sites in developing their comment. Again, a large majority of commenters are seeking out information, even those who submit form letters.

Commenters also review others' comments. Surprisingly, 68% said that they had read the comments of others at some point. As these comments are only available either in person in the agency docket rooms in Washington, DC, or on the newly developed agency websites, it may be that all types of commenters are using the agency websites to examine the docket, when such comments are available.[12] For those that specifically reported using the agency websites, 69% said that the site helped them review other citizens' comments. Overall reporting of the review of others' comments is high regardless of submission type, illustrating attention to the positions of others in the rulemaking process.

---

[12] Then again, as only 50% say they visited agency websites, and it seems unlikely that 18% physically visited a docket room, this number needs further explanation. It may be that some who report reading others' comments saw samples on interest group websites.

Reading of other citizens' comments is not just for information. Commenters report that they gain an *understanding* of the positions of others as well. Overall, nearly 75% say they get a better understanding of the positions of other citizens by reading their comments, and more than 41% say that they have found the comments of other citizens persuasive. Of the commenters who said that they visited and used agency websites, a very large percentage (72%) said that they somewhat or strongly agreed with the statement that the agency websites helped them to understand the positions of others. As the difference across types of commenters is insignificant, this finding suggests that commenters in general are gaining an understanding of the positions of other citizens commenting on a rule. Agency websites seem to have added to this particular indicator of democratic deliberation.

Finally, over 36% report that their position on an issue changed after reading others' comments. That is less than the 47% who report no change in their position. But the percentage that acknowledges such change is significant and serves as yet another indicator that the limited discourse made possible by access to others' comments is having an impact on the reasoning of citizen commenters. All of these findings suggest that elements necessary for deliberation—namely openness to information, willingness to understand others, and the possibility of preference transformation—are already present and information technology has made these opportunities more accessible.

Differences Between Original and Form Commenters

The most significant differences in this study are between those who submit original comments and those who submit form-based comments. A better understanding of these differences may impact how agencies respond to public comment and how interest groups refine their campaigns. Numerous civil servants have reported at workshops, focus groups, and interviews over the last four years that agencies are required to respond to substantive comments but not to sheer numbers. Notice and comment rulemaking was designed to bring diverse information into the rulemaking process not to be a referendum (Shulman 2004a).

Many interest groups, in addition to drawing on their legal and scientific staff to draft detailed comments, respond to the rulemaking process with an aggregative approach, soliciting mass numbers of identical or nearly duplicate comments from their members and other interested citizens. By all accounts, new ICTs have enabled the number of comments to increase well beyond the capacity of agencies to cope without expensive, outside private consulting firms to report on the content of citizen comments. A key question is whether or not this technology improves or degrades citizen discourse (Shulman 2004b).

In the survey findings, the differences between original and form commenters start with the use of information. More than 54% of original commenters report having used an agency website to read information on a proposed rule. This compares to only about 44% of the form commenters, a significant difference. Original commenters are also significantly more likely to report gaining a greater understanding of the positions or arguments of other citizens by reading their comments. While both sets of commenters read the positions of others, original submitters are more likely to report having a better understanding of those positions.

In addition to these differences, there are significant differences between original and form commenters on a number of indicators of trust in the process and the agency involved. For example, original commenters (both paper and electronic) are significantly more likely to believe their comments were actually read by a government employee, compared to form commenters. Electronic form commenters appear to be the most cynical in terms of their feeling that their participation will have an impact on their satisfaction with the final rule. Conversely, those who sent paper original comments are the most satisfied with their participation and the outcome. Not only are form submitters more cynical about having their comments read and making a difference, they are also more likely to say that their participation led to a negative view of the agency running the rulemaking. Original commenters are more likely to report a positive view of the agency and are slightly more satisfied than form commenters with agency decisions on issues on which they have commented. Users of form letters are simply more negative about the government in general and are significantly more likely to 'rarely' or 'never' trust the government to do what is right.

Overall, the survey illustrates the belief that form letters are less likely to be read by government employees or have an actual impact. It may be the case that a negative view of the agency and government in general was one of the reasons for commenting in the first place. A central question here is whether a lack of faith in the agency has led to some citizens' refusal to take the time to write an original letter.

On the Value of Electronic Comment and Mass E-Mail Campaigns

There is one other key finding regarding the difference between form and original commenters. Though it contradicts the lack of trust in government noted above, form commenters are more likely than original commenters to think that groups that organize mass mail campaigns have the ability to change proposed rules. This may partly explain why form commenters are much more likely to submit comments more often than original commenters. This faith that mass email campaigns have an impact has led to the increase in the popularity of the tactic. Nearly 50% of those surveyed said they submitted their last comment through an interest group website, and almost 40% reported that this method will also be how they comment next time. While agencies such as the EPA and DOT have worked to improve the information on their Web-based docket systems, and the Federal government continues to develop a Federal Docket Management System as a single Web-based public comment portal, very few commenters plan to use such systems—only 12% versus the nearly 40% who plan to use interest group websites.

This practice should be worrisome for those interested in the potential of the Web to increase discourse on important issues in the rulemaking process. Commenters who submitted using form emails via interest group websites were the least likely to look at other information and the least likely to report that their positions have changed as a result of reading others' comments. In other words, electronic form commenters show the lowest scores on many deliberative indicators. Mass email campaigns, as they are currently designed, are only useful in an aggregative form of democracy. Such an approach is better suited to pressuring legislators than to influencing agency personnel.

In addition, there is little evidence to support the belief that mass email campaigns actually do change proposed rules. While the proposed Waters rulemaking was dropped, other highly controversial rulemakings went forward while tens of thousands and sometimes hundreds of thousands of comments came in against them. Interviews with agency rule writers show that agencies do not value and often openly resent form letters. The EPA, in fact, simply prints and stores an inaccessible hard copy of all but one example of each identical or similar mass email. Importantly, however, our interviews and focus groups show that these same officials would welcome more substantive and original comments, as they could return the rulemaking process to that designed by the APA—one based on the collection of information and substantive input from interested parties outside of the government.

5 Democracy, Online Deliberation, and E-Rulemaking

The distinction between paper and electronic commenters, which was the basis of our original set of hypotheses, simply does not exist as we imagined it might. A majority of commenters, regardless of the medium of submission, are using electronic means of researching an issue. Comparing paper and electronic commenters on recent rules does not help us understand whether the new electronic systems are more deliberative than past paper-based notice and comment processes.

That said, the issue of the difference between original and form-based mass participation is obviously at the forefront of the questions regarding the potential for deliberative activity in the rulemaking process. Original commenters embody many of the deliberative qualities we hypothesized given the move to an accessible open docket system. The range of significant differences between original letter writers and form letter submitters might be partially explained by the introduction of a large number of commenters (mostly form users) who are new to the rulemaking process. The ease with which interest groups can spread information to constituents about proposed rules open for public comment, and the sophistication of email action alert systems that allow individuals to 'participate' by doing little more than clicking the 'send' button on an interest group's website, means agencies are getting more comments, especially from people who have not participated in the process in the past. Though many of these participants, even electronic form submitters, reported to us that they seek out information before sending in their comments, form submitters are nevertheless much more cynical about the process, and much less deliberative in their engagement. This leads us to conclude that there might be a certain amount of political capability that must be acquired before these new participants have a level of efficacy and trust in the process that will justify the effort required to become more deliberative participants.

Interest groups could develop this capability, so why don't environmental groups, in particular, solicit more original, substantive, deliberative comments? Certainly, it is true that it is very easy to respond to a mass email by clicking 'send'. It takes substantially more effort to participate in a deliberative process, but the existing deliberative shortfall could reflect movement strategy and assumptions rather than a lack of citizen interest or capability. Environmental groups simply respond to the rulemaking process with an aggregative approach, soliciting mass numbers of identical or near-duplicate comments, which the agencies then ignore. Yet, according to the survey, a good part of the environmental constituency has shown an interest in more deliberative participation—reading others' comments, learning, and participating in something more substantive than mass emails. Environmental groups favoring mass email campaigns have been unable to take advantage of technological changes or the professed willingness of some of their constituents to be more deliberative.

Environmental groups simply need to use Web technology to solicit more substantive comments. For example, they can challenge members to think up new categories for agency cost-benefit analyses. They could also ask members to enter postal codes, and then prompt them to report something about a local stream, mercury emitting industry, or health problems.

Groups could also distribute parts of a proposed rule, and ask constituents to comment substantively on a specific section of interest.

From the agency side, the easiest way to improve the process would be to develop a better user interface in the open dockets. Agencies could also randomly respond to comments online during the rulemaking process, or supplement the formal comment process with online dialogues. Federal agencies do not necessarily need to figure out how to get more people to comment through their websites, but they do need to figure out how to get more commenters to trust the process and invest time in enhancing deliberation on a proposed rule.

The potential to increase both political capacity and deliberation exists in the practices of both agencies and interest groups. Perhaps as the very technology that has brought more participants into the process is better utilized to handle increased levels of participation, all types of participants—from paper original letter writers to electronic form submitters—will feel their participation is meaningful. In turn, theoretically, these participants will invest time in becoming more educated, thoughtful, and deliberative commenters.

So we conclude by noting the potential of electronic rulemaking to enhance democratic deliberation on key issues in the American polity. Certainly, we see that some citizens are interested in rules, information surrounding various issues, and what other citizens have to say in the comment process. Many citizens are also willing to have their own positions challenged and possibly transformed in the engagement with others. We also see that technology exists both to enhance the deliberative process (the open dockets and access to information on agency websites) and to degrade discourse (the easy click-to-send Web pages on interest group websites). Obviously, the technology will not stand still. We only hope that research like this will push the agencies and interest groups alike to develop systems that meet the ideals of both the APA notice and comment process and deliberative democracy to increase the amount of information, expand the exchange of views, and improve the democratic process in the development of better policy.

Acknowledgements.

This project was funded by a grant (SES-0322622) from the National Science Foundation Program on Social Dimensions of Engineering, Science and Technology (SDEST). Any opinions, findings, conclusions, or recommendations expressed in this material are those of the authors and do not necessarily reflect those of the National Science Foundation. The authors wish to thank Cary Coglianese and Vincent Price for their insightful comments on previous versions of this paper. A more comprehensive version of this study is available as Schlosberg, Shulman, and Zavestoski (2007).

References

American Political Science Association (APSA). 2004. American Democracy in an Age of Rising Inequality. Available at http://www.apsanet.org/imgtest/taskforcereport.pdf (last accessed October 1, 2008)

Andrews, R. N. L. 1999. *Managing the Environment, Managing Ourselves: A History of American Environmental Policy*. New Haven: Yale.

Barber, B. 1984. *Strong Democracy: Participatory Politics for a New Age*. Berkeley: University of California Press.

Beierle, T. C. 2004. Digital Deliberation: Engaging the Public Through Online Policy Dialogues. *Democracy Online: The Prospects for Political Renewal Through the Internet*, ed. P. M. Shane, 155-166. New York: Routledge.

Bohman, J. 1996. *Public Deliberation: Pluralism, Complexity and Democracy*. Cambridge, MA: MIT Press.

Brinkley, J. 2004. Out of the Spotlight, Bush Overhauls U.S. Regulations. *New York Times* (August 14, 2004): A1.

Coglianese, C. 2004. E-Rulemaking: Information Technology and Regulatory Policy. *Regulatory Policy Program Report No. RPP-05*.

Coglianese, C. 2003. *The Internet and Public Participation in Rulemaking*. Paper presented at the conference on Democracy in the Digital Age, Yale Law School, New Haven, CT, April 4-6 2003.

Dahl, R. 1961. *Who Governs?* New Haven: Yale University Press.

Dahlbergh, L. 2001. Computer-Mediated Communication and the Public Sphere: A Critical Analysis. *Journal of Computer-Mediated Communication* 7(1). Available at http://jcmc.indiana.edu/vol7/issue1/dahlberg.html (last accessed October 1, 2008)

Dryzek, J. S. 2000. *Deliberative Democracy and Beyond: Liberals, Critics, Contestations* New York: Oxford University Press.

Froomkin, A. M. 2004. Technologies for Democracy. *Democracy Online: The Prospects for Political Renewal Through the Internet*, ed. P. M. Shane, 3-20. New York: Routledge.

Froomkin, A. M. 2003. Habermas@Discourse.Net: Toward a Critical Theory of Cyberspace. *Harvard Law Review* 116(3): 751-873.

Government Accountability Office (GAO). 2004. Electronic Government: Initiatives Sponsored by the Office of Management and Budget Have Made Mixed Progress. Washington, DC: author. Available at http://www.gao.gov/new.items/d04561t.pdf (last accessed October 1, 2008)

Goldstein, A. and S. Cohen, 2004. Bush Forces a Shift in Regulatory Thrust. *Washington Post* (August 15, 2004): A1.

Habermas, J. 1996. *Between Facts and Norms: Contributions to a Discourse Theory of Law and Democracy*. Cambridge, MA: MIT Press.

Janssen, D. and R. Kies. 2004. *Online Forums and Deliberative Democracy: Hypotheses, Variables and Methodologies*. Paper presented at the Conference on Empirical Approaches to Deliberative Politics, European University Institute, Florence, May 22-23, 2004. Available at http://edc.unige.ch/publications/e-workingpapers/onlineforums.pdf (last accessed February 28, 2005)

Lubbers, J. S. 2002. The Future of Electronic Rulemaking: A Research Agenda. *Administrative and Regulatory Law News* 27(4): 6-7, 22-23.

Paehlke, R. 1989. *Environmentalism and the Future of Progressive Politics*. New Haven: Yale University Press.

Schlosberg, D, S. W. Shulman, and S. Zavestoski. 2007. Democracy and E-Rulemaking: Web-based Participation and the Potential of Deliberation. *Journal of Information Technology and Politics* 4(1): 37-55.

Schlosberg, D., S. W. Shulman, and S. Zavestoski. 2005. Virtual Environmental Citizenship: Web-Based Public Participation on Environmental Rulemaking in the U.S. *Environmental Citizenship: Getting from Here to There*, eds. A. Dobson and D. Bell, 207-36. Cambridge, MA: MIT Press.

Schlosberg, D. and J. S. Dryzek. 2002. Digital Democracy: Authentic or Virtual? *Organization & Environment* 15(3): 332-335.

Shane, P. M. 2004. Introduction: The Prospects for Electronic Democracy. In *Democracy Online: The Prospects for Political Renewal Through the Internet*, ed. P. M. Shane, xi-xx. New York: Routledge.

Shulman, S. W. 2004a. The Internet Still Might (but Probably Won't) Change Everything: Stakeholder Views on the Future of Electronic Rulemaking. Available at http://erulemaking.ucsur.pitt.edu/doc/reports/e-rulemaking_final.pdf (last accessed April 11, 2005)

Shulman, S. W. 2004b. Whither Deliberation? Mass e-Mail Campaigns and U.S. Regulatory Rulemaking. Available at http://erulemaking.ucsur.pitt.edu/doc/papers/Smarttape12.04.pdf (last accessed April 11, 2005)

Shulman, S. W. 2003. An Experiment in Digital Government at the United States National Organic Program. *Agriculture and Human Values* 20(3): 253-265.

Shulman, S. W., D. Schlosberg, S. Zavestoski, and D. Courard-Hauri. 2003. Electronic Rulemaking: New Frontiers in Public Participation. *Social Science Computer Review* 21(2): 162-178.

Sunstein, C. R. 2001. *Republic.com*. Princeton, NJ: Oxford: Princeton University Press.

Truman, D. 1960. *The Governmental Process: Political Interests and Public Opinion*. New York: Knopf.

Witschge, T. 2004. Online Deliberation: Possibilities of the Internet for Deliberative Democracy. *Democracy Online: The Prospects for Political Renewal Through the Internet*, ed. P. M. Shane, 109-122. New York: Routledge.

Young, I.M. 2000. *Inclusion and Democracy*. Oxford: Oxford University Press.

Zavestoski, S., S. Shulman, and D. Schlosberg. 2006. Democracy and the Environment on the Internet: Electronic Citizen Participation in Regulatory Rulemaking. *Science, Technology & Human Values* 31(4): 383-408.

Zavestoski, S. and S. W. Shulman. 2002. The Internet and Environmental Decision-Making. *Organization & Environment* 15(3): 323-327.

10

Turning GOLD into EPG: Lessons from Low-Tech Democratic Experimentalism for Electronic Rulemaking and Other Ventures in Cyberdemocracy

PETER M. SHANE

1 Introduction

For cyberdemocrats—researchers and activists who champion the potential for new information and communication technologies (ICTs) to improve upon our practice of democracy—electronic rulemaking seems a tantalizing prospect. Federal agencies engrafting Web-based tools onto notice-and-comment rulemaking are operating across a domain of policy making that affects the lives of every American. Within this domain, U.S. federal law already mandates, even if indirectly, that agency experts and their politically accountable supervisors take some deliberative account of public input. The federal commitment to electronic rulemaking thus seems to hold out the potential to enlarge significantly a genuine public sphere in which individual citizens participate directly to help to make government decisions that are binding on the entire polity.

Central to this vision of what might be called 'Government On-Line Deliberation', which I abbreviate 'GOLD', are values of democratic

Online Deliberation: Design, Research, and Practice.
Todd Davies and Seeta Peña Gangadharan (eds.).
Copyright © 2009, CSLI Publications.

collaboration and participation. These values align the project of cyberdemocracy with a family of reforms that political scientist Archon Fung and sociologist Erik Olin Wright call 'Empowered Participatory Governance', or EPG. EPG is a style of deliberative democracy that seeks to 'deepen the ways in which ordinary people can effectively influence policies that shape their lives' (Fung and Wright 2003b: 5). Although writers on EPG have yet to consider seriously the political role of ICTs in such reforms, their work can be of enormous use to cyberdemocrats. That is because EPG theory attends thoughtfully to the issue that, so far, is the least usefully addressed in the burgeoning literature on electronic democracy, namely, the conundrum of power. Researchers and activists have persuasively demonstrated the theoretical potential for ICTs to undergird more robust democratic practices, strengthening both the deliberative and representative aspects of our institutional life (Froomkin 2004). What has been less successfully addressed is the question of how to get 'there' from 'here'. In particular, what are the social conditions and conditions of political power that would make it practicable to implement and sustain some version of GOLD that is genuinely collaborative, participatory, and democratic?

With this question in mind, I will now briefly do three things. First, I will sketch the theory of EPG. Second, I will argue for the centrality of the issues of power to any realistic assessment of the future for electronic rulemaking. I will do this by elaborating on how questions of power pervade every aspect of the electronic rulemaking agenda as it is currently being both studied and implemented, and consider the lessons of EPG research for the future of this particular form of GOLD. Finally, I will discuss whether there is a role for GOLD or other ICT initiatives in EPG projects other than electronic rulemaking. That is, to the extent researchers have identified obstacles to EPG in low-tech democratic initiatives, what might be the role of ICTs in addressing those obstacles?

2 What is EPG?

EPG is a model of governance that Fung and Wright derive partly from democratic theory and partly from the study of 'real world' attempts to institutionalize 'transformative strategies' for democratizing social and political decision making (Fung and Wright 2003b: 4). The model seeks to connect a set of normative commitments for strengthening democracy with a set of institutional design prescriptions intended to meet that objective. Such a project necessarily highlights what Joshua Cohen and Joel Rogers (2003) call the 'conditions of background power' (240) that make more or less reasonable 'the hopeful, radical-democratic assumption' (241) that underlies EPG. This is the assumption 'that ordinary people are capable of reducing the political role of untamed power and arbitrary preference and, through the exercise of their common reason, jointly solving important collective problems' (Cohen and Rogers 2003: 240). Doubts about that assumption are not only, or even primarily, a reflection on the capacities of the participating citizens themselves. Rebecca Neaera Abers (2003) has posed the key issue: '[W]hy would governments transfer decision-making power to deliberative spaces in which 'ordinary people' have influence and why would those ordinary people, most of whom have little political experience beyond the occasional vote, voluntarily subject themselves to time-consuming and often frustrating deliberative processes?' (201).

Most generally, as seen by Fung and Wright, EPG is a form of institutionalized deliberative democracy. That is, it is a way of producing legitimate governmental decision making through reasoned public dialogue that is conducted under conditions of equality. As they describe it, EPG projects seek to involve those people who are affected by specific, tangible problems in addressing those problems through the deliberative development of solutions that are actually implemented by institutions of state power (Fung and Wright 2003b: 15). The emphasis on specific, tangible problems is intended to facilitate collaboration in democratic decision making among erstwhile policy competitors who are enabled to focus their problem solving attention on a constrained set of issues (Fung and Wright 2003b: 16). The direct engagement of ordinary citizens assumes that their experiential knowledge and immediate participation will improve problem solving through enhanced information, as well as increasing accountability for the implementation of any solutions developed. Experts remain deeply engaged in such institutions, but, ideally, as enablers, not deciders.

There are three design features on which EPG initiatives generally rely in order to stabilize and deepen the practice of its animating principles. First, EPG seeks to 'devolve' decision making authority to empowered local units. This reflects the skepticism among many contemporary activists about the problem-solving capacities of highly centralized state organizations (Fung and Wright 2003b). On the other hand, because local units cannot solve all problems themselves and can also benefit from the sharing of insights and from objective oversight, EPG initiatives tend, as a second feature, to depend upon 'formal linkages of responsibility, resource distribution and communication' between local units and central state offices (Fung and Wright 2003b: 16). Finally, EPG must be embodied in state institutions that actually make decisions and are capable of implementing an allocation of public resources that is both more effective and more equitable in addressing public problems. EPG thus envisions a kind of 'inside' revolution. EPG is distinguishable from wholly voluntary and spontaneous organizational efforts that seek to influence state outcomes through outside pressure alone.

Of course, EPG projects cannot be expected to arise or be sustained solely by good intentions or noble aspirations. The likelihood of engaging citizens successfully in such ventures will depend, for example, on their own attitudes and capacities, such as literacy. Attitudes and capacity are, however, presumably not insurmountable obstacles. Even at an early stage in this field of research, evidence shows it is possible to mobilize ordinary citizens, including those of profoundly modest means, into genuinely deliberative institutions that effectively make significant public decisions.

The tougher hurdle is one of political context, namely, the existing allocation of political decision making power in the domain over which activists might wish to achieve EPG. Existing power structures are likely in all societies to reflect some imbalance of influence and control, in which relatively advantaged groups are disproportionately able to direct the distribution of social resources in their favor. As Fung and Wright (2003a) recognize, these 'inequalities of background power can subvert the democracy-enhancing potential of institutional designs such as EPG' (260). The question is, what can be done about it?

Fung and Wright do not so much offer a confident answer to this question as underscore its significance. They elaborate on the possibility of what they call, 'countervailing power', meaning that 'variety of mechanisms that reduce, and perhaps even neutralize, the power advantages of ordinarily powerful actors' (Fung and Wright 2003a: 260). Mechanisms of countervailing power may include such things as effective grassroots organizing or a judicial order requiring some powerful institution to respond in particular ways to less powerful interests. Fung and Wright do not yet have a theory as to the mobilization of countervailing power or how much is enough to achieve the democratic potential of EPG institutional designs. They do, however, assert four relevant propositions:

> EPG will not yield its intended benefits in a context without a substantial presence of countervailing power;
>
> The sources and forms of countervailing power that are efficacious in the collaborative exercise of power are likely to differ from those sources or forms that are effective in redressing power imbalances under conditions of adversarial interest group pluralism;
>
> The adversarial and collaborative forms of countervailing power are not easily converted to one another, so that actors effective in mobilizing for the underrepresented in one context may not have the 'skills, sources of support, and bases of solidarity' necessary for success in the other; and

> Well designed public policies and institutions can facilitate, but will not themselves generate the countervailing power needed for collaborative governance (Fung and Wright 2003a: 266-267).

Fung and Wright point to political parties, 'adversarial organizations', and social movements as sources of countervailing power.

The facial plausibility of Fung and Wright's cautionary propositions might alone be thought sufficient to generate a fair amount of pessimism about the future of EPG. But it may be a mistake to think about transformation in general, or EPG specifically, in entirely categorical terms. Rebecca S. Krantz (2003) has suggested it is most helpful to understand EPG reforms as part of a larger trend towards direct participatory innovation, a trend that may be advanced by steps more partial or gradual than the case studies Fung and Wright highlight. The key question, she posits, is not whether EPG can erupt full-blown, but whether 'gradualist forms of participatory civic innovation might contribute to more widespread adoption of EPG' (225). Under the Krantz view, what is needed to nudge things forward is only a political context in which sufficient countervailing power is present to trigger some degree of participatory institutional reform.

In this way, there might be hope, in the words of Fung and Wright (2003b), for a 'reorganization of formal state institutions [to] stimulate democratic engagement in civil society, and so form a virtuous circle of reciprocal reinforcement' (15). This could happen, for example, if institutional reform yielded benefits to both those traditionally empowered and those traditionally disempowered. As expressed by Rebecca Abers: '[T]he success of participatory institutions depends on a dual-process of commitment-building'. The key is for each round of reform to intensify the motivation of 'state actors (ranging from politicians to bureaucrats) and ordinary people... to support, take part in, and respect EPG experiments' (Abers 2003: 201).

In sum, EPG researchers offer a model of politics under which institutional reforms would truly deepen democratic effectiveness and legitimacy. They offer a sensible rubric for conceptualizing conditions under which reforms tending towards EPG are likely, at least, to be plausible. They identify the obstacles likeliest to impede the realization of those conditions. These elements provide a firm basis for asking the question: What is the role of GOLD in the future of EPG?

3   Electronic Rulemaking and EPG

At first blush, electronic rulemaking of the sort now either implemented or on the 'drawing board' of the federal 'E-Rulemaking Initiative', does not easily fit the EPG model.[1] Current electronic rulemaking resembles a global suggestion box, appended to an electronic library. Agencies use the World Wide Web as a vehicle for facilitating both citizen access to information about rulemaking and the capacity to submit comments efficiently. But electronic rulemaking does not yet involve actual dialogue among citizens or between citizens and agencies about either proposed rules or about comments already submitted. Neither does anything about the process provide assurance that agencies will give greater weight to electronically transmitted citizen comments than to citizen views conveyed in the days of predigital notice-and-comment rulemaking. Nor is there any necessary connection between the citizens who participate in electronic rulemaking and some set of specific problems that the rules address and that affect the commenting citizens in specific and tangible ways. Rulemaking operates on a national scale; there is no devolution at work. The interest a rule elicits may have more to do with abstract ideology than actual problem solving.

The barriers to moving towards an EPG model are not technological. Software tools already exist that could be deployed to support online democratic deliberation (Noveck 2005: 21). It is already possible to imagine, with currently available software, the following model of electronic rulemaking: a government agency—perhaps the Environmental Protection Agency—sets up deliberative groups around the country with access to software for conducting online deliberations both asynchronously and in real time. Various of these groups are invited, depending on the issues presented, to develop deliberative recommendations concerning issues on the agency's agenda. The EPA would support 'formal linkages' among these deliberative groups; it might even convene regional and national online assemblies of representatives elected from local and regional discussions, respectively. Even if the deliberative groups were not empowered with formal decisional influence, as full-blown EPG would require, such a network of deliberative bodies would much more closely resemble the style of democratic governance that Fung and Wright have in mind.

The reason this scenario seems so unlikely is because of the inertial force exerted by the current allocation of power with regard to federal rulemaking decisions. This is true at every level. First, insofar as rulemaking is an exercise in what Fung and Wright (2003a) call 'top-down adversarial governance' (259-262), there are numerous firms and organized groups,

---

[1] Links to key documents explaining the Federal E-Rulemaking Initiative appear at http://www.regulations.gov (last accessed November 14, 2008). Additional background information and research may be found at E-Rulemaking Resource Web Site maintained by the Regulatory Policy Program at Harvard University's Kennedy School of Government, http://www.hks.harvard.edu/m-rcbg/rpp/erulemaking/home.htm (last accessed November 14, 2008).

representing business interests, government entities, and like-minded citizens that have mastered the current system. They are able either to elicit substantive results satisfactory to their clients or to persuade their clientele sufficiently of the importance of their adversarial activity as to remain viable actors on the current political stage. In addition, within each agency, there is an existing equilibrium of power for the management of rulemaking that the infusion of new information technologies necessarily threatens to disturb. There are presumably people within every agency who have succeeded at managing the predigital rulemaking process; they might not have the same level of capacity or effectiveness when it comes to managing an electronically enabled process.

This does not mean that proponents of a more transformative version of electronic rulemaking are utterly without current and potential sources of countervailing power. Deregulatory forces might become enamored of deliberative forms of electronic rulemaking if they think that more deliberative policy making will actually delay new regulations, an end that many powerful interests will likely find attractive in itself. Moreover, if deliberative processes hold the promise of sensitizing agencies to adopting regulatory alternatives in a variety of contexts that are more palatable to small business and to state, county, and local entities, that, too, would be a boon for federal legislators. Agency decision makers could come to see genuinely deliberative electronic rulemaking as a way of building public support for an agency. And there may exist reform entities, such as the American Bar Association or the Administrative Conference of the United States, who might be mobilized to nudge government forward in a more participatory direction.

One also should not underestimate the possible influence of peer reputation. The trend towards online citizen consultation is global and is likely to accelerate. Agency policy makers travel in international professional circles, where innovation gives rise to bragging rights. For example, in reporting to Congress on its regulatory activities, the Office of Management and Budget routinely refers to the regulatory affairs research of the international Organisation for Economic Co-operation and Development (OECD), headquartered in Paris (Office of Management and Budget 2004: 31). The OECD has been a strong champion of cyberdemocracy efforts (OECD 2003).

Things also look more promising if we ask a question less ambitious than whether electronic rulemaking is likely itself to be so transformative as to generate EPG. Following Rebecca Krantz's (2003) analysis, the better question is whether, and under what circumstances, electronic rulemaking could come to represent one of those 'gradualist forms of participatory civic innovation [that might] contribute to more widespread adoption of EPG' (225). It may be that the greatest contribution of electronic rulemaking to EPG would be the imitative effort it spawns at the state and local levels. Rather than pursuing forms of electronic rulemaking now that will immediately shake our adversarial, pluralist system of federal notice-and-comment rulemaking into something collaborative and participatory, the federal government could assess tools and develop model processes for online citizen deliberation which, in turn, would be available for adoption by local governments that would not otherwise have the resources to launch such an effort.

Of course, it may well be that the burgeoning of ICT-infused deliberative democracy at the local level is better seen as a precondition, rather than as an objective of federal transformative efforts. It seems all but inevitable, however, that well-publicized federal experiments in online citizen consultation, even if episodic, would stimulate local efforts along the same lines to invigorate citizen input into public policy making. People would begin to ask, 'If they can do it, why can't we?' It also seems predictable that, the more local the effort, the greater would become the likely expectation that the formal processes of actual decision making would have to take account of the input gleaned from online citizen forums. That is, for the very reasons Fung and Wright tie EPG to local decision making, the pressures to give online citizen consultation genuine decisional influence would seem greatest for smaller government units.

In sum, the obstacles to the promulgation of genuinely deliberative electronic rulemaking strongly resemble the obstacles Fung and Wright identify as facing EPG generally. Those obstacles seem quite powerful enough, in the near-term, to rebuff any serious movement towards an ICT-enabled paradigm shift in the role of citizens in federal administrative rulemaking. They seem less daunting, however, if the objective is not near-term federal transformation, but only sufficient innovation at the federal level to both inspire and facilitate local efforts. A spread of local participatory policy making could, of course, create a new round of pressure on the federal government to intensity its democratic ambitions as well. Whether any of this is plausible will require more substantial analysis. It is clear, however, that Fung and Wright provide helpful conceptual tools for assessing the possibilities.

4   GOLD and EPG

The foregoing analysis, urging that electronic rulemaking be understood as a possible prod to local Government On-Line Deliberation, or GOLD, necessarily leads to the question: Would local versions of GOLD be helpful in institutionalizing EPG? In Fung and Wright's collection of papers on EPG, *Deepening Democracy*, the only reference to ICTs is the potential, noted by political scientist Craig W. Thomas, for a Web-based library of draft and final Habitat Conservation Plans to facilitate public input, monitoring, and the diffusion of expertise in this Department of Interior-sponsored experiment in collaborative environmental planning and management (Thomas 2003: 164). But, of course, virtually every democratic initiative would benefit from online repositories of expertise, relevant data, and records of past decisions. Given the ease at which vast amounts of critical information can be made available cheaply to unprecedented numbers of people, one would wish that some sort of online library were incorporated into every effort at democratic reform.

Information technology could also be of profound utility with regard to training, data gathering, and monitoring. Training is critically important to empowering citizens with the mastery of both data and deliberative processes critical to sustaining effective deliberative problem solving at the local level. Much of this training would surely be amenable to presentation in the form of online tutorials and simulations. GIS-oriented websites would enable citizens to visualize much more richly the resources, opportunities, and challenges confronting particular neighborhoods, towns, and counties.[2] Interactive GIS tools could enable citizens to upload information to a community website about the location of environmental hazards, roads in need of repair, traffic safety problems, or other geographically based public needs.

Similar tools could vastly improve the quality of monitoring efforts during the implementation phase of EPG governance. Projects could be publicly tracked online. Complaints could be channeled more efficiently to relevant administrators. Individual citizens could check on the progress of local agencies in responding to specific needs. Perhaps most famously, the advent of process-tracking software in Seoul, Korea not only enhanced government efficiency but greatly reduced suspicions of 'irregular' practices and municipal corruption.[3]

On top of all this, the proliferation of Web-based organizing tools among civil society groups could greatly magnify their capacity to provide the checking and balancing of more powerful interests that is a necessary

---

[2] 'GIS' stands for 'geographic information system', which is a combination of hardware and software designed to enable the storage, retrieval, mapping, and analysis of information tied to specific physical locations.

[3] Seoul's project is called OPEN, which stands for Online Procedures Enhancement for Civil Applications. For an archived version of the OPEN system, see http://web.archive.org/web/20060628204152/http://www.unpan.org/training-open-manual.asp (last accessed November 14, 2008, original site http://www.unpan.org/training-open-manual.asp, is no longer available).

element of EPG under the theory of countervailing power. The deployment of Web-based tools in the 2004 presidential election in the United States enabled the Democrats to compete with Republican fundraising, turn out enormous numbers of volunteers, schedule countless planning meetings, and elicit more voters for a presidential challenger than in any prior presidential election in American history.[4] The same tools, deployed locally, could have effects of equally profound importance, focused on a smaller venue.

What, then, would GOLD add? All of the tools I have mentioned already would help provide a context for sustaining deliberative democracy, but would not extend deliberation itself. Among the most profound potential contributions ICTs can make to EPG is precisely that—to extend deliberation beyond the limited times and limited venues of face-to-face deliberation. I am not suggesting the substitution of one for the other but an augmentation of face-to-face encounters through computer-mediated discussion. The reliance of deliberative democratic institutions solely on face-to-face meetings necessarily imposes a drastic limitation on the scale of possible citizen participation. Webcasting face-to-face meetings (and perhaps receiving online input even in those sessions), and then allowing conversations to be extended through both asynchronous bulletin boards and self-scheduled real-time online meetings, would permit large numbers of citizens to participate who otherwise could or would not.

It is easy to anticipate four possible objections to the recommendation of GOLD-enhanced EPG institutions: GOLD costs money. The 'digital divide' will distort the population of online discussants. The formats for online discussion privilege those categories of citizens who prefer the modes of communication that work most effectively online. Finally, online deliberation is less likely than face-to-face discussion to induce the feelings of mutual respect and solidarity on which long-term EPG depends.

The first point is undeniable. Even if GOLD is sustained by open source software—avoiding any issue of licensing fees—all software needs support, whether in-house or contracted to others.[5] Any worthwhile system will entail monitoring and the updating of content. The cost of hardware systems administration will go up. These costs, however, are not likely to be pro-

---

[4] 'From Jan. 1 through June 30, Kerry and Democrats raised $292 million, compared with $272 million for President Bush and Republicans' (VandeHei and Edsall 2004: A1).

[5] Delibera, an open source software product to support online deliberation, was developed at Carnegie Mellon University for the purpose of enabling users to access a rich menu of online deliberative options. See http://virtualagora.org/ (last accessed November 14, 2008). Its developers, including this author, provided a royalty-free license for educational, research, and civic uses. The software has received little use, however, because it would be difficult to implement without the help of a skilled programmer.

hibitive and need to be weighed against the benefits. Government agencies may well be able to negotiate favorable terms for some of the necessary services given the volume of business involved. And EPG may lead to ideas for accomplishing sufficient economies in the spending of public resources to generate any additional revenues that might be needed to sustain GOLD.

The digital divide question seems more serious because it runs counter to the aspiration for genuinely democratic vitality on which EPG rests. But, as long as the legitimacy of EPG depends in part on its inclusion of substantial numbers of citizens, it is difficult to see that empowering larger numbers of citizens to contribute through online participation hurts more than it helps. This is true even if not every mechanism for expanding participation reaches every segment of the population with equal success. Moreover, there is no a priori reason to believe that the online participating population will always be less representative than the face-to-face participating population. Low-income single parents, people of limited physical mobility, citizens uncomfortable with speaking in public—these are just a few of the population subgroups likely to be underrepresented in face-to-face deliberations. More than half of all U.S. households now have Internet connections (U.S. Department of Commerce 2004: 4). There is virtually no access-based 'digital divide' by gender (U.S. Department of Commerce 2004: A-1). Even underrepresented populations on the Internet—for example, Latinos and African-Americans, non-college educated Americans, and low-income Americans—nonetheless participate at significant rates (U.S. Department of Commerce 2004). Computers and free Internet service are both common features of increasingly large numbers of libraries, senior centers, and community centers of all sorts.

The more profound long-term 'digital divide' issue may pertain not to physical access but to an unequal distribution of the skills necessary to motivate civic engagement through the Internet. Research is showing that a potential participant's lack of confidence in using the Internet in a way that will yield a rewarding experience may be a more significant barrier to Internet use than is the lack of home computer access (Muhlberger 2004). This only underscores the importance of combining GOLD efforts with the proliferation of computer literacy training for all adults.

The third likely objection to GOLD, that formats for online discussion will privilege certain categories of citizens over others, based on their preferred modes of communication, hugely underestimates the potential of new technologies. This might be a more serious concern if we were stuck with text-only, English-language Internet communications. New tools, however, already support text, audio, and video inputs. Language translation software can enable multilingual exchange to a degree never before possible. Protocols for online meetings, such as software-enforced time limits to individual comments, can prevent domination of real-time discussions.

Finally, the objection that online deliberation is less likely than face-to-face discussion to induce feelings of mutual respect and solidarity is far from proven. Even more to the point, this concern is all but irrelevant to institutions where face-to-face and online encounters supplement and reinforce each other. Not only do face-to-face interactions strengthen the community-building potential of online interaction, but the possibility of continuing discussions online means that the momentum and sense of common purpose generated by face-to-face meetings can be supported even in the necessary hiatus between such occasions.

ICTs can also be used to create and sustain favorable circumstances for the maintenance of EPG, as well as bolstering its structural features. Deploying ICTs for community organizing will foster the countervailing power that provides EPGs sustaining context. The Internet can support the 'formal linkages of responsibility, resource distribution and communication' (Fung and Wright 2003b: 16) that Fung and Wright take to be essential to EPG design. Providing online documentation of local government decision making and enabling citizens to contribute their knowledge through both deliberative and data-gathering applications will insure enhanced levels of transparency and accountability. For all of these reasons, development of ICTs aimed at strengthening EPGs effectiveness ought to enjoy high priority on the agenda of EPG researchers and activists.

5   Conclusion

EPG represents a model of democratic governance that links significant objectives, namely, effective problem solving, increased equity, and broad participation, to particular features of real-world institutional design. Its proponents offer reasonable hypotheses as to the potential superiority of EPG in terms of problem solving and implementation. They make the case that a commitment to real-world problem solving, together with the institutionalization of modes of decision making that include more direct participation by the poor and disadvantaged, and in which decision procedures are governed by reason (not power), should tend towards more equitable outcomes (Fung and Wright 2003b).

These will not be easy outcomes to achieve, but the EPG vision is clear and compelling enough to inspire considerable interest among cyberdemocracy researchers and activists. From a cyberdemocratic perspective, there readily appears an extraordinary fit between the capacities of new ICTs and the needs of EPG, in terms of both accomplishing a supportive context and actually implementing the recommended institutional designs. It is not certain whether electronic rulemaking will prove a significant way station towards EPG. What does seems clear, given the promise of the EPG experimental agenda and the need to enlarge opportunities for meaningful citizen participation in decisions that affect their lives, is that the future of GOLD at least deserves to be bright.

Acknowledgements

Portions of this chapter are drawn from Peter M. Shane, *Turning GOLD into EPG: Lessons from Low-Tech Democratic Experimentalism for Electronic Rulemaking and Other Ventures in Cyberdemocracy*, 1 ISJLP 147 (2004-05), and are reprinted by permission.

References

Abers, R. N. 2003. Reflections on What Makes Empowered Participatory Governance Happen. *Deepening Democracy: Institutional Innovations in Empowered Participatory Governance*, eds. A. Fung and E. O. Wright, 200-207. New York: Routledge.

Cohen, J. and J. Rogers. 2003. Power and Reason. *Deepening Democracy: Institutional Innovations in Empowered Participatory Governance*, eds. A. Fung and E. O. Wright, 237-255. New York: Routledge.

Froomkin, A. M. 2004. Technologies for Democracy. *Democracy Online: The Prospects for Political Renewal Through the Internet*, eds. P. M. Shane, 3-20. New York: Routledge.

Fung, A. and E. O. Wright. 2003a. Countervailing Power in Empowered Participatory Governance. *Deepening Democracy: Institutional Innovations in Empowered Participatory Governance*, eds. A. Fung and E. O. Wright, 259-289. New York: Routledge.

Fung, A. and E. O. Wright. 2003b. Thinking About Empowered Participatory Governance. *Deepening Democracy: Institutional Innovations in Empowered Participatory Governance*, eds. A. Fung and E. O. Wright, 3-42. New York: Routledge.

Krantz, R. S. 2003. Cycles of Reform in Madison and Porto Alegre. *Deepening Democracy: Institutional Innovations in Empowered Participatory Governance*, eds. A. Fung and E. O. Wright, 225-236. New York: Routledge.

Muhlberger, P. 2004. Access, Skill and Motivation in Online Political Discussion: Testing Cyberrealism. *Democracy Online: The Prospects for Political Renewal Through the Internet*, ed. P. M. Shane, 225-237. New York: Routledge.

Noveck, B. S. 2005. The Future of Citizen Participation in the Electronic State. *I/S: A Journal of Law and Policy for the Information Society* 1: 1-32.

Organisation for Economic Co-operation and Development (OECD). 2003. *Policy Brief: Engaging Citizens Online for Better Policy-making*. Paris: author.

Office of Management and Budget. 2004. *Informing Regulatory Decisions: 2004 Draft Report to Congress on the Costs and Benefits of Federal Regulations and Unfunded Mandates on State, Local, and Tribal Entities.* Washington, DC: author.

Thomas, C. W. 2003. Habitat Conservation Planning. *Deepening Democracy: Institutional Innovations in Empowered Participatory Governance*, eds. A. Fung and E. O. Wright, 144-172. New York: Routledge.

United States Department of Commerce. 2004. *A Nation Online: Entering the Broadband Age.* Washington, D.C.: author.

VandeHei, J. and T. B. Edsall. 2004. Democrats Outraising the GOP This Year But Republicans Still Have Financial Lead. *Washington Post* July 21, 2004: A1.

11

Baudrillard and the Virtual Cow: Simulation Games and Citizen Participation

HÉLÈNE MICHEL AND DOMINIQUE KREZIAK

1 The Development of Citizen Relationship Management

We have defined three modes of local citizenship management using ICTs (Michel 2005). In 'e-administration', the citizen is considered a 'consumer of rights' claiming personalized and efficient public services. 'E-government' reflects a vision of a relatively passive citizen-agent who responds to his duties. In 'e-governance', the citizen is considered an active agent of local democracy. (See Table 1 below.)

When trying to promote this kind of participation in public debate ('e-governance'), public organizations face persuasion challenges. Participation requires both motivation and perceived capacity. Simulators may thus prove to be efficient communication channels by providing both, leading in turn to a higher elaboration likelihood of the message content (Petty and Cacioppo 1984).

Online Deliberation: Design, Research, and Practice.
Todd Davies and Seeta Peña Gangadharan (eds.).
Copyright © 2009, CSLI Publications.

	E-administration	E-government	E-governance
French Republican principle	Government for the people	Government of the people	Government by the people
Citizenship's component	Rights	Duties	Participation
Role given to the citizen	Consumer	'Passive' agent	Actor 'Active' agent
Underlying logic	Delivering services, improving satisfaction of citizens	Improving the chance of a policy's success	Encouraging deliberation, participation
Role of local elected	Improving administration performance	Understanding the opinion of the citizens using consultation	Protecting free expression,
Corresponding ICTs tools	Online administrative services	Electronic consultation	Collaborative tools Simulation games?

Table 1. Three types Citizen Relationship Management using ICTs

2 Entering the Vacheland World

Every day, more than 490,000 people visit Vacheland ('cow country') to take care of their virtual cow.[1] Vacheland, originally developed by the Poitou-Charentes regional council in France, is a unique simulation game focusing on agricultural issues and designed as a communication tool for citizens. Agriculture is a key asset to economic development for this region. Has playing Vacheland changed anything about players' attitudes towards farming? To address this question, an exploratory study was conducted through forum analysis, exploratory interviews, and 'netnography' (Kozinets 2002).

---

[1] See http://www.vacheland.com (last accessed September 16, 2008).

Participating in Vacheland could be considered an example of a significant modern ritual, a quest for authenticity (Cohen 1979; Pretes 1995; Corrigan 1997). Participants might then experience the game less as a way of learning about 'real' agricultural conditions and more as what Rheingold (1993) calls 'hyperreality'. For Rheingold, 'hyperrealists' see the use of ICT as a route to the total replacement of the natural world and the social order with a technologically mediated world. The experience of hyperreality is a quest for the lost reality of a more authentic life (Corrigan 1997). For hyperrealists, reality and authenticity are located elsewhere, in another, healthier historical period, culture, or lifestyle (MacCannell 1976).

3   Results and Questions

Vacheland players seem to seek two different types of recreated authenticity, consistent with Baudrillard's (1981) framework on simulation and simulacra. For some people Vacheland is related to something that once existed, or still exists, or is perceived as having existed once, such as one's past or childhood, with a strong nostalgic dimension. It can therefore be interpreted as simulation, a symbolic representation of reality. For other players, the references underlying Vacheland are already fictional. Vacheland can then be interpreted as a form of simulacrum: 'I come from the city. I know very little about the countryside and agriculture. It is mostly from movies (e.g., *Babe*), television shows, or books (e.g., *Animal Farm*)'.

Vacheland is seen as a potentially powerful tool to raise people's awareness about agriculture, but it has not significantly changed players' attitudes. Virtual farming does not interfere with their real consumption. The connection between virtual breeding and consumer behavior is strongly symbolic; it applies mostly to gadgets related to the animals. Thus, for the question 'Can we use simulation games as a tool to help build political opinion and change citizens' behavior?' the results seem ambivalent. On the one hand, simulated phenomena could be a way to re-enchant political life (Ritzer 1999). On the other hand, this could lead to a 'disneylandisation' of political life, in keeping with the 'society of spectacle' described by Debord (1967).

References

Baudrillard, J. 1981. *Simulacres et Simulation*. Paris: Galilée.

Cohen, E. 1979. A Phenomenology of Tourist Experiences. *Sociology* 13(2): 179-201.

Corrigan, P. 1997. *The Sociology of Consumption*. Thousand Oaks, CA: Sage Publications.

Debord, G. 1967. *La Société du Spectacle*. Paris: Buchet-Castel.

Kozinets, R. 2002. The Field Behind the Screen: Using Netnography for Marketing Research in Online Communities. *Journal of Marketing Research* 39(February): 61-72.

MacCannell, D. 1976. *The Tourist: A New Theory of the Leisure Class*. Berkeley: University of California Press.

Michel H. 2005. *On the Way to the Learning City? A Typology of Citizen Relationship Management*. Paper presented at the ECEG Conference, Antwerp, June 16-17, 2005.

Petty, R. E. and J. T. Cacioppo. 1984. The Effects of Involvement on Responses to Argument Quantity and Quality: Central and Peripheral Routes to Persuasion. *Journal of Personality and Social Psychology* 46: 69-81.

Pretes, M. 1995. Postmodern Tourism—The Santa Claus Industry. *Annals of Tourism Research* 22(1): 1-15.

Rheingold, H. 1993. *The Virtual Community: Homesteading on the Electronic Frontier*. Reading, MA: Addison-Wesley.

Ritzer G. 1999. *Enchanting a Disenchanted World: Revolutionizing the Means of Consumption*. Thousand Oaks, CA: Pine Forge Press.

12

Using Web-Based Group Support Systems to Enhance Procedural Fairness in Administrative Decision Making in South Africa

HOSSANA TWINOMURINZI AND JACKIE PHAHLAMOHLAKA

1 Introduction

The Republic of South Africa's Promotion of the Administrative Justice Act, No. 3 (2000), or the 'PAJA', mandates that government decision making be justified to those negatively affected by administrative decisions. The PAJA has been put forward as a demonstration to democratic ideals, social fairness, and fundamental human rights.

We are investigating whether Web-based Group Support System (GSS) tools can support and enhance procedural fairness in administrative decision making in South Africa. We report here on work that emanates from a masters dissertation by the first author. The work formed part of a larger project led by the second author that investigates the use of Web-based collaboration processes and tools to enable citizens to interact effectively with government and public bodies in South Africa.

Online Deliberation: Design, Research, and Practice.
Todd Davies and Seeta Peña Gangadharan (eds.).
Copyright © 2009, CSLI Publications.

2 The Promotion of the Administrative Justice Act 3 of 2000

The PAJA, whose Code of Good Administrative Conduct is similar to the European Code of Good Administrative Behaviour, has its origin in section 33 of the 1996 Constitution of South Africa (South Africa 1996). The PAJA both empowers and constrains the power of administration, aiming for a delicate balance between paralyzing effective administration and encouraging lawful, reasonable, and procedurally fair decision making. The goal of procedural fairness is to reach decisions which are impartial or free from any real or apparent bias.

Currently, there are no online tools for an individual to communicate with the government when affected adversely by administrative decision making. Procedural fairness is accomplished through a letter sent by post to the affected person. On the other hand, the government encourages and extensively uses Web-based applications as a medium of communication within itself and with the public (Department of Public Service and Administration 1997).

3 Group Support Systems and their Potential in Facilitating the Implementation of PAJA

In this study, we define a GSS as a combination of approaches, software, and technology constructed to bring together and reinforce the dialogue, deliberations, and decision making of groups (Shen et al. 2004; see also Denis et al. 2001). We considered two case participants, one with a disability grant and the other with a child welfare grant. Because of the unavailability and possible costs of formal Web-based GSS tools, we used Web-based email.[1] Thus, we were able to facilitate interaction between the participants and the administrator to deal with the application process.

Key findings included:
- Web-based GSS resulted in lower costs and lower time in the appeal process;
- Case participants had an increased awareness of PAJA;
- There was faster feedback on the application progress;
- There is a lack of technology infrastructure, and where it exists there are no skills to fully utilize it;

---

[1] The key available infrastructure that could be used to facilitate online deliberations in South Africa is the Multi Purpose Community Centre framework (MPCC) and the Batho Pele Gateway Portal. Our continuing work recognizes this.

- Case participants need training for using the technology;
- There is a fear of challenging those in authority;
- Case participants generally appreciated being included in the study as they could see the benefits thereof;
- The rejection letter was misinterpreted due to illiteracy;
- The information in the rejection letters as required by the PAJA was incomplete.

4   Limitations

The research described here was limited in its scope to two case participants. A larger sample size in terms of demography and gender would have generated a better representation of the potential of Web-based GSS to enhance procedural fairness in administrative action. Additionally, we did not use a formal GSS tool such as GroupSystems© for reasons given in the previous section. The use of a wider demographic sample and a formal Web-based GSS tool are currently being pursued.

References

Dennis, A. R., B. H. Wixom, and R. J. Vandenberg. 2001. Understanding Fit and Appropriation Effects in Group Support Systems via Meta-Analysis. *MIS Quarterly* 5(2): 167-193.

Department of Public Service and Administration. 1997. Batho Pele—'People First': White Paper On Transforming Public Service Delivery. *Government Gazette*. Pretoria: Author. Available at http://www.info.gov.za/whitepapers/1997/18340.pdf (last accessed August 2, 2008)

Promotion of the Administrative Justice Act—No. 3. 2000. *Government Gazette*. Pretoria: Author. Available at http://www.info.gov.za/gazette/acts/2000/a3-00.pdf (last accessed August 2, 2008)

Shen, Q., J. K. H. Chung, H. Li, and L. Shen. 2004. A Group Support System for Improving Value Management Studies in Construction. *Automation in Construction* 13(2): 209–224.

South Africa. 1996. *The Constitution of the Republic of South Africa*. 1996. Available at http://www.info.gov.za/documents/constitution/index.htm (last accessed August 1, 2008)

13

Citizen Participation Is Critical: An Example from Sweden

Tomas Ohlin

1 Introduction

Lack of citizen interest in democratic participation is one of the most severe problems for democracy in the twenty-first century. Can modern technology help? Surely there are a number of models and theories about new forms of citizen participation, but much of this has not been tried empirically yet. It is difficult to get political support for experiments that try to move some influence towards the citizen.

However, looking at the concept of citizen participation, we find several possibilities. Participatory democracy can include acquisition of knowledge, discussion about the decision process, citizen initiatives, participation in agenda setting, deliberative dialogue concerning alternatives, concern for minorities, participation in preparatory decisions, actual decision making, built on representativeness, and citizen participation in analysis of the effects of a decision.

Participation need not be restricted to heavy and long-term decisions. On the contrary, it may be quite local and limited in scope. Mere presence in decision making, although small in scope, often generates citizen satisfaction. This in turn tends to avoid later problems of dissatisfaction with the results. It therefore seems advisable for politicians to try this kind of sharing of power. Citizen influence can be increased on both sides of a decision. Many of the planning sessions that take place before decision making

Online Deliberation: Design, Research, and Practice.
Todd Davies and Seeta Peña Gangadharan (eds.).
Copyright © 2009, CSLI Publications.

contain space for participatory citizen presence. Information communication technology (ICT) can support such citizen presence in several ways, including distribution of background knowledge, simplified access to initiatives and discussions, simplified participation in agenda setting, easier formulation of alternatives, online support for deliberative sessions, participation in preparatory decision making, and participation in analysis of the effects and feedback related to the decision.

It is amazing that so few of these possibilities are being tried in European countries at present. Planners seem to be frightened to approach the topic. Politicians are not unaware of reform possibilities. At a meeting with the Council of Europe in 2004 in Barcelona, a number of possibilities were presented. Among these were: support for citizen initiatives, encouragement of citizen participation, warnings around citizen passiveness, organizing and financing of citizen panels, definition of local space for citizen decision making, intelligent registering of political participation, smart voting (voting on issues with pre-prepared alternatives), and many more. Organized citizen movements may be needed in order to get the ball rolling.

2   Cybervote and the Kista Project

The Cybervote project (http://www.eucybervote.org) was a research project (partly funded by the European Commission) that included representatives from seven European countries. It was carried out from 2001 to 2003. Participants represented users, researchers, and providers of technology. The focus was originally placed on the development of secure Internet voting software, and this focus remained central for most of the participating countries during the duration of the main project. However, in the Swedish version, this was complemented by an interest in participation, discussion, and agenda setting. Such a social approach differed from the other nations, which mostly concentrated on technology.

There were three 'user' projects in the main project, one of which was carried out in Kista, a northern suburb of Stockholm. It concentrated on citizen involvement in city planning. A unique aspect of the Kista project was that it only engaged elderly citizens, in an attempt to deal with the 'digital divide' between the oldest and younger generations.

With the help of local organizations of the elderly, invitations were distributed that said: 'Do you want to join in the shaping of history?' The invitation mentioned the use of new technologies, and prospective participants were told that they would be instructed in how to use the equipment. This was a general appeal to senior citizens to get them involved in helping develop part of a new city plan for where they lived.

A sizable group turned up for the first meeting, where the discussion centered on a variety of possible project topics to be addressed later. Through this process a list of about a dozen topics emerged. The next step was to get a smaller sample of the participants to use new communication and voting technology to go through the list and establish their own priorities. This included deliberation, plus testing new and more secure software.

The priority topics that were agreed on through this process were: (1) local planning (parks or commercial), (2) public transportation (trams, buses, or trains), and (3) art and culture (a cultural center or not). These were then disseminated through printed materials and via the Internet. Two young researchers carried out a specific study of this part of the project. It showed that these elderly citizens did encounter certain practical problems in using what for them were new PCs, particularly in the voting software, but that they appreciated the possibility to take part in agenda setting.

The main Kista trial project then took place in January 2003. Everyone who had preregistered was invited to come to discuss and vote. Two hundred thirty-six elderly participants showed up. Each person who came was given a password that they could use once at the final vote via the Internet. Their choices concerned the three topics listed above, from the earlier agenda setting process. There were discussion facilities available. The electronically supported voting was done without major problems. The results showed majorities for a green environment, a new train line, and a cultural center. In fact, the participants were very pleased with their project experience, and several indicated that they would like to do it again in the future.

Part IV

Online Deliberation in Organizations

14

Online Deliberation in the Government of Canada: Organizing the Back Office

ELISABETH RICHARD

1 Introduction

A number of increasingly complex metaphors have inspired governments over the last decade of Internet presence. Starting with the static single-window, followed by the front door, a more welcoming metaphor, the emerging metaphor at the end of the first decade of the millennium, may well become the sand-box. With new Web applications known as Web 2.0, information can be gathered and remixed in new ways by users themselves. The public space is open for citizens and stakeholders who want 'in'. Online deliberation and groupware such as: discussion forums, chats, webinars, surveys, and collaboration and social networking tools are being deployed in the Government of Canada. There is more to online deliberation, however, than online applications: citizens cannot expect to become partners in the governance process without new public management frameworks. New consultation, communication, correspondence, and program management models are needed to ensure that public administrations are adapted to the network age.

As the role of government in western economies shifts from direct service provision to increased regulation in a wider variety of social-economic domains, a more direct and open engagement of external opinions and resources from citizens and experts is needed in specific phases of decision-making. In parallel, outside of government, a practice of online deliberation

Online Deliberation: Design, Research, and Practice.
Todd Davies and Seeta Peña Gangadharan (eds.).
Copyright © 2009, CSLI Publications.

is growing. Nongovernmental organizations, some directly connected to political parties or with clearly aligned ideologies, others striving to be neutral, are all contributing to deliberation in the public sphere. Some argue that just like the mass media is becoming fragmented, public discussion is affected by the fact that the Web is splintered. But new Web 2.0 tools provide integration mechanisms that help harness the collective intelligence of civil society.

Citizens expect government to enter the sphere. The Internet provides them with a direct channel to government, an option preferred over relying solely on intermediaries. Citizens need to know that their efforts will influence an outcome. Evidence shows that involvement of public servants is essential to the success of a consultation both internally—among project planning teams—and publicly—when engaging Canadians directly. Citizens wish to see government representatives acknowledge their comments, pose questions, and aid in the orientation of the discussion, either directly, or by forwarding their comments to the moderator.

Building on the history of public deliberation and citizen participation in Canada, this paper describes how the government of Canada organizes the back office to sustain an efficient culture of deliberation. It also draws from the experience of public servants in other Western democracies. The focus is on the work units, where content is generated, and relationships are nurtured so that sound policies are developed. The system dynamics enabled by the Internet allows public servants to take full advantage of connections with citizens and stakeholders. Without the proper processes in government, the many hopes generated by the Internet to renew democratic processes are at stake.

2 Systems Dynamics Enhance a Tradition of Consultation and Participation

With the Internet linking millions of personal computers, modern culture has taken a new focus on connections rather than computations. The Internet enhances multiple overlapping networks and allegiances. The multiplication of groups—ad hoc or issue-specific—is felt in government policy and service delivery. The Canadian federal government taps into the knowledge and resources of the market and civil society. Policy webs are created and lead to the design of more relevant programs and services. Networks of individuals, small groups, and teams at all levels of the organization, as well as interorganizational networks have been added to the bureaucratic mix. This evolution was felt at the dawn of the Internet Age, when White and Green Papers—the classic tools for input gathering on policy development—became more frequent. The Mulroney Government's Green Plan or Finance Minister Paul Martin's public consultations on Budget measures are two examples. The Department of Finance, for one, published reports on the Internet for outreach purposes at the very onset of the Web in 1994. During the following ten years, departments conducted a number of online consultations, gathering significant expertise. In 2002, for example, over 28,000 Canadians participated in the twenty-minute online workbook and worked through scenarios for the future of health care (Canadian Policy Research Networks 2005). In 2004, the revision of the Treasury Board Government Communication Policy led to a permanent Consulting with Canadians portal, along with a suite of procedures for consultation and citizen engagement online and off-line.

Simultaneously, there has been a growing trend of decentralization of power from the federal government to the provinces. The federal government has had increased difficulty creating new national programs. Many analysts feel that a tangible democratic deficit has been created at the federal level. Citizens are looking for new ways to define democracy. The policy making process allows many opportunities. The problem identification phase at the beginning of the policy process, for example, gives nongovernmental organizations and interested citizens a unique opportunity to mobilize interest in the implementation phase. Community capacity building and education is considerable.

Networks affect government-to-citizen and citizen-to-government relationships at all levels of the bureaucracy. Responding to this increase, policy analysts and program managers, with the help of increasing ranks of information management professionals, are using networks to increase their expertise and the efficiency of their program delivery. Web 2.0 confirms the more active user role for citizens and has an impact of back-office domains of government such as regulation, cross-agency collaboration, and program management.

3 The People

Skill sets are evolving in the public service. A new mix of conceptual and emotional intelligence is required in the work units of the information age. Public servants must be able to translate concepts from one discipline to the next, working horizontally, in multidisciplinary teams. They trade data and terminologies so that they can be translated into meaningful intelligence across organizations. They must also have the ability to establish and maintain effective relationships. They lead groups and serve as facilitators and negotiators.

Six main profiles participate in the culture of online deliberation at the working level in the Government of Canada's back office. Network Conveners, Educators, Moderators, and increasingly Subject Matter Experts are in direct contact with the stakeholders at one point or the other. Issue Managers and Content Managers work more in the background.

The Network Convener

In the network of networks, the systems view is prevailing. Public servants are drawn beyond their roles of gatekeeper or benefactor. What matters is not only their organization but also the concerns of the whole network. The term Network Convener (Svensen and Laberge 2005) best describes this reality. The Data Liberation Initiative is an exemplary group of Statistics Canada users advising the department on the use of statistical data. A listserv is used to seek feedback from users, answer questions, and foster discussions. It has allowed statisticians to improve major products and programs like the Census. The Persons with Disabilities Online cluster, which engages in ongoing discussions with users and continuously garners their feedback, is another example.

The Network Convener develops a sensitivity and nurtures a group zeitgeist. This is particularly important in virtual networks. Network Conveners are responsible for that deep sense of connection that transcends the commitment of physical communities. It comes with holding the space, the belief that the space where people share their values will generate high outcomes. Persistence is key, but with holding the space also comes the ability to let go: when natural leaders emerge, the Network Convener sometimes works him/herself out of the job of leader.

The job also has a very down-to-earth side. Network Conveners are the stewards of transparent, accountable decision-making. Community building involves creating rules of engagement and conducting traditional administrative tasks of collecting data and planning events. Network Conveners stay close to their networks: they know 'who's who' and what is on everyone's mind. This detailed work helps them with one of their most delicate functions: to define who is in the network. Health Canada's Office of Public Involvement and Consumer Affairs has a number of public servants who perform this role. Broader information sources are now available through content syndication and social networking. Ongoing relationships and communications can be fostered on the basis of shared competencies and expertise. Niche competencies are much easier to identify and nurture. Active listening is one of the Network Convener's most complex skills. By acknowledging and naming issues, they set the ground for deliberation that feels authentic. Efficient naming brings on creative deliberation so that naming can take precedence over blaming.

Often, consultations and deliberations are run within a short timeframe. There is little time for initial guesswork and history. The Network Convener must rely on the solid background processes provided by the Issue Manager.

The Issue Manager

Issue Managers often work in the background, tracking such things as stakeholders' websites and newsletters. Although they might not be in direct conversation with stakeholders, they often know stakeholders most intimately. Some are like historians: they have a passion for the struggles and challenges of stakeholders, and they track the long-term record of a topic. They track their areas of interest, the lists of meetings they attended, and record their comments. Blogs and other self-publishing tools enhance their work. They provide Issue Managers with their favourite material: clearly delineated points of view and verbatim quotes. These are particularly useful to senior executives and elected officials to understand stakeholders' positions and motivations.

In departments focused on social affairs like Social Development Canada, Issue Managers are a dedicated community resource comprised of skilled and invaluable researchers and analysts. Issue Managers can provide guidance to the policy branch on the specific needs of one community. They also help frame the issues, advising on what specific information a community needs to understand. Finally they can help implement the consultation results: in some consultations, findings can be very rich and detailed, particularly when questions are very specific, and many stakeholders are involved.

Issue Managers are increasingly found in new horizontal networks emerging within the bureaucracy. These internal networks support the scope and complexity of interdepartmental coordination. In Australia, in the Queensland Department of Employment and Training, a network of official contacts has been recruited across government to provide responses to questions that young people have emailed to the site. This role has expanded to include providing reports on outcomes achieved as a result of issues raised by young people; information within departments about the opportunities to incorporate online consultation processes; and advice on proposed site developments (Oakes 2004).

Wikis like the CIA's Intellepedia allow analysts from different agencies to produce joint reports and augment the quality of the issue management. These horizontal networks enhance the need for standardized information management practices, such as tracking information and comparing and reporting on outcome calls for enterprise processes. Content management becomes a cornerstone of an efficient deliberation practice.

The Content Manager

The proper naming of issues all stems from a shared body of knowledge and sound information management practices. Information is a public good, and citizens should have ownership of it. Sorting through and learning how to manage the flow of government information is a challenge for public servants as much as it is for the general public. Information management professionals are growing through the ranks of the public service to tap into the information resources and tailor them to a specific group. Content Managers, information brokers, and content aggregators are children of the network age and did not exist ten years ago in government. They are most commonly located in departments that do active market research or close to policy centers in scientific departments. They are slowly spreading through the various policy and service delivery work units. In the international policy website of the Department of Foreign Affairs, Content Managers participate in the content governance.

With Web 2.0 applications, Content Managers become gardeners. Tools that promote folksonomies—user-generated taxonomies for categorizing Web content—add a very popular layer on structured information architecture. The content grows by consensus. In the Government of Ontario, tag clouds are carefully gardened to care for inconsistencies created by multiple users (i.e., search terms). Content Managers develop a deep understanding of their knowledge base in order to identify the best content. The Canadian Government's Business and Consumer website, Strategis, is an example of how information can be packaged for public education of specific audiences.

The role of Content Managers will grow as syndication allows end-users to reach content via any particular path. Each piece of content stands on its own and may require careful attention. Content Managers act as the natural librarians in the organization, mapping pockets of knowledge. They are also the bridge between expert terminologies, able to translate the jargon of one set of experts so that a different set of experts can use the information in their endeavours. They help set the stage for the new stars of deliberation and government information: the Subject Matter Experts.

The Subject Matter Expert

The legitimacy of Subject Matter Experts (SMEs) is increasingly questioned in the networked world because of the amount of information that is shaped to serve particular interests. The multiplication of sources of information is creating confusion. In Canada and abroad, citizens want neutral sources, and they turn to government experts to provide them. They identify government resources as the most credible (EKOS 2003). The Canadian Health Network is an example of a trusted knowledge base to which many Canadians turn. The department of Natural Resources Canada has created a massive architecture to support access to three layers of information: raw data; instructions to access a first level of general information; and highly specialized knowledge.

Networked technologies and processes help to showcase the knowledge of SMEs: webcasting, webinars, video streaming, metadata to access data summaries, and fact sheets. An increasing number of policy experts and scientists are brought into to the deliberation space for information or opinions. At Health Canada, the Office of Consumer and Public Involvement, recruits SME coworkers across the country to participate briefly on specific subjects and answer technical questions only. At Industry Canada and Canadian Heritage, SMEs have strong experience and master the legal consequences of specific topics such as legal copyright.

SMEs, however, are often difficult to locate. Names circulate in policy shops and word of mouth prevails until the right expert is found. They must be involved without having enough time to distill their material and sift through the specialized jargon. Web 2.0 applications allow self-appointed experts to chip in and contribute, with collaborative filtering acting as the vigilance mechanism. Social discovery tools such as Twitter and Friendfeed pull in the niche experts who often prefer recognition and visibility from their peers to monetary compensation.

For public servants conscious of their neutrality, this is not always a comfortable setting. This feeling is not limited to countries that follow the Whitehall model. In Finland, although public servants are expected to be active in the dialogue as SMEs, there is uncertainty about how freely they may answer or comment and to what degree their statements should be approved by their superiors (Latvanen 2004). In the online world in general, it is much easier to forget one's identity as SME, because the context is more informal than face-to-face. One's personal opinions are more likely to surface. In addition to feeling uncertain or uncomfortable with how involved they should be, public servants are also concerned about the amount of time they can spend on the exercise. New intermediaries are needed.

The Educator

The Educator has been brought to the front lines as an intermediary to deliver the expertise to the public and serve as gatekeepers to scientific experts. With masses of information available through networked government, education is an important facet of the public sector value model (Accenture 2005). Continuous learning is a corollary result from the network environment. It is embedded in Canada's Service Delivery for Canadians Framework, as well as the new Communication Policy.

Outreach and education plays an important role in the engagement continuum, often at the onset or in the implementation phase of a policy. The online environment can be a rich medium for learning and outreach because it allows participants to experience issues at their pace, with a variety of learning mechanisms. Health Canada (2005) recently concluded an e-consultation on 'Measures to help ensure Canadians' continued access to an adequate supply of safe and affordable drugs' that employed two online workbooks and more than twenty questions to help Canadians provide specific answers.

Alberta's Department of Agriculture has brought educators into call centers and uses them as an efficient alternative to outreach and in-person public education programs, which helps reduce the number of people in the field (Richard 2003). The French term *vulgarisateur*, meaning 'populariser', describes this growing function.

The function of Educator can be brought to the front line for outreach purposes in the early stages of policy development. When the deliberation phase starts, however, the dynamic changes. Citizens have learned enough and now want to be heard. They need to speak directly to the senior policy executive who acts as a spokesperson, a role similar to the Educator. In many stakeholder consultations, the senior policy executive must be prepared to take on this role. The more the decision-makers are able to speak clearly and explain the policy, the better that message gets through. A recent history of budget cuts in the policy centers has challenged this capacity in the Government of Canada. Often the senior executives end up at a public meeting without enough briefing on the subject matter and cannot properly fulfill the Educator's role. If, at the same time, the Subject Matter Experts are too specialized, an opportunity for real dialogue is missed.

With Web 2.0 structure, discussions can be integrated alongside content and can happen right at the place in the site where people need them. This facilitates outreach. Multi-directional flows create a rich form of public involvement but they require a lot of maintenance. As the information flows move to the highest levels of public involvement, another intermediary is required: the Moderator.

The Moderator

Networks allow new and interesting forms of computer-assisted moderation. Popular sites Slashdot, Plastic, and Kuro5hin have all developed karma points systems in which contributions are peer-ranked, giving users an opportunity to build up a reputation as a knowledgeable, trustworthy source of information and also allowing users to quickly identify and filter out poorly-ranked comments and contributions.

Multi-stakeholder communications, however, whether online or face-to-face, require a live human intermediary to orchestrate the voices. There is considerable debate about the role of moderators. Some argue moderators skew results by forcing common ground and influencing opinions. A great deal of trust is placed in the judgment of the moderator. Not all government moderators have had success. There is persistent fear that governments will restrict freedom of discussion. Moderators of the Downing Street website (http://www.number-10.gov.uk) were criticized for their interpretation of the rules of engagement (Wright 2005). But experience shows the moderator has a positive role in promoting the levels of discussion and bringing in users from outside (Trénel 2005).

In general, the stronger the authentification process is at the onset, the weaker the moderation needs to be, but in collaboration projects that have a strong expert community, moderation, and quality assurance is left to participants. The vigilance of the crowd for example, protects Wikipedia or projects like Peer to Patent. Debates continue over whether the discussion should happen on neutral ground with an independent facilitator or whether a public servant can moderate. Participants are caught between the need to trust judgment and the need to ensure that the discussion is well connected within the machinery of government.

Using clear rules and objectives developed by the public service, some departments have had positive experiences with external moderators, who were considered more neutral. Public servants themselves often prefer to limit their role in a deliberation to sponsors or content providers only. An example of this was a recent online consultation on sustainable development in Scotland, where public servants developed and signed off all the background information but did not make any further contribution once the consultation started.[1] In Scotland Yard, the Metropolitan Police, the police authority and the police service each hosted consultations on their websites but deliberately chose an outside organization to run their public consultations. This approach was used in the interest of transparency and to avoid being accused of guiding the way.[2] When conversation should be focused on wide citizen-to-citizen interaction, external moderation might be best.

Co-moderation between a public servant and a trusted representative of a nongovernmental organization (NGO) is a formula that has proven very successful. The public servant's knowledge and mandate is bridged with the NGO representative's ability to speak freely, without the risk of being mistaken for the voice of the entire public service. Status of Women Canada, in

---

[1] Interview with Ann Macintosh, Director of the International Teledemocracy Centre, June 8, 2004.

[2] Interview with Jane Wilkin, Consultation Officer with Scotland Yard, July 12, 2004.

the Beijing +5 consultation that led to Canada's contribution to a United Nations document at the U.N. General Assembly Special Session in June 2000, used a co-moderation model. One moderator was from Status of Women Canada. The other was from an NGO.

In the Government of Canada, online discussions on very specific policy issues are sometimes conducted with stakeholder groups of various sizes. A Subject Matter Expert who is dedicated to the exercise often moderates these discussions. He/she is empowered to: create the discussion agenda and framework; help market the consultation through his/her contacts; stimulate discussion; and provide rapid response in vetting comments (Darragh 2003).

There are also a number of moderating functions that happen in the background. In the Department of Indian and Northern Affairs, where online collaboration is used intensively in Treaty Negotiations, project moderators take on an important record management role. This is a new responsibility: skimming through the discussion threads material, cleaning them up (i.e. sorting and organizing the comments), and making sure that it is recorded and searchable. Methodical process modeling from start to finish is essential so that keywords and quick summaries are available. The job also involves editorial judgment.

Finally, the moderation functions are sometimes split. The National Dialogue on Foreign Policy lists a number of roles that were shared by many individuals, including public servants and volunteers. These roles included: animators, who incited discussions when online activity began to slow; moderators, who made the decisions of which posts could or could not be posted on the site; a cybrarian, who gathered information; and analysts who rolled data out of answers to open-ended questions (Jeffrey 2004).

Continuing Role Definition

In Canada and around the world, public servants have been brought into the online public space. The breadth and depth of the online consultation framework, still mostly uncharted territory, shows there are many new roles and processes emerging. The roles of Moderators, Network Conveners, Issue and Content Managers, Subject Matter Experts, and Educators are all key to supporting a culture of online deliberation in government. Roles will become clarified as experience is gathered. A greater understanding of the value-added role that public servants can play helps overcome many of the cultural barriers.

The institutionalization of public involvement also includes new structures. The Office of Consumer and Public Involvement within the Health Products and Food Branch at Health Canada, for example, created a Public Advisory Committee in 2002. A community of practice and Centre of Expertise among interested departments have emerged to reinforce the use of consultation online and off-line in the ongoing processes of government. The new processes and structures are a test ground for the relationship skills of public servants. Codes of conduct are evolving such as the 10 principles for public sector social media.[3]

4 Structures and Processes

Online consultation brings a specific challenge: it is a multi-disciplinary function that links program managers, policy makers, information management professionals, communicators. This is sometimes a difficult mix. The lead responsibility for online consultation can change from one department of the other. Flexible combinations of skills are needed, within the public service or at arm's length.

The Editorial Board

An Editorial Board of senior public service officials and stakeholders can provide a sober, impartial frame. The Editorial Board tackles fundamental questions on content. The concept stands whether for small, focused deliberation or large-scale ones. The idea is to determine the issues and select the sources of information for deliberation. Membership is based on the type of consultation and should be composed at the minimum of the Network Convener, Subject Matter Expert, and Content and Issue Managers, and chaired by the senior executive responsible for the consultation. This model has proven to be successful at the Canadian Cultural Observatory, where the Editorial Board is comprised of members from the Observatory, plus members of the cultural professionals community; these members include heads of think tanks, private consultants, policy experts, and advocacy employees. The Network Convener can provide insight when selecting an Editorial Board.

A similar model is being tested at the Department of Foreign Affairs, where an ad hoc editorial committee composed of senior officials from the policy and the communications functions is the final authority on which policy documents are made available for public discussion on the Canadian Foreign Policy Strategic Policy website.

The Editorial Board exists to ensure the process for the selection of content is fair and not purely government-driven. Because essentially all areas in the editorial process exist in various shades of grey, a wide range of

---

[3] See http://psnetwork.org.nz/blog/2007/02/19/principles-public-sector-socialmedia/ (last accessed November 1, 2008).

knowledge and experience allows the board to come up with fair and representative solutions, creating an unbiased framework for deliberation.

Issue Framing

Under the leadership of the Editorial Board, a range of information products are selected or developed. Deliberation guides developed in teams outline a number of scenarios. This is where Subject Matter Experts, Content and Issue Managers, Network Conveners, and Educators get into the nitty-gritty of the issue at hand.

The naming and framing of an issue is where 'bureaucratese' stops: the issue must be presented according to the way the public identifies the problem. All discussions will be based on the way these issues were framed. The role of the Issue Manager is significant in this stage. It is enhanced by the folksonomy, which contributes key information about how the stakeholders access the information.

One of the challenges with multi-stakeholder online consultation is the lack of common grounds. Time devoted to convening networks, where members in turn explain their knowledge on issues, is a good investment. A common body of knowledge develops from acknowledging issues, while still framing democratically and being sensitive to all stakeholders involved.

Issue framing brings organizational challenges. Horizontal issues that span across many departments are difficult to address quickly. In this context, the relationships between public servants are essential: Issue Managers keep tabs on the language that matters; Network Conveners foster the circulation of this common language; and Content Managers know where the information to substantiate the issues lies.

Content Analysis

There is still considerable fear and mistrust in the policy shop about rolling out coherent reports from the mass of data generated by an online consultation. This issue becomes especially difficult when dealing with large amounts of qualitative data, such as the individual comments and postings from consultation participants. Public servants are concerned about the need to capture text-strings in a storable format and the lack of a database to collect comments and produce reports. Many consultation practitioners do not discover the pitfalls in their planning processes until it comes time to analyze the data they have collected during the online consultation.

Experience shows that information management practices at the planning stage are well received, and citizens do not mind self-sorting the content. Emoticons are popular to categorize feelings. Participants seem to like choosing predetermined post types, categories, headings, and topics.

The review of threads posted in a particular forum is also an extremely resourceful way of finding out what is most useful in verbatim comments. For example, the level of interest surrounding a particular topic or issue can be determined by examining the number of comments posted per thread, the average word count per thread, the thread depth (threads per reply), and thread length (length of time between first and last contribution) (Whyte and MacIntosh 2002). The increasing use of tags provides key metadata about content.

Simple practices between the Subject Matter Expert and junior staff can help the process of summaries considerably. A common problem is knowing what information to include. Summaries may not represent the key elements well unless the policy Subject Matter Expert writes them. The policy Subject Matter Expert might create a first synthesis that can then be used as a guideline by the more junior staff that does the bulk of the analysis. A tight evaluation grid can also be developed; this method proved successful for Mortgages and Housing Ontario's Rent Reform Consultation in 2004 (Hendriks 2005).

Although summaries are useful to produce a report, the full submissions are also very important.

Stakeholder Management

In deliberation, momentum is key. For all the fears of network avalanches and Slashdot effects, many deliberation spaces remain ghost towns. Policy shops still commonly have very limited stakeholder lists with outdated information.

The growing practice of issue management is bringing to light new opportunities. The Office of Consumer Affairs and Public Involvement in Health Canada for example, has started a stakeholder management system to identify common ground among stakeholders and directorates alike. Many stakeholders might be willing to take action on issues related to the primary issue with which their organization is involved. Good stakeholder information allows consultation staff to identify lateral similarities and identify both existing and possible outside coalitions (Online Consultation Centre of Expertise 2004).

5 Strategic Considerations

A number of initiatives have set the ground for a culture of deliberation in the government of Canada. Not all deliberations are on the scale of new, large national policies. Information technology enables deliberation on many scales, including: local, very specific regulatory issues, or services for a targeted stakeholder group. Small-scale deliberation is blossoming in the program corridors. The nature of these deliberations is multidisciplinary: they require public servants to act as bridges, set the tone, and feed the process of networking. The system must empower them to do so. But some roles do affect traditions. The clear line between neutral information and debate is blurred. 'Faceless bureaucrats' are being brought into this grey zone in order to do their job and gather the best evidence and advice for their respective ministers.

Networks allow policy experts and program managers to create an environment of continuous learning so that Canadians are fully engaged in shaping government. Public servants are walking a fine line: the more efficient they are in creating and nurturing online conversations, the closer they become to advocates. Risks that their neutrality will be challenged are increasing. Public servants can get caught in the noise just like anybody else on the Internet.

At the same time, many of these roles strengthen the traditions of the public service. In a context of a splintered web, the value of public service neutrality increases considerably. Public servants are the keepers of a solid body of information increasingly recognized as a key public resource. Authoritative information, an information sovereignty of sorts, is a key mechanism of government in the network age. But too many information professionals remain the underestimated intelligence agents in offices managed by an older, less technologically literate, population. Issue Managers and Content Managers must be empowered so that data on the Web is truly used as a public resource. Emerging issues identified by Issue Managers are key to a culture of deliberation. The high content value located by Content Managers can be integrated and reused across various applications. This is a first step towards a semantic Web where data can be shared and processed by automated tools as well as by people. Until the third-generation Web is in full bloom and content is gracefully aggregated on-the-fly, Content Managers will be needed to bring the right content for deliberation. Currently, however, they have not yet been able to mature into their full potential.

Many of these roles are not related to large-scale deliberations. Regulatory details of policies and the designs of new programs are not all major blocks of democratic renewal. They often affect only a small group of stakeholders. But online deliberation allows geographically dispersed people to be involved in the specific issue that matters to them, in their world. Tocqueville declares, 'One measures the health of society by the quality of functions performed by local citizens' (quoted in Wyman, Shulman, and Ham 1999). There must be, at the other end of the line, public servants who are ready to listen, interpret, and record this involvement. With Web 2.0 allowing users—citizens and public servants—to take a more active role, the simplicity, transparency, cohesiveness of government increases.

References

Accenture. 2005. Leadership in Customer Service: New Expectations, New Experiences. Available at http://www.accenture.com/xdoc/ca/locations/canada/insights/studies/leadership_cust.pdf (last accessed October 7, 2008)

Canadian Policy Research Networks. 2005. Trends in Public Consultation in Canada. Available at http://www.cprn.com (last accessed October 7, 2008)

Darragh, I. 2003. *A Step-by-Step Guide to Successful Web Consultations.* Paper presented at Web and New Media at Public Works and Government Services Canada.

EKOS. 2003. *Citizens and Government in a Digital Era.* Available upon request from Ekos.

Health Canada. 2005. *Measures to Help Ensure Canadian's Continued Access to an Adequate Supply of Safe and Affordable Drugs.* Available at http://www.hc-sc.gc.ca/ahc-asc/branch-dirgen/hpfb-dgpsa/public-rev-exam/cons-resul-eng.php (last accessed November 1, 2008)

Hendriks, L. 2005. *Rent Reform Consultation and Technology: A Review of the Submission Database.* Presented at Online Consultation: Analyzing the Outcomes at Public Works and Government Services Canada.

Jeffrey, L. 2004. *Foreign Policy Dialogue.* Presented at Practical Applications of e-Consultation at Public Works and Government Services Canada.

Latvanen, M. 2004. *Personal Communication June 13, 2004.* Online Consultation Research Project.

Oakes, K. 2004. *The Impact of 'E' on the Public Sector.* Paper presented at the Australian Electronic Governance Conference at the University of Melbourne, April 14-15, 2004.

Online Consultation Centre of Expertise. 2004. Practical Applications of e-Consultation.

Richard, E. 2003. *Archetypes of the Network Age.* Ottawa: Public Policy Forum.

Svensen, A. and M. Laberge. 2005. *Convening Stakeholder Networks: A New Way of Thinking, Being and Engaging.* Vancouver: Simon Fraser University Centre for Collaborative Management. Available at http://www.sfu.ca/cscd/cli/jcc-2005.pdf (last accessed November 1, 2008)

Trénel, M. 2005. *Facilitating Deliberation Online: What Difference Does it Make?* Paper presented at the Second Conference on Online Deliberation: Design, Research, and Practice, Stanford, CA, May 17, 2005.

Whyte, A. and A. MacIntosh. 2002. Analysis and Evaluation of E-Consultations. *e-Service Journal* 2(1): 9-34.

Wyman, M., D. Shulman, and L. Ham. 1999. Learning to Engage: Experiences with Civic Engagement in Canada. Available at http://www.cprn.com/en/doc.cfm?doc=86 (last accessed October 7, 2008

15

Political Action and Organization Building: An Internet-Based Engagement Model

MARK COOPER

1 Introduction

The 2004 presidential election signaled the possibility and the early phase of the 2008 election leaves little doubt that the Internet is changing the face of American politics as a means of fundraising and communication and as a fact-checking part of the journalistic fourth estate (Cornfield 2004). The general growth of participation and collaboration over the Internet has been widely noted (Benkler 2006; Coleman and Gøtze 2002), challenging the fears that the Internet would contribute to the social isolation of 'bowling alone' in physical space (Putnam 2000). It is not yet clear, however, the extent to which blogging will become a new form of meaningful social engagement or the Internet will become a vehicle for political organization building and sustained citizen participation in the political process.

This chapter examines the economic, social, and political challenges for organizations that use an online environment internally to deal with members and aim to strengthen their capacity to use the online environment externally and influence the political process.

Online Deliberation: Design, Research, and Practice.
Todd Davies and Seeta Peña Gangadharan (eds.).
Copyright © 2009, CSLI Publications.

2 Physical Space, Cyberspace, and Political Action

The Internet and traditional political institutions should be seen as two planes that intersect along the axis of political action. Figure 1 identifies analogous activities in physical space and cyberspace that are intended to mobilize people through information, support, and persuasion to act politically. The processes of reinforcement and coordination in physical space are augmented by processes of viral communications and collaboration in cyberspace.

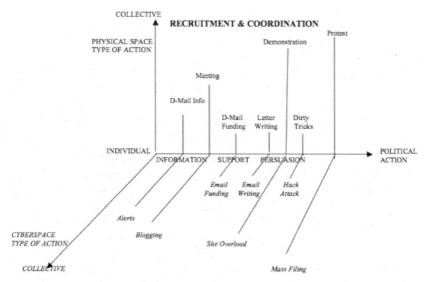

Figure 1. Physical space and cyberspace intersecting on the axis of political action

At one level, Web tools can be used to make physical space activities work better. Face-to-face contact is the lifeblood of politics but a highly labor intensive and decentralized activity. As a coordinating tool, the Internet shifts politics away from local control, allowing local volunteers to spend more of their time in face-to-face contact. The Internet also facilitates promotion, scheduling, enrollment, and gathering/targeting of local data, where centralized messages can be branded locally and delivered to specific areas.

At another level, technology can be used to enrich large-scale political activities in cyberspace. Software-based approaches to queuing, speaking, cross-talking, and decision making give a qualitative feel of an in-person meeting. The empirical evidence on group formation and persistence on the Internet shows that networks become groups through communication processes that also support the political activities of organizations. Members and participants become more deeply engaged through collateral communication, which expands on the messages that are sent to stimulate specific actions, when they forge bonds directly with one another outside of the official channels of communications between the leadership of the organization and the membership. 'Insurgent media', such as blogging, viral fact checking, etc., offer a new form of collective action. These collaboration-based media support both the organization, as an organization, and specific political activities. An interactive process in which values, norms, and boundaries are defined, collaboration implies a fundamentally deliberative democratic process of communications among peers.

3   Institutional Models for Internet-Based Organizations

Participatory decision making in an Internet-based organization, i.e. those that rely primarily on the Internet to initiate and maintain contact and relationships between members and conduct organizational activities and functions, is crucial to its success, although it is difficult to accomplish. The problems of achieving civic engagement in a large democratic nation resemble the problems confronting the institutionalization of an Internet-based organization on a large-scale and long-term basis. In both cases, the challenge is the impossibility of frequent face-to-face interaction.

Several contemporary models are useful sources of insight into the potential for politically oriented Internet based organizations—deliberative polling, peer-to-peer production, and cooperatives. Perhaps the most directly relevant to political action-oriented Internet based organization is the concept of enhanced deliberation offered by James Fishkin (1997). Fishkin identifies four key characteristics of what he calls 'a democracy of civic engagement': equality, participation, deliberation, and non-tyranny:

> *Political equality:* citizens' preferences count equally in a process that can plausibly be viewed as representative of everyone. *Deliberation*: a wide range of competing arguments is given careful consideration in small-group, face-to-face discussion. *Participation*: A significant portion of the citizenry is engaged in the process. *Non-tyranny*: the political process avoids, wherever possible, depriving any portion of the citizenry of rights or essential interests (Fishkin 1997: 34).

From the Internet point of view, peer-to-peer production of presents itself as another instructive model. One could hardly think of four characteristics that better describe the peer-to-peer production of information or the nature of cooperatives. Recent analyses of peer production in the open source community suggest the solutions to organizational challenges blend cooperation at the base with light-handed authority and hierarchy (Weber 2004). Leaders, lieutenants, maintainers, and gatekeepers organize production and innovation. Rules of democratic deliberation draw members in and bind them to the organization. The essential elements of the new form of organization include: (1) technologies that rely on distributed intelligence and that support intensive open communications, (2) decentralized collaborative economic relations where distribution and sharing take precedence over exclusion and market transactions, (3) norms that rest on voluntary nonhierarchical, nondiscriminatory interpersonal social relations, and (4) authority relations that are noncoercive and egalitarian based on participatory deliberation (Cooper 2006, 2002; Lessig 1999).

The essential problems of civic engagement are parallel to the peer-to-peer problem: sampling to ensure representativeness (making sure the important tasks are identified), scheduling to get all the participants in the right place (getting tasks done), and coordination and management of interactions so that people can hear and be heard. They must solve the problem of creating order, without undermining the essential open, democratic nature of the enterprise. Far from a 'free-for-all', deliberative policymaking requires trusted facilitation—rules for discussion, an attempt to reach a conclusion, an account of what happened, and feedback. The characteristics of the deliberative forum are the antithesis of media driven, one-way dissemination.

The deliberative poll melds the traditional function of a poll—signaling preferences to representatives—with the engagement of citizens in action. While its use has been focused on external relations (gathering citizens to deliberate on broad public policies), it is ideally suited to create the democratic processes internal to the Internet-based organization, particularly as online deliberation is enriched to bind members to organizations.

Engagement in political acts is facilitated by Internet-based or Web-based representative democracy: communicating with officials through email, volunteer solicitations, fundraising, and visits to websites for information and voter instructions. Web-based protest movements have captured a great deal of attention.

Cooperatives are a third, more common type of institution that provides insight for the institutionalization of collaborative production in Internet-based organizations. In fact, some argue that because of their nature, cooperative organizations may play a larger role in the information and knowledge economy (DiMaggio and Anheier 1990; Normark 1996). As Weisbrod points out, 'There is increasing demand for trustworthy institutions as a geographically mobile population and an array of increasingly complex goods pose problems for consumers who seek assurance that they expect' (Weisbrod 1998: 69).

This element of trust makes the cooperative well-suited to the goals, values, and practices of the nonprofit. The types of goods and services considered most conducive to nonprofit suppliers are qualitatively complex products where the purchaser of the service may lack expertise or the ability to monitor institutional behavior. The difficulty of identifying and monitoring product quality creates a transaction cost problem that arises from an asymmetry of information between the consumer and the producer (Handy 1997; Nilsson 1996; Bonus 1986). The difficulty in assessing the quality or quantity of service delivered results can result in a contract failure between the supplier and the consumer, so the trust relationship can fill the gap between consumers and producer.

Figure 2. Characteristics of cooperatives that create trust and credibility

A cooperative, however, meets the need by building trust between the parties to a transaction.[1] It provides a solution to information and monitor-

---

[1] In analyzing producer cooperatives, similar information problems arise out of conflicts of interest between owners and workers that feed into information asymmetries, raise costs, and provide an opportunity for lower cost production where conflict and monitoring problems can be eliminated (Ben Nur 1988).

ing problems by creating trust and credibility (see Figure 2) (Hansmann 1987). For example, cooperatives most commonly signal trust to the public and secure credibility by: (1) curtailing profit-maximizing activities and (2) making decisions according to a model of participatory governance (Handy 1997). As Ellman (1982) writes, 'The opportunity to choose management oneself is at least as reassuring as the stricter fiduciary obligations, which are themselves only a partial solution' (1044). Consumer/producer control afforded by the cooperative model also allows a flow of information that the marketplace cannot achieve.

An additional factor that is frequently invoked not only in explaining the existence of cooperatives, but also in justifying their social support, is values (Gomes and Owens 1988). Some argue that organizations can be created around different sets of values, independent of economic motivation. These institutions may arise and persist for purely value-laden reasons (DiMaggio and Anheier 1990; Gassler 1996; Rose-Ackerman 1986).

Based on different values, organizations seek to achieve different goals (Weisbrod 1998). A variety of principles have been suggested including community (Krashinsky 1998), democracy (Kelly and Rosenman 1995; Eisenberg 2000), altruism (Gassler 1986), service to a disadvantaged population (Normark 1996), focus on service quality (Hansmann 1981), pricing in a consumer friendly fashion (Lynk 1995), cooperation (as opposed to competition) (Normark 1996), maximization of output (Steinberg 1993), and satisfying behavior (as opposed to maximizing, greedy behavior) (Weisbrod 1998). Societal values also receive attention, such as institutional diversity, civic development, and human capital.[2]

These goals become a recruitment mechanism, particularly in recruiting management. Managers with values that are especially supportive of these unique organizational characteristics can be selected and attracted to organizations (Handy 1997; Normark 1996). Specifying management roles and functions with values that are consistent with an organization contributes substantially to the ability of that organization to achieve its unique goals because they possess particular values and ethics which suggest that they are less likely to cheat consumers (Handy 1997).

4 Functions and Relationships in the Internet Based Organization

A key challenge to building a model for engagement in political activity based primarily on the Internet is to provide a rhetoric and structure that

---

[2] These institutional factors can also be considered to be ecological explanations at the societal level (Abzug and Turnheim 1998; Clarke and Estes 1992).

assures potential members that they will be able to constructively promote their ideas and target their energy in an organized, reliable environment that shares reputational similarities to the world outside of cyberspace. The Internet engagement process as a two-way flow of information and resources between the organization and its members. The organization must array roles and functions to meet member needs, giving them reason to commit time, effort, and resources to the organization (Saint-Onge and Wallace 2003). The organization can then use the financial and human resources made available to it to accomplish shared goals (Rheingold 2002: 114). This means members must experience frequent results, no matter what form or medium they are delivered in (Cornfield 2004).

Diversifying the nature of the results and defining early on what members will experience in terms of information and collaboration, enhance satisfaction and commitment of members. It is the responsibility of the organization to provide the initial goals and calls to action for its Members and to constantly update those goals based on the developing interests of its Members as well as the changing political climate around them. Beating the drum once every four years will not keep the rhythm; collective action must be amassed on a continuous basis to create the collective culture.

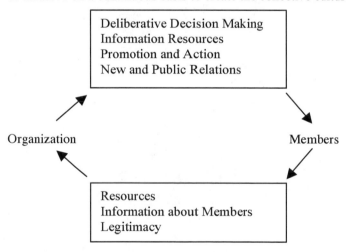

Figure 3. Functions and activities in the Internet-based engagement model

There are three critical functions that support the efforts of the Internet-based organization (see Figure 3). The **Information Resource** builds the technical systems of vertical and horizontal communications. Information flows in a multi-way dialogue with members and leadership to create a shared sense of purpose. Everyone at every level of the organization will be able to contact all others. The necessary, open dialogue will be established by information flows (Saint-Onge and Wallace 2003: 103) and will enlighten facilitators and contacts on how to keep the systems performing.

It is imperative to recognize that within the American communications and political cycles, **Promotion of Action** have become intimately linked, since most of what is done and said is captured, reworked, and re-released into the wild for reinterpretation and regurgitation by the public, resource creation is now broad and constant. Promotion is carried out with the familiar array of tools: emails, outreach, online events that add fanfare and increased attention, and advertising.

The **Publicity** function packages and broadcasts the organization's goals, initiatives, and accomplishments to members, the public-at-large, the mainstream and independent media. It attempts to solidify and project the message and outward appearance of the organization with an overall promotional scheme (O'Keefe 2002: 58). In the past few years, online newsrooms have become an essential public relations tool. The packaging and publication of members' concerns and achievements aids in the expansion and recognition of the community as an efficient, influential body of citizens, strengthening its potential for future dialogue and impact.

Political campaigns provide targeted moments of high visibility for Internet-based organizations, but it is in the period between elections and for issues tied to policy not politics where the new models of organizing for political action will go farthest to transforming the political process.

References

Abzug, R. and J. K. Turnheim. 1998. Bandwagon or Band-Aid? A Model of Nonprofit Incorporation by State. *Nonprofit and Voluntary Sector Quarterly* 27(3): 300-322.

Ben Nur, A. 1988. Comparative Empirical Observations on Worker-Owned and Capitalist Firms. *International Journal of Industrial Organization* 6(1): 7-31.

Benkler, Y. 2006. *The Wealth of Networks*. New Haven: Yale University Press.

Bonus, H. 1986. The Cooperative Association as a Business Enterprise: A Study in the Economics of Transactions. *Journal of Institutional and Theoretical Economics* 142: 310-339.

Clarke, L. and C. L. Estes. 1992. Sociological and Economic Theories of Markets and Nonprofits: Evidence from Home Health Organizations. *American Journal of Sociology* 97(4): 945-969.

Coleman, S. and J. Gøtze. 2002. *Bowling Together: Online Public Engagement in Policy Deliberation*. London: Hansard Society.

Cooper, M. 2002. Inequality in Digital Society: Why the Digital Divide Deserves All the Attention it Gets. *Cardozo Arts & Entertainment Law Journal* 20(1): 73-134.

Cooper, M. 2006. From Wifi to Wikis and Open Source: The Political Economy of Collaborative Production in the Digital Information Age. *Journal on Telecommunications & High Technology Law* 5(1): 126-58.

Cornfield, M. 2004. *Politics Moves Online: Campaigning and the Internet.* New York: Century Foundation Press.

DiMaggio, P. J. and H. K. Anheier. 1990. The Sociology of Nonprofit Organizations and Sectors. *Annual Review of Sociology* 16: 138.

Eisenberg, P. 2000. The Nonprofit Sector in a Changing World. *Nonprofit and Voluntary Sector Quarterly* 29(4): 603-9.

Ellman, I. M. 1982. Another Theory of Nonprofit Corporations. *Michigan Law Review* 80: 1044.

Fishkin, J. S. 1997. *The Voice of the People: Public Opinion and Democracy.* New Haven: Yale University Press.

Gassler, R. S. 1986. *The Economics of Nonprofit Enterprise—A Study in Applied Economic Theory.* Lanham, MD: University Press of America

Gomes, G. M. and J. M. Owens. 1988. Commercial Nonprofits, Untaxed Entrepreneurialism, and 'Unfair Competition'. *Journal of Small Business Management* 26: 10.

Handy, F. 1997. Coexistence of Nonprofit, For-Profit and Public Sector Institutions. *Annals of Public and Cooperative Economics* 7: 208.

Hansmann, H. B. 1981. Reforming Nonprofit Corporation Law. *University of Pennsylvania Law Review* 129(3): 497-623.

Hansmann, H. B. 1987. The Effect of Tax Exemption and Other Factors on the Market Share of Nonprofit Versus For-profit Firms. *National Tax Journal* 40: 71-82.

James, E. 1983. How Nonprofits Grow: A Model. *Journal of Policy Analysis and Management* 2(3): 350-365

Kelly, M. and M. Rosenman. 1995. *Nonprofits, Commerciality, and Democracy.* Washington: Office for Social Responsibility, Centre for Public Policy.

Krashinsky, M. 1998. Does Auspice Matter? The Case of Day Care for Children in Canada. *Private Action and the Public Good*, eds. W. W. Powell and E. S. Clemens, 114-123. New Haven: Yale University Press.

Lessig, L. 1999. *Code and Other Laws of Cyberspace.* New York: Basic Books.

Lohmann, R. A. 1992. The Commons: A Multidisciplinary Approach to Nonprofit Organization, Voluntary Action, and Philanthropy. *Nonprofit and Voluntary Sector Quarterly* 21(3): 309-324.

Lynk, W. J. 1995. Nonprofit Hospital Mergers and the Exercise of Market Power. *Journal of Law and Economics* 38(2): 437-61.

Nilsson, J. 1996. The Nature of Cooperative Values and Principles. *Annals of Public and Cooperative Economics* 67(4): 633-653.

Normark, P. 1996. A Role for Cooperatives in the Market Economy. *Annals of Public and Cooperative Economics* 67: 430.

O'Keefe, S. 2002. *Complete Guide to Internet Publicity: Creating and Launching Successful Online Campaigns.* New York: John Wiley.

Putnam, R. 2000. *Bowling Alone.* New York: Simon and Schuster.

Rheingold, H. 2002. *Smart Mobs: The Next Social Revolution.* Cambridge: Perseus Publishing

Rose-Ackerman, S., ed. 1986. *The Economics of Nonprofit Institutions: Studies in Structure and Policy.* New York: Oxford University Press.

Saint-Onge, H. and D. Wallace. 2003. *Leveraging Communities of Practice for Strategic Advantage.* Burlington, MA: Elsevier Science.

Steinberg, R. 1993. Public Policy and the Performance of Nonprofit Organizations: A General Framework. *Nonprofit and Voluntary Sector Quarterly* 22: 13-31.

Weber, S. 2004. *The Success of Open Source.* Cambridge: Harvard University Press.

Weisbrod, B. A. 1998. *To Profit or Not to Profit.* Cambridge: Cambridge University Press.

16

Wiki Collaboration Within Political Parties: Benefits and Challenges

KATE RAYNES-GOLDIE AND DAVID FONO

1   Introduction

We report here a case study of the only wiki that, at the time of writing, had been significantly used by a political party: the Green Party of Canada's (GPC's) Living Platform. The GPC is a quickly growing federal party whose mandate is to address environmental issues and improve the democratic process. The party created the Living Platform to engage Canadian citizens in the development of its political platform. Anyone was free to view and edit the document. We interviewed several major participants about their experiences with and reflections on the project. Our analysis of these interviews is intended to guide future initiatives that employ a wiki towards a similar end.

2   Effectiveness of the Wiki

The main advantage of the Green Party's use of a wiki to develop its platform was that it effectively facilitated distributed writing, editing, and document sharing. Users were able to work on discrete portions of the document while at the same time observing ongoing development of other portions. Furthermore, multiple users working on a single portion could work asynchronously and without any confusion as to the most recent status of the document. Distributed and parallel document development were particularly advantageous in this case because they helped to overcome the

Online Deliberation: Design, Research, and Practice
Todd Davies and Seeta Peña Gangadharan (eds.).
Copyright © 2009, CSLI Publications.

'political bottleneck' involved in creating a document based on consensus, where a large number of decisions must be made by a small group of individuals. The wiki allowed decisions to be distributed over a larger number of people.

Another benefit of the wiki was that it facilitated 'doing' rather than simply talking, as is often the case with other collaborative technologies. The wiki's focus on editing a document directly rather than just discussing it meant that the platform actually got built rather than remaining in the limbo of dialogue about what it should be. The flipside of this advantage was that the wiki often did not facilitate an effective dialogue around the platform development process. For example, users would often make changes to the document without any consultation with other users.

Consequently, a number of interviewees emphasized that the wiki should augment rather than replace traditional modes of communication such as phone calls and face-to-face meetings. Based on these observations, it appears most appropriate that wikis serve as a 'secondary tool' for similar collaborative work.

3 Technological Barrier

There was near consensus that the Living Platform presented some degree of a technological barrier involved in using. Even those participants with strong technical backgrounds reported needing some initial training.

The main function of this training was not only to help participants learn an unfamiliar technology but also to change the way they thought about writing and authorship. According to one interviewee:

> There is a substantial learning curve that goes against [the] way people use the Web and what an author is. You're really cranking over a paradigm in people's heads... The first time people use [a] wiki they turn it into a discussion board. The challenge of the technology is to overcome people's preconceptions.

After the initial learning period, all of the interviewees seemed to like using the wiki. These reports suggest that the required skills are more of an initial barrier than an ongoing problem for users.

4 Issues of Transparency

Another major point of contention among the people we spoke to was the issue of transparency. One of the goals of using a wiki was to increase the transparency of the GPC's platform development process. However, party members disagreed about how transparent the process should actually be.

At one point, members posted on the wiki criticisms of the party, spurring conflict among members and party leaders. Advocates for reduced transparency argued that as a political party the GPC needs to be careful about what happens on the wiki. For example, certain elements of the platform may need to be kept hidden from other parties so that the other parties do not gain an advantage in an election. There were also concerns about the party's public image, as well as liability issues.

Those who advocated for a completely transparent process argued that content regulation defeats the purpose of the Living Platform and goes against the very culture of the GPC. Furthermore, if there is a legitimate criticism of the party, the Living Platform could be used as a way to create positive change. The solution is not to suppress the criticism, but instead to address the issues that are raised.

Conflict on the Living Platform tangibly demonstrates what other parties who choose to use wikis for public discourse will likely face. While the most apparent solution would be to strike an appropriate balance between transparency and privacy, this may not be the best course of action for parties with mandates to reinvigorate politics.

5 'Function Creep'

Party leaders originally intended members to use the Living Platform exclusively for platform development. However, the site became a vehicle for other activities as well. For example, the wiki became a forum for users to air their grievances regarding party leadership and related issues. The wiki was also being employed towards less controversial ends, such as for administrative purposes and policy development.

The flexibility of wiki technology makes it very easy for users to appropriate a single wiki for a number of purposes but very difficult for administrators to restrict usage to a single area. The implications of function creep can be both positive and negative. On the one hand, unofficial or unintended usage may result in disagreements over what constitutes appropriate use, and can become an excuse to censor or control content. On the other hand, it can be advantageous to permit 'function creep' because it allows users to utilize the tool in a variety of helpful and novel ways. Thus, those who employ wikis in similar initiatives should be prepared for users to take advantage of the tool in unexpected ways.

17

Debian's Democracy

GUNNAR RISTROPH

1 Introduction

The Debian project is likely the largest and longest-lived online deliberative body. Debian is an organization of slightly more than a thousand volunteers who collaborate over the Internet to package roughly eighteen thousand separate open source software projects into a single freely distributed complete operating system (Debian 2007). Over the past decade, an intricate and documented set of democratic rules has been created to govern Debian.

2 History

During the early years of Debian, the only official authority came from Ian Murdock, who founded Debian in 1994. When he stepped down as Debian Project Leader, he simply appointed a successor (Murdock 1996). The developers occasionally used ad hoc means to draft statements and take votes. While many developers supported the dictatorship, there were vocal and persistent calls for democracy (Perens 1997a).

Between 1995 and 1998, membership was doubling each year (Brief 2007), and discussion of a constitution began. Ian Jackson, who became project leader in late 1997 (Perens 1997b), led the drafting and revising of the constitution over the Debian email mailing list (Jackson 1998). The constitution was ratified at the end of 1998, according to the procedure described in the constitution itself and received unanimous support of the eighty-six developers who voted (Debian 1999).

Online Deliberation: Design, Research, and Practice.
Todd Davies and Seeta Peña Gangadharan (eds.).
Copyright © 2009, CSLI Publications.

3   Membership

For many years, eligible voters were simply those who had recently maintained a package, a task for which anyone could volunteer. The constitution does not address the question of membership.

As Debian grew, an account manager was created to verify and oversee new members. The project growth was unchecked and many developers felt that the new members were just creating new projects, not working on old bugs, and the overall quality was suffering. New applicants complained that the wait to become a member was too long (O'Mahony 2004). Some members anticipated this problem of controlling membership (Jackson 1998), but no solution was found and the issue simmered for many years (O'Mahony 2004).

In October 1999, the situation finally culminated with the project leader halting all new applications until a new membership process could be created. Six months later, a new membership committee began processing applications under its own guidelines. A complicated bureaucratic application process was designed to make sure that applicants were skilled, philosophically agreeable, and dedicated (O'Mahony 2004).

The interview, verification, and assessment process takes months and is subject to long delays. Nearly all applications which are pursued diligently result in successful completion, but many have complained that the process takes too long and often applicants give up (Byfield 2005).

4   Political Structure

In addition to authority over their own work, members—called 'developers' by the constitution—can propose, sponsor, and vote on general resolutions. Members have immense power by way of general resolution. They may overrule or even remove the project leader, amend the constitution, and rule on any technical or non-technical issue. Members may also run for project leader and vote in the yearly elections (Debian 2008a). The project leader must make urgent decisions and is the public and internal figurehead of the organization (Debian 2008a).

The technical committee acts as a last resort arbiter of technical disagreements between developers. With help from the leader, the technical committee appoints members and usually serves for several years (Debian 2008a). Prior to 2007, the committee was only occasionally asked to resolve a problem and handed down an average of one or two decisions per year (Debian 2008c). The lack of referrals to the committee indicate to some that the members lack confidence in it, but others explain this by saying that disputes are resolved well by other means (Robinson 2005). The committee handed down several formal decisions in 2007 (Debian 2008c), but some, including Ian Jackson, remain frustrated (Jackson 2008).

The project secretary oversees votes and handles constitutional disputes. The leader and incumbent secretary appoint the next secretary annually (Debian 2008a).

Many important decisions are made outside the constitutional structure, such as changes to the *Debian Policy Manual*, a detailed compendium of software requirements. Revisions are discussed on a mailing list until consensus is reached, but only a few policy maintainers can change the document (Debian 2004). How policy is shaped was the subject of controversy in the early years of the constitution (Srivastava 1999). In principle, a deadlocked policy dispute could be referred to the technical committee, but this has never happened (Debian 2008c).

5 Deliberation

The Debian Constitution prescribes the 'Standard Resolution Procedure' as a generic way to decide questions by proposal, discussion, amendment, and voting—all through email. The procedure is used for many processes within the constitution and establishes principles that are used informally as well.

Any member may formally propose a resolution which then becomes subject to discussion and amendment.[1] If the original resolution author accepts a proposed amendment, the resolution is immediately changed and the discussion period continues. If the original author rejects the amendment, it remains as a separate option and will be voted on as an alternate to the original. Amendments may not be amended (Debian 2008a).

Once a minimum discussion period (usually two weeks) has elapsed, the resolution's author or the author of any amendment may call for a vote. The original resolution, a default or 'further discussion' option, and all amendments are presented on a single ballot. Voters are instructed to rank the options and return their ballots in a fixed time (usually two weeks). A quorum requirement must be met for the counting to proceed (Debian 2008a). The counting method used to determine a winner from all the voters' ballots is a variant of Condorcet Voting with Schwartz Sequential Dropping.[2] In most situations, there is one option that beats all other options in pairwise matchups, and so there is a clear winner (Voss 2005).

---

[1] Sometimes sponsors or seconds or required.

[2] For a complete discussion of the intricacies of the Debian voting protocol, see 'The Debian Voting System' by Jochen Voss (2005).

Sometimes an election under the standard resolution procedure is simply managed by a secretary or chair. For elections in which all developers participate, custom software for automated balloting is used.

Email

Most discussion, and all deliberations using the standard resolution procedure, occurs on dedicated email lists. The *debian-devel* list hosts technical and political discussion and sees between 50 and 100 emails each day. The *debian-vote* list is used for formal action. The technical committee and many large undertakings have their own mailing lists (Debian 2008b).

Chat

Technical questions and politics are also discussed over Internet Relay Chat (IRC). A proposal by general resolution to give IRC legitimacy and subject it to control failed to gain support (Debian 2001). An official, moderated debate for the project leader elections has been conducted over IRC in most years since 2001 with much participation.

6   Conclusions

Because Debian has been actively and successfully engaged in online deliberation for a decade, a careful study of Debian's governance is useful in developing tools and standards for online democratic decision making.

The Debian experience confirms established lessons about both democracy and online interaction. The importance of defined procedures and member empowerment shine clear. Asynchronous text-based communication is not an obstacle to deliberation. Rather it offers new convenience. The Debian Constitution offers hope and a specific structure for taking democratic deliberation to new effectiveness and participation.

References

Byfield, B. 2005. Becoming a Debian Developer. Linux.com. February 3, 2005. Available at http://www.linux.com/articles/42155 (last accessed September 26, 2008)

Debian. 1999. *Proposal-0: Constitution.* Available at http://www.debian.org/vote/1999/vote_0000 (last accessed September 26, 2008)

Debian. 2001. *IRC as a Debian Communication Channel.* Available at http://www.debian.org/vote/2001/vote_0002 (last accessed September 26, 2008)

Debian. 2004. *Debian Policy Manual.* Version 3.6.1.1. http://www.debian.org/doc/debian-policy/ (last accessed September 26, 2008)

Debian. 2007. *A Brief History of Debian.* Available at http://www.debian.org/doc/manuals/project-history/ (last accessed September 26, 2008)

Debian. 2008a. *Debian Constitution.* Version 1.4. Available at http://www.debian.org/devel/constitution (last accessed September 26, 2008)

Debian. 2008b. *Debian Mailing Lists Index for Developers.* http://lists.debian.org/devel.html (last accessed September 26, 2008)

Debian. 2008c. *Debian Technical Committee.* Available at http://www.debian.org/devel/tech-ctte (last accessed September 26, 2008)

Jackson, I. 2008. *Functionality of the Committee, and Maintainership disputes.* March 9, 2008. http://lists.debian.org/debian-ctte/2008/03/msg00000.html (last accessed September 26, 2008)

Jackson, I. 1998. *Re: Initial Draft Proposed Constitution (v0.2).* March 19, 1998. http://lists.debian.org/debian-devel/1998/03/msg01778.html (last accessed September 26, 2008)

Murdock, I. 1996. *My Role in the Project.* March 4, 1996. http://lists.debian.org/debian-announce/debian-announce-1996/msg00003.html (last accessed September 26, 2008)

O'Mahony, S. 2003. *Managing the Boundary of an 'Open' Project.* Santa Fe Institute Workshop on The Network Construction of Markets.

Perens, B. 1997. *Debian Dissent Mailing List Formed.* August 27, 1997. Available at http://lists.debian.org/debian-announce/debian-announce-1997/msg00027.html (last accessed September 26, 2008)

Perens, B. 1997. *Ian Jackson is the Next Debian Project Leader.* December 1, 1997. Available at http://lists.debian.org/debian-announce/debian-announce-1997/msg00037.html (last accessed September 26, 2008)

Robinson, B. 2005. *The Technical Committee (Was: Question to All Candidates).* March 12, 2005. Available at http://lists.debian.org/debian-vote/2005/03/msg00558.html (last accessed September 26, 2008)

Srivastava, M. 1996. *Bug 30036: Debian-Policy Could Include Emacs Policy.* January 20, 1999. Available at http://lists.debian.org/debian-policy/1999/01/msg00153.html (last accessed September 26, 2008)

Voss, J. 2005. *The Debian Voting System.* April 2005. Available at http://seehuhn.de/comp/vote.html (last accessed September 26, 2008)

18

Software Support for Face-to-Face Parliamentary Procedure

DANA DAHLSTROM AND BAYLE SHANKS

1 Introduction

Parliamentary procedure of the sort codified in *Robert's Rules of Order* is a widely used system of rules for group decision making. Unfortunately, in many settings where parliamentary procedure is used, unfamiliarity with the rules inhibits participation, working against the aim of giving due consideration to each member's opinion.

This chapter describes a software interface that supports face-to-face parliamentary procedure by publicly displaying information about items under consideration and about actions available under the rules. These features facilitate shared context among the participants, encourage adherence to the rules, and help novices engage and learn the process.

2 Motivations

Parliamentary procedure is used in many different organizations ranging from small boards and committees to governmental legislative bodies. A group meeting using *Robert's Rules of Order* is called a deliberative assembly and requires that all members communicate synchronously by voice, normally face-to-face. A deliberative assembly may have from a few to a few hundred members.

Online Deliberation: Design, Research, and Practice
Todd Davies and Seeta Peña Gangadharan (eds.).
Copyright © 2009, CSLI Publications.

Central to *Robert's Rules of Order* are motions, by which a member may propose that the assembly take certain actions. The 'Table of Rules Relating to Motions' in the 1915 version of *Robert's Rules of Order Revised*, now in the public domain, includes forty-five different motions that fall mostly into four classes: main motions, subsidiary motions, incidental motions, and privileged motions. Precedence among and within the classes specifies which motions are in order—that is, permitted by the rules—depending on which motions are currently pending.

Each class of motions has general characteristics, and many individual motions have peculiarities of their own. Some motions are debatable. while others are not. Some are amendable. Some allow subsidiary motions applied to them. Some can be reconsidered. Most require first obtaining the floor, being seconded, and a majority vote in the affirmative to be adopted; others may interrupt a speaker, need not be seconded, and require no vote; yet others require a two-thirds vote. In short, the rules are many and difficult to remember, especially in a lively meeting.

Procedural Difficulties

The complexity of parliamentary procedure can be challenging for anyone, and particularly stifling to a novice participant who knows little or nothing of the rules. He or she may have opinions to voice or objectives to accomplish, but not know how. *Robert's Rules of Order* allow a parliamentary inquiry by which a member may ask for advice on such matters, but the member must know this option is available and the chair must be prepared to give an appropriate response.

In many organizations that nominally use parliamentary procedure, even the chair of an assembly is only vaguely familiar with the rules, often having learned mainly from experience in meetings and never having studied a manual. One problem that can arise in such circumstances is that the assembly may take action without due process, and in doing so violate fundamental rights of the minority, of individual members, or of the assembly itself.

For example, one common misbelief about parliamentary procedure is that any member may halt debate and initiate a vote at any time by shouting, 'I call the question'! In fact, to 'call the question' or, more properly, to move the previous question, one must obtain the floor in order to make the motion, and it must be seconded and finally itself receive a two-thirds vote in the affirmative. *Robert's Rules of Order* consistently emphasize that suppressing debate requires the support of two thirds. This requirement protects the fundamental right to have questions thoroughly discussed before taking action. Absent knowledge of the rules, this fundamental right is easily violated.

Even when members have a working knowledge of the rules and their fundamental rights are intact, participants can lose track of the proceedings for a variety of reasons. Parliamentary procedure is formally linear and verbal and relies on shared context. When one loses context in a deliberative assembly, one may rise to a point of information in order to ask questions, but this may be socially awkward. If participants miss something, it is easy to become confused about what has happened or what is happening.

Our Software

We have built software that can run on a portable computer connected to a digital projector. A single user enters events as they transpire, such as motions and votes. Based on this input, the software keeps track of the meeting state and updates the large display so that at any time, assembly members can see information such as currently pending motions, motions currently in order, and transacted business.

The prototype application shown in Figure 1 (below) is operated in a face-to-face meeting conducted according to *Robert's Rules of Order*. It is written using the Parliament module (Shanks and Dahlstrom 2009) and is freely available.[1]

3   Design Considerations

A main concern is which information to display in the interface, especially as there are too many motions to display at once.

A second design goal is to serve the secretary's needs. Under Robert's *Rules*, the duties of the secretary include preparing of an order of business for the chair; keeping track of business that is postponed, laid on the table, or left unfinished; and producing the minutes. Our system is intended in part to aid the secretary in executing these duties.

Assisting the secretary is not merely ancillary. As Grudin (1994) has pointed out, the disparity between who does the work and who gets the benefit is often a barrier to acceptance of groupware systems. While it aims to benefit many individuals and the group as a whole, this system requires someone to do work: continually and promptly entering meeting proceedings into a computer. Helping get the secretary's job done is a key incentive for this work.

---

[1] See http://parliament.sourceforge.net (last accessed September 28, 2008).

A third requirement for the interface is that it be quick and flexible enough to keep up with live action. The user must not get backlogged entering events; a public display of obsolete information is worse than useless.

Finally, the interface must gracefully handle at least two kinds of irregularities: mistakes by the user, which must be promptly correctable; and deviations from the ordinary rules, either by a motion to suspend the rules or by mistake.

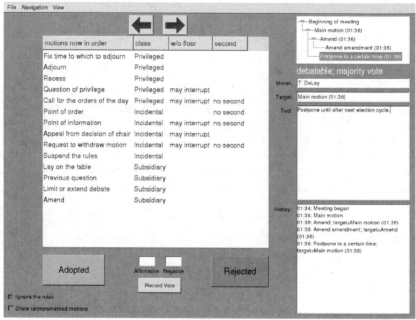

Figure 1. User interface

Use Considerations

When software support for parliamentary procedure is introduced, it should be made clear that the chair, not the software, presides over the assembly. However, to prevent confusion, it is crucial for the chair to monitor the output of the software to ensure that the information being recorded and displayed to the assembly is correct.

The software should not be considered a parliamentary authority or a substitute for knowledge of the rules. One of the chair's responsibilities is to advise members on how to achieve their aims; in most cases, simply ruling a motion out of order will not do. Because *Robert's Rules of Order* are intricate and rely on subjective determinations, the software's capacity to settle parliamentary questions is necessarily limited. The chair should be familiar with the rules and have a copy of the assembly's parliamentary authority at the meeting.

Computers are oblivious to social conventions, which makes them less fit for many tasks of chairmanship but perhaps more fit for others. For example, enforcing time limits can be socially awkward, but is often appreciated so long as it is done fairly.

4 The User Interface

Figure 1 depicts the user interface, designed for a single user such as an organization's secretary. The window which is displayed on the projector is different.

'Motions now in order' are only those motions that are in order at the present time. The user may activate any of these motions to indicate that that motion has been moved in the meeting. There are text fields for the number of affirmative and negative votes and a button to compare the tallies to the proportion of votes required by the rules. Adopted and rejected buttons allow the user to indicate the fate of the immediately pending motion directly when votes are not counted. Back and forward buttons navigate through meeting history, providing a multiple undo/redo mechanism.

The currently pending motions in the tree diagram can be selected, populating several other fields with information about the selected motion. In addition to the text of the motion, these also include its mover and its target. All of these fields are editable by the user.

The interface also provides an event log with a record of each motion and whether that motion was adopted or rejected.

Real-world assemblies sometimes deviate from the rules. To be useful, the software must continue to track the state of the meeting. Hence the interface provides an 'Ignore the rules' checkbox that allows the user to record actions and motions despite these being out of order according to the module's interpretation of the rules.

5 Results of Preliminary Trials

The prototype has been pilot-tested in meetings of the Graduate Student Association Council at the University of California, San Diego (GSACUCSD). One problem was the physical arrangement of the room. Since members spend much of the meeting looking toward the chair, who faces them, it seemed fitting to place the projected display behind the chair. However, this meant that the chair could not see the display. That made it difficult for the chair to realize when the software was displaying inaccurate information.

A projector screen displaying inaccurate information about the state of the meeting is potentially disastrous and should be avoided. Meeting participants may rely on the projected information which, if inaccurate, will hinder rather than help. Therefore, the chair should keep aware of what the software is displaying and see that it is corrected when necessary. One solution is for the system's operator (perhaps the secretary) to sit next to the chair. This way, though the projected display may not be visible to the chair, the computer screen will be.

Preliminary experience confirms that when a computer and projector are introduced into a meeting, people want to put the equipment to various uses. Members of the GSAUCSD Council asked us to launch other software on the computer in order to display their governing documents and long resolutions under consideration.

6   Relation to Other Work

There is a considerable body of work on electronic meeting systems and systems to support group decision making, whether face-to-face or otherwise, but much less work has focused on parliamentary procedure.

A group decision support system (GDSS) employs technology to facilitate group decision making. A GDSS is groupware, in that it is designed for multiple people working collaboratively. As a field, GDSS is related to decision support systems (DSS), although the latter typically focus on information gathering and analysis for a single individual.

A GDSS to apply parliamentary procedure was envisioned at least as early as 1987 by DeSanctis and Gallupe. In their nomenclature, such a system is called a Level Three GDSS. While Level One GDSSs aim only to facilitate communication and Level Two GDSSs passively offer tools and models, Level Three GDSSs actively apply rules regulating the decision process.

In their survey of systems for cooperative work and group decision support, Kraemer and King (1998) argue that 'most of the efforts to apply these technologies have affected decision processes too much or too little to provide a good assessment of their effects' (130). On one hand, audiovisual presentation and teleconferencing technologies merely speed up process without improving the quality of decision making; on the other hand, technology that imposes structured collaboration techniques also imposes the designers' views of the decision process on the participants.

Our software aims to improve group decision making without externally imposing structure; many organizations have already adopted a parliamentary authority such as *Robert's Rules of Order*.

A number of GDSSs have been built. For example, Davies et al. have built an online deliberation environment, Deme (Davies et al. 2009), primarily to support the activities of groups that already meet face-to-face.

Work Related to *Robert's Rules of Order*

Some aspects of parliamentary procedure are oriented toward a face-to-face setting, but the underlying principles and many of the rules can be applied to decision-making groups using various other modes of communication. One group designed a document-based collaboration system based on an 'agenda item life cycle' inspired by *Robert's Rules of Order* (Zhang et al. 2003). Horan and Benington (2000) describe a protocol for conducting deliberations by email in academic committees using *Robert's Rules of Order*. Robert's Rules in Motion[2] is a commercially available single-user application that simulates meetings in order to train the user in the use of parliamentary procedure. Schuler (2009) describes a system similar to ours, e-Liberate.

7 Conclusions

The technology described herein shows promise for improving the practice of parliamentary procedure in face-to-face meetings. Assemblies with members not well practiced in the rules can especially benefit from such a system.

Software support for parliamentary procedure fills a unique niche among similar research. By supporting group work while having a single user operating the interface, it avoids many pitfalls of groupware applications. By aiming to improve group decision making without externally imposing structure, software for parliamentary procedure offers opportunities to study effects on groups that were obscured by the more dramatic interventions of other group decision support systems.

Software for parliamentary procedure should run on common portable computers and be easy for any organization's secretary to learn and use, streamlined enough to keep pace with live meetings, and flexible enough to handle the adaptive circumvention of rules that inevitably occurs in real assemblies. The software should generate a record from which official minutes can be produced and which may in the future be a medium for interoperation with online deliberation systems.

Preliminary experience with a prototype system in real meetings has met with enthusiastic response. Further development and experimentation is underway.

---

[2] See http://www.imovethat.com (last accessed September 28, 2008).

References

Davies, T., B. O'Connor, A. Cochran, J. J. Effrat, B. Newman, and A. Tam. 2009. An Online Environment for Democratic Deliberation: Motivations, Principles, and Design. *Online Deliberation: Design, Research, and Practice*, eds. T. Davies and S. P. Gangadharan, 275-292. Stanford, CA: CSLI Publications.

DeSanctis, G. and R. B. Gallupe. 1987. A Foundation for the Study of Group Decision Support Systems. *Management Science* 33(5): 589–609.

Grudin, J. 1994. Groupware and Social Dynamics: Eight Challenges for Developers. *Communications of the ACM* 37(1): 92–105.

Horan, S. M. and J. H. Benington. 2000. A Protocol for Using Electronic Messaging to Facilitate Academic Committee Deliberations. *Journal of Higher Education Policy and Management* 22(2): 187–197.

Kraemer, K. L. and J. L. King. 1988. Computer-based Systems for Cooperative Work and Group Decision Making. *ACM Computing Surveys* 20(2): 115–146.

Schuler, D. 2009. Online Civic Deliberation with E-Liberate. *Online Deliberation: Design, Research, and Practice*, eds. T. Davies and S. P. Gangadharan, 293-302. Stanford, CA: CSLI Publications.

Shanks, B. and D. B. Dahlstrom. 2009. Parliament: A Module for Parliamentary Procedure Software. *Online Deliberation: Design, Research, and Practice*, eds. T. Davies and S. P. Gangadharan, 303-307. Stanford, CA: CSLI Publications.

Zhang, J., C. K. Chang, K. H. Chang, and F. K. H. Quek. 2003. Rule-mitigated Collaboration Framework. *Proceedings of the Eighth IEEE International Symposium on Computers and Communication* 1: 614–619.

Part V
Online Facilitation

19

Deliberation on the Net: Lessons from a Field Experiment

June Woong Rhee and Eun-mee Kim

1 Introduction

The emergence of the Internet and its potential for creating a public sphere has sparked renewed interest in the concept of deliberative democracy. Efforts have begun to test whether such online activities actually produce the prerequisites of deliberative democracy, and to explore the effects of Internet discussion in general (Corrado and Firestone, 1999; Norris 2000; Price and Cappella 2002; Price et al. 2002; Rheingold 1993).

However, the results have not been consistent enough to reach a conclusion about the positive or negative potential of online deliberation (Delli Carpini, Cook, and Jacobs 2004). Conflicting results on the political prospects of Internet discussion call for a clarification of empirical conditions under which Internet discussion substantially contributes to deliberative democracy. We reasoned that if discussions, offline or online, do bring about effects, they must come from a specific set of structural and regulative conditions of communication. In other words, what invokes the effect of deliberation might not be the mere fact of talking but the specific conditions surrounding discussion—the methods, norms, and rules by which people talk to each other. To further simplify, there is beneficial talk and harmful talk depending on the potential goal.

The 'virtual' nature of the Internet permits us to monitor communication behavior under varying circumstances. It can be easily transformed into

Online Deliberation: Design, Research, and Practice.
Todd Davies and Seeta Peña Gangadharan (eds.).
Copyright © 2009, CSLI Publications.

a testing field to account for the systematic effects of a focal variable by, for example, devising the webpage to operate in specific ways. Exploiting this 'virtual' nature of the Internet, we reasoned that a field experiment is a powerful research method for testing the effects of structural and regulative conditions of communication in an online deliberation forum.

Previous empirical studies on the effects of online deliberation (Fishkin 2003; Hansen 1999; Iyengar, Luskin, and Fishkin 2003; Price et al. 2002) showed that various online deliberative activities do bring about positive effects on democracy, with heightened convenience but less cost compared to offline. The virtuous effects on which such studies have focused include increased political knowledge, higher opinion quality, increased social capital, and greater trust. However, these studies did not represent the natural conditions of online political conversation. In addition, they usually focused on the outcomes of online deliberation, without paying much attention to the process through which discussions were carried out.

This chapter reports on the theoretical assumptions, methodological considerations, and major findings of a field experiment. The experiment, carried out as a part of the *Daum Deliberative Democracy Project*, attempted to examine the structural and regulative conditions of Internet deliberation which bring about outcomes related to deliberative democracy.[1] The study as a whole suggests a new theoretical approach to deliberative democracy, by emphasizing the processes and conditions that mediate between political discussion and ideals of deliberation.

2 Structural and Regulative Conditions of Communication

Deliberation can be divided into two dimensions: the formal frame and the content. Although the two dimensions are inseparable in the actual communication process, they must be separated for analytical purposes. In our conceptual model, the two dimensions, in fact, interact with one another to constitute the dynamic nature of human communication. The former renders the structural and regulative frame of the latter, while the latter enables the former.

---

[1] The Daum Deliberative Democracy project was a series of field experiments to explore the impacts of online deliberation on Korean voters' political activities within the context of the 2004 Korean General Election. After the presidential election in 2002, Korean voters, renowned for the heaviest Internet use in the world, utilized the medium as a main channel for expressing their political opinions. Daum Communications Corporation, a provider of Internet communities, search engine, e-commerce, and media, runs the portal site (http://www.daum.net, last accessed September 19, 2008), which was ranked number one in terms of visitors, and registered users during the 2004 election.

It is the formal frame of communication that functions as a structural and regulative ideal of democracy. That is, deliberative democracy assumes that the ideals of inclusion, openness, uncoerciveness, and rationality of communication are realized in talks, discussions, and argumentation (Dryzek 1999; Habermas 1996). Thus, when deliberation is said to have worthwhile effects, this means that the structural and regulative conditions (the formal frame dimension) of communication in deliberation exerts influences in such a way that the ideals of inclusion, openness, uncoerciveness, and rationality are realized in the outcomes of deliberation (the content dimension). To substantiate this assumption, the connection between the structural and regulative conditions of communication and deliberative actions has to be confirmed. In this study, we are particularly interested in exposure of social identity cues in deliberation, intervention of moderators in deliberation, and reinforcement of discussion efficacy.

Social Identity Cues

Physical appearance or social status (perceived) in face-to-face interactions often function as 'gates' that control human interaction. Anonymity in computer-mediated communication frees interaction participants from potentially feeling socially inferior to their counterparts and, thus, facilitates expression for everyone. On the other hand, the presence of other people in an interaction creates inherent 'publicness' of the communication context. But it is not clear whether a higher level of interaction leads to improvement of the process or its consequences, such as attention, rationality, and persuasion. Revelation of social identity cues in computer-mediated communication is likely to make discussants more attentive to messages and possibly to lead them through cognitively higher elaboration. At the same time, it may make group identity more salient, leading people to conform to a salient group norm rather than to attend to the informative argument (Lea, Spears, and de Groot 1991). There is still a possibility that having to reveal social cues could cause chilling effects. Thus, anonymity in online discussion seems to be a double-edged sword.

Moderator

Lack of discussion structure and lack of leadership both contribute to the failure to improve the quality of online discussions (Rice 1984). Coleman and Gøtze (2001) emphasized the role of moderation, such as setting up rules for discussion, ensuring fair exchanges among parties, offering a balanced summary of the discussion, and giving feedback to participants. In this way, moderators contribute in a pivotal way to shaping the democratic potential of online discussion by actively intervening in debates (Edwards

2002; Trénel 2009). Moderators who perform effectively in online discussions seem likely to improve the deliberative process.

Reinforcement of Deliberation Efficacy

Coleman and Gøtze (2001) sought to ensure that participants received feedback so that they did not feel their contributions were in vain. In the same way, this study instituted a 'point-reward system', through which online activities were monitored, indexed, and rewarded as 'points' to the individual. The points were then shown next to their login ID whenever they talked online. A participant would observe his/her points adding up in the course of active participation, which was expected to increase the person's efficacy and thus provide further motivation.

Research Model

Along with the conditions of communication discussed above, predispositions or characteristics of communicators should also be considered in a research model of communication effects. Online deliberation could be influenced by availability of Internet access, computer related skills, motivation to communicate, or, more generally, socioeconomic status. In addition, deliberative behavior may vary according to individual differences such as communicative competence, motivation, political involvement, political information consumption, and Internet literacy.

Our research framework incorporates the above considerations and reflects the stages of a generic communication process: sociopolitical context, communicator, communicative action, and effects. The theoretical components address sociopolitical differences in online deliberation, effect of individual characteristics, structural and regulative conditions of communication on deliberation, and effects on quantity and quality of online deliberation, as well as political discussion efficacy, tolerance, and trust. Thus, we can ask whether the structural and regulative conditions of communication have any effects on the quantity and quality of online deliberation and other outcome measures when the effects of sociopolitical differences and individual characteristics are controlled for (see Table 1).

Note that the model attempts to integrate communicator characteristics and social conditions as Internet users communicate under specific communication conditions. We manipulated these conditions in the field experiment to predict communication outcome measures such as quantity and quality of political discussion, political discussion efficacy, and other outcome variables.

Model Components	Functional Constructs	Observations
Moderators (Control Variables)	Sociopolitical conditions	Gender Age Region
	Individual knowledge and competence	Internet literacy Political involvement Political ideology Media information consumption
Experimental Treatments	Structural and regulative conditions of deliberation	Social identity cues (showing gender, age, and region vs. anonymity) Moderator (Moderated Vs. Unmoderated) Reinforcement of deliberation efficacy ('discussion points system' vs. no points system)
Outcome Measures	Quantity and quality of discussion	Quantity (frequencies of posting) Quality of discussion (argument repertoire and other quality indices) Discussion engagement (agreement, disagreement)
	Consequences of discussion	Political discussion efficacy Civility Tolerance Trust Political participation

Table 1. The research model

3 Methods

A pre-/post- field experiment was conducted on three stimuli. These three different structural features of online discussion settings included: social identity cues (showing social identity cues vs. anonymity), moderation (moderated vs. nonmoderated), and reinforcement of efficacy (point reward system vs. no such system). The combination of these resulted in eight different experimental conditions.

First, in the 'social identity cue' condition, individuals writing messages to the discussion group were required to reveal their social identities: gender, age, and region. These social identity cues were displayed next to the user nickname at each posting. Second, in the 'moderation' condition, moderators greeted the participants. Three trained moderators shared the work of 'management and regulation' of the four 'moderated' groups, providing 'supplementary information and other materials' collected from mass media or the Internet on a regular basis, posting rules and etiquette guidelines for the discussion, and sending 'warnings' to ill-mannered participants. Finally, where the efficacy reinforcement condition was applied, each participant received an icon in the shape of a cylindrical barometer. The barometer 'reading' changed as the participant accrued points, based on the frequency of postings, frequency of being read by someone else, and number of favorable replies. The more the participants wrote, were read by others, and received favorable replies from others, the higher the reading on the barometer icon.

Procedures

When users logged on to the Daum portal site and visited the 'Discussion Plaza' page set up for the 2004 Korean general elections, they were asked to 'sign in'. At the point of initial sign-in, participants were randomly assigned to one of the eight experimental conditions, i.e., the discussion groups. This process was preprogrammed in such a way that subsequent visits were automatically directed to the preassigned experimental group.

The plaza launched on February 9, sixty-six days before the general election in Korea (April 15, 2004), and people began to post messages or replies. An online survey (pre-test) through email to discussion plaza participants ran from March 8 through March 18. The survey posed questions on communicator characteristics such as communication competence, Internet literacy, and political involvement as well as questions about the person's demographics, ideological tendency, and mass media usage, including Internet. By April 15, the number of participants who signed on to the plaza totaled 36,485. Among these, 15,996 participants actually left more than one message on the discussion group. That is, more than half of the participants were just lurking at the site rather than posting any messages.

In the post-test survey, more than two million email surveys were sent out to the Daum portal users, and 52,419 were completed (return rate 2.4%). Among the participants who signed on to the discussion group, 6,542 completed the survey. On April 15, the final day of the experiment, those who had completed the survey and left more than one message on the message board totaled 2,777.

Stimulus Evaluation Tests

We employed to two methods to evaluate whether the experimental treatments produced the kinds of responses that were theoretically expected.

First, during the early period of experimentation, two student samples (one of thirty-one students, the other containing forty-four) among the participants were recruited to report on the distinctiveness, effectiveness, and conventionality of the discussion plaza. After, the experimenters analyzed the reports and drew implications for management of the experiment. The reports suggested few difficulties in assuming the kinds of effects that this experiment was expected to produce. Secondly, three questions regarding the evaluation of the Daum Communication Service were included in the post-test. Detailed analyses of the data revealed no sign of significant differences in evaluation across the experimental conditions in terms of distinctiveness, ease of use, or satisfaction.

4 Key Findings

The major findings reported in three papers (Kim and Rhee 2006; Rhee and Kim 2006; Rhee, Kim, and Moon 2004) can be summarized as follows:

Reading Versus Writing

In the online discussion plaza, participants were more likely to be engaged in reading than writing. Among 32,647 participants, who read other participants' postings an average of 30.7 times, only 15,996 (49.0%) actually wrote for the discussion plaza. The number of postings per participant averaged 1.5. Reading was significantly associated with communicative competence, political liberalism, political knowledge, and political information seeking in newspapers and television news, even after controlling for positive effects of gender (male), age, and education. By contrast, writing was correlated only with communication competence and political liberalism. More importantly, reading was significantly predicted by civility, tolerance, and political participation. By contrast, writing was accounted for by political discussion efficacy and political participation.

Quantity and Quality of Discussion

The presence of a moderator was found to *decrease* the number of message postings. Participants in the moderated condition seemed to be more cautious than their unmoderated counterparts in writing about the election. A borderline effect was found in the reinforcement of deliberation efficacy on the number of message postings. The treatment variables of social identity/anonymity and inclusion/noninclusion of a moderator produced significant effects on a surrogate measure of quality. In addition, participants in the moderated group wrote messages that were read more often than those written by counterparts in other groups.

There were significant interactive effects between moderation and other experimental treatments. Participants in both the moderated and social identity cues groups were most likely to be read by other participants. Anonymity, as opposed to displaying social identity cues, produced more engagement in deliberation. Reinforcement of deliberation efficacy (through 'points') also increased the frequency of responses generated by a message.

Political Discussion Efficacy

Display of social identity cues was found to be significant in increasing political discussion efficacy. The effect of the reinforcement/points system on political discussion efficacy was positive but only borderline significant. Discussion quantity and quality significantly affected political discussion efficacy. However, tests for interaction effects between the experimental conditions and the quantity and quality variables did not approach significance.

Considering that some people were more sociopolitically and psychologically disposed to demonstrate political discussion efficacy than others, such factors are included in the analysis. When controlling for these variables, the effect of 'display of social identity cues' and 'discussion quality' on political discussion efficacy remained significant while all of the other main effects and interaction effects showed no significance.

Tolerance, Trust, and Other Outcome Measures

No significant findings were obtained as the main effects of the experimental treatments on civility, tolerance, and trust. However, positive empirical associations between reading and civility and between reading and tolerance were found to be significant. Further analyses of possible interaction effects between the experimental conditions and other mediating variables on the outcome measures remain to be conducted.

5 Conclusion

Based on the assumptions that various communication channels offer different structural and regulative conditions of communication and that they affect deliberative behavior and its consequences, we conducted a field experiment on the Internet to examine whether these conditions of communication affect not only the quantity and quality, but also other outcome measures of online deliberation. The three experimental conditions on which this study focused have produced some nuanced effects on the quantity and quality of online deliberation. It was also found that the 'social identity cue' factor showed the most significant effect on political discussion efficacy followed by the 'reinforcement system' factor.

The findings in this experimental project taken together provide strong support for the role of structural and regulative conditions of communication in producing better deliberation outcomes. The conditions under which deliberation is conducted have significant impacts on its quantity and quality and also on its consequences, such as political discussion efficacy. The effects were confirmed through a field experiment which controlled for the impacts of sociodemographic conditions and individual differences in Internet use.

A field experiment on the Internet clarifies the empirical conditions under which Internet discussion substantially contributes to deliberative democracy. Deliberative actions and their consequences differ depending on the specific process of communication, which can be effectively explored by experimental research whose conditions can be manipulated and tested. What invokes the effect of deliberation is not the talk itself but the specific process of talking—that is, the way people talk to each other. Future studies are expected to explore various potential outcomes of online deliberation such as content of discussions, flaming behaviors, knowledge gains, attitude change, participatory acts, the level of trust, and others. In this way, empirical findings can effectively be transformed into theories of deliberation.

References

Corrado, A. and C. Firestone. 1999. *Elections in Cyberspace: Toward a New Era in American Politics*. Washington, DC: The Aspen Institute.

Coleman, S. and Gøtze, J. 2001. *Bowling Together Online: Public Engagement in Policy Deliberation*. Available at http://www.bowlingtogether.net/about.html (last accessed August 21, 2008)

Delli Carpini, M. X., F. L. Cook, and L. R. Jacobs. 2004. Public Deliberation, Discursive Participation, and Citizen Engagement: A Review of the Empirical Literature. *Annual Review of Political Science* 7: 315-344.

Dryzek, J. S. 1990. *Discursive Democracy: Politics, Policy and Political science*. Cambridge, UK: Cambridge University Press.

Edwards, A. 2002. The Moderator as an Emerging Democratic Intermediary: The Role of the Moderator in Internet Discussions About Public Issues. *Information Polity* 7(1): 3-20.

Fishkin, J. S. 2003. *Deliberative Polling: Toward a Better-Informed Democracy*. Available at http://cdd.stanford.edu/polls/docs/summary (last accessed August 21, 2008)

Habermas, J. 1996. Three Normative Models of Democracy. *Democracy and Difference: Contesting the Boundaries of the Political*, ed. S. Benhabib, 22-30. Princeton: Princeton University Press.

Hansen, K. M. 1999. *The Deliberative Poll*. Paper presented at the conference of Elites and Democracy, Copenhagen, Denmark, December 1999.

Iyengar, S., R. C. Luskin, and J. Fishkin. 2003. *Facilitating Informed Public Opinion*. Available at http://cdd.stanford.edu/research/papers/2003/facilitating.pdf (last accessed August 21, 2008)

Kim, E. and Rhee, J. W. 2006. Rethinking 'Reading Online'. *Korean Journal of Journalism and Communication Studies* 50(4): 65-94. (In Korean)

Lea, M., R. Spears, and D. de Groot, D. 1991. Knowing Me, Knowing You: Anonymity Effects on Social Identity Processes Within Groups. *Personality and Social Psychological Bulletin* 27(5): 526-537.

Norris, P. 2000. *A Virtuous Circle: Political Communication in Post-Industrial Societies*. Cambridge: Cambridge University Press.

Price, V. and J. Cappella. 2002. Online Deliberation and Its Influence the Electronic Dialogue Project in Campaign 2000. *IT & Society* 1(1): 303-329.

Price, V., D. Golthwaite, J. Cappella, and A. Romantan. 2002. *Online Discussion, Civic Engagement, and Social Trust*. Paper presented at the annual meeting of the International Communication Association, Seoul, July 17, 2002.

Rhee, J. W. and E. Kim. 2006. *The Effect of Online Deliberation on Political Discussion Efficacy: A Field Experiment on Internet Discussion Groups*. Paper presented to the Political Communication Division at the annual meeting of the International Communication Association, Dresden, June 23, 2006.

Rhee, J. W., E. Kim, and T. Moon. 2004. *The Effects of Structural and Regulative Conditions of Communication on the Quantity and Quality of Online Deliberation: Preliminary Results from the Daum Deliberative Democracy Project*. Paper presented to the Theory and Methodology Division at the annual meeting of the Association for Education in Mass Communication and Journalism, Toronto, August 21, 2004.

Rheingold, H. 1993. *The Virtual Community: Homesteading on the Electronic Frontier*. New York; HarperCollins.

Rice, R. E. 1984. Mediated Group Communication. *The New Media: Communication, Research, and Technology*, eds. R. E. Rice and Associates, 129-56. Beverly Hills, CA: Sage.

Trénel, M. 2009. Facilitating and Inclusive Deliberation. *Online Deliberation: Research, Practice, and Design*, eds. T. Davies and S. P. Gangadharan, 253-257. Stanford, CA: CSLI Publications.

20

The Role of the Moderator: Problems and Possibilities for Government-Run Online Discussion Forums

SCOTT WRIGHT

1 Introduction

Governments at all levels, and across many continents, have adopted online discussion forums as a means to promote democratic participation. These vary greatly in structure and may encourage a two-way link between government and people and/or help create a virtual public sphere (Wright 2002). Asynchronous forums might facilitate the kind of large-scale discussion often considered unrealistic. Thus, they have the potential to facilitate broader-based interactive policy making (Coleman and Gøtze 2001; Wright and Street 2007). New technologies do not, however, deterministically produce idealized conditions for discussion. There are many potential problems such as flaming and polarized debates. Moderators, it is sometimes suggested, are crucial to shaping the democratic potential of online discussion, because they help to mitigate many problems by actively intervening in the debates (Edwards 2002; Coleman and Gøtze 2001; Wright 2006b, 2007). There is, however, a great deal of confusion about exactly what roles moderators should, and do, perform (Barber 2003). This, in turn, leads to disputes about the nomenclature for such activities: are they moderators, facilitators, or censors?

Online Deliberation: Design, Research, and Practice.
Todd Davies and Seeta Peña Gangadharan (eds.).
Copyright © 2009, CSLI Publications.

This chapter develops two models that take account of the different roles which moderators perform in government-run online discussion forums. Two case studies, approximate to these models, are then presented. First, the Downing Street website. This featured a large-scale moderated discussion forum. Second, Citizen Space's E-democracy Forum, which was a smaller, policy-linked forum with interactive moderation. The case studies will highlight the practical positives and negatives of these models and lead to the generation of a series of policy suggestions about how the e-discussion agenda can be taken forward.

2 The Necessity of Moderation

Moderation is generally thought to positively influence the quality and usefulness of government-run online debates. For Kearns et al. (2002): 'The use of moderators is important in keeping citizen engagement focused and in consequently ensuring that such engagement adds value to services, to policy, and to citizens' (26). This is because: 'Free speech without regulation becomes just noise; democracy without procedure would be in danger of degenerating into a tyranny of the loudest shouter—or, in the case of e-democracy, the most obsessive, loquacious poster' (Blumler and Coleman 2001: 17-18). Barber (2003) likewise supports this position. He states: 'The question is not whether or not to facilitate, mediate, and gate-keep. It is *which* form of facilitation, *which* mediation, and *which* gatekeeper? The pretence that there can be none at all, that discourse is possible on a wholly unmediated basis, breeds anarchy rather than liberty and data overload rather than knowledge' (42). For Edwards (2002), 'the moderator can be characterized as a democratic intermediary' but must be independent of government in order to avoid a 'shadow of control' (5).

Blumler and Coleman (2001) argue for the creation of a civic commons in cyberspace, under the umbrella of 'a new kind of public agency' that would 'connect the voice of the people more meaningfully to the daily activities of democratic institutions' (16). This organization would be funded publicly but would be independent of government. Although such a proposal has many potential benefits, it is unclear how the summaries produced by such a body would be fed into the political process and what is meant, in practice, by the requirement that public bodies would 'be expected to react formally to whatever emerges from the discussion' (16). Secondly, it is questionable whether the rules and reports produced by an overarching body would be suitable across all government contexts.

3 The Fear of Moderation

In general, there is neither an acceptance of moderators as enhancing democracy, nor of what activities a moderator should perform. In fact, moderation does not come without potential costs if it is poorly structured, and can be very counterproductive (Coleman, Hall, and Howell 2002). Noveck (2004) has argued that: 'To be deliberative, the conversation must be free from censorship' and this 'includes any distortion or restraint of speech that would hinder the independence of the discussion or cause participants to self-censor' (22).[1] But I argue that we must be very careful not to automatically demonize the censorial role of the moderator: there are legitimate reasons for censoring the content of online discussion forums. This is because in the online world, constitutive (and/or self) censorship is arguably weakened by perceived anonymity.[2] Moral and social cues that shape speech acts are missing, and this gives people greater freedom to use profanity.

The fear remains, however, that the power to moderate the content of online forums will be abused. This could be done by setting overly restrictive rules or by ignoring 'fair' rules and deleting messages that are critical of the authority involved. It is, thus, necessary to draw a line between legitimate and illegitimate censorship. Determining what constitutes legitimate censorship is dependent on the context and is thus hard to define except in broad terms. Legitimate censorship could be defined as occurring when messages are deleted that do not meet specific, and open, rules for debate that have been discussed and agreed upon by a range of stakeholders. Illegitimate censorship occurs, then, when the rules are either too restrictive or are ignored by the moderator. To avoid value judgments, the analysis here will concentrate on whether or not the given rules were enforced.

The development and enforcement of moderation rules must be seen as fair—a complicated endeavor given that censorship can appear arbitrary. A great deal of trust has to be placed in the judgment of the moderator not to unduly censor messages. However, who should moderate discussions? Should it be independent, trained moderators, relevant policy experts, or 'unbiased' software? Because it is difficult to know when messages are being censored, these sorts of questions prove complicated to answer.

---

[1] Despite such an unequivocal statement against censoring discussions, the Unchat software, which was designed in relation to the values listed, contained a number of flexible censorship tools, potentially open to both individual participants and site administrators

[2] Constitutive censorship relates to the latent, taken-for-granted rules by which discourse is structured (McGuigan 1996).

4 The Form of Moderation

Moderators can perform a range of duties. These are shaped by administrative aims, the technology used, the institutional context, the funding given to support the moderator, and by the moderator's decisions which determine the extent to which rules are followed. The list of potential roles presented below can be used interchangeably by moderators dependent on the specific aims and context:

- Greeter: making people feel welcome
- Conversation Stimulator: posing new questions and topics, playing devil's advocate in existing conversations
- Conflict Resolver: mediating conflicts towards collective agreements (or agreeing to disagree)
- Summarizer of debates
- Problem Solver: directing questions to relevant people for response
- Supporter: bringing in external information to enrich debates, support arguments
- Welcomer: bringing in new participants, either citizens or politicians/civil servants
- 'Cybrarian': providing expert knowledge on particular topics
- Open Censor: deleting messages deemed inappropriate, normally against predefined rules and criteria. Feedback is given to explain why, and an opportunity to rewrite is provided
- Covert Censor: deleting messages deemed inappropriate, but without explaining why
- Cleaner: removing or closing dead threads, hiving off subdiscussions into separate threads

Two broad models have been developed that take account of the potential forms of moderation. These are not fixed models. Moderation policies evolve and change in response to events. For example, if consensus is the goal, mediation strategies come to the fore (Morison and Newman 2001). They are, thus, intended as guides. A third possible model is unmoderated forums, e.g. Usenet. This is not explored here as no government-run forum was found to have adopted this policy.[3]

---

[3] A further independent variable is the use of mechanized moderation on top of human moderation. Mechanized moderation is an electronic filter that blocks specific barred words. It is also possible for individual users to control the content that is made visible to them through 'kill files' on some forums. These block messages on particular topics or from specific people.

5 Content Moderation: The Downing Street Website

One model is human-based content moderation. The rules for moderation are set by the institution. This is a silent form of moderation because no feedback is given either to posters or to the institution. Silent moderation can create a conspiratorial atmosphere as messages are removed without explanation (Coleman, Hall, and Howell 2002). This is exacerbated if debates are not fed into the decision making process. Coleman (2001) describes this as 'tokenism', arguing that it is very counterproductive because: 'rational citizens seek outcomes from their participation and meaningful outcomes often depend upon there being a link between the virtual world of open discussion and the physical world of complex political relationships and institutions' (120).

The Downing Street website's online discussion forums differed from this model in two important ways. First, it used post-moderation: messages went straight onto the discussion forum before being moderated. Second, at least during the early stages of the forum, a mechanical filter was used in combination with human moderation.

The Downing Street website was redesigned on the February 10, 2000, and two discussion forums, 'Speaker's Corner' and 'Policy Forum', were added in an attempt to create a 'two-way link between government and people'.[4] In contradiction to the aim, limited resources meant only a selection of posts received Official Responses: around 0.27% in the Speaker's Corner and these were primarily to questions about the discussion board itself (Wright 2002). This is unsurprising as the forums were moderated by the website team rather than by people with a direct policy making background.

The primary task for Downing Street's moderators was moderating the content of messages. Determining whether messages breach posting rules is subjective. One person might consider the word 'prat' acceptable while another might not. The degree of subjectivity can be limited by having clear and detailed guidelines. In this case, the rules were quite vague. Initially, the site carried only a warning not to swear because children may visit the site. This was subsequently strengthened, in line with government guidelines: 'Please do not make inappropriate postings, including those containing offensive, defamatory or libelous comments'.[5] Nevertheless Kevin Webster, Chairman of the site's Independent Users Group, noted that the

---

[4] This quote forms part of the original stated aim of the site.

[5] See http://www.cabinet-office.gov.uk/moderngov/download/modgov.pdf (last accessed October 6, 2008).

Downing Street discussion forum had 'become a haven for people to post offensive and meaningless messages'.

To give an idea of the number of abusive messages and thus highlight exactly why content moderation was necessary, a search for various offensive words was conducted on a random sample of seven forums from the second version of the discussion board.[6] In total, there were 256 messages (out of 20,540 total, including all 'missing' messages) that featured one or more of the words (some messages contained literally hundreds of swear words, but are counted here as one). The findings suggest that the government was justified in moderating the content of the discussions as there were numerous offensive messages—although arguably the use of profanity was surprisingly small given the volume of messages involved.

The problem for Downing Street was drawing a line between 'abuse' and legitimate criticism of the government. The site was, after all, designed to make government more transparent and accountable. The moderators noted: 'it is often a difficult line to tread to ensure that the debate is kept as open as possible, while removing inappropriate postings. The emotive topics which are discussed on this forum make that task particularly challenging'.[7] Indeed, a number of mistakes were recognized: 'The Magna Carta was deleted in error, I know that it has caused a lot of irritation and please accept my apologies for the mistake'.[8]

We have seen that censoring the content of online discussion is necessary if debates are not to be fractured by rude language. There is still a fear that moderators might abuse this power and censor messages that legitimately criticize the government. Such a fear would appear to have been at least partially upheld. There were numerous claims that Downing Street officials censored discussions inappropriately, particularly in the first incarnation of the forum. The IR35 discussion forum was particularly heated and many critical messages 'magically disappeared overnight'.[9] This created bad publicity for the government, leading to accusations of excessive control and censorship in the Times and technological naivety in The Observer.

---

[6] The discussion board collapsed on May 12, 2000, after the message number field exceeded 32,767. The site designers took this opportunity to improve the software. Unfortunately, all the messages that were made to the forum before this crash were lost—except for the http://no10.quiscustodiet.net/ (last accessed October 6, 2008) cache, which had copies of all the messages that were sent to the forum.

[7] See http://archive.cabinetoffice.gov.uk/moderngov/download/modgov.pdf (last accessed October 6, 2008).

[8] See http://no10.quiscustodiet.net/cgi-bin/show_archive2?fid=13&mid=31968 (last accessed October 6, 2008).

[9] See posts in the IR 35 Forum 15/03/2000 (IR 35 refers to income taxation and the self-employed). Archived at: http://no10.quiscustodiet.net/cgi-bin/archive2?fid=73 (last accessed October 6, 2008).

Two deleted messages are presented below, taken from the first incarnation of the forum at the time by the Quiscustodiet team:[10]

> Shouldn't this website be independent of any particular party? It definitely tries to give the impression that the labour party and the government are the same thing whereas they are merely the current 'majority shareholders'. Is there an independent alternative to this site?

And:

> What is the point of this website if the points made and questions posed are not responded to by government?
>
> If we cannot expect some level of response we may as well make the point with a paint can on the nearest wall!! Government must do more than just provide the 'wall' and then pretend they are a listening open government because they opened a website.

In the light of the rules, it is difficult to explain why these messages were deleted. Removing them appears to be politically motivated: they criticize the government/website without the use of foul, racist, libelous, or offensive language.

Moderators do not just delete messages because of their content, however. They also perform housekeeping functions such as deleting stale threads. Such legitimate activities heavily shaped the discussions: 53.9% of messages sent to the Downing Street website were not visible at the end. Undoubtedly the majority of these deletions were legitimate. However, there was still the potential for this to lead to accusations of censorship: several moderation practices were not listed in the rules. Most importantly, if a message did not receive a reply within three days, it was automatically deleted and messages that replied to a deleted message were also deleted in an attempt to maintain the coherence of the discussions. Thus, in contradiction to the rules, many legitimate messages were deleted. This was further complicated by the use of a language filter that operated on the first version of the site.[11] It was initially set to block messages containing words such as 'bomb', 'anarchy', and 'fairy', but these were significantly reduced after complaints. Such practices explain much of the controversy about political censorship.

---

[10] A systematic analysis of censorship during the first incarnation is not possible because of the way the data was stored.

[11] See http://no10.quiscustodiet.net/cgi-bin/show_archive2?fid=13&mid=33800 (last accessed October 6, 2008).

6 Interactive Moderation: The E-democracy Forum

A second model is interactive moderation. In this model, the communication is two-way and the moderator far more interventionist. This model is approximate to Edwards' conceptualization of the moderator as a democratic intermediary (Edwards 2002). The moderator brings both new citizens and political institutions into the discussion, encourages existing users to respond, moderates the content of messages and attempts to maintain civility, where possible, by persuasion and not censorship, frames the debate and sets subtopics, provides feedback to the institution, and participates in the debates.

The E-democracy forum, hosted on Citizen Space, was a small-scale, policy-linked discussion board that included 427 posts in 73 separate threads. A system of interactive pre-moderation was adopted, mitigating the problem of inappropriate posts being aired publicly before being removed. Moderators gave ongoing feedback and generally guided the discussions by providing topics for debate. Although the moderator initiated the most new threads, these topics also produced the most responses: 31.9% of all discussion.[12] The moderator was also successful in getting politicians to participate.

Moderators adopted stricter rules and regulations than found on the Downing Street website, yet fewer messages were censored: 26.3% (152 of 579). These were censored either because messages were repeats, used foul language, had inappropriate Web links, or were considered off-topic.[13] The lower levels of censorship can probably be explained by this forum's lower profile and less emotive topic.

Despite the time and resources invested in premoderation, the results could be considered ambiguous. It was 'not possible to conclude that the provision of the consultation on the Internet significantly increased the number of people included or the spread of the e-democracy debate'.[14]

---

[12] This is only a rough guideline, because it does not take into account the number of initiated topics. Secondly, discussions within a topic tend to have a life on their own and move on from the initial post. Thus, people are often not responding to the initial post.

[13] See http://web.archive.org/web/*/http://www.edemocracy.gov.uk/feedback/responses/edemocracy_discussion_final_summary.doc (last accessed November 15, 2008, original site, http://www.edemocracy.gov.uk/feedback/responses/edemocracy_discussion_final_summary.doc is no longer available).

[14] See http://web.archive.org/web/*/http://www.edemocracy.gov.uk/downloads/your_response_report.doc (last accessed November 14, 2008, original site, http://www.edemocracy.gov.uk/downloads/your_response_report.doc is no longer available). The online provision was, however, 'particularly successful in distributing the consultation

Moreover, it is not clear what effect the forum had. A consultation report was developed which showed that messages were analyzed at some length, but the development of a formal policy has floundered (Wright 2006a).

7 Conclusion

This analysis has highlighted the problems and possibilities when moderating government-run online discussion forums. Interactive moderation can promote discussion and bring in new participants and can, thus, produce democratic/discursive benefits. The extent to which benefits outweigh financial costs depends on the aims and size of the discussion. The value of this model decreases for larger discussion forums.

On the downside, numerous problems were discovered, particularly with the large, content-moderated Downing Street website. Most prominent were allegations of censorship that dogged the forum. This was primarily a structural problem caused by poorly designed and poorly advertized rules. To resolve this, following Blumler and Coleman, and Edwards, I argue that the censorial power of the moderator would most fruitfully be enforced by an independent body following detailed (and openly available) rules set by the institution in negotiation with a range of stakeholders. This proposal differs from their models in which there is a link to policy making. I argue that it would be beneficial to separate the roles of the moderator into two clearly defined areas. Independent censors would be supplemented by civil servant facilitators. This would stop the facilitator (and government) being tainted by accusations of censorship. It would also mean that the facilitator would have direct experience of, and links with, the governmental body concerned—mitigating both the problems experienced on the Downing Street website, and with Blumler and Coleman's model wherein the summarizer does not have direct experience of the policy being discussed.[15] The moderator can, thus, perform important democratic functions, but such practices are not without problems and must be carefully planned and thought through.

---

document' with 22,000 copies of the main document being downloaded and about 18,500 copies of the background and summary.

[15] This is not to say that this model must always be used. The strategy must be adopted in relation to the aims—one can envision situations where having completely independent facilitators would be appropriate.

Acknowledgements

A longer version of this chapter was published in 2006: Government-run Online Discussion Fora: Moderation, Censorship and the Shadow of Control. *British Journal of Politics and International Relations* 8(4): 550-568.

References

Barber, B. 2003. Which Technology and Which Technology? *Democracy and New Media*, eds. H. Jenkins and D. Thorburn, 33-47. Cambridge, MA: MIT Press.

Blumler, J. G. and S. Coleman. 2001. *Realising Democracy Online: A Civic Commons in Cyberspace*. London: Institute for Public Policy Research.

Coleman, S. 2001. The Transformation of Citizenship. *New Media and Politics*, eds. B. Axford and R. Huggins. London: Sage.

Coleman, S. and J. Gøtze. 2001. *Bowling Together: Online Public Engagement in Policy Deliberation*. London: Hansard Society.

Coleman, S., N. Hall, and M. Howell. 2002. *Hearing Voices: The Experience of Online Public Consultations and Discussions in UK Governance*. London: Hansard Society.

Edwards, A. 2002. The Moderator as an Emerging Democratic Intermediary: The Role of the Moderator in Internet Discussions about Public Issues. *Information Polity* 7(1): 3-20.

Kearns, I., J. Bend, and B. Stern. 2002. *E-participation in Local Government*. London: Institute for Public Policy Research.

McGuigan, J. 1996. *Culture and the Public Sphere*. London: Routledge.

Morison, J. and D. R. Newman. 2001. On-line Citizenship: Consultation and Participation in New Labour's Britain and Beyond. *International Review of Law, Computers and Technology* 15(2): 171-194.

Noveck, B. S. 2004 Unchat: Democratic Solution for a Wired World. *Democracy Online: The Prospects for Political Renewal through the Internet*, ed. P. M. Shane, 21-34. London: Routledge.

Wright, S. 2002. Dogma or Dialogue? The Politics of the Downing Street website. *Politics* 22(3): 135-142.

Wright, S. 2006a. Electrifying Democracy: 10 Years of Policy and Practice. *Parliamentary Affairs* 59(2): 236-249.

Wright, S. 2006b. Government-run Online Discussion Fora: Moderation, Censorship and the Shadow of Control. *British Journal of Politics and International Relations* 8(4): 550-568.

Wright, S. 2007. A Virtual European Public Sphere? The Futurum Discussion Forum. *Journal of European Public Policy* 14(8): 1167-1185.

Wright, S. and J. Street. 2007. Democracy, Deliberation and Design: The Case of Online Discussion Forums. *New Media and Society* 9(5): 849-869.

21

Silencing the Clatter: Removing Anonymity from a Corporate Online Community

GILLY LESHED

1 Introduction

As we evaluate various arrangements in online communities, one crucial question is how anonymity impacts discussion. This chapter describes a closed intra-corporate message-board community, which upon establishment allowed anonymous participation, but at a certain point, following a managerial decision, enforced identity exposure. The policy change is analyzed through an examination of participation and discussion style, worker and management attitudes, and employee-employer relationships. This case study illuminates issues of privacy in the face of both managers and co-workers, revealing the power of online anonymity policy to facilitate or inhibit open discussion in a community.

2 Privacy in the Information Age

Privacy encompasses a wide range of beliefs as to what this concept means in different contexts. In terms of personal information exposure, the definition of privacy has developed over many years from 'the right to be let alone' (Warren and Brandeis 1890), to the right to control one's information disclosure, 'with only extraordinary exceptions in the interest of so-

Online Deliberation: Design, Research, and Practice.
Todd Davies and Seeta Peña Gangadharan (eds.).
Copyright © 2009, CSLI Publications.

ciety' (Westin 1967). In recent years, intricate variations of information privacy ideas have evolved, regarding individuals' expectations for fairness of use and control over personal information, anonymity when surfing the Web, and confidentiality of communicating parties (Berman and Mulligan 1999).

The evolution of the definition of information privacy reveals how charged this issue is, caused in part by constantly increasing surveillance capabilities. Present communication systems are no longer private. From cell phones to electronic messaging systems, transactional data is collected and stored, and can later be accessed, analyzed, and shared (Dempsey 1997). Berman and Bruening (2001) suggest that privacy today means the protection of the individual's autonomy as it relates to collecting and using personal information, particularly by the government. As surveillance tools become pervasive and standard practices involve personal data collection, keeping individuals unreachable is a great challenge and requires a change in public awareness (Nissenbaum 1999).

One way to consider privacy relationships involving authorities and individuals is by translating this relationship to that of employer-employee and examining the workplace setting. While it is important to protect employees' privacy, the employer is generally able 'to do what is necessary to earn profits' (King 1994). Employers are armed with tools capable of collecting information about their employees' Web surfing and email transactions, and there are different views as to whether employers should use these tools (Koprowski 1997). Employees have diverse views regarding the types of information they tolerate their employers to monitor or prefer to keep private (Edmonds and Braasch 2001).

3   Online Anonymity

The scale of online privacy runs from complete identifiability to complete anonymity. Providing complete anonymity allows communicators to decide which pieces of their identity to expose. Alternatively, knowing the identity of one's interlocutor is not only essential for understanding and evaluating the interaction but also plays a role in motivating people to participate in the discussion (Donath 1999). When identity is concealed, people learn about their interlocutors from such cues as writing style and the ways they interact with others in the online environment.

Online anonymity helps individuals feel free to participate and express thoughts and, at the same time, lessens ridicule and embarrassment (Nissenbaum 1999). This suggests that the Internet as a communication medium must allow its users the right to remain anonymous online (Oakes 1999). Conversely, online anonymity might also be detrimental. The main risk of anonymity is the loss of accountability. Those responsible for any misconduct cannot be identified and brought to justice (Wallace 1999), as in Dibbell's (1993) 'rape in cyberspace' where the real user behind 'Mr. Bungle' was not punished for his online misbehavior. The price may be, as Davenport (2002) suggests, an incremental breakdown of the fabric of society. In discussing the tradeoffs of anonymity and accountability, the online context should be carefully analyzed for making decisions about anonymity policy (Teich et al. 1999).

The role of anonymity can be analyzed empirically by observing the effects of an online venue's anonymity policy on various dimensions of the discussion. The case described in the following section presents an online community within a workplace, meaning that online discussants may actually be colleagues. Further, the online anonymity policy was changed at a certain point of time, requiring the community to adjust accordingly, and providing an opportunity for pre- and postchange analysis of the consequences of anonymity policy for online deliberation.

4   The Young and Fresh Community

Located in a high-tech corporate intranet, *The Young and Fresh* is a message board-style website, comprised of various discussion boards called *forums*. The forums are all non-work related topic threads, covering topics such as items for sale, recipes, sports, and so forth. Unlike other communities in the company targeting professional subsets of workers, this community aims to meet the needs of a few thousand company workers distributed across a few campuses. Workers use the forums to publish announcements, ask questions and receive answers, and share thoughts and opinions. A worker who accesses a forum sees on a webpage a listing of all the recent messages with their responses, including title, content, poster name, and posting date and time.

One factor that impacts *The Young and Fresh's* activity is that the company's intranet is an isolated network: Workers cannot access the Internet from their desktops inside the company's sites, and the intranet cannot be accessed from outside. This makes *The Young and Fresh* a closed community, and the only venue to communicate online with others about nonwork issues during the workday.

The Anonymity Policy Change

The Young and Fresh launched in December 2002, featuring anonymity on all of its forums. Each message included a free text 'name' field into which writers could type any name, or leave it blank. The typed name (if any) was then displayed with the message in the forum. However, users were aware that postings were not truly anonymous. All postings were saved in a database server with their posters' logged-in user names. The community moderator and a few system administrators had direct access to the posters' identities. Despite this caveat, I use the term 'anonymous forum' to indicate that anonymity for a poster existed with respect to the majority of workers who accessed the forums as ordinary members.

During the second half of 2003, following a series of personal defamations, sexual allusions, and blatant commercial advertisements, the company's management began deliberating on ways to cope with these troubling phenomena not observed previously in any of the online communities on the company's intranet. Management considered alternatives such as leaving the community as is, hoping for it to quiet down by itself, or shutting down the community entirely. The final decision, led by the Chief Knowledge Officer, was to remove anonymity from newly posted messages in the forums. Administered in October 2003 on eleven forums, the new practice automatically attached the name of the poster to every message, consisting of the worker's first and last name, retrieved from the database according to the login user name.

Only one forum, titled *Just Talking*, remained anonymous. The management chose to permit anonymity in *Just Talking* as it frequently carries political debates and complaints against the management. The management decided that this would allow workers to safely expose their opinions but that anonymity would remain only as long as language was properly used.

Before and After: Participation Patterns

Immediately after the anonymity policy change, posting frequency dropped by an average of 25% per month. Conversely, workers accessed the forums 20% per month more frequently than before the change. The increase in the visiting frequency can be explained by considering the time frame of the study: the first year of the community was a launching period during which workers discovered the forums and a critical mass of use was established (Markus 1987). Furthermore, forums were added over time, before as well as after the change, attracting new audiences. Along these lines, one could predict an increase in the posting frequency, whereas the opposite was observed.

The decrease in the posting frequency was observed in all the forums that turned identifiable after the change. For instance, the *Recipes* forum dropped from being one of the most popular forums before the change to one of the least popular after the change. The only exception was the *Just Talking* forum, which remained anonymous after the change and increased in its posting frequency. This implies that the new policy had an impact on reducing participants' desire to post messages.

Before and After: Discussion Style

Not only did workers post fewer messages after the change, the manner of discussion changed as well. First, excluding *Just Talking*, discussion threads turned flatter after the change: whereas before the change a posted message was likely to initiate a hierarchic chain of messages deliberating on an argument, after the change messages often remained solitary with no responses.[1]

Furthermore, conversations in the newly identifiable forums turned from dialogues with small talk often straying away from the forum's topic, into narrowly focused discussions. For example, the *Restaurants* forum hosted several conversations about a specific seafood restaurant. In the anonymous period these conversations typically started with general information about the restaurant and then drifted toward anecdotes of visits to that restaurant with zealous exchanges between seafood detesters and ardent fans. In contrast, conversations about the same restaurant in the identifiable period were short and conveyed only dry information about the restaurant location, menu, and prices.

Standpoint of Employers

After the change, several conversations about the anonymity removal were held in the *Just Talking* forum. The enduring anonymity along with this forum's theme made it the only venue that generated such discussions. Messages discussed issues such as the decreased traffic in the other forums, opinions regarding the new policy, and speculations about reasons for it. The following message thread is part of a conversation held two weeks after the change:

> Did you notice that since there is no anonymity, most of the forums, except this one, are empty?
>
>> I am not in favor of the anonymity. Whoever wants anonymity either wants to hide something or did something illegal... he'd better not talk at all...
>>
>>> The anonymity issue is important and undoubtedly influential, otherwise how can you explain the situation before and after? It may be that people just don't want everybody to know that they asked/answered/referred to something in the forum, concerned that their boss is noticing their postings...

This piece of conversation exemplifies the kind of concerns employees had about the anonymity removal. Interestingly, some of these discussions

---

[1] In the twelve forums that existed both before and after the change, there was a decrease of an average from 0.69 responses per message (SD=0.13) before the change to 0.50 responses per message (SD=0.21) after the change (t(11)=5.39, p<0.001).

emerged as a result of messages posted by the moderator, reminding members to use the *Just Talking* forum appropriately. The moderator participated in the discussions that arose, not explicitly expressing his opinion about the change but also noting the importance of keeping the *Just Talking* forum clean so that *'they don't cancel **our** anonymity in this forum as well'* (bolding added by author). With this wording, he staged himself as an ordinary community member rather than as one of the managers and implicitly signaled his adverse stance toward the change.

One issue that emerged was a concern for the death of the community. The employees believed that people's willingness to post messages was a direct consequence of the policy change. Direct managers and colleagues introduced new opportunity for surveillance of the exposed identities. The identifiability allows others to judge posters not only according to the contents of their messages but also to the volume of messages they post. Workers whose names appear frequently in the forums are considered loafers, writing messages instead of doing the work they are paid for.

Second, workers felt various satisfaction levels from the new policy that compels disclosing their identity. Some felt disappointed, angry, or cynical, expressing loss of interest and attractiveness of the community and feeling that their mouths were shut. In contrast, others welcomed the new policy they believed introduced honesty and accountability, appreciating the reduction in idle talk and inappropriate language use.

Third, workers put forward a variety of speculations regarding the reason for the policy change, as management did not publicly announce the reason. Some conjectured that the reason was improper language use. Others speculated about purposes such as cutting down irrelevant messages, limiting criticism against the management, and reducing time spent at work on nonwork activities. These opinions suggest that when a new policy is introduced, visibility of the motivations and the process may facilitate acceptance by the community participants that are influenced by it.

Management Standpoint

According to the management's official position, they were not concerned about misusing the forums for idleness, time wasting, criticism, or small talk. Instead, they respected the community participants as responsible workers who know how to manage their time and workload. Realizing the importance of the community in the workplace, they looked for a solution to keep it working, eliminating only inappropriate expressions in messages. The management was not interested in *who* was saying *what* and *how much* but rather concerned about *how things were said*. Deciding to remove anonymity, however, had further effects beyond controlling language use.

The chief knowledge officer, representing the management, believed the change defeated the community's ills and raised the level of discussion. On the contrary, the moderator felt that the decision was too extreme and that other methods to confront misbehavior could have been applied. In fact, he occasionally used his ability to identify posters, sending emails to those who posted extreme expressions. These emails adopted a personal worker-to-worker rather than supervisor-to-subordinate style, reminding the recipient of the ability to identify posters and that there is no guarantee that the management will never want to use this ability. The moderator believed that these emails were effective and that the impact of anonymity was too powerful for the community to endure its earlier and more open form.

5 Conclusions: The Effects of Online Policy Change

The management of the company stated a single purpose upon deciding on removing anonymity: to eliminate inappropriate language use in messages posted on the forums. The results exemplify how this simple policy change had a wider range of effects on participation, discussion structure and content, and workers' attitudes toward the workplace. Removing anonymity increased accountability, the effect that the management sought to achieve, and some of the workers appreciated that. However, it also affected responsible workers, taking away their sense of protection from gossip by their coworkers.

This understanding accords with the claim that careful contextual analysis should be carried out to balance between the benefits and costs when making a decision about online anonymity policy (Teich et al. 1999). The decision to *change* online policy, however, should involve even more comprehensive consideration, as the change is likely to have further effects beyond decisions made at the establishment of the community. For instance, the management's intervention in a venue considered to be the workers' territory was understood by some community members as a means to remove democratic attributes in the community and to control their voices.

Studies of online anonymity typically refer to Internet communities, referring to identity exposure toward the authorities (Davenport 2002) and the public (Donath 1999). Narrowing the discussion to the workplace often moves the discussion to employee-employer relationships (Westin 1996). The case of *The Young and Fresh* provides us with insight into the effects of online anonymity policy changes on a larger range of variables: the online setting, the participating individuals, and their relationships with each other and with policy makers.

Acknowledgments

I thank the people from the company who cooperated in obtaining materials for the study. Advice from Geri Gay and Tarleton Gillespie is gratefully acknowledged.

References

Berman, J. and P. Bruening. 2001. Is Privacy Still Possible in the Twenty-first Century? *Proceedings of Social Research, Special Issue on Privacy* 68(1): 306-318.

Berman, J. and D. Mulligan. 1999. Privacy in the Digital Age: Work in Progress. *Nova Law Review* 23(2): 551-582.

Davenport, D. 2002. Anonymity on the Internet: Why the Price May Be Too High. *Communications of the ACM* 45(4): 33-35.

Dempsey, J. X. 1997. Communications Privacy in the Digital Age: Revitalizing the Federal Wiretap Laws to Enhance Privacy. *Albany Law Journal of Science and Technology* 8(1): 65-120.

Dibbell, J. 1993. A Rape in Cyberspace. *The Village Voice* 38(51): 36-42.

Donath, J. S. 1999. Identity and Deception in the Virtual Community. *Communities in Cyberspace*, eds. P. Kollock and M. Smith, 29-59. London: Routledge.

Edmonds, P. and A. Braasch. 2001. Workplace Privacy: A Thing of the Past? *Techies.com*. (February 21, 2001). (Site no longer functional.)

King, D. N. 1994. Privacy Issues in the Private-Sector Workplace: Protection from Electronic Surveillance and the Emerging Privacy Gap. *Southern California Law Review* 67(2): 441-474.

Koprowski, G. J. 1997. Is Big Brother—or His Server—Watching You? *Wired News*. Available at http://www.wired.com/politics/law/news/1997/06/4184 (last accessed September 22, 2008)

Markus, M. L. 1987. Toward a 'Critical Mass' Theory of Interactive Media: Universal Access, Interdependence, and Diffusion. *Communications Research* 14(5): 491-511.

Nissenbaum, H. 1999. The Meaning of Anonymity in an Information Age. *The Information Society, Special Issue: Anonymous Communications on the Internet* 15(2): 141-144.

Oakes, C. 1999. Study: Online Anonymity Critical. *Wired News* (June 29, 1999). Available at http://www.wired.com/politics/law/news/1999/06/20480 (last accessed September 22, 2008)

Teich, A., M. S. Frankel, R. Kling, and Y. Lee. 1999. Anonymous Communication policies for the Internet: Results and recommendations of the AAAS conference. *The Information Society, Special Issue: Anonymous Communications on the Internet* 15(2): 71-77.

Wallace, K. A. 1999. Anonymity. *Ethics and Information Technology* 1: 23-35.

Warren, S. and L. Brandeis. 1890. The Right to Privacy. *Harvard Law Review* 4: 193-220.

Westin, A. F. 1967. *Privacy and Freedom*. New York: Atheneum.

Westin, A. F. 1996. Privacy in the Workplace: How Well Does American Law Reflect American Values. *Chicago-Kent Law Review* 72: 271-83.

22

Facilitation and Inclusive Deliberation

MATTHIAS TRÉNEL

1 The Problem of Internal Exclusion

While scholars of citizen deliberation frequently consider problems that participants face in accessing deliberative environments (see Cohen 1997), they often fail to address a more subtle form of exclusion that occurs within deliberative environments. As Young (2000: 53-65) explains, some participants may be marginalized *during* deliberation if they have lower chances to be heard, introduce topics, make contributions, or suggest or criticize proposals. In other words, they may face the problem of 'internal exclusion' (see also Habermas 1996).

To challenge this problem, facilitation may serve as an important means for inclusive deliberation. For example, facilitators or moderators can structure group communication in a way that empowers disadvantaged participants (Fung 2004; Fulwider 2005).[1] Still, evaluations of facilitation are infrequently studied (Sunwolf and Frey 2005). The study described here looks at the effects of different types of facilitation.

2 A Field Experiment in Facilitation

In 2002, the local municipal authorities sponsored Listening to the City Dialogues (LTC), a series of town hall meetings in New York, to gather populations. Among the 826 participants in the LTC-O, 45% were

---

[1] The words 'facilitator' and 'moderator' are used interchangeably here.
Online Deliberation: Design, Research, and Practice.
Todd Davies and Seeta Pena Gangadharan (eds.).
Copyright © 2009, CSLI Publications.

Manhattan residents, 9% were family members of 9/11 victims, and 12% classified themselves as survivors of 9/11. Participants were then assigned to twenty-six discussion groups aimed at gender and demographic heterogeneity within each group. With the exception of two groups which began later, all worked through the same five-step agenda (introductions, hopes and concerns, rebuilding and revitalization, creating a memorial, wrapping up) in parallel over the course of two weeks. While participants could read in all discussion groups, message posting was allowed only in the group they belonged to. Five hundred ninety-three participants contributed one message or more, leading to a total of 9036 messages.

Since the role of facilitators was not entirely consensual among the group of LTC-O conveners, a field experiment was designed (Figallo, Miller, and Weiss 2004). Discussion groups were evenly assigned to one of two conditions. In the *basic facilitation* condition, the task was to keep participants focused on the agenda and ensure rules of civility. Participants were notified by email when a new agenda item was scheduled. Also, deliberations were monitored, and, if necessary, a facilitator intervened to make sure that interpersonal conflicts did not disrupt discussion. However, as this was not often the case, facilitators remained invisible for the most part. The *advanced facilitation* condition augmented the basic condition with professional facilitators who were recruited for each discussion group, in order to balance participation, create a respectful climate, and stimulate, clarify, and summarize discussions (see Pyser and Figallo 2004).

3   The Difference That Facilitation Makes

LTC-O discussion archives were analyzed to assess the degree of inclusion of traditionally underprivileged groups. Figure 1 shows the percentage of women and non-whites among the population of New York City, among the upper quartile posters, who contributed about 80% of all messages in each discussion group.[2] A first comparison between population and registered participants indicates the degree of external exclusion. The 'exclusion curve' marks a significant decrease in inclusion for women and even more so for non-whites. A second comparison between registered and most involved participants suggests the degree of internal exclusion: Inclusion dropped further for women in the basic facilitation condition, but not in the advanced facilitation condition. The results for non-whites on internal inclusion and facilitation effects mirrored the pattern found for women.[3]

---

[2] Population figures are based on data from the US Census Bureau (2000).

[3] So did the pattern for participants with lower education and lower income. However, unlike for women, differences between the basic and advanced facilitation condition for

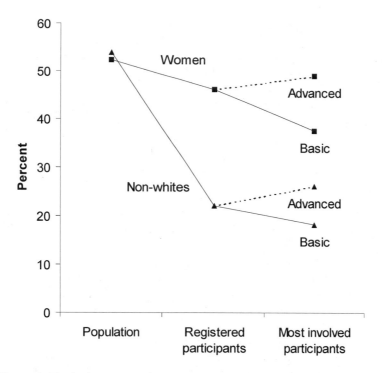

Figure 1. Exclusion curves for women and non-whites in the basic and advanced facilitation condition

These results suggest that the problem of internal exclusion is only serious under the condition of basic facilitation. This result is particularly troubling, as the basic facilitation approach seems to be the most common in the field of face-to-face and online deliberation (Rhee and Kim 2009; Wright 2009; Rosenberg 2004). Although basic facilitation may be inexpensive, require few specialized skills, and is easy to standardize and automate, it proves ineffective in avoiding further exclusion in deliberation.

Why then was the advanced facilitation approach more successful in empowering women to engage in deliberation? One possible explanation is that women felt more motivated because their specific use of rhetorical forms—they used narratives almost twice as often as men did in the LTC-O

---

nonwhites (as well as for lower education and lower income) failed to reach statistical significance. Still, there is good reason to believe that the problem of internal exclusion becomes equally acute for nonwhites (and people with low income or low education) once external exclusion is mitigated for them to the level women faced in the LTC-O.

(Polletta and Lee 2006)—was better accommodated. Thus, the challenge for facilitators in (online) deliberation is not only to provide a space for citizens with different interests and opinions but also to provide a space where citizens with different ways of expressing themselves feel equally welcome.

Advanced facilitation may include various facilitator competencies (Lieberman Baker and Fraser 2005) and forms of facilitation, such as Rosenberg's (2004) facilitation strategies for reason and transformation oriented deliberation, or Edwards' (2002) conceptualization of the moderator as a democratic intermediary. Further studies are needed to identify which of these are most effective in reducing internal exclusion.

References

Cohen, J. 1997. Deliberation and Democratic Legitimacy. *Contemporary Political Philosophy: An Anthology*, eds. R. Goodin and P. Pettit, 143-155. Oxford: Blackwell.

Edwards, A. E. 2002. The Moderator as an Emerging Democratic Intermediary: The Role of the Moderator in Internet Discussions about Public Issues. *Information Polity* 7:3-20.

Figallo, C., J. Miller, and M. N. Weiss. 2004. Listening to the City Online Dialogues: Overview and Observations. *Group Facilitation* 6(4): 25-32.

Fulwider, J. 2005. *Do Moderators Matter? Answering a Jury Deliberation Challenge to Deliberative Democracy*. Paper presented at the Annual Conference of the American Political Science Association, Washington, DC, September 1-4, 2005.

Fung, A. 2004. Deliberation's Darker Side: A Discussion with Iris Marion Young and Jane Mansbridge. *National Civic Review* 93(4): 47-54.

Habermas, J. 1996. *Between Facts and Norms: Contributions to a Discourse Theory of Law and Democracy*. Cambridge: MIT Press.

Lieberman Baker, L. and C. Fraser. 2005. Facilitator Core Competencies as Defined by the International Association of Facilitators. *The IAF Handbook of Group Facilitation*, ed. S. P. Schuman, 459-472. San Francisco: Jossey-Bass.

Lukensmeyer, C. J. and S. Brigham. 2002. Taking Democracy to Scale: Creating a Town Hall Meeting for the Twenty-First Century. *National Civic Review* 91(4): 351-366.

Polletta, F. and J. Lee. 2006. Is Telling Stories Good for Democracy? Rhetoric in Public Deliberation After 9/11. *American Sociological Review* 71(5): 699-723.

Pyser, S. N. and C. Figallo. 2004. The Listening to the City Online Dialogues Experience: The Impact of a Full Value Contract. *Conflict Resolution Quarterly* 21(3): 381-393.

Rhee, J. W. and E. Kim. 2009. Deliberation on the Net: Lessons from a Field Experiment. *Online Deliberation: Design, Research, and Practice*, eds. T. Davies and S. P. Gangadharan, 223-232. Stanford, CA: CSLI Publications.

Rosenberg, S. W. 2004. *Examining Three Conceptions of Deliberative Democracy: A field Experiment*. Paper presented at the conference Empirical Approaches to Deliberative Politics, Florence, May 21-22, 2004.

Schuman, S. P., ed. 2005. *Listening to the City: Public Participation and Group Facilitation in Redeveloping the World Trade Center Site*. College Station: VBW Publishing.

Sunwolf and L. R. Frey. 2005. Facilitating Group Communication. *The Handbook of Group Research and Practice*, ed. S. Wheelan, 485-510. Thousand Oaks: Sage.

United States Census Bureau. 2000. Available at http://www.census.gov/main/www/cen2000.html (last accessed November 1, 2008)

Wright, S. 2009. The Role of the Moderator: Problems and Possibilities for Government-Run Discussion Forums. *Online Deliberation: Design, Research, and Practice*, eds. T. Davies and S. P. Gangadharan, 233-242. Stanford, CA: CSLI Publications.

Young, I. M. 2000. *Democracy and Inclusion*. New York: Oxford University Press.

23

Rethinking the 'Informed' Participant: Precautions and Recommendations for the Design of Online Deliberation

KEVIN S. RAMSEY AND MATTHEW W. WILSON

One of the benefits of public deliberations often cited by practitioners and theorists alike is the potential to help participants become more informed about an issue, by providing them with relevant information and competing arguments. While the act of deliberation alone is often argued to provide this benefit (Eveland 2004), many deliberative forums also emphasize additional resources such as pamphlets, videos, or expert testimony to ensure all participants have access to balanced information (e.g., Fishkin and Farrar 2005). A growing trend in the field of public participation is to incorporate computers to enable participants to view and explore interactive maps and other multimedia information resources (Craig et al. 2002). These kinds of resources can be particularly useful in deliberations about urban planning or environmental issues, where they are used to help communicate complex ideas such as spatial equity or the predicted environmental impacts of a proposed action. One of the great promises of designing forums to support deliberations on the Internet is the ability to cost-effectively share multimedia resources with a far greater number of participants than can be done in face-to-face settings.

While this development is often interpreted as another positive step in narrowing the divide between citizens and experts, there has been very little research examining the impacts these information resources may have on

Online Deliberation: Design, Research, and Practice
Todd Davies and Seeta Peña Gangadharan (eds.).
Copyright © 2009, CSLI Publications.

the participants in public deliberations or on the dynamics of deliberative process. In this chapter, we bring a theoretical perspective to the questions: How is it that information resources made available in online deliberative forums help to create informed participants? Or in other words, what are the relationships between these information resources and the creation of informed deliberation participants? And, what does it mean to be an 'informed' participant?

To explore these questions, we are influenced by the work of Michel Foucault, specifically the notion that all information is located in networks of power through which information is produced and legitimized; and therefore information is not only partial and biased but also always political (Foucault 2003). We illustrate this point by examining the map—a commonly used information resource in deliberative forums. Drawing on geographic theorists we demonstrate how the map necessarily represents a privileged and politicized reality, while simultaneously enjoying an aura of objectivity that is not as readily given to textual evidence. We describe how this theoretical perspective problematizes the role of information resources in deliberation. We argue for a re-thinking of the ideal informed participant as someone who is not merely aware of the various facts and arguments about a given issue but able to critically assess and position those 'facts' and arguments in relation to shifting landscapes of power relations. We also describe significant implications of this theoretical perspective for the field of online deliberation. This is followed by a series of specific recommendations for the designers of online deliberative forums that may help orient participants to this kind of critical political awareness. Finally, we conclude with a set of precautions for researchers.

1   Rethinking Information and Politics

Supporting deliberation can be thought of as a project of shifting and controlling power relations among participants in such a way that results in a 'level playing field', where civil and equitable discussions over political matters can take place. The design of deliberative forums is often concerned with reducing obstacles to participation and ensuring that all background information is balanced and factual. Efforts are often made to reduce antagonisms and partisan politics, to ensure that discussions are reasoned and sensitive to multiple points of view. We wish to make a distinction between this more conventional treatment of *politics*—as something to be managed and minimized—with a conceptualization that acknowledges how politics permeates the very project of deliberation. Here, we draw on postfoundational approaches in order to resist fixed notions of the political in deliberative situations (see Sparke 2005).

We advocate the analysis and design of deliberations where all efforts of informing (the inclusion or exclusion of certain language or voices) are conceptualized as always-already political and produced through power. Therefore, the concern is not how to control the information and activities of the participants to reduce 'power struggles' and account for any difference but to realize that all information provided and all structuring of activities have political status. This section proposes a rethinking of information and politics in three discussions, around: a different conceptualization of power, a multiplicative approach to information, and the implications for this rethinking in the realm of the map.

Providing information during deliberative situations is *a priori* political. By this we specially mean that all information is produced through operations of power. Power enables certain closures and openings during the creation, packaging, and distribution of information resources. This production of information occurs through particular normalizations (including proficiencies, controlled vocabularies, relations of truth, ways of knowing). These normalizations work to politically produce an *informed* participant. Moreover, this idealized informed participant is entirely contingent upon power relations, including particular and situated knowledges (technical, social, cultural, political, or other ways of rationalizing and systematizing meaning). Many questions assist in making these relations more visible. What particular knowledges facilitated the material production of information resources before and during deliberation? How were these information resources presented during deliberation?

In order to recognize power in this way, a political project must be undertaken where power is understood as a capillary process—Foucauldian notions of power as 'neither given, nor exchanged, nor recovered, but rather exercised' (Foucault 1977: 89). Specific to our interest in deliberation, power is not to be conceived as something held by deliberation planners and to be obtained by participants in the course of best procedure or best argument (i.e. to empower). Nor should power be conceived as something that necessarily restricts or oppresses participants during the deliberation and thus requires an erasure of power from the idealized process. Rather, information resources are produced within relations of power and knowledge: a complex ether producing and positioning truths, expertise, participants' knowledges, discourses, and normalizations within multiple frameworks of subjugation. What we are after is not (and should not) be an arresting of power; rather, our approach is toward a realization that information always already constitutes the 'playing field' and the 'players' through power's enabling. For example, information resources always employ normalizing discourse—legitimizing certain knowledges over others. Conceptualizing information in this way, demonstrates how the notion of the 'level playing field' (where, presumably, power imbalances are temporarily bracketed) is problematic when not analyzed as always already a political operation of power.

One approach to taking a critical perspective of power pluralizes the meaning of information and expands the possibilities for (re)interpretations and (re)examinations of information resources. This multiplicative approach to information is reminiscent of Nancy Fraser's (1992) critique of Habermas' (1989) public sphere, where she describes the ways in which Habermas' enablisms of participants (via 'universal pragmatics') during these specified procedures oversimplify and constrain the activities of the individuals taking part, as well as stricture the information provided. Key to Fraser's critique is the implication that Habermas' supposed transformation of participants from 'private' individuals into a 'public' oppresses the 'private' (which is precluded from 'public'). As Fraser (1992) explains, that which is 'private' is conceived as some 'prepolitical starting point' (130). In the field of online deliberation, designers often conceptualize information resources in a similar way, as having a 'prepolitical' role to play in the transformation of participants into *informed* deliberators. However, as Fraser's work suggests, it is important to identify the political status of 'prepolitical': information resources.

In recent work, critical cartographers have repoliticized the map as an information resource by using techniques of (re)interpretation and (re)examination. Like all information, maps are productions that privilege certain perspectives on reality, and this privileging is a political act (Crampton 2001). Maps, by definition, represent the world by portraying some aspects of reality while hiding others. For example, a road map represents highways, exits, cities, and other items useful to car travelers while omitting elements like ecosystems, hair salons, and burial grounds. Such privileging of information in maps is necessary to make them useful for particular tasks. However, in the context of deliberations, this privileging often has major implications. John Pickles (2004) draws attention to three different perspectives on how to read maps as productions that are necessarily political: the map is an interpretative act, the map has a particular gaze, and the map constructs a sense of realities.

Map as Interpretation

Pickles (2004) is interested in reconstructing the map as a product of interpretation, deconstructing what seems to be a dominant notion of the map as a technical product. His point is to situate our notion of this information resource within the context of the author's intention, values, and identity, whether conscious or unconscious, therefore debasing notions of the map as singular fact or truth.

Map as Gaze

Critical cartographers forward the notion of the 'cartographic gaze', which calls attention to the map's (and map readers') perspective (i.e., a view from somewhere rather than nowhere) (Pickles 2004). This 'gaze' is a notion of reduction and control coming from some position of purpose when maps (and information) are produced. The concern is with complexity and perspective; maps reduce complexity to simply the object of the author's intent, while manipulating the perspective from which the observer also gazes onto the map. These 'technical' decisions, while not seemingly political ones, have directly political implications.

Map as Reality

Drawing on King (1996), Pickles (2004) traces how maps are understood as reality—maps in interesting ways produce a reality. The boundaries, territories, and hill shading in the map construct a particular understanding, stricturing the way in which the observer can 'see' the world and community.

2 Implications for Online Deliberation

By acknowledging that all information is political and thereby power-laden, the introduction of information into a deliberative forum is realized as a political act. Furthermore, if we acknowledge that maps work to construct our sense of reality, then we should also recognize that particular maps privilege certain types of reality and thus certain types of arguments about how to best address a problem over others. More generally, when we introduce a map into a deliberative forum, we fundamentally shift the political dynamics of that deliberation.

A useful illustration of this point is Ramsey's (2008) case study into the use of a geographic information system (GIS) to inform a deliberative process intended to identify acceptable solutions to a conflict over water shortages in southern Idaho. The state water management agency developed this system, which visualizes measured and predicted water flow through a valley in the form of an interactive map, in hopes of introducing a 'credible' and 'objective' information resource that could serve as the basis for discussions. They developed the system to track the flow of water based on what they found to be the best available information. However, based on the data available, the GIS could only be used to tell a particular kind of story about the water shortage problem—one focused on efficiency of water use by farmers in the valley. It was silent regarding other major arguments in this dispute, such as theories about the causes of diminished spring water flows that feed the valley water system. As a result, attempts to focus deliberation around the information provided by the GIS prevented and precluded certain arguments from being made and hindered the process of collectively constructing alternative understandings of the problem. Recognizing the development of the GIS and its introduction into the deliberative process as inherently political is central to analyzing the context within which it was received and the way in which it worked to privilege and marginalize certain discourses and ways of knowing.

Of course, we are not suggesting that information resources, such as maps or the GIS described above, should be banned from deliberative forums. Such resources play an important part in enabling certain understandings of complex problems, but they must be presented in a manner that foregrounds, rather than hides, their politics. For example, deliberation forums and facilitators should draw attention to the origins of maps and the perspectives they represent. Participants should discuss the *political* meaning of these maps as well as their relevance to science or policy making. By repoliticizing information and the deliberative forum more generally, facilitators can help foreground shifts in political dynamics and the privileging of some perspectives over others, encouraging the critical political awareness of participants and, perhaps, motivating efforts by participants to call for (or create their own) alternative maps that present alternative stories, and that thereby also enable multiple interpretations.

This issue is particularly salient in online contexts. By comparison, face-to-face deliberations such as Deliberative Polls® often feature experts clearly representing particular political perspectives on an issue who present evidence (information), thereby cueing participants to the fact that evidence needs to be considered in relation to the presenter's perspective. However, online evidence (e.g. maps) can easily be presented and/or received out of context, potentially appearing to participants as a window on reality that represents no particular perspective (i.e. viewed from nowhere). For this reason, designers of online deliberation environments need to be particularly careful to qualify maps and other information resources as political products within complex power relations by foregrounding the 'gaze' and supporting maps' multiple interpretations.

We recognize that the idea of politicizing a deliberative process might appear to be inviting conflict and therefore seem counter to the goal of providing space for reasoned and civil discussions among participants with different points of view. However, we argue that efforts to artificially construct a depoliticized environment in this way works only to disguise processes of privileging and marginalization such as those described above. We also argue that a repoliticized deliberative forum is not necessarily incompatible with many of the normative goals of deliberative democratic process, such as respectful and reasoned debate and the quest to identify shared stories about how the polity (however defined) should address the political problem at hand. However, such a forum calls for (and, we hope, can foster) participants who are not only 'informed' about various facts and arguments relevant to an issue but who are also able to critically assess and position this information in relation to the shifting political landscape of power relations. It is for this reason that we call for a reimagination of the ideal informed participant as somebody who recognizes that all information is political and that the project of deliberation is designed to shift power relations in particular ways.

3 Design Recommendations for Online Deliberation

We propose a few recommendations for how to design and structure online deliberative forums that may cultivate a critical political awareness among participants. At the time of publication, these recommendations are currently being used to motivate the development of an online deliberative forum called 'Let's Improve Transportation', part of a larger research endeavor exploring ways to support public participation in regional transportation improvement decision making.[1] Below we highlight a few of the design decisions and explain how they might help orient participants to a more critical approach to deliberation.

- **Foreground how information resources were produced.** Call attention to the author(s) of a map and how (and why) the data were collected.
- **Demonstrate that information resources have multiple interpretations.** Invite specialists with alternative points of view to write critical analyses/reviews of a map.
- **Include multiple and conflicting information resources.** Provide multiple maps depicting different elements of a problem and emphasize how each represents a different story (which potentially conflict).
- **Encourage critical evaluation of information resources.** Orient questions and discussion around the critical evaluation of the perspective, intention, meaning, validity, and relevance of a map and map data. Encourage participants to consider whose story the map is telling, and whose story is not represented.

---

[1] See http://www.pgist.org and http://www.LetsImproveTransportation.org (both last accessed November 1, 2008) for more information.

4   Conclusions

The designers of online deliberative forums should continue to problematize ways in which certain 'offline' or 'technical' decisions around the handling of information resources are political actions, worthy of active reflection. Here we have attempted, somewhat briefly, to draw out some themes of this problematization to emphasize the work carried out when attempts are made to 'level' the field of deliberation through the introduction of information resources. In particular, we advocated a notion of power which exposes the politicized production of all information and knowledge, as illustrated by critical re-readings of the map. We proposed an alternative handling of information resources that opens space for multiple interpretations. Our implications and recommendations for online deliberation are centered on a key notion—being an informed participant requires a critical political awareness not emphasized by many in the field of deliberation. While realizing that this somehow 'critical' participant is idealized, we argue that the design of deliberative forums should support (not hinder) the participants' process of developing a critical political awareness.

Acknowledgements

The authors would like to thank the support of the Participatory Geographic Information Systems for Transportation research project funded by the National Science Foundation, Division of Experimental and Integrative Activities, Information Technology Research (ITR) Program, Project Number EIA 0325916, funds managed within the Digital Government Program.

References

Craig, W. J., T. M. Harris, and D. Weiner. 2002. *Community Participation and Geographic Information Systems*. New York: Taylor & Francis.

Crampton, J. W. 2001. Maps as Social Constructions: Power, Communication and Visualization. *Progress in Human Geography* 25(2): 235-252.

Eveland, W. P., Jr. 2004. The Effects of Political Discussion in Producing Informed Citizens: The Roles of Information, Motivation, and Elaboration. *Political Communication* 21: 177-193.

Fishkin, J. and C. Farrar. 2005. Deliberative Polling: From Experiment to Community Resource. *The Deliberative Democracy Handbook*, ed. J. Gastil and P. Levine, 68-79. San Francisco, CA: John Wiley & Sons, Inc.

Foucault, M. 2003. *Society Must Be Defended: Lectures at the Collège de France, 1975-76*. New York: Picador.

Fraser, N. 1992. Rethinking the Public Sphere: A Contribution to the Critique of Actually Existing Democracy. *Habermas and the Public Sphere*, ed. C. Calhoun, 109-42. Cambridge, MA: MIT Press.

Habermas, J. 1989. *The Structural Transformation of the Public Sphere: An Inquiry into a Category of Bourgeois Society, Studies in contemporary German Social Thought*. Cambridge, MA: MIT Press.

King, G. 1996. *Mapping Reality: An Exploration of Cultural Cartographies*. New York: St. Martin's Press.

Pickles, J. 2004. *A History of Spaces: Cartographic Reason, Mapping, and the Geocoded World*. New York: Routledge.

Ramsey, K. 2008. A Call for Agonism: GIS and the Politics of Collaboration. *Environment and Planning A* 40: 2346-2363. Available at http://www.envplan.com/abstract.cgi?id=a4028 (last accessed August 31, 2008)

Sparke, M. 2005. *In the Space of Theory: Postfoundational Geographies of the Nation-State*. Minneapolis: University of Minnesota Press.

24

PerlNomic: Rule Making and Enforcement in Digital Shared Spaces

MARK E. PHAIR AND ADAM BLISS

1 Introduction

In *Smith v. United States* (1993), the defendant attempted to sell firearms to undercover officers. He requested to be paid with drugs, and the prosecutors attempted to invoke a statute relating to the 'use' of a firearm in a drug crime. Did the legislation mean 'use' as a weapon, or did it simply mean 'carry'? Ambiguity in statutes is a common occurrence, leading different judges to interpret them in different ways. To mitigate these problems, citizens can exercise influence on statutes (and, in some cases, judges) through the electoral process.

In digital shared spaces, governing is typically performed by one or more administrators of the community. In most online communities, users cannot change certain aspects. Even if they can request that the system administrator change a few rules, very rarely do they have access to the 'laws' of the community. These laws are built into the computer programs that make up the system and controlled only by the system's owners or administrators. Offline governments, by contrast, provide a means of modifying the laws themselves. Article V of the Constitution of the United States exemplifies this.

The system presented here, called PerlNomic, allows its users (players) to modify the core of the system itself by making proposals in the form of

Online Deliberation: Design, Research, and Practice.
Todd Davies and Seeta Peña Gangadharan (eds.).
Copyright © 2009, CSLI Publications.

computer code on which the community can vote; if accepted, the proposal is executed and the rules are changed. All rules are interpreted by a strictly 'letter of the law' judge: the Perl programming language interpreter.

The core ideas of the system are based on the game of Nomic, which was invented by Peter Suber and described in an appendix of his book (Suber 1990). The essence of Nomic is captured in the motto that 'to play the game is to change the rules.' The initial rule set outlines mechanics for play, but these rules are changed by play itself. Initially, players make proposals to change rules which are put to a vote. Points are awarded for successful proposals.

2 System Description and Game Summaries

The authors have implemented a novel game called PerlNomic,[1] begun in 2002. PerlNomic runs on a Web server. Each webpage comprises a Perl script that takes certain actions when requested by players. One script allows players to submit proposals (which are arbitrary pieces of code). A second script allows players to vote on pending proposals. A third allows a player to activate (run) a proposal that has sufficient votes in its favor. PerlNomic is not turn-based, but rather any player can submit a proposal at any time and vote on whatever is pending. When proposals are activated, points are awarded to the player who wrote the proposal and to the players who voted on it. Although they can potentially contain anything, the typical proposal changes the way in which future proposals are interpreted.

The initial code base featured an unrefined user interface. In the first game, the players became dissatisfied with this and proposed changes which would make the system more usable. Any proposal that improved the interface was likely to gain large support among the other players, and proposals that passed rewarded the author with points.

With a mind towards giving the game broader appeal, PerlNomic 2.0 was supplemented with PatchMaker. PatchMaker allows any user to download a local copy of the then-current PerlNomic code base, make changes to that code base in a *sandbox*, create a file summarizing the differences between the sandbox and the live code base, and craft a proposal which would use the patch program to implement these changes on the live code base.

PerlNomic 3.0 was the first game to see transferable points. This created an economy wherein points could be traded for votes or other actions. However, as one player approached a winning score of 100 points, the other

---

[1] See http://www.nomic.net/~nomicwiki/index.php/PerlNomic (last accessed September 13, 2008).

players passed an 'inflation' proposal which increased the winning condition from 100 points to 1000 points, obstructing his possible win.

One issue raised in PerlNomic 4 was a dispute over the problems caused by the point reward system. The rules were initially set up to allow players to vote against good proposals in order to receive extra points. Out of the discussion came two proposals. The first simply proposed to remove the extra awarded points. The second proposed that an attribute be added to players that tracked their so-called 'ethos,' a measure of how inclined the player is to support law and order that could later be used to punish or reward players. The first proposal became too outdated to function before it received enough votes to pass (an indication that it did not have much support), but the second passed quickly. Many proposals followed with plans to deal with low ethos individuals.

3   Summary and Conclusions

The ambiguity of laws in the 'real' world leads to an uneven and often unpredictable application of those laws. By applying the concept of a consistently enforced legal corpus to the rule making game Nomic, a much more consistent system can be achieved, especially in the context of digital shared spaces. We have introduced PerlNomic, a novel realization of these concepts. Shirky (2004) asked whether or not a game of this nature could be fun. PerlNomic has had international appeal, with over 3000 visitors from at least six continents, and the authors hope that the ongoing interest in the game has answered Shirky's question with a resounding 'Yes'!

References

Shirky, C. 2004. *Nomic World: By the Players, For the Players.* First published May 27, 2004, on the Networks, Economics, and Culture mailing list. Available at http://www.shirky.com/writings/nomic.html (last accessed April 1, 2005)

Smith v. United States. 113 SCt. 1050, 1993.

Suber, P. 1990. *The Paradox of Self-Amendment.* New York: Peter Lang Publishing. Available at http://www.earlham.edu/~peters/writing/psa/ (last accessed April 1, 2005)

United States Constitution. 1787. Article V.

Part VI

Design of Deliberation Tools

25

An Online Environment for Democratic Deliberation: Motivations, Principles, and Design

TODD DAVIES, BRENDAN O'CONNOR, ALEX COCHRAN,
JONATHAN J. EFFRAT, ANDREW PARKER, BENJAMIN NEWMAN,
AND AARON TAM

1 Introduction

We have created a platform for online deliberation called *Deme* (which rhymes with 'team'). Deme is designed to allow groups of people to engage in collaborative drafting, focused discussion, and decision making using the Internet.

The Deme project has evolved greatly from its beginning in 2003. This chapter outlines the thinking behind Deme's initial design: our motivations for creating it, the principles that guided its construction, and its most important design features. The version of Deme described here was written in PHP and was deployed in 2004 and used by several groups (including organizers of the 2005 Online Deliberation Conference). Other papers describe later developments in the Deme project (see Davies et al. 2005, 2008; Davies and Mintz 2009).

Demes were the divisions or townships of ancient Attica (from the Greek word *demos*—the populace). In ecology, a deme is a local population of closely related plants or animals, and in modern Greece a deme is a commune (OED 1989). The name was chosen to reflect our focus on providing an online tool for small to medium-sized groups that (1) have a substantial face-to-face existence that predates or is independent of any interaction on the Internet, (2) are geographically limited so that all members

Online Deliberation: Design, Research, and Practice
Todd Davies and Seeta Peña Gangadharan (eds.).
Copyright © 2009, CSLI Publications.

can meet each other face to face, and (3) have difficulty meeting face to face as much as they need or would like to. Examples of such groups include neighborhood associations, places of worship, community interest groups, university groups (e.g., dormitories), and coalitions of activists.

Targeting this type of group suggested a distinct set of design criteria from those that govern groupware for 'virtual' (Internet-based) groups, businesses, or large organizations. The decline in participation, within the U.S., in small, community-based civil society groups such as the ones we are targeting has received considerable attention from political scientists and sociologists (see Putnam 2000; Skocpol 2003).

2   Background

In January of 2002, students and faculty affiliated with the Symbolic Systems Program at Stanford University began a consultative partnership with staff of the newly forming East Palo Alto Community Network. East Palo Alto is a vibrant, low-income, multi-ethnic, and multi-lingual community of 29,506 residents (U.S. Census 2000), located three miles from the Stanford campus. The East Palo Alto Community Network[1] comprises a community website or 'portal' (EPA.Net) and technology access points ('TAPs' — public computer clusters located throughout the city).

Over the first year (2002) of this partnership, which became the Partnership for Internet Equity and Community Engagement (PIECE), projects included studies of how the needs of the area's diverse groups related to the Internet, and of the realized and unrealized role of Internet tools in improving civic engagement.[2] In the second year (2003), we focused on (1) outreach to the community, (2) follow-up data collection to assess the impact of the community website one year after its launch, and (3) designing a tool for online deliberation, which is the topic of this chapter.

3   Motivations

In an earlier paper (Davies et al. 2002), members of our team argued that East Palo Alto residents and community organizations could gain a great deal through the use of the Internet. This was one of the motivating principles behind the Community Network and other recent technology initiatives in East Palo Alto. Our research looked especially at barriers that keep resi-

---

[1] The community network has been funded primarily by grants from Hewlett Packard and the National Telecommunications and Information Administration's Technology Opportunities Program (TOP), with software donations from Microsoft.

[2] These and other projects, including Deme, are discussed on the PIECE website (http://piece.stanford.edu, last accessed January 18, 2009).

dents from knowing about, participating in, and influencing decisions that affect them, and at how Internet tools could reduce or eliminate those barriers.

Our early research drew two broad conclusions concerning the use of Internet tools for enhancing democratic decision making in East Palo Alto:

- The ability to use computers and the Internet was distributed very unevenly within the community, and was especially absent among Spanish-speaking residents who do not speak English very well (68% of the Latino population, which is 59% of the city; U.S. Census 2002; Sywulka 2003). We refer to eliminating 'digital divides' as the goal of *Internet equity*.

- When the ability to use the Internet is commonplace among members of a group, Internet communication can address many of the difficulties associated with democratic participation in East Palo Alto's organizations and the City Government, for that group of Internet users. Using both the existing community website (EPA.Net) and developing new networking tools appear necessary to best achieve the goal we refer to as *community engagement*.

Much of the Community Network's expenditure and effort, and some of PIECE's work, has been aimed at improving Internet equity (the focus of the first conclusion) through, for example, providing hub computer access and training open to all residents, making the content and functionality of the EPA.Net website motivating and accessible (e.g., through community news coverage and automatic translation), and reaching out to community network users and potential users.

The present chapter primarily concerns the *second* conclusion. The PIECE team explored community engagement through both research and tool development. We began by attending several types of meetings, including those of advisory boards for nonprofit organizations, informational and feedback meetings open to community or neighborhood members, and official functions of the City Government, and by subscribing to both organizational and community email lists in East Palo Alto.

Through participant-observation, reading, and interviews, we found that most group decisions made in East Palo Alto occurred in face-to-face meetings, often involving volunteers or people who received little compensation for participating. Residents had, in many cases, very little free time (e.g., they worked double shifts or had long commutes to their jobs). There was a widespread perception that decisions were made by a handful of people who served on multiple committees, were well connected, and sometimes had their own agendas, and that groups were not empowered in proportion to their population. Although our observations generally indicated a high level of interest, effort, and public spiritedness among the city's leaders, this substantive reality was sometimes undermined by perceptions of procedural injustice (see Tyler 1988).

This situation is mirrored in many communities. We found a number of recurring community engagement difficulties that Internet tools might address (see also Davies et al. 2002):

1. *Attendance and representation.* When attending a face-to-face meeting is the only way to have input into a decision, many people are disenfranchised because they cannot attend, because of work or family obligations or other engagements, and this is likely to make attendees collectively less representative of all stakeholders.

2. *Meeting duration and frequency.* When meetings are not held very frequently (frequent meetings being difficult for everyone to attend), or when the time available for meetings is scarce, groups are less able to act in ways that are timely, or with adequate discussion.

3. *Communication between meetings.* When groups lack efficient means for communicating between meetings (e.g., if they do not have an email list, or if not everyone is on the list), meeting quality suffers because attendees are likely to be under prepared, or worse, they may not know the time/location of the next meeting.

4. *Available information during meetings.* When decisions are made in a setting where some or all attendees are unable to access information that may be relevant to a decision (e.g., a room with no computer or Internet connection, or the relevant experts not present), meeting quality suffers because attendees must rely on memory, common knowledge, or the word of others who may persuade them, rather than basing opinions on the best information.

5. *Communication between groups.* When groups' decisions affect each other (e.g., subcommittees, groups in coalition, or multiple stakeholders), traditional means of communication between them are often inadequate, leading to conflicts, duplicated effort, and uninformed decisions.

6. *Group records.* Groups making decisions in face-to-face meetings often have inadequate records of their own past deliberations and decisions when they meet, which can lead to disputes, conflicting decisions that must be revisited, and duplication of previous effort.

7. *Decision procedures.* Face-to-face meetings often lead to streamlined, time-saving procedures for making a decision, which may not fit the complexity of what the group must decide, or which may unduly empower the chair or agenda committee (e.g., presentation-sensitive

procedures, voting that does not take into account relative preferences among multiple options, etc.).

8. *Transparency*. Face-to-face meetings are difficult to record or to broadcast, so that those who cannot be present are often left unable to know exactly what has happened. This can lead to mistrust, side dealing, and general disenfranchisement.

The above findings point to a clear role for Internet communication as either a supplement to, or in some cases a replacement for, face-to-face decision making. Many of the above observations would apply to more affluent communities, and we have observed them in many settings outside of East Palo Alto. But the difficulties posed by an almost exclusive reliance on face-to-face meetings are amplified in East Palo Alto because, in comparison to the more affluent residents of neighboring communities: (1) East Palo Alto's residents are more dependent on community resources; (2) they have more experience with being disenfranchised or otherwise being victimized (and are therefore more likely to break off trust relationships); and (3) they have fewer means to participate outside of public forums, which they may be unable to attend. Prior to EPA.Net, East Palo Alto did not have its own media (newspapers or a broadcast station).

Some of the challenges we have identified for community engagement in East Palo Alto were addressed through already existing features of the Community Network: e.g., getting organization members access to the Internet and email accounts, setting up email lists, collecting relevant information about groups and the city on the community website, and publicizing important meetings. But to address the above challenges fully requires a kind of groupware that did not appear to exist before we began this project.

4 Principles

The challenges listed above (1 through 8) led easily to the idea that Internet tools could improve group decision making, if the group's members each had regular Internet access. Attendance and participation would be easier because members would not have to travel to participate, and if the tool allowed asynchronous communication, members could participate at their convenience instead of needing all to be present at the same time. Discussion comments could be composed at a more leisurely pace and with more care, and the group would not be constrained by its announced meeting times and durations. Even if face-to-face meetings were to continue to be the primary setting for decisions, Internet communication could occur between meetings, and relevant outside information as well as communication with other groups could be more easily incorporated into discussions through linking. An online archive of the group's activities would make it less likely that the group would get bogged down due to a lack of collective memory, and, since the Internet can be used as a form of broadcasting, all stakeholders could follow what was happening in the proceedings of a group.

The observation that Internet communication could address challenges 1-8 was, however, just a starting point. How could the Internet best be used to address these difficulties, serving the general goal of enhancing the ability of group members and/or stakeholders to participate in decisions that affect them? We concluded that the design of a platform or toolset for groups that have a substantial non-Internet existence, should ideally satisfy four top-level criteria. The criteria take the form of outcome goals that we intended to be evaluated with respect to a particular group or set of groups.

The first criterion required that online interaction enhance, or at least not diminish the group's overall effectiveness, on- and offline. We called this the criterion of supportiveness.

> *Supportiveness.* The platform should support the group overall, so that there is either an improvement or no decline in the ability of the group to meet the needs of its members or stakeholders.

The second criterion (comprehensiveness) expressed a desire to liberate the group from a dependence on having face-to-face meetings. While groups might still choose to meet face to face, eliminating the need to *rely* on face-to-face meetings would mean that there would no longer be an excuse for inner-circle, closed-door decision making, because no task would require it.

> *Comprehensiveness.* The platform should allow the group to accomplish, in an online environment, all of the usual deliberative tasks associated with face-to-face meetings.

The third criterion expressed a desire to make decision making more participative relative to what occurs in face-to-face meetings.

> *Participation.* The platform should maximize the number of desired participants in the group's deliberations, and minimize barriers to their participation.

Finally, the fourth criterion (quality) was aimed at the group's satisfaction with the process and substance of its decisions.

> *Quality.* The platform should facilitate a subjective quality of interaction and decision making that meets or exceeds what the group achieves in face-to-face meetings.

Combining these four criteria with general principles of design yielded a richer set of design principles. These derived principles were closer to the level of actual design, and provided an outline of the functionality for our platform. In the subsections below, we discuss the design principles and goals (highlighted in *italics*) that we derived from each of the four outcome criteria listed above.

Supporting the Group

The criterion of supportiveness is analogous to Hippocrates' famous dictum 'do no harm'.[3] We interpreted supportiveness, in part, to mean that groups should have *autonomy* over the toolset that they use for deliberation, so that group members can determine as much as possible for themselves when and how to use online tools, how and whether to modify them, and what resources should be devoted to their maintenance. Inasmuch as tools can be made available as *free and open source* software, supportiveness does not seem consistent with a model that draws resources away from groups (e.g., monetary payments by the group that exceed or are not tied to fair compensation for labor and other costs), or that limits access to online tools for commercial purposes or to benefit the provider at the expense of groups. Open access to the code seems especially important for software that is going to be used for decision making (e.g., elections), where group members may worry whether they can trust the results.

Supportiveness also implies that online deliberation should not lead to reduced satisfaction with the group on the part of its members or stakeholders. The online platform should therefore *build in feedback and assessment* from group members, shared both within the group and with tool providers, at different stages during and after tool adoption.

As a guiding principle, a supportive platform should not take away capabilities that the group possessed before its adoption, but should *integrate with existing practices* as much as possible. If group members are using email as a group communication tool, for example, and want to continue doing so, supportiveness implies that any new platform should incorporate email usage where it can be accommodated, without also diminishing the effectiveness of the earlier practice (e.g., by maintaining the option to communicate with the group by email and not creating a separate interaction space that is unnecessarily inaccessible through email).

Comprehensive Deliberation

The criterion of comprehensiveness implies that we can map the usual activities of face-to-face deliberation onto the design of an online toolset. Meetings in organizations feature discussion that is typically *focused on*

---

[3] This appears not in the Hippocratic Oath itself but rather in Hippocrates' *Epidemics*, Dk. I, Sect. XI.: 'As to diseases, make a habit of two things—to help, or at least to do no harm' (http://www.geocities.com/everwild7/noharm.html, last accessed December 20, 2008).

particular agenda items. These items give structure to the meeting, and are usually discussed in some order. One type of agenda item is simply a topic of discussion, such as a question about which members of the group brainstorm or express their opinions. Discussion items are often well suited to traditional online forums (e.g., Web message boards or even listservs) because the topic can generally be specified simply (e.g., by posting a question). But organizations often must go beyond exchanges of opinion to *numerical polling or formal decisions,* in which some agreed upon procedure is applied, such as voting or testing for consensus. Furthermore, each group has its own procedures for decision making, and if an online platform is to provide comprehensive support for the group's deliberations, it must give the group *options for decision making procedures* that are sufficiently close to its offline practice.

A general design principle of *flexibility and customizability* derives from the goal of comprehensive deliberation support. This can also be applied to another important type of agenda item: the drafting of a document. Documents such as bylaws, flyers, press releases, and budgets, should ideally be expressions of a group's will. *Collaborative drafting* is a cumbersome process that often gets delegated to one or a few people who can meet face to face. But the power that is delegated in such cases can be considerable. Even if the whole group must ultimately approve a document, those who participate in drafting it in its earlier stages are likely to have disproportionate influence on its content. At a minimum, an online platform should support the same level of document collaboration as can occur in face-to-face meetings. At best it offers the possibility of exceeding that standard.

Documents (including nontextual material such as images and video recordings) can be objects of discussion in meetings both as part of collaborative drafting and as the centerpieces of debate (e.g., as evidence that bears on a decision). An important feature of face to face meetings, in contrast to the lists of messages that usually comprise online discussion, is that a document can be placed in the common view of a meeting's participants, by distributing copies or projecting it onto a screen, and oral discussion can center on the document through synchronizing references (such as: 'Everyone look at the paragraph beginning with "Maria said...".'). The importance of common views or WYSIWIS ('What you see is what I see') has been stressed from the early days of research on computer-supported cooperative work (see Stefik et al. 1987). The ability of meeting participants to function simultaneously in two discourse spaces—the document and the discussion, generally by applying separate perceptual modalities (visual and auditory), is a formidable advantage of face-to-face meetings that must somehow be captured in a fully online platform if the criterion of comprehensiveness is to be met, to allow *document-centered discussion* (Davies et al. 2008).

The structure of both civil society and government groups typically resembles a network of clusters, exhibiting relatively high levels of connectivity within groups (clusters), and low (though important) connectivity between groups. This argues for *each group having its own online space,* with the ability to close access for nonmembers, but also to establish lines of communication with other groups. Groups usually include subgroups such as committees, or they may segment meetings into different topics. These observations imply that each group should be able to create *separate online spaces for different subgroups or meeting topics.* Often, groups of representatives from different groups form coalitions, which implies that *meeting areas should be able to be linked across groups* as well.

Collaborative drafting, document-centered discussion, rich support for decision procedures, and hierarchical and network structuring of group meeting spaces are all cumbersome in standard message-list online environments. We therefore emphasized these in our design principles/goals for an online deliberation environment. There are many other activities associated with face-to-face group meetings that were well supported in groupware prior to 2003, such as *announcements,* the keeping of a *common calendar,* the *sharing of personal information* by group members, and *the ability to share files and links.* Since we assumed that groups would desire minimal inconvenience in moving between these capabilities, we inferred that they should be integrated with a deliberation toolset so that groups could have an all-purpose online space to call their own.

Maximizing Participation

The participation criterion has a number of consequences for the design of a deliberation platform. Maximizing the number of people who can participate implies that communication should be *asynchronous* so that group members can participate at their own convenience. The software should be *compatible and interoperable* with the widest possible range of server and user environments, so that those who might participate are not prevented from doing so for technical reasons.

Participation is affected by other factors that determine how comfortable group members feel using the platform, e.g., *familiarity of features, design simplicity* and *intuitiveness, accessibility to those with special needs, execution speed* and *robustness,* trustworthy *privacy protection,* and *secure communication.*

For those who can use an online deliberation tool, overall participation may be enhanced merely by this fact. A number of authors have noted the tendency of computer-mediated communication to equalize participation (see Kiesler et al. 1984; Price 2009). Of course, accessibility is key in realizing this potential.

High Quality Deliberation

The criterion of quality could be assessed subjectively, through the kind of *built-in feedback* referred to above under 'Supporting the Group'. There are also numerous principles that have been proposed for creating sound deliberation, such as the conditions of the 'ideal speech situation' defined by Habermas (1990; Horster 2001; see also Kiesler et al. 1984), and other theorists of 'deliberative democracy' (see Gutmann 1997). In general, enhancing decision quality seems to call for greater *structure around which discussion can take place*. Farnham et al. (2000) demonstrated that more structured discussion in a chat room (i.e. preauthored scripts) improves the ability of a group to come to consensus.

A full treatment of the theory of deliberation is beyond the scope of this paper, but it seems possible for an online platform to support good discourse practices through, for example, *built-in tutorials* and *models of practice*, as well as *features that encourage directed discussion* (e.g., encouragement to quote comments being responded to, when possible, rather than to paraphrase them; clear options for one-on-one replies when a more visible discussion is not justified, etc.).[4]

5 Design

Applying the above principles within what is technically and otherwise feasible for us led to the creation of Deme: an online environment for group deliberation. In this section and the next, we describe the early design of Deme and attempt to relate its features to the design principles and goals derived in the previous section. The early design of Deme was refined through a series of meetings with prototypical target groups: the Community Network staff in East Palo Alto, prospective users at Stanford, and a grassroots group of labor activists organizing a labor media/technology conference. These groups provided valuable input to the design, and Deme's features reflected their comments.[5]

---

[4] For an excellent discussion of the relationships between deliberative democracy and the design of groupware, see Noveck (2003).

[5] The version of Deme described below can be used at http://www.groupspace.org/wordpress/?page_id=54 and downloaded at http://www.groupspace.org/wordpress/?page_id=28.

We organized Deme around *group spaces*: subsites that were each de-voted to a particular group. A *group* was assumed to be either a well-defined set or a looser cluster of individuals who identified themselves with a *group name*, which also named their online group space. Entry into each group space was provided through the *group homepage* (see Figure 1). The group homepage showed the group's name (e.g., 'Labortech') and an *intro-ductory description* at the top. It also identified the user (if logged in) and provided the user entry into his/her *member profile*, or a link for joining the group if the user was not a member.

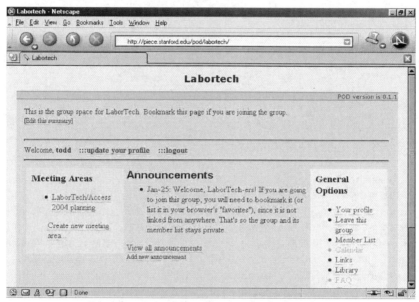

Figure 1. A Group Homepage from Deme (then 'POD') v0.1.1

These were familiar features to those who had used sites such as Yahoo! Groups. The somewhat novel feature of the group homepage was the avail-ability of an arbitrary number of meeting areas. Each meeting area link took the user to a new page (a *meeting area viewer*), where group members could interact and/or deliberate. A meeting area might correspond to a committee or working group that was either a subgroup or a group con-nected to the group on whose homepage the meeting area was linked, or it might be set up around a topic for discussion or decision of interest to the group as a whole. A meeting area viewer is shown in Figure 2.

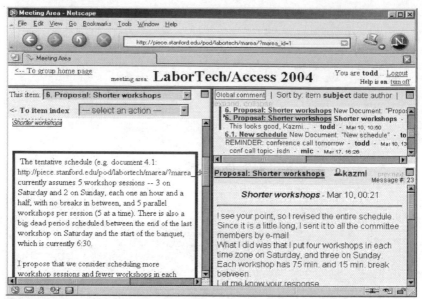

Figure 2. A meeting area from Deme v0.1.1

Beneath the *meeting area banner* at the top of the viewer page in Figure 2, the browser window was divided into three *panes*. Each pane could be viewed and operated upon either in the part of the screen shown (which was the *standard view* of a meeting area), or it could be made to fill most of the browser through the *enlarge button* located in the upper right corner of each pane. Under the banner, the standard view of a meeting area was divided vertically into the *discussion viewer* on the right side of the screen (consisting of a *comments index* pane that sat above a *comment reader* pane), and, on the left side of the screen, a pane known as the *folio viewer*. These left and right side viewers in the standard view were used to view and manipulate the two main types of objects in a meeting area: *items* and *comments*. Items comprised a meeting area's *folio*. Items were intended to be focuses of attention for the participants in a meeting area. The types of items included *documents, links, discussion items, nonbinding polls,* and *decisions*. Comments comprised a meeting area's *discussion*. A comment could be posted in reference to a particular item, or as a response to another comment, or as a *global comment*. In general, the meeting area was designed so that items were the objects of comments, and comments could refer to items. [6]

---

[6] This feature and some of the others described here persist in the latest version of Deme (Davies and Mintz 2009).

When a comment referred to an item, the *comment header*, as shown in both the comments index and comment reader, contained an *item reference*. Item references are shown as underlined red links at the beginning of the comment header in Figure 2. When an item reference was clicked on, it became *active* and the item to which its comment refers was loaded into the *item display*, which took up the bulk of the folio viewer and was located just beneath the *folio viewer control panel*. If an item reference was active, it was highlighted using both green shading and a small arrow in both the comments index and the comment reader. Clicking on a comment header, either via its item reference or via its *subject line*, made the comment itself (as opposed to the item reference) active. If there was an active comment, its subject line was highlighted in yellow in both the comments index and comment reader.

Comments could be viewed independently of the active item reference by clicking on their subject lines. But when an item reference was first clicked on, both the item reference and the comment that had been first associated with the item reference became active. Right after a click on an item reference, the referenced item was loaded into the item viewer so that the *comment reference* that was tied to the item reference could be seen in the display of the item, the comment was loaded into the discussion viewer, and the comment reference was highlighted in yellow inside the item display to indicate that both the comment and its associated item reference were active. A comment could reference an item either as a *general comment on the item* or as an *in-text comment*. In-text comments were unique to documents. The comment reference of an in-text comment could appear in any blank space within the document, and the document and the location of the comment reference together became the comment's item reference, indicating to Deme what the user should see in the folio viewer when an item reference was clicked on in the discussion viewer. All items could have general comments that referenced them.

As an example, in Figure 2 the user has clicked on the item reference '6. Proposal: Shorter Workshops', which is highlighted in green with a small arrow pointing to it in the comments index. This item reference appears in the comment header for the comment 'Shorter workshops', which was posted by 'kazmi'. The document itself appears on the left in the folio viewer, with the active comment reference highlighted in yellow above the text of the document. Documents could be entered directly (typed or pasted in as plain text), which allowed in-text commenting, or they could be uploaded in any format and made available for general comments.

There were additional features and subtleties in the design of the meeting area viewer. The main point was that the meeting area viewer was designed to embody the principles discussed in the section above on 'Comprehensive Deliberation'. Through a division between items and comments, and an architecture for referring to each, the meeting area viewer more closely approximated the processes of collaboration and item-centered discussion that happen in face-to-face meetings. Additional item types— discussion items, Web links, nonbinding polls, and decisions (e.g., majority, approval, plurality, and consensus procedures) were integrated into the meeting area to allow a full range of deliberation activities.

Consistent with our conclusions about how best to support groups, all versions of Deme have been free/open-source software (under the Affero General Public License) that can be accessed either through the server that we maintain or else installed on a group's own server.

6   Experience and Follow-up

An early release version of Deme was made available on Freshmeat.net in January of 2004, and group spaces were set up on Groupspace.org for tutoring new users, for internal development discussion, and for a group planning the LaborTech 2004 conference at Stanford. Over the following year, about a dozen groups used Deme on a regular basis, and many others created group spaces for trial. The response from users was generally positive, with many new users commenting that Deme had great potential to enhance participation in groups of which they were members. By 2005, however, the frame-based interface of the early Deme was behind the times, as frames gave way to more nimble user experiences based on AJAX. Deme has been rewritten a few times since the first version in order to keep up with advancing Web technology. But our experience with the first version taught us some enduring lessons for the design of an online deliberation platform:

- *Complexity demands visual guidance.* While users appreciated the functionality of Deme once they learned how it worked, the complexity of the early Deme interface proved too confusing for most new users, leading to lower levels of adoption and use. A redesigned interface (Figure 3) addressed this problem through affordances, icons, and labels (Davies et al. 2005; 2008).
- *Commenting must be integrated with email.* Because our first test group's Deme space was set up as a supplement to its regular email list, members continued to use the email list in addition to the group space, which caused confusion and duplicated effort. We concluded that Deme must offer to groups the ability to transfer their email list wholesale into Deme, with support for posting to

(not just reading and being notified of) meeting area discussions via email. This feature was added in version 0.5 in July 2005.

* *Codebase must be built for incremental improvement.* Advances in Web technology and experiences with users dictated many changes to the software, but these proved difficult for new student programmers to implement in the PHP version. The advent of Web application frameworks such as Ruby on Rails and Django made possible a new way of designing complex websites that addresses this problem, and recent versions of Deme have been written in these frameworks.[7]

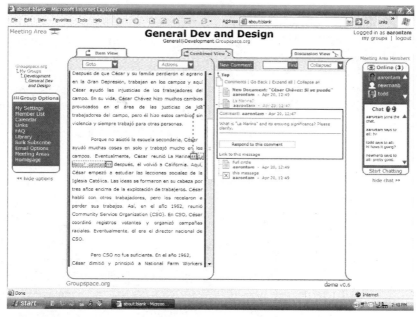

Figure 3. Meeting area redesign (mockup) from January 2006

7 Related Work

Many of Deme's features appeared in some form prior to the first version of Deme. Web-based tools existed for document-centered discussion (e.g., Quicktopic), collaborative authoring (e.g., TWiki), polling and integrating email with message boards (e.g., in Yahoo! Groups and phpBB), petition signing (e.g., PetitionOnline), survey design (e.g., Zoomerang), event scheduling (e.g., Meetup), and many other useful applications for groups.

---

[7] The latest version is at http://deme.stanford.edu (last accessed December 20, 2008).

Previous research prototypes had explored in-text comments of the type implemented in Deme (see Cadiz et al. 2000). Furthermore, interface designs had been developed to address the multiple points of focus that characterize group meetings; e.g., flexible split-screen interfaces in desktop applications such as the FreeAgent newsreader and the D3E discussion environment. We wanted to develop a platform that integrated many of these functional and interface ideas and was entirely Web-based, so that, ideally, a group's members could log into the platform from any computer on the Internet. Another project with goals broadly similar to ours has been the Communities of Practice Environment (CoPE) reported in Thaw, Feldman, and Li (2008) and Thaw et al. (forthcoming).

In the context of social science, our work generally aligns with the perspective known as 'deliberative democracy' (see Fishkin 2009; Gutmann and Thompson 1997), which holds that democracy can be enhanced by tying social decisions to thoughtful, fair, and informed dialogue among stakeholders, rather than through the filtering and manipulation of raw public opinion by power holders.

8 Conclusion

A common theme of participant-observations leading up to the design of Deme was that the need to make group decisions in face to face meetings often serves as an excuse for inner-circle, nontransparent decision making at many levels in society, ranging from small informal activist organizations to the U.S. Government. Our goal is to eliminate that excuse, so that stakeholders can legitimately demand to be included in decisions even if they cannot be present at face-to-face meetings or are not in an executive body. Our hope is that tools like Deme will eventually change the culture of democracy to one in which we expect more participatory inclusion from institutions and more participation from ourselves.

9 Acknowledgments

We are grateful for the assistance of many people who have contributed to Deme during the period reported in this chapter, including Mic Mylen, Rolando Zeledon, Bayle Shanks, Kent Koth, Art McGee, Sally Kiester, Laurence Schechtman, and David Taylor.

This work was funded by a Public Scholarship Initiative grant from the Vice Provost for Undergraduate Education (VPUE) at Stanford administered by the Haas Center for Public Service, by a VPUE Departmental Grant to the Symbolic Systems Program, and an unrestricted gift to the

Symbolic Systems Program by the late Ric Weiland, to whom we dedicate this chapter.

References

Cadiz, J. J., A. Gupta, and J. Grudin. 2000. Using Web Annotations for Asynchronous Collaboration Around Documents. *ACM 2000 Conference on Computer-Supported Cooperative Work (CSCW 2000)* (Philadelphia, PA, December 2-6, 2000), 309-318. New York: ACM Press.

Davies, T. R. and M. D. Mintz. 2009. Design Features for the Social Web: The Architecture of *Deme*. *Proceedings of the 8th International Workshop on Web-Oriented Software Technology* (IWWOST 2009), eds. L. Olsina, O. Pastor, G. Rossi, D. Schwabe, and M. Winckler, 40-51. CEUR Workshop Proceedings, Vol. 493. Available at http://www.stanford.edu/~davies/IWWOST09-Davies-Mintz-websiteversion.pdf (last accessed August 20, 2009)

Davies, T., B. Newman, B. O'Connor, A. Tam, and L. Perry. 2008. Document Centered Discussion: A Design Pattern for Online Deliberation. *Liberating Voices: A Pattern Language for Communication Revolution*, ed. D. Schuler, 384-386. Cambridge, MA: MIT Press.

Davies, T., B. O'Connor, A. Cochran, and A. Parker. 2005. *'Groupware for groups': Problem-driven design in Deme.* Position paper from the Beyond Threaded Conversation Workshop at CHI 2005 (Portland, Oregon, April 2005). Available at http://www.stanford.edu/~davies/Groupware-for-Groups.pdf (last accessed December 20, 2008)

Davies, T., B. Sywulka, R. Saffold, and R. Jhaveri. 2002. *Community Democracy Online: A Preliminary Report from East Palo Alto.* Paper presented at the American Political Science Association Annual Meeting, Boston, August 29-Sept 1. Available at http://www.stanford.edu/~davies/APSA-2002.pdf (last accessed December 20, 2008)

Farnham, S., H. R. Chesley, D. E. McGhee, and R. Kawal. 2000. Structured Online Interactions: Improving the Decision-Making of Small Discussion Groups. *ACM 2000 Conference on Computer-Supported Cooperative Work (CSCW 2000)* (Philadelphia, PA, December 2-6, 2000), 299-308. New York: ACM Press.

Fishkin, J. S. Virtual Public Consultation: Prospects for Internet Deliberative Democracy. *Online Deliberation: Design, Research, and Practice*, eds. T. Davies and S. P. Gangadharan, 23-35. Stanford, CA: CSLI Publications.

Gutmann, A., and D. Thompson. 1997 *Democracy and Disagreement.* Cambridge, MA: Harvard University Press.

Habermas, J. 1990. *Moral Consciousness and Communicative Action.* Cambridge, MA: MIT Press.

Habermas, J. 2001. *On the Pragmatics of Social Interaction.* Cambridge, MA: MIT Press.

Horster, D. 1992. *Habermas: An Introduction*, Philadelphia: Pennbridge Books.

Kiesler, S., J. Siegel, and T. W. McGuire. 1984. Social Psychological Aspects of Computer-Mediated Communication. *American Psychologist* 39:1123-1134.

Noveck, B. S. 2003. Designing Deliberative Democracy in Cyberspace: The Role of the Cyber-Lawyer. *Journal of Science and Technology Law* 9(1):1-91.

Price, V. 2009. Citizens Deliberating Online: Theory and Some Evidence. *Online Deliberation: Design, Research, and Practice*, eds. T. Davies and S. P. Gangadharan, 37-58. Stanford, CA: CSLI Publications.

Putnam, R.D. 2000. *Bowling Alone: The Collapse and Revival of American Community*. New York: Simon and Schuster.

Skocpol, T. 2003. *Diminished Democracy: From Membership to Management in American Civic Life*. Norman, OK: University of Oklahoma Press.

Stefik, M., G. Foster, D. Bobrow, K. Kahn, S. Lanning, and L. Suchman. 1987. Beyond the Chalkboard: Computer Support for Collaboration and Problem Solving in Meetings. *Communications of the ACM* 30(1): 32-47.

Sywulka, B., T. Davies, R. Saffold, and R. Jhaveri. 2003. Computers and Community in East Palo Alto. Available at http://piece.stanford.edu/piece-computer-survey.pdf (last accessed December 20, 2008)

Thaw, D., J. Feldman, and J. Li. 2008. CoPE: Democratic CSCW in Support of e-Learning. *Proceedings of the 2008 International Conference on Complex, Intelligent and Software Intensive Systems*, 481-486. Washington, DC: IEEE Computer Society.

Thaw, D., J. Feldman, J. J. Li, S. Caballé. Forthcoming. Communities of Practice Environment (CoPE): Democratic CSCW for Group Production and e-Learning. *Intelligent Collaborative e-Learning Systems and Applications*, eds. T. Daradoumis, S. Caballé, J. M. Marquès, F. Xhafa. Berlin, Germany: Springer-Verlag.

Tyler, T. 1988. What is Procedural Justice?: Criteria Used by Citizens to Assess the Fairness of Legal Procedures. *Law and Society Review* 22: 301-305.

26

Online Civic Deliberation with E-Liberate

Douglas Schuler

1   Online Civic Deliberation

Online deliberation is the term for a network-based (usually Internet) computer application that supports the deliberative process in some way. At present, very few examples exist, although the number is slowly increasing. Online deliberation has advantages and disadvantages relative to face-to-face deliberation. Broad criteria of success for either approach include access to the process, efficacy of the process (including the engagement of the participants and the process as a whole), and integration within the social context (including legal requirements, etc.). Of course these criteria overlap to some degree and influence each other.

Online deliberation is a difficult service to provide and support optimally. Low literacy rates and the lack of access to appropriate networked computer facilities and services including support for non-English languages notwithstanding, there are three main reasons for this. The first reason is that very few applications are available for use. Of course, this challenge illustrates a 'chicken and egg' problem: if the applications do not exist, people will not use them. If people do not use them, programmers will not develop them. Systems and the culture of the communities who use them should coevolve. But deliberation applications are difficult to design and implement, and there is seemingly little money to be made with online deliberation. E-commerce, for example, has a larger potential user base, is easier to program, and is more lucrative.

Online Deliberation: Design, Researach, and Practice.
Todd Davies and Seeta Peña Gangadharan (eds.).
Copyright © 2009, CSLI Publications.

The second reason is that deliberation is difficult to do. It is time consuming and confusing in many cases due to complexity of content and process, such as knowing when to 'call the question'. Potential participants often perceive the 'payoff' as far less than the effort expended within the process. As a point of comparison, consider voting in the United States as one form of civic participation that citizens can use. Half of all eligible voters are registered to vote and, of those, on the one day in the four-year span that separates voting opportunities, fewer than half of them make the effort to visit their polling place or drop their ballot in the mail.

The third reason is that meaningful civic deliberation plays a miniscule role in most societies. Unfortunately with few exceptions, governmental bodies from the smallest towns to the highest national and supranational levels seem unable (or, more accurately, unwilling) to support or promote public deliberation in a genuine way, whether it is online or not.

Although the requirement of Internet access in online deliberation adds hurdles of cost, geography, and some degree of computer fluency, this may be offset by the advantages that online deliberation provides, especially depending on the characteristics of the attendees. If, for example, the meeting attendees are drawn from Western Europe and the United States, the costs associated with computer communication will be less than transportation costs. As a matter of fact, online deliberation makes possible the prospect of more-or-less synchronous discussions among people around the world. Unfortunately this seems to allow attendees on one side of the planet to make decisions while the other attendees are asleep. The very fact, however, that worldwide meetings become possible provides an enormously fertile ground for civil society opportunities.

Although face-to-face deliberation is generally 'low-tech', physically getting to meetings may involve costly, 'high-tech' travel. Once attendees are physically present at a face-to-face meeting, effective participation depends on the skills (including, for example, how to use a specific meeting protocol like *Robert's Rules of Order*), intentions, and knowledge of participants as well as the chair. Online environments, however, have the potential of alleviating, at least to some degree, some of the disadvantages that are intrinsic to face-to-face settings. For example, online environments can be developed that only display actions that are allowable within the process at that time, thereby reducing the challenges faced by participants not thoroughly familiar with *Robert's Rules* or whatever system of rules is being used. Online systems can also provide online 'help systems'. For example, within e-Liberate (discussed below) users can view descriptions of how and when specific actions are used. Also, deliberative systems can automatically create meeting transcripts and support a voting process as well.

2   E-Liberate: A Tool for Online Civic Deliberation

Motivated by a long-term desire to employ computing technology for social good, particularly among civil society groups who are striving to create more 'civic intelligence' in our society, I proposed that *Robert's Rules of Order* could be used as a basis for an online deliberation system (Schuler 1989, 1996, 2001). The rationale was based on the widespread use of *Roberts's Rules* (at least in the United States) and its formalized definitions. A network-based application that provided nonprofit, community-based organizations with technology that facilitated deliberation when members couldn't easily get together in face-to-face meetings would be very useful. Face-to-face meetings are still very important, but appropriate use of online deliberation could hopefully help organizations with limited resources.

In 1999, at The Evergreen State College, a team of students (John Adams, Amber Clark, Cory Dightman-Kovac, Neil Honomichael, and Matt Powell) developed the first prototype of an online version of *Robert's Rules of Order*. In 2003, Evergreen student Nathan Clinton, working with me, designed and implemented the system which is now being beta-tested with actual users. Greg Feigenson, Allen Williams, Fiorella De Cindio, and Antonio Marco (De Cindio et al. 2007) have done follow-up work. Schuler and Clinton named the system e-Liberate, which rhymes with the verb *deliberate*. Ideally, the technology would increase the organization's effectiveness while requiring less time and money to conduct deliberative meetings.

Beginning in the late 1800s, Henry Robert devoted over forty years to the development of *Robert's Rules of Order*, a set of directives that designated an orderly process for equitable decision making in face-to-face meetings. One of the most important design objectives was to guarantee every attendee's opportunity to make his or her ideas heard while ensuring that the minority could not prevent the majority from making decisions. These rules work at a variety of scales, from small groups of five to groups numbering in the hundreds. Thousands of organizations around the world now use *Robert's Rules of Order* every day and, in fact, governments and civil society organizations have legally mandated its use in meetings.

Robert's Rules of Order is a type of protocol-based, cooperative work system. It is related to Malone et al.'s (1987) work on semi structured messages and Winograd and Flores' (1987) work which builds on the concept of the speech act (Austin 1962). Those examples all employ what is known as 'typed messages'. The message 'type' is, in effect, a descriptor of the message content, and because of its discreteness, is more easily handled by computer applications than natural language.

In designing e-Liberate, we took into consideration the importance of imposing a strict regimen over communication. Typically, control over communication is appropriate when trying to handle contention over resources. In face-to-face deliberation, contentious moments include the time available for speaking and the existence of explicit objectives and/or formal constraints placed upon the venue, such as in a courtroom or parliament. Using a simple criterion of efficiency, participants will often gauge whether the benefits of making a contribution outweigh possible drawbacks, not being allowed to speak later, for example. In voluntary assemblies such as those employed by civil society, this translates into individuals making a conscious or subconscious calculation of whether the effort of learning the rules (such as *Robert's Rules of Order*) and participating in the assembly is justified by the perceived benefits. As mentioned above, Robert worked on his rules for many years, and each adjustment was intended to remedy a particular problem that Robert observed. Furthermore, Robert—and, after Robert's death, his son—answered via letters all queries from people with questions or comments about the rules. To a computer programmer, this is analogous to meeting user needs by providing user support, fixing bugs, and issuing new releases. In either case, the change process is intended to make the system more amenable incrementally to the needs and preferences of its users.

E-Liberate is intended to be easy to use for anybody familiar with *Robert's Rules of Order*. The system employs a straightforward user interface (Figure 1), which is educational as well as facilitative. The interface shows only the legal actions that are available to the user at that specific time in the meeting. (For example, a user cannot second a motion when there is no motion on the table to second.) Also, at any time during a session, users can click an 'about' button to learn what each particular action will accomplish, thus gaining insight to information not readily available in face-to-face meetings. In addition, meeting quorums are checked, voting is conducted, and the minutes are automatically taken and archived.[1]

The system currently supports meetings that take place in real-time over an hour or so, as well as meetings that are less intense and more leisurely. Meetings could, in theory, span a year or so, making it necessary for meeting attendees to log in to e-Liberate once or twice a week to check for recent developments and perhaps vote or make a motion. E-Liberate currently supports the roles of *chairs, members,* and *observers,* and these meeting participants can be anywhere where Web browsers exist. The system uses the AJAX paradigm to update the meeting transcript and the meeting monitor including meeting status and current allowable actions for each participant without page refreshes.

---

[1] See http://www.publicsphereproject.org/e-liberate/demo.php (last accessed November 1, 2008) for a transcript of an entire sample meeting.

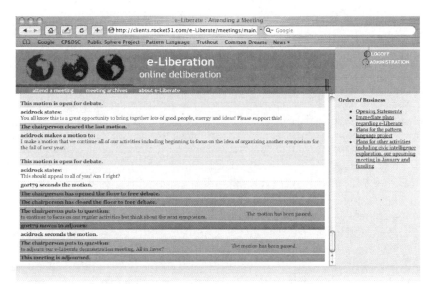

Figure 1. E-Liberate main user interface

By providing cues to permissible actions and online help for all features, e-Liberate is intended to be educational as well as being utilitarian. Meeting attendees should become more knowledgeable about *Robert's Rules* and the use of e-Liberate over time through normal use of the system. Having said that, however, it is still important to acknowledge that some knowledge of—and experience with—*Robert's Rules* is critical to successful participation in e-Liberate meetings. Groups intending to use e-Liberate should work to ensure that all meeting attendees have a basic understanding of the various motions and the basic rules, and we have developed an online manual for that purpose. Additionally, the meeting chair should be prepared to assist attendees whenever possible. Finally, the developers have agreed to be available during some meeting sessions to assist attendees.

Thus far, we have begun working with groups who are interested in using the system to support actual meetings. The hope is that nonprofit groups will use e-Liberate to save time and money on travel and use the resources they save on other activities that promote their core objectives. We are enthusiastic about the system but are well aware that the system as it stands is likely to have problems that need addressing. For this reason, we continue to host meetings with groups and gather feedback from attendees and intend to study a variety of online meetings in order to adjust the system and to develop heuristics for the use of the system. At some point, we plan to make e-Liberate freely available for online meetings and to release the software under a free software license.

3 Preliminary Findings and Outstanding Issues

The first version of e-Liberate has been used in a handful of actual meetings (sometimes conducted as a way to see how well the system worked). The users have expressed positive reactions about the usefulness of the system as well as shortcomings in the system. Our admittedly minimal amount of experience with e-Liberate has nevertheless helped expose a broad range of issues which need to be investigated over time. Unfortunately, there is only room for brief discussion of these shortcomings and issues.

One drawback of online deliberative systems is that computers cannot—or are very unlikely to—facilitate collaboration appropriately based on the *content* of messages. For that reason, the contributions of online deliberations are *typed* to allow automated management of the interactions. In e-Liberate, for example, the typed messages are part of a grammars which specifies allowable 'moves' in a conversation. For example, a move of message type 'seconding a motion' is only legal directly after another participant in a deliberative setting makes a 'making a motion' move. Computers, with their penchant for following rules, can be invaluable for imposing the discipline of an immutable protocol. This is not always agreeable to users. In an infamous incident in the history of computer-supported cooperative work, disgruntled users of the Coordinator, a groupware application based on the ideas developed by Winograd and Flores (1987), proclaimed that the program was 'Nazi-ware' and angrily cast the disks out of their offices (Twidale and Nichols 1998). It is possible, of course, that if the users had derived enough benefit from the Coordinator, they would have helped transform it over time into a less dictatorial program.

Another issue concerned the developers. The objective of e-Liberate was to move beyond chat, premature endings, and unresolved digressions. We wanted to support groups already working for social change and mimic their existing processes as closely as possible. This approach attempted to minimize disruption by integrating the online system as unobtrusively as possible into their actual work lives. However, this strategy was met with unexpected resistance: developers seemed to be constitutionally opposed to implementing existing systems. The few developers I asked stated that supporting *Robert's Rules* was a bad idea (although they in general were not familiar with it) and several advanced the suggestion that meeting participants should be able to make motions *in parallel*. This capability could easily lead to a variety of problems, including the possibility of several competing motions being discussed and amended simultaneously.

Developers and researchers may disregard the existing user base and the important lessons about deliberation that came to be embodied in the rules that they use. From the beginning we've acknowledged that additional or modified functionality in the *Robert's Rules* implementation may be necessary but changes should generally be made only as a response to Feedback from group members.

One set of issues is related to the role of chair, which *Robert's Rules of Order* explicitly specifies for every meeting. The role includes enforcing 'rules relating to debate and those relating to order and decorum', determining when a rule is out of order and to 'expedite business in every way compatible with the rights of members' (Robert 1990). In all, the main reason that a chair is needed at all is due to the fact the rules alone will not suffice. A variety of situations require the chair's input, notably when human judgment is required. Another reason that Robert called upon the services of a chair in his deliberative universe is that meeting attendees may attempt to 'game the game' by invoking rules, which although strictly legal, violate the spirit of the meeting.

The special status of the chair dictates that the human assuming that role needs to be particularly vigilant, especially in light of conniving participants. But what if the attendees do not tend to be connivers? What if they are extremely fair minded and conciliatory? Should not the chair be allowed to put his tasks into an 'auto pilot mode' which could approve nonproblematic requests? If this mode existed, the chair could, say, allow one 'point of order' per attendee an hour or other unit of time, or even as some fraction of the total number of points of order made by all participants. Of course this could also lead to 'gaming'. At that point, of course, the chair would need to be brought back from retirement to reassert his or her 'human touch'. We initiated a form of 'auto pilot' in e-Liberate after we ascertained that the chair could actually be an impediment to progress and seemed less necessary in the online environment—at least the particular configuration of our meeting. When an attendee requests the floor, he or she is automatically 'recognized' by the automated proxy of the chair.

Another set of issues, when meeting attendees are unseen and distributed, arises in the process of adapting face-to-face processes in online environments. For example, how do we know when a quorum is present? This is part of the larger issue of how do we know who is online? Establishing the identity of a person who is interacting, sight unseen, via the Internet is important and certainly not trivial, such as in the case of online voting. We also would like to know whether, for example, members are offline by choice or whether they want to participate but are unable to connect for technical reasons? And, if not connected and/or not paying attention to the meeting at any given time, does that mean they are not in attendance and, consequently, a quorum may no longer exist?

All of these issues are interrelated and influence each other in obvious and subtle ways. For example, since attendees are no longer at a single shared location, where they would be (presumably) attending solely to the business of the assembly, the question of meeting duration comes up. Should meetings be relatively intense affairs where all attendees interact, and business is conducted in one or two hours? Or should/could the meeting be more leisurely, perhaps stretching over one or two weeks? The values assigned to a particular meeting (which act as constraints enforced by the deliberation tool) probably need to be established in relation to each other and to the characteristics of the individual meeting. These characteristics could include the number of attendees, distribution of attendees across time zones, deadlines for decisions, and so on.

The distribution of attendees across time zones highlights and helps bring forward a variety of 'problems' that humankind's earth-based orientation and social institutions (like the work day or work week, and family obligations) place in the way of Internet-enabled 'always-on' opportunities. These problems add considerable complexity to an already complex undertaking. Addressing these issues will require social as well as technological approaches. It may be advisable to establish a certain span of time as a 'recess' which prevents user input or only permits a maximum length and/or number of comments that an attendee can submit on any given motion. E-Liberate's 'meeting configuration' page is currently fairly sparse, but this can change over time to better reflect the needs of its users.

How well will e-Liberate perform when used by larger groups? The only way to learn is to host meetings with larger numbers of people—50, 100, 1000—observe the results and interview the participants. Finding groups this large with a strong enough interest seems unlikely in the short term, but if trials work out well with smaller groups, increasing the size of the groups willing to invest the time should also increase.

A final set of issues is related to the legal and other aspects of the social environment in which the system operates. In many cases, for example, meetings of nonprofit groups are required to be public. Does an online environment that allows for 'observers' (as e-Liberate does) meet this requirement? The law sometimes requires a certain number of meetings every year. A system like e-Liberate could help organizations do this more easily, by automatically sending out meeting notices, for example. In addition, developers must face the issue of cultural biases. We encourage collaborative projects that address these issues.

4   Next Steps

E-Liberate, after some modification, is likely to be useful for groups who want to conduct online meetings using *Robert's Rules of Order*, and we will continue to pursue this end by working with actual groups. In addition to improving the usability of e-Liberate with basic adjustments, we will pursue two additional lines of development: (1) working with outside groups to continue development, and (2) working on ways to augment the system—while leaving the fundamental model intact. In other words, although the system would be extended in various ways meeting attendees would still be able to employ *Robert's Rules of Order* to arrive at decisions in an equitable, collective manner. One of the most interesting lines of development involves the employment of a separate 'protocol language' which would allow modifications (as well as replacements) to the Roberts Rules foundation including, at least ultimately, other collaborative tools like brainstorming to be added to the meeting process. This approach would hopefully help hasten the evolution of useful online deliberative technology.

References

Austin, J. 1962. *How to Do Things With Words*. Cambridge, MA: Harvard University Press.

De Cindio, F., A. De Marco, and L. A. Ripamonti. 2007. Enriching Community Networks by Supporting Deliberation. *Communities and Technologies. Proceedings of the Third Communities and Technologies Conference, Michigan State University, 2007*, ed. C. Steinfield, B. T. Pentland, M. Ackerman, N. Contractor, 395-417. New York: Springer

Malone, T., K. Grant, K. K. Lai, R. Rao, and D. Rosenblitt. 1987. Semistructured Messages are Surprisingly Useful for Computer-Supported Coordination. *ACM Transactions on Office Information Systems* 5(2): 115-131.

Robert, H. 1990. *Robert's Rules of Order—Newly Revised*. New York: Perseus Books.

Schuler, D. 1989. A Civilian Computing Initiative: Three Modest Proposals. *Directions and Implications of Advanced Computing*, eds. J. Jacky and D. Schuler, 167-74. Norwood, NJ: Ablex.

Schuler, D. 1996. *New Community Networks: Wired for Change*. New York: Addison-Wesley.

Schuler, D. 2001. Cultivating Society's Civic Intelligence: Patterns for a New 'World Brain'. *Community Informatics*, ed. B. Loader, 284-304. Routledge. 2001.

Schuler, D. and A. Namioka, eds. 1993. *Participatory Design: Principles and Practices*. Hillsdale, NJ: Lawrence Erlbaum and Associates.

Twidale, M. B. and D. M. Nichols. 1998. *A Survey of Applications of CSCW for Digital Libraries. Technical Report CSEG/4/98.* Computing Department, Lancaster University. http://www.comp.lancs.ac.uk/computing/research/cseg/projects/ariadne/docs/survey.html (last accessed September 18, 2008)

Winograd, T. and F. Flores. 1987. *Understanding Computers and Cognition: A New Foundation for Design.* Reading, MA: Addison-Wesley.

27

Parliament: A Module for Parliamentary Procedure Software

BAYLE SHANKS AND DANA DAHLSTROM

1 Introduction

Parliament is an open source software module that can be used to build programs that follow or moderate the conduct of a deliberative assembly using parliamentary procedure. Parliament encapsulates logic and bookkeeping functions necessary for the function of parliamentary procedure and can be embedded in applications for face-to-face meetings or for synchronous or asynchronous computer mediated communication.

Parliament's central functions track meeting state aspects of the meeting, such as pending motions, the relationships among them, and business already transacted. The outer application (see Figure 1) is responsible for informing the Parliament module about events as they occur in the meeting, such as 'member X made motion Y' or 'motion Y failed.' Parliament answers queries such as 'Which motions are presently valid?' or 'Which motions have been adopted in this meeting?' It is also capable of answering questions about hypothetical situations, such as 'Which motion will be pending if the immediately pending motion is adopted?' The Parliament module does not incorporate the details of parliamentary procedure, such as the motions and customs described in *Robert's Rules of Order Revised* (Robert 1915). Instead, Parliament requires an external rule specification, allowing the user or developer to modify the rules independently and even to develop whole new rule systems.

Online Deliberation: Design, Research, and Practice,
Todd Davies and Seeta Peña Gangadharan (eds.).
Copyright © 2009, CSLI Publications.

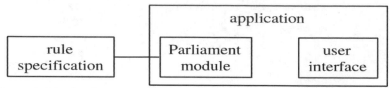

Figure 1. The Parliament module is embedded in an application, and uses an external rule specification[1]

2 A Reusable Model

Many software applications could share a common software implementation of parliamentary procedure; for example, applications that:

- (for online, synchronous meetings)
  - o assist meeting participants during the meeting
  - o assist meeting officers during the meeting
  - o train people before the meeting
  - o provide a networked application which participants use to request the floor and to make and vote on motions
- (for online, asynchronous meetings — Web or other)
  - o assist a human chair
  - o automatically chair a meeting
  - o moderate a large discussion board or wiki according to formal meeting rules
  - o automatically update a set of organizational bylaws according to the instructions of an online deliberative assembly

We offer the Parliament module for use in other programs (applications), since it would be inefficient to reimplement the core logic of parliamentary rules and sets of motions for each software project.

3 Modular Rule Specifications

Robert's Rules of Order Revised is the most common parliamentary authority in the United States, but there are others. Older, public domain versions of *Robert's Rules of Order* and Sturgis's *Standard Code of Parliamentary Procedure* are examples. Each branch of the U.S. Congress uses its own rules, which are broadly similar to others just mentioned.

Rather than choosing a specific set of parliamentary rules and 'hard-coding' them, we designed a single module to accommodate many different parliamentary rule sets. The user or developer may describe new rule sets in a specification language understood by the Parliament module, and the specification is then loaded at runtime (see Figure 1 above). There are many advantages to this approach:

- Different deliberative assemblies use different meeting rules.

- Unconventional meeting settings such as the Web or Internet relay chat (IRC) demand new innovations in parliamentary rules.

- Allowing the rule set to be modified gives each assembly complete flexibility to adapt the software to its needs. Assemblies should not be forced to follow a particular set of meeting rules just because their software cannot support the rules that they prefer.

- Research on group decision making support systems (GDSS) is hindered by the difficulty of isolating the effect of individual components of the group decision making process. A configurable parliamentary rule set will serve as the ideal platform for testing fine-grained modifications to a group's process.

4 The Rule Specification Language

The rule specification language has a quasi-English syntax. A rule set is typically written in a separate file and then loaded into the Parliament module upon initialization.

The rule set is specified in terms of 'actions' that participants can take at certain times in the meeting.

The rule set specification can be arbitrarily expressive: if there is no other way to express some desired behavior, Python code can be embedded into the rule set.

5 The Robert's Rules Parliamentary Rule Set Specification

We have written a partial rule set specification for the 1915 (now public domain) fourth edition of *Robert's Rules of Order Revised*. The rule set includes over twenty-five of the most common motions and their important attributes—such as when they are debatable and what vote is required for them to carry—as well as most of the precedence relations between the motions and some of their semantics.

This specification was initially based on Henry Prakken's formalization of Robert's Rules (Prakken 1998), which he kindly provided to us in machine-readable form. We made many changes to Prakken's formalization, including the addition of the complicated logic of precedence.

6   Conclusion

The Parliament module provides the central infrastructure for parliamentary-procedure software. A reusable module, it implements and interprets parliamentary rules, tracks meeting state, and infers important information such as which motions are in order at a given time. The module is flexible, accommodating any properly codified set of parliamentary rules.

```
NAME: Lay on the table
MOTION TO FORM OF NAME: "Motion to lay on the table"

TYPE: Subsidiary motion

SUMMARY: "The objective of this motion is to temporarily lay a question aside"

motion precedence: 1
debatable: NO
amendable: NO
subsidiaries allowed: NO
reconsiderable: ONLY WHEN (WAS_ACCEPTED)

TARGET: ancestor motion
ON PASS: table target

category: "scheduling"
purpose: "delay"

# comments can be embedded like this

RRO section ref: "19"

RROR section ref: "28"

{
def example_method(self):
print 'This is embedded Python code'
}
```

Figure 2. The motion to 'Lay on the table' defined in the rule specification language (note that in the actual code there would be no word-wrapping)

Figure 2 shows the definition of an example motion in the rule specification language, taken from the Robert's Rules rule set.

A concise specification language allows others to create and modify rule sets efficiently. A usable partial specification of Robert's rules has been created, and a prototype Robert's rules meeting assistant has been built and used in real face-to-face meetings (Dahlstrom and Shanks 2009).

The Parliament module shows potential for use in many contexts, including both face-to-face and online meetings. It is hoped the module will lead to a variety of useful parliamentary software.

References

Dahlstrom, D. and B. Shanks. 2009. Software Support for Face-to-Face Parliamentary Procedure. *Online Deliberation: Design, Research, and Practice*, eds. T. Davies and S. P. Gangadharan, 213-220. Stanford, CA: CSLI Publications.

Prakken, H. 1998. Formalizing Robert's Rules of Order: An Experiment in Automating Mediation of Group Decision Making. *Tech. Rep. REP-FIT-1998-12*, GMD.

Robert, H. M. 1915. *Robert's Rules of Order Revised*. Public Domain.

Sturgis, A. 2001. *The Standard Code of Parliamentary Procedure*, 4th ed. New York: McGraw-Hill.

28

Decision Structure: A New Approach to Three Problems in Deliberation

RAYMOND J. PINGREE

1 Introduction

Offline discussion is often assumed to be the gold standard for deliberation. As a result, online deliberation environments are typically designed with the goal of creating something as close as possible to offline discussion. This has caused us to neglect certain possibilities unique to the online environment. Deliberation is an ideal form of discussion in which participants share their considerations in order to make decisions of higher quality and democratic legitimacy (Chambers 1996; Cohen 1989; Delli Carpini, Cook, and Jacobs 2004; Fearson 1998; Fishkin 1991, 1995; Gastil 2000; Gutmann and Thompson 1996). Because deliberation is an ideal that is not automatically achieved in offline discussion, it seems unwise to assume that the best that online deliberation can do is to mimic offline discussion. Designers of online forums should instead strive to take advantage of the unique design flexibility of the online discussion environment. Instead of mimicking offline discussion, online discussion environments should be designed with the goal of more closely approximating the ideals of deliberation.

This chapter will review three problems for achieving ideal deliberation that can be addressed by forum design, and introduce a forum design intended to solve each of them. First is the problem of scale, which seems to limit coherent and efficient deliberation to very small groups. Second are problems of memory and mental organization which interfere with the

Online Deliberation: Design, Research, and Practice.
Todd Davies and Seeta Peña Gangadharan (eds.).
Copyright © 2009, CSLI Publications.

purpose of the deliberative norm of open-mindedness. The third problem is that there can be an apparent conflict between the desire for organization of discussion topics and democratic legitimacy, which can make large groups feel they must accept undemocratic control over the agenda to make any progress at all.

2   Problems in Deliberation

Several of the most commonly discussed problems in deliberation are independent of the design of a deliberative forum, because they address the nature of participants, such as their diversity of views (Mutz and Martin 2001), their willingness or tendency to follow deliberative norms (Conover, Searing, and Crewe 2002), or the kind of content that should be encouraged or allowed in deliberation, such as public-spirited reasons (Chambers 1996; Knight and Johnson 1994; Young 1996) and testimony (Sanders 1997). This section will enumerate a different set of problems from those usually discussed, because it focuses on those that could plausibly be affected by forum design. These include problems of coordination and ability, which are more fundamental and perhaps more important than problems of intent and motivation, particularly if one sees deliberation as a form of ideal group decision making that is not limited to politics. In nonpolitical decision making discussions, it is easier to imagine that most participants want to reason together with open minds.

The Problem of Scale

Large groups of people often want to make decisions deliberatively. However, large group sizes seem to create a conflict between the goals of coherence and efficiency. Coherence seems to demand *full reception*: that all participants receive all messages sent. However, in large groups full reception can be painfully inefficient. In a spoken discussion, full reception means one speaker at a time, which gives each participant a decreasing fair share of speaking time as group size grows. Written online discussion does not automatically solve this problem, although it does allow any number of people to compose messages at once without a loss of comprehensibility. In written discussions, the problem of scale manifests as a difficulty in keeping up with all messages being sent. In both spoken and written contexts, as group sizes grow, the coherence of the discussion is threatened as it begins to break up into subdiscussions.

Problems of Memory and Mental Organization

Theories of deliberation often seem to assume that human memory is a perfectly reliable and uniform storage bin for all information a person is exposed to (Lupia 2002). Proponents of deliberation must confront the real limitations of unassisted human memory in order to design deliberative forums to effectively assist memory.

Even those who have the best of intentions to be open-minded may find it difficult to do so because of the limitations of human memory and the complexity of decisions. Following through with the ultimate purpose of the deliberative ideal of open-mindedness is a lot to ask given what we know about unassisted human memory. This purpose is to form an opinion at the end of deliberation based on all relevant considerations expressed. To do this, one must not only remember all of these considerations but also remember the structure of how they relate to one another. Even if one makes the very questionable assumption that people pay perfect attention to all considerations they hear, each consideration must also remain in short term memory long enough to have a chance to be stored in long-term memory (Lupia 2002). Then, even if all considerations are in fact stored in long-term memory, when participants attempt to form an evaluation by searching their memory for considerations, they are likely to recall only a sample of them (Zaller 1992). This can create systematic biases towards using more recently or more frequently expressed considerations (Price and Tewksbury 1997). Finally, even if all considerations are not only stored in long-term memory but also cognitively accessible at the point of decision making, their structure may not have been understood, remembered, or sampled. One can remember an argument without remembering what it argues against.

The Conflict between Organization and Democratic Legitimacy

Organization is a central problem not only within individual heads but also at the group level. In any deliberation, but particularly with larger numbers of participants discussing a complex topic, it often seems necessary to impose some form of agenda or organization of discussion topics in order to get anywhere at all. However, if the specific topics and decision goals of the deliberation are imposed undemocratically, this can limit the range of possible outcomes of the deliberation and thus embody undemocratic control. The potential open-endedness of decision goals in deliberation is a key argument for its superior legitimacy over mere voting. Through discussion a group can discover the appropriate ballot. With mere voting, those who determine the ballot have enormous power.

3 A New Solution

A new theoretical model of deliberation called Decision-Structured Deliberation (DSD) may be used to design asynchronous online forums that address each of these problems. DSD is a theoretical model not tied to any particular technology. For a more detailed description of DSD and its theoretical implications, see Pingree (2006). How this is expected to solve each of the three problems above will be explained in more detail below, after describing the proposed forum.

HeadsTogether

This chapter describes a particular proposed online implementation of DSD called HeadsTogether. A HeadsTogether forum is like other asynchronous online forums in that participants post messages that other participants can read later at any time. It is also like some other asynchronous online forums in that it uses a hierarchical structure of messages, meaning that each message can have any number of messages within it and that this nesting can continue to any depth. However, the relationships between messages that constitute this hierarchy are more specific than the mere reply relationships found in existing forums. They can specify, for example, that a particular message is a: solution to a problem stated by another message, reason why a problem is important, or reason why another reason is not valid.

Because this structure is created by participants during the deliberation itself, authoring messages in a HeadsTogether forum involves specifying these relationships. Message authors must first choose what type of message they are posting. The available types are specified by an administrator and can be specific to the deliberation context or a more general purpose set of types such as problems, solutions, and causes. The type of a particular message determines the ways other messages can be connected to that message. These allowed relationships between types can also be configured by a forum administrator. For example, a problem message can have solutions, causes, and reasons for and against the importance of the problem. The set of types allowed can, and usually should, include a catchall message type such as 'comments' for free-form discussions about any message of the other types.

Message authors also choose where a message fits into the structure by specifying what it relates to and how. Some message types are appropriate at the top level. Again, which types are allowed at the top level can be configured by the forum administrator. In the above example, problems would be a top level type, while solutions would not. In other words, one can post a problem without solutions, but all solutions must be solutions to at least one problem.

Any number of messages can be colocated at any point in this structure. For example, within each problem message there can be any number of solution messages. By default, HeadsTogether presents lists of colocated messages in rank order based on past participant votes on their quality. As a result, greater prominence is given to messages judged by participants to be of higher quality, although all messages remain available.

The main page for a HeadsTogether forum is a ranked list of top level messages. In our example, this would be a list of problem messages posted by past participants, rank ordered based on votes on the importance of each problem message. After clicking on a top level message, users see lists of messages contained in that message—one list for each type that can be contained in that message. For example, after clicking on a problem message, users will see a ranked list of solution messages, a ranked list of cause messages, and a ranked list of reasons for and against the importance of the problem. After clicking on a solution, users would see a ranked list of reasons why that solution should or should not be used to solve the problem.

HeadsTogether and Self-Organization

The structure of messages in HeadsTogether is a *decision structure*: a hierarchy of decisions and subdecisions the group makes collectively (Pingree 2006). Each message is a decision. For example, for each problem, the group must decide how important a problem it is, and for each reason, the group must decide how strong a reason it is. The state of this structure at any point in time can be seen as the agenda for the deliberation. Because these decision messages can be added by any participant at any time, and because they achieve prominence through the votes of other participants, this agenda is democratically determined within the discussion itself. This provides a highly detailed organization of the collective decisions without sacrificing democratic legitimacy.

HeadsTogether as a Memory and Organization Aid

Recall that deliberative norms ask that participants make their final decisions based on all relevant considerations expressed in the deliberation. Because deliberation contains many subdecisions, this is best thought of as a decision-specific requirement. When making each decision or subdecision, participants should have access to all considerations directly relevant to that decision. Because of decision structure, this exact set of messages is available to participants when viewing any decision message in HeadsTogether. When viewing a problem message at the end of deliberation in order to make a final vote on its importance, all messages marked as reasons for the problem are conveniently listed in one place. Because any of these reasons might be worth considering as a subdecision prior to a final decision on the problem's importance, a participant can click on any reason and then see a list of subreasons directly relevant to the validity of that reason. This can continue to any depth.

Note that existing asynchronous online message boards that use hierarchical structures of replies do not provide the same benefits of organization and decision-specific memory. Instead of organizing all considerations relevant to a decision in one place, reply structures tend to bury many of those considerations deep in long chains of replies and within messages that discuss multiple topics.

HeadsTogether at Large Scales

With large numbers of participants, it is inefficient for every message to be received by every participant. This is true in HeadsTogether forums as in any other discussion. However, in HeadsTogether forums, a breakdown in full reception does not necessarily cause a breakdown in coherence. This is because coherence is a decision-specific concept. As argued elsewhere in greater depth (Pingree 2006), coherence for any given decision means that all who made that decision had access to all considerations offered for it. In other words, because of the decision structure of HeadsTogether, users can make coherent contributions to (or deliberative decisions about) one part based only on knowledge of the status of that part and its relationship to the whole, without being aware of the internal details of other parts of the deliberation. The ultimate purpose of sharing considerations in deliberation is to benefit from the pooled considerations of the group about each decision. HeadsTogether forums allow people to benefit from the considerations left by all other users who have ever visited a particular decision before, without having to synchronize with those participants or any others. Because of this, HeadsTogether forums are expected to allow much larger numbers of participants to have an efficient and coherent deliberation.

4 Conclusions

> [Online forums are] a development of historic significance, for there has been practically no innovation in many-to-many communication in over two thousand years (Klein 1999: 213).

Early assessments of the Internet noted the novel possibility of cheaply and quickly gathering large numbers of geographically scattered people virtually 'into one room' (Klein 1999). The hope was that this would remove the physical constraints that the ancient Athenians thought of as the most serious limits to the size of discussion-based democratic decision making (Dahl

1989). Because this has not automatically resulted in dramatically different possibilities for democratic decision making in large groups, it has laid bare the fundamental coordination limits of discussion processes and fundamental cognitive limits of human participants. The true promise of the Internet lies not merely in its ability to bring large numbers of people *into* 'one room' but in its ability to structure that room in ways that no physical room could be structured. As HeadsTogether demonstrates, it is possible to structure an online space to resolve coordination problems for large groups and complex decisions. Face-to-face discussion spaces are, of course, more real. If the goal is social bonding or understanding of other people or groups, offline discussion may well be the gold standard. However, these are not the goals of deliberation. Instead the goal is group decisions that are of higher quality and higher democratic legitimacy.

The DSD model does not, of course, provide any magical solution to problems of intent or motivation. If people do not want to reason together, nothing can force them to do so. HeadsTogether is designed to solve the often-overlooked problems that concern the *ability* of groups of well-intentioned people to have an effective, coherent, and democratically legitimate deliberation. Even with the best of deliberative intentions, unassisted human memory is imperfect, the need for organization may make people feel they must accept undemocratically imposed agendas, and as group sizes grow, discussions may lose coherence by effectively breaking up into unrelated subdiscussions.

References

Chambers, S. 1996. *Reasonable Democracy*. Ithaca, NY: Cornell University Press.

Cohen, J. 1989. Deliberation and Democratic Legitimacy. *The Good Polity: Normative Analysis of the State*, eds. A. Hamlin and P. Pettit. Cambridge, UK: Basil Blackwell.

Conover, P. J., D. D. Searing, and I. M. Crewe. 2002. The Deliberative Potential of Political Discussion. *British Journal of Political Science 32:*21-62.

Dahl, R. 1989. *Democracy and Its Critics*. New Haven, CT: Yale University Press.

Delli Carpini, M. X., F. L. Cook, and L. R. Jacobs. 2004. Public Deliberation, Discursive Participation, and Citizen Engagement: A Review of the Empirical Literature. *Annual Review of Political Science* 7: 315-44.

Fearson, J. 1998. Deliberation as Discussion. *Deliberative Democracy,* ed. J. Elster, 44-68. Cambridge, UK: Cambridge University Press.

Fishkin, J. 1991. *Democracy and Deliberation*. Binghamton, NY: Vail-Ballou Press.

Fishkin, J. 1995. *The Voice of the People*. Binghamton, NY: Vail-Ballou Press.

Gastil, J. 2000. *By Popular Demand.* Berkeley: University of California Press.

Gutmann, A. and Thompson, D. 1996. *Democracy and Disagreement*. Cambridge, MA: Harvard University Press.

Klein, H. 1999. Tocqueville in Cyberspace: Using the Internet for Citizen Associations. *The Information Society* 15: 213-220.

Knight, J. and J. Johnson. 1994. Aggregation and Deliberation: On the Possibility of Democratic Legitimacy. *Political Theory* 22: 277-296.

Lupia, A. 2002. Deliberation Disconnected: What It Takes to Improve Civic Competence. *Law and Contemporary Problems* 65: 133-50.

Mutz, D. C. and P. S. Martin. 2001. Facilitating Communication Across Lines of Political Difference: The Role of Mass Media. *American Political Science Review* 95:97-114.

Pingree, R. J. 2006. Decision Structure and the Problem of Scale in Deliberation. *Communication Theory* 16: 198-222.

Price, V. and D. Tewksbury. 1997. News Values and Public Opinion: A Theoretical Account of Media Priming and Framing. *Progress in the Communication Sciences*, eds. G. Barnett and F. J. Boster, 173-212. New York: Ablex.

Sanders, L. M. 1997. Against Deliberation. *Political Theory* 25: 347.

Young, I. M. 1996. Communication and the Other: Beyond Deliberative Democracy. *Democracy and Difference*, ed. S. Benhabib, 120-135. Princeton, NJ: Princeton University Press.

Zaller, J. 1992. *The Nature and Origins of Mass Opinion*. New York: Cambridge University Press.

29

Design Requirements of Argument Mapping Software for Teaching Deliberation

Matthew W. Easterday, Jordan S. Kanarek, and Maralee Harrell

1 Introduction

Argument mapping software can be used to teach the (much needed) argumentation skills required for deliberation (van Gelder 2003, 2001; Harrell 2005b; Kirschner, Buckingham Shum, and Carr 2003; Kuhn 2005, 1991). But widespread usability problems among current tools have prevented teachers from using these tools in their classrooms (Harrell 2005a). In a comparative usability evaluation of argument mapping software in an introductory university philosophy course, we found that even the most popular tools fail to meet six key criteria: correct representation, flexible construction, 'visualogic', automation of nonsemantic operations, simultaneous display of multiple diagrams, and cross platform compatibility. Using our prototype, we show how a tool can satisfy these requirements by achieving the proper balance of drawing-based interaction and automation.

2 The Problems With Argument Mapping Software

The following scenarios illustrate the most common problems (with example packages exhibiting each problem noted):

Online Deliberation: Design, Research, and Practice.
Todd Davies and Seeta Peña Gangadharan (eds.).

317

1. A teacher wants to diagram an argument from a text but the software does not run on the school's operating system (Omnigraffle, Reason!Able, Argutect).

2. The teacher attempts to diagram the first claim in the text, but the tool does not allow the claim to be added unless the conclusion has been specified (Araucaria, Reason!Able).

3. The teacher reads the remaining text for the conclusion and enters it but has now forgotten the reasons supporting the conclusion and must start rereading. The teacher abandons the tool and draws the diagram on paper.

4. After copying the paper diagram into the tool, the teacher wants to represent a 'linked' reason: but the tool does not allow representation of linked reasons. (Argutect, Athena, Belvedere, Inspiration).

5. The teacher wants to move a reason a little to the left but moving the reason requires redrawing every arrow connected to the reason. (Illustrator).

6. The teacher tries to move the conclusion to the upper-left and enlarge the entire diagram so that it is legible when projected but the tool does not allow the size, layout or text format to be manipulated (Araucaria, Argutect, Athena Standard, Belvedere, Inspiration, Reason!Able).

7. Finally, the teacher tries to display two diagrams side-by-side for comparison, but the tool only displays one diagram at a time, (Araucaria, Belevedere, Reason!Able).

3 Design Requirements

The usability breakdowns illustrated in the previous scenario suggest six criteria that even the best argument mapping tools often overlook:

1. **Correct representation:** Tools must provide visual representations of structures unique to arguments such as 'linked reasons' and 'rebuttals'.

2. **Flexible construction:** Tools must allow input of elements in any order, e.g., claims before conclusions.

3. **'Visualogic':** Teachers need some control over the visual properties including size, layout, and typeface because they have semantic connotations, e.g. size may indicate importance, layout may in-

dicate order, or type might simply need to be larger to be visible to students when projected on a screen.

4. **Automation of nonsemantic operations:** General purpose drawing programs often require operations unnecessary for argument mapping, for example in Adobe Illustrator, moving a claim (box) might require redrawing all the arrows connected to the claim.

5. **Multiple diagrams:** Tools should allow simultaneous presentation of multiple diagrams for comparison.

6. **Cross platform compatibility** Programs that satisfy all of the above criteria still might not run on school computers.

The table below summarizes the requirements satisfied by different argument mapping tools:

Tool	Represent.	Construct.	Visualogic	Automation	Multiple	Platform
Special purpose argument mapping tools						
Araucaria	*			*		*
Argutect		*		*	*	PC
Athena		*		*		*
Belvedere		*		*		*
Inspiration		*		*	*	*
Reason!Able	*			*		PC
General purpose drawing tools						
Omnigraffle	*	*	*	*	*	Mac
Illustrator	*	*	*		*	*

Table 1: Design requirements met by different tools

4 The iLogos Prototype

We developed a prototype that satisfies all of the requirements by balancing the flexibility, interaction, and 'visualogic' of a general purpose drawing program with the automation and specialized representations required for argument mapping. The following scenario illustrates the improvements, by reiterating the teacher's workflow, this time using the prototype (with the satisfied criterion noted at each step):

1. The teacher opens the argument mapping program. iLogos runs on Windows, Macintosh, and Linux *(cross platform)*:

2. The article begins with the claim before stating the conclusion. The prototype allows the teacher to enter claims in any order *(flexible construction)*:

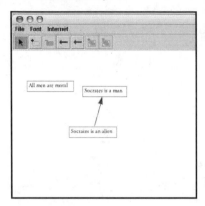 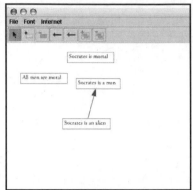

3. After the argument is entered into the tool, the teacher wants to show that some reasons are 'linked'. The prototype allows the teacher to create the desired argument representation by clicking on the 'linked reasons' button *(correct representation)*:

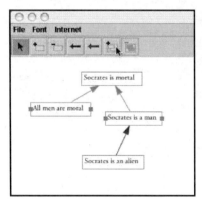 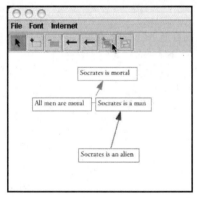

4. The teacher moves a reason a little to the left. Arrows between reasons are automatically redrawn *(automation)*:

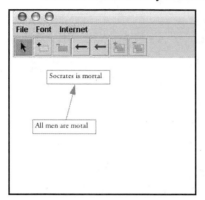 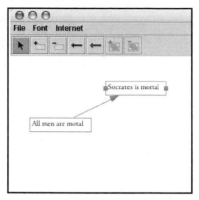

5. The teacher wants to move the conclusion nearer to the top of the screen, making it large enough to be seen when projected. The prototype allows manipulation of visual properties such as layout, text, and size using standard drawing conventions *('visualogic')*:

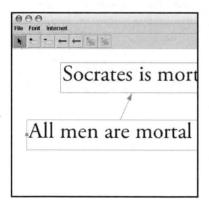 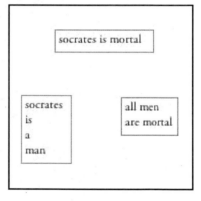

6. Finally, the prototype allows the teacher to compare diagrams by displaying two of them simultaneously *(multiple diagrams)*:

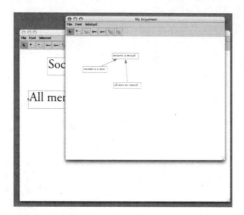

5 Conclusion

By balancing the interaction of a drawing program with automation and support for visual representation of argumentation structure, iLogos satisfies the six design requirements allowing argumentation teachers to successfully use the software in the classroom. By demonstrating how to overcome the functional and usability obstacles of argument mapping software, we hope it will lead to improved usability in other tools and open the door to widespread use of argument mapping software for teaching deliberation.

References

Adobe Illustrator 9 (Version CS2) [Computer software]. 2005. San Jose, CA: Adobe Systems Incorporated.

Argutect (Version 3.0) [Computer software]. 2002. Pittsburgh, PA: Knosis.

Araucaria (Version 3.0) [Computer software]. 2005. Scotland: University of Dundee, Department of Applied Computing.

Belvedere (Version 4.0) [Computer software]. 2002. University of Hawai'i at Manoa, Laboratory for Interactive Learning Technologies.

Kirschner, P. A., S. J. Buckingham Shum, and C. S. Carr, eds. 2003. *Visualizing Argumentation: Software Tools for Collaborative and Educational Sensemaking.* New York: Springer.

Kuhn, D. 1991. *The Skills of Argument.* New York: Cambridge University Press.

Kuhn, D. 2005. *Education for Thinking.* Cambridge: Harvard University Press.

Harrell, M. 2005a. Using Argument Diagramming Software in the Classroom. *Teaching Philosophy* 28(2): 163-177.

Harrell, M. 2005b. *Using Argument Diagrams to Improve Critical Thinking Skills in 80-100 What Philosophy Is*. (Tech. Rep. CMU-PHIL-176). Pittsburgh, PA, Carnegie Mellon University.

Inspiration (Version 7.6) [Computer software]. 2005. Portland, OR: Inspiration Software.

Omnigraffle (Version 4) [Computer software]. 2005. Seattle, WA: Omni Group.

Reason!able (Version 1.1c) [Computer software]. 2001. Australia: University of Melbourne.

Rolf, B. and Magnusson, C. 2005. Athena (Version 2.5) [Computer software]. Karlskrona, Sweden: Blekinge Institute of Technology.

van Gelder, T. 2001. How to Improve Critical Thinking Using Educational Technology. *Meeting at the Crossroads: Proceedings of the 18th Annual Conference of the Australian Society for Computers in Learning in Tertiary Education*, eds. G. Kennedy, M. Keppell, C. McNaught, and T. Petrovic, 539-548. Melbourne: Biomedical Multimedia Unit, University of Melbourne.

van Gelder, T. 2003. Enhancing Deliberation through Computer Supported Visualization. *Visualizing Argumentation: Software Tools for Collaborative and Educational Sense-making*, eds. P. A. Kirschner, S. J. Buckingham Shum, and C. S. Carr, 97-115. New York: Springer.

30

Email-Embedded Voting with eVote/Clerk

Marilyn Davis

1 Motivation

In a democracy, political power lies only nominally in the vote. The primary power is proposing the subject of the vote. The secondary power is being listened to, getting your points considered. The weakest power is listening and voting. We are accustomed to the weak power, to listen and vote. Email lists and a plethora of Web-based collaboration tools provide the secondary power, to be listened to.

The focus of the eVote®/Clerk software project was to provide a tool for dispersing the primary power: the power to compose a poll that a group of people can vote on. Embedded into an email list, eVote gives each member of an online community all three powers.

2 Petition Plebiscites

The software has been used for a few plebiscitary petitions. In a petition, most community members are not involved in discussion or creating the text of the declaration, they only read and sign. EVote/Clerk petitions feature a webpage that facilitates participation by generating and sending an Email message to the email interface. Typically, half the signatures have been gathered via the Web interface and half from direct email.

Online Deliberation: Design, Research, and Practice.
Todd Davies and Seeta Peña Gangadharan (eds.).
Copyright © 2009, CSLI Publications.

Notable among the eVote petitions were Zapatista Consulta and Kopilli Ketzalli.[1] However, participation in these petitions was meager. Zapatista Consulta drew 210 votes, compared to a million votes collected in the streets. Kopilli Ketzalli has drawn 235 votes thus far, while several hundred thousand have been collected for this cause. Nevertheless, many of the few who did participate online commented that they were grateful for the opportunity.

While there has been considerable academic interest in the primary power available through eVote, such as composing a poll, very few people have actually used it. Laurent Chemla translated eVote/Clerk to French and implemented it for the AUI (Association des Utilisateurs d'Internet), the French Internet Society. Opposition to eVote was immediate and strident. First there was opposition to the dispersion of the primary power, especially by the president of the group. In response, the group decided that only committee members could poll the email list. Also, there was surprising opposition to the fact that, until a poll is closed, members can change their votes. John J. Jacq in Australia runs a successful eVote email list for his extended family. Different members of the family have set polls, and John has made nice webpages to accompany them.

3 Election Voting

Interest in the eVote/Clerk software took an unexpected turn toward election voting because of the security features inherent in its architecture. 'The Clerk' is a specialized vote server, a database server designed solely for vote-keeping. Because there is no flexibility in the types of data that it serves, it enables extreme flexibility in 'eVote', the user interface that communicates with The Clerk. In addition to handling polls and storing ballots, The Clerk also stores a link to the voter's identity with the ballot. Storing the link with the ballot is important so that a vote can be changed at the voter's instruction and votes can be made visible for external checking and recounting.

The practice of storing votes with the voter's identity is antithetical to a common assumption about voting: a vote must be secret, therefore, the link from the ballot to the voter must be broken. However, if we do not break the link to the voter, and if we trust technology to keep the link secret, then voting run by cooperating Clerks provides absolute accuracy of the vote tally. An election administrator is not able to tamper with an election (Davis 2001). Even without secrecy, networked Clerks provide a perfect medium

---

[1] See http://www.deliberate.com/consulta (last accessed September 22, 2008) and http://www.deliberate.com/aztec (last accessed September 22, 2008).

for signature gathering for ballot referendums, because secrecy is not needed for our direct democracy facility (Davis 2000). A simple solution to providing secrecy is for each voter to be given an anonymous email address for voting. This method, along with EVote/Clerk, was successfully used for online elections for Computer Professionals for Social Responsibility in 2006.[2]

4 Conclusions

EVote/Clerk has been used sucessfully, technically, for a number of groups. However, almost always, it brings much discomfort and opposition. Possibly this is because many people, especially powerful people, are firmly attached to a hierarchical model of social organization. EVote/Clerk displaces that model with the 'cooperative' model (see Eisler 1987). This sudden displacement of the older, more violent model is disturbing for many. However, cooperation with people, while using a computer, is an increasingly important skill. Through the electronic medium, which is our collective organ for communication and collaboration, the cooperative model is growing. I believe that democracy will emerge.

References

Davis, M. 2001. *Protecting A System From Attack From Within*. Workshop on Trustworthy Elections, Tomales Bay, California, August 26-29, 2001. Available at http://www.deliberate.com/wote01/wotetext.html (last accessed September 22, 2008)

Davis, M. 2000. The First Step: Petitions. Available at http://www.deliberate.com/deliberate/eVote/papers/petition.html (last accessed September 22, 2008)

Eisler, R. 1987. *The Chalice and the Blade: Our History, Our Future*. New York: Harper Collins Publishers.

---

[2] See http://www.deliberate.com/cpsr (last accessed September 22, 2008).

Epilogue

Understanding Diversity in the Field of Online Deliberation

SEETA PEÑA GANGADHARAN

1 Introduction

For designers, scholars, and practitioners, the term 'online deliberation' holds many different meanings. Words or phrases like 'consensus', 'participation', 'access to information', 'voting', 'project management', 'learning', and 'collaboration' inflect the vocabularies used by those developing, assessing, or disseminating digital technologies that facilitate deliberation. Within this book alone, online deliberation has been variously applied to collectively editing a document on a political party's wiki (Raynes-Goldie and Fono 2009), collaborating among programmers to package thousands of open source software projects into a single operating system (Ristroph 2009), and using electronic voting software (Davis 2009).

Where do these different perspectives on online deliberation come from? And what does this diversity suggest for the future of the field? To answer these questions, this chapter proceeds in two main parts. First, I explore the multiple histories of the field to enumerate the various forms and practices of online deliberation. I cast a purposefully wide net over cross-disciplinary scholarship that has used the term 'online deliberation'. In many cases, I even consider literature that does not explicitly refer to either deliberating or being online, but which has since been cited as intellectual forerunner of the current field of online deliberation. Much of this literature alludes to deliberative activity, such as group decision making,

Online Deliberation: Design, Research, and Practice.
Todd Davies and Seeta Peña Gangadharan (eds.).

formation of consensus, group learning processes, collaborative authoring, editing, or content creation, and virtual meeting spaces or conferences.

Second, based on these histories, I create a taxonomy that aims to make sense of the field's diversity. This taxonomy focuses on the levels at which online deliberation occurs, such as deliberative processes that take place within a software agent versus deliberative projects that are institutionally managed. By focusing on the level at which online deliberation occurs, the taxonomy subsumes disciplinary boundaries that have often separated the study, design, and practice of online political deliberation, on the one hand, from that of deliberation for more general purposes, on the other.

By laying out multiple histories of the field and presenting a taxonomy of online deliberation, this epilogue brings together the seemingly disparate areas of interest within the field, exposing similarities and differences between them. In doing so, I hope to lay the groundwork for future inquiries and experiments with the idea, tools, and practices of online deliberation.[1]

2   Democratic Theories and Political Deliberation

For many, talk of online deliberation is synonymous with talk of changing or improving democracy and seeing it work via digital media. To fully understand this political focus, it is helpful to recall the rise in interest in deliberative democracy. The study of online political behavior, social forms, and cultural processes has emerged alongside inquiries into a new style of democratic practice that values collective interest or group dynamics in political discussion and decision making.

Deliberative democracy became a popular concept in the wake of a chorus of concern for liberal democracy (Bohman and Rehg 1997). In 1980, political scientist Joseph M. Bessette published a chapter titled 'Deliberative Democracy: The Majority Principle in Republican Government', which outlined a plan for the renewal of civic life based on citizen participation and debate. Bessette called for participation that goes beyond voting and includes dialogue of controversial issues among citizens. His model was republican in the sense that it encouraged the formation of the common good and shared civic culture. Subsequently, Sunstein (1985) and others began crediting Bessette with having first used the term 'deliberative democracy' and, furthermore, extolling the merits of republican designs. A new direction of scholarship opened, urging that the value of communal life be restored through public communication, protection of public spaces, and

---

[1] An annotated list of past and current forms and practices in online deliberation can be found as an appendix to this chapter. The list is also publicly available and will be updated on the website for this book at http://www.Online-Deliberation.net.

identification of a communal ethos (Sandel 1982, 1984; Taylor 1989, 1992; see also Gutmann 1985).[2]

Increased attention to deliberative democracy also resulted from the publication in 1989 of the English translation of Habermas's *Structural Transformation of the Public Sphere* (*STPS*). The work, which had been available but less well known in German since the 1960s, argued for the necessity of procedural norms in democratic practice. According to Habermas, only the establishment of criteria for communication within a group, or what is also referred to as public communication, leads to legitimate outcomes. His work subsequent to *STPS* further developed norms of public communication—first at the level of moral philosophy (Habermas 1990, 1993) and then later in terms of democratic theory (Habermas 1996).

By the late 1990s and early 2000s, deliberative democratic theories had ascended. Bohman (1998) wrote about the 'coming of age' of deliberative democracy, noting the evolution of deliberative democratic theory into deliberative democratic theories, plural. Bohman claimed that as writings on the topic expanded, key theorists were responding to criticism concerning the impossibility—or heady idealism—of the deliberative ideal. Or, as Fishkin (2003) described, 'the move from imaginary thought experiments to real (or at least possible) institutions' (2) confronted political theorists with many pragmatic considerations. With these considerations came the revelation that not all deliberative democrats embraced the same vision. Bohman suggested that the diversity of models of deliberative democracy reflected a measure of their acceptance. Dryzek (2002) claimed 'the essence of democracy itself is now widely taken to be deliberation' (1).

Against the growing visibility and acceptability of deliberative democratic theories in law, philosophy, political science, and communication, scholars began exploring technologically mediated democracy. With innovation in digital technologies, development of the World Wide Web protocol, and wider availability of the Internet, these scholars studied information and communication technologies (ICTs) as agents—and emblems—of change, heralding a new era in democratic and soon-to-be-democratic societies. By the late 1980s, social scientists were using terms like 'cyberdemocracy', 'virtual democracy', and 'electronic democracy' to denote the potentially democratizing effect of new technologies.[3]

---

[2] There is a tradition of participatory democracy that deals with renewing citizen power (Pateman 1970; for a practitioner's perspective, see Arnstein 1969). However, these works do not focus on deliberation or deliberative processes as intently as they focus on participation and influence.

[3] Carey (1997) has written a compelling history—and critique—of the recurring theme of technology as a democratizing force.

In time, scholarly discourse on cyberdemocracy grew multifaceted (see Shane 2004). It discussed computer-mediated communication as a remedy for lackluster rates of participation in politics (Johnson 1998), and included criticism of the assumption of digital media's liberatory power and of techno-centric society (Barbrook and Cameron 1998). It also ranged from an interrogation of 'cyborg politics' (Poster 1995, n.p.), in which disembodied, decentralized, and often anonymous forms of argumentation and interaction alter democratic practice, to a comparative examination of online civic experiments in Western cities (Tsagaroursianou, Tambini, and Bryan 1999).[4]

As scholarly interest in cyberdemocracy expanded, some scholars began to explore the idea of deliberation in an online setting. Early works did not use the specific term 'online deliberation' but nevertheless implicitly dealt with the idea of deliberation. Whether from a techno-determinist or socio-determinist perspective, or somewhere between utopian and skeptic, scholarship probed the nature of argumentation, debate, and decision-making; inclusion and participation in spaces for deliberation; and architecture or structures for online public communication, such as the virtual town hall or common space. For example, against the backdrop of different models of deliberative democracy, Friedland (1996) explored emergent forms of citizenship in an age of computers and the Internet. According to Friedland, electronic public journalism, government-community online projects, community-based computer networks, and advocacy networks offer new paths to social capital formation not anticipated in theoretical models.

Since the start of the new millennium, the expression 'online deliberation' has become more widely used. As the term 'cyberdemocracy' gave way to 'digital democracy', 'e-democracy', or 'Internet democracy',[5] and the volume of digital democracy studies grew, political scientists and political communication scholars, in particular, began taking a greater interest in deliberative activity in computer-mediated settings. Sunstein (2001) took stock of the dangers of personalized communication technologies and countered the 'daily me' (Negroponte 1995) with a republican model of democracy, calling for, among other things, a public sidewalk in virtual space where individuals could encounter competing viewpoints. Looking at a predominantly Western European political context, Coleman and Gøtze (2001)

---

[4] Throughout the 1990s, researchers also engaged with the idea of virtual communities. This work, pushed into academic discourse in part by practitioners such as Rheingold (1993), explored community computer networks (Cohill and Kavanaugh 1997; Kollock and Smith 1996). While their work was not grounded in debates about deliberative democracy, their analyses evolved in a context of optimism for the renewal of civic life.

[5] In the era of the Xbox, iPod, and iPhone, it would not be surprising if the terms 'i-democracy' or 'x-democracy', became part of the jargon.

considered several different cases of public consultation, i.e., citizen engagement in deliberation over public policies. Meanwhile, Price et al. (2001) employed the specific term 'online deliberation', to probe the notion of citizen deliberation online. Their study examined a large-scale electronic dialogue on American electoral politics and found that individuals who were older, predominantly white, more educated, more politically knowledgeable, interested, and active, and more trustworthy demonstrated the ability to better argue political positions (see also Price and Cappella 2002).

As we near the end of the first decade of the new millennium, enquiries into the nature and possibility for online political deliberation have become much more diverse. But this explicit merging of deliberative democratic and technological interests has by no means been homogeneous. Many have adopted or are influenced by competing normative views of deliberative democracy or, more accurately, competing notions of deliberation in different models of democracy. Some scholars emphasize a Habermasian approach to deliberative democracy. For example, Froomkin (2004) questioned whether new forms of online discourse could achieve what the bourgeois public sphere did in 18th century Western Europe. Despite Habermas's 'tall order' (8), Froomkin argued that the diversity of discursive forms holds promise for the revitalization of public communication.

Others, however, part ways with the notion of the public sphere or proceduralism implied by Habermas. For example, Fishkin's (1997, 2009) Deliberative Poll is concerned with aggregate changes in individuals' political preferences that result from both large and small group discussions. Transferred to an online setting, the design of the D-Poll harmonizes the ideal of group discussion with that of the calculated, opinion-forming individual. Drawing from John Stuart Mill and James Madison, the D-Poll uses aspects of liberal and federalist (i.e., republican) democratic theory as a way to structure—and establish criteria for the evaluation of—online political discussion.

Still others embrace variations on the theme of deliberation in participatory democracy. Shane's (2009) appraisal of empowered participatory governance borrows from Fung and Wright (2003, 2004) to consider the formation, mobilization, and inclusion of citizen-led policy forums in the United States. Meanwhile, Noveck's (2008) writing on wiki-government proposes innovations in direct citizen participation in political decision making, questioning all the while who is considered an expert. Like other approaches to analyzing online political deliberation, Shane's and Noveck's approaches embrace their own brand of deliberative democracy.

The plurality of models for online political deliberation implies different criteria for success or failure. The model of democracy that is instantiated in an online setting influences what types of political behavior will be emphasized, studied, celebrated, or criticized. As Barber (1998) wrote, 'unless we are clear about what democracy means to us, and what kind of democracy we envision, technology is as likely to stunt as to enhance the civic polity'. Thus, the differences between competing models of deliberative democracy 'are not only theoretically crucial, but have radically different entailments with respect to technology' (584-5).

3   A General Purpose Approach to Online Deliberation

Social scientists with a political interest in deliberation constitute only one strand in the evolution of the field of online deliberation. For years, computer scientists, along with cognitive scientists, linguists, social psychologists, information scientists, organizational sociologists, and scholars in management science and engineering have explored deliberation by computers themselves, by people and computers interacting, and by people interacting with each other nonpolitically in computer-mediated environments. There are four main areas of general purpose online deliberation: the design of intelligent computer systems/agents, group decision support software or groupware, computer supported cooperative work, and group learning.

Deliberation by Artificial Agents

The first area of general purpose online deliberation relates to the study of artificial intelligence. As early as the 1950s, computer scientists began exploring the simulation of argumentation in artificial intelligence (AI) systems. As Wooldridge and Jennings (1995) described, computer scientists have long focused their attention on the design and implementation of an 'agent'—a hardware or software-based computer system capable of exhibiting specific types of intelligent behavior.[6] This work has included the design and implementation of deliberative reasoning processes in agents, or in shorthand terms, 'deliberative agents'.[7] Distinguished from reactive agents, which respond directly to inputs rather than engage in complex reasoning

---

[6] A robot serves as a good example here.

[7] Wooldridge and Jennings (1995) explained that, 'The term "deliberative agent" seems to have derived from Genesereth's use of the term "deliberate agent" to mean a specific type of symbolic architecture (Genesereth and Nilsson, 1987, pp325–327).) We define a deliberative agent or agent architecture to be one that contains an explicitly represented, symbolic model of the world, and in which decisions (for example about what actions to perform) are made via logical (or at least pseudo-logical) reasoning, based on pattern matching and symbolic manipulation' (24).

processes, deliberative agents are designed to make autonomous decisions, without the presence of humans.

The link between online deliberation and the deliberative reasoning processes of artificial agents may be difficult to grasp—especially for someone who comes from the deliberative democratic tradition. The types of mathematical formalism used as the basis for agents' programming languages resemble little of the deliberative reasoning processes theorized by deliberative democrats. However, the implementation or instantiation of deliberation is nonetheless integral to the development and refinement of intelligent systems. Work on autonomous agents represents a specific type of online deliberation, where 'online' might be understood in relation to computational logics rather than an electronic public forum or computer-mediated space in which humans interact. The type of online deliberation implied by work on autonomous agents doing complex reasoning is indifferent to the nature of inputs (political or otherwise) into an intelligent system (see also Love and Genesereth 2005).[8]

Group Software

The second area concerns groupware (group collaboration software) and decision or group decision support systems (DSS and gDSS, respectively). Like intelligent computer systems, the design and study of groupware, DSS, and gDSS differs dramatically from the focus of online deliberative democrats. Beginning in the 1960s and 1970s, decision support software was primarily concerned with organizational decision making and interactive computer systems (Power 2003; Keen 1978). GDSS emerged later and was exemplified by computer conferencing, interactive software, and distributed networks, aiding organizations in tasks such as identifying issues, assumption surfacing, brainstorming, aggregating data, modeling, team building, policy writing, voting, and more (Straub and Beauclair 1988; Nunamaker 1989; Gavish and Gerdes 1997).

Although initially this trajectory of scholarship did not use the term online deliberation, some writing on DSS and gDSS nevertheless referred to processes in which individuals and groups discuss, debate, and decide in computer-mediated settings. As early as 1969, Churchman and Eisenberg (1969) had argued for the need to understand deliberation and judgment before 'grinding through a mathematical model or computer algorithm' (53) in order to facilitate organizational behavior. By the 1980s, gDSS scholars

---

[8] Mike Ananny has suggested that the study of embodied conversational agents (see Cassell 2001; Cassell et al. 2000), which use deliberative reasoning processes and which are prevalent in virtual reality environments, also links to the history of non-political deliberation. For space constraints, I have not dealt with them here.

were using the term 'computer-aided deliberation' to explore group decision making within—and across—institutional settings (Kraemer and King 1988; Nunamaker et al. 1988; Nunamaker 1989). Many scholars, however, relied on the more generic expression computer-mediated communication in their treatment of group dynamics in the formation of consensus (Kiesler et al. 1984; Siegel et al. 1986; Watson et al. 1988). Others simply focused on problem solving, decision making, and other forms of group interaction that can be linked to deliberative behavior (DeSanctis and Poole 1994; Poole and DeSanctis 1989).

Computer Supported Cooperative Work (CSCW)

Overlapping with the task orientation of DSS/gDSS, the third area refers to computer supported cooperative work (CSCW) and software-assisted group behavior. As Grudin (1994) explained, CSCW grew out of the interests of an interdisciplinary group of researchers and developers in the dynamics of group activity. CSCW deals predominantly with small groups, not the design and implementation of large group systems that, for example, help automate large corporations and assist in corporate managerial decision making. Applications like 'desktop conferencing and videoconferencing systems, collaborative authorship applications, electronic mail and its refinements and extensions, and electronic meeting rooms or group support systems' (Grudin 1994: 20) were originally included in the CSCW domain.

Although a large field with many areas of specialization, CSCW research and development links to issues of deliberation by virtue of its interest in cooperation. Cooperation requires that individuals identify their positions, beliefs, goals, claims, and so forth, recognize differences, evaluate differences, and eventually act upon them. Some degree of deliberation is involved—both within individuals' own minds, as they decide what to think and how to act—and between individuals as they move forward towards agreement, disagreement, or compromise. In the late 1980s, for example, Conklin and Begemann (1988) studied how a hypertext tool, gIBIS, affected computer system designers through the early stages of their work process, including designers' hierarchical work relationships and the collection and sharing of informal design information. Baecker et al. (1993) explored collaborative writing software in both asynchronous and synchronous settings, paying attention to the different roles participants assume in writing projects.

Group Learning Systems

Finally, in addition to intelligent computer systems, DSS/gDSS, and CSCW, general purpose online deliberation also has roots in theories and practices of group learning, participation, collaboration, and teaching in relation to computational media. Drawing from fields such as cognitive science, philosophy, instructional design, and education, online learning experts are concerned with augmenting processes of human reasoning. The idea of augmentation links back to one of online learning's forefathers, Douglas C. Engelbart. Engelbart's (1962) discussion of 'augmenting human intellect' presaged many of the attempts at designing, developing, and analyzing learning among groups in online settings. Augmentation includes the development and design of technologies for distributed intelligence and computer-supported visualization of argumentation, whereby reasoning processes of individuals are visualized to assist in problem solving, document creation, and other forms of collaboration.

As with online political deliberation, intelligent systems, decision support systems, and collaborative systems, the field of online learning is vast and multi-layered. For example, while earlier discussions of distributed intelligence (Pea 1993) or groupware communities (Engelbart 1992) did not expressly take an interest in deliberation, their work engaged with problems of consensus, collaboration, and knowledge sharing in virtual spaces.[9] Today, that legacy is manifested in a variety of ways, from the use of text-based conferencing systems for deliberation about adult education curriculum by adult literacy stakeholders (Herod 2005) to the benefits of argument mapping tools in professional and educational settings to enhance individuals' ability to present better-founded claims and arrive at the truth. Others have investigated design issues when using argument software to teach deliberation (Easterday, Kanarek, and Harrell 2009).

4 Agents, Applications, Systems

The above treatments of intelligent computer systems, group decision support software, and online learning reveal a complexity in the field of online deliberation across political and more general purposes. The latter type of online deliberation involves educational institutions, transnational corporations, and even less formally organized, but geographically dispersed, groups. By contrast, political deliberation typically occurs in government or civic spaces, where individuals are equated as citizens (or citizens-in-the-making), political decision makers, or political administrators, as opposed to students, teachers, managers, employees, or consumers.

---

[9] For a more explicit discussion of Engelbart's legacy in online learning, see van Gelder (2002).

Types of Online Deliberation

Based on the different intellectual forerunners discussed above, the following represents my classification of both political and general purpose types of online deliberation.

Online *political* deliberation is classified as follows:

A *virtual governmental debate hall* consists of an online space that facilitates the state's consultation of its citizens for political decision making. It is manifested more often than not in the form of an official government website that gather information from citizens and provide information to citizens. Online town halls convened by the state for the purposes of political decision making fall into this category. Examples: Australian Defense Department, Regulations.gov

Given that the state does more than merely consult the public, a *virtual government-citizen space* differs slightly from the agency discussed above. The purpose of this forum is to introduce or welcome the citizen to civic life (at least as it is defined by the state), provide them with information about public services, or connect with other citizens (Friedland 1996; Tsagaroursianou et al. 1998). Examples: community computer networks

A *virtual civil society* centralizes deliberative activity by creating an online space for discussion, debate, learning, and so forth. Here, nongovernmental groups/civil society organizations, rather than governmental agencies, manage deliberative activity.[10] Examples: online Deliberative Polling®, Electronic Dialogues

An *online news media space* also centralizes, manages, and stimulates debate on issues of political importance and informs governmental decisionmaking. Online news media may be unconventional (featuring a devolved, user-driven process of newsmaking) or traditional (exercising control over their editorial process). Examples: BBC Online, NYTimes.com, OhMyNews International

An *online public-private sphere* is another form of online political deliberation, where expressive individuals generate public opinion. Managed by for-profit corporations, these virtual spaces contain design features that facilitate deliberative activity and that transform a virtual private sphere into a public square. Corporate social networking sites and virtual worlds often play host to this type of quasi-public sphere activity. Examples: Facebook, Youtube, Second Life

By contrast, *general purpose* online deliberation includes the following:[11]

---

[10] Though virtual civil society organizations may not be explicitly politicized, they hold the potential to shape and encourage civic behavior (Putnam 1993, 2000).

[11] This list is partly inspired by the work of online learning scholars. See Jonassen et al. (1995).

A *virtual meeting space* allows individuals to access an online environment remotely, asynchronously/synchronously, in an embodied/disembodied manner. The entire space may be expressly designed for deliberation or merely feature tools within the space that can facilitate deliberative behavior. Issues of authority, transparency, and accountability often come into play if this type of virtual environment allows individuals to adopt anonymous or pseudonymous identities. Examples: chatrooms, forums

A *collaborative writing tool* allows a set of individuals working remotely to produce, edit and finalize a piece of writing. Whatever technology is used, collaborative writing can be seen as deliberative to the extent that the group works toward a common objective, dealing, for example, with issues of consensus, transparency, and dissent. Examples: Google Docs, Wikipedia

An *argument visualization tool* refers to a specific feature that can fit into any number of online group decision-making systems. Argumentation visualization helps one to propose arguments, review the reasonableness of claims, and select or support a particular claim based on its reasonableness. For example, in a school environment, argument visualization can be used to help structure a student's learning of reasoning. In a professional (corporate) environment, argument visualization can be used to organize competing viewpoints on work-related proposals (see also Horn 1999). Examples: Reason!able, Austhink

A *preference aggregation tool* is software that collects, processes, and represents/reports individuals' preferences on an item that a group must debate and decide upon. The tool may collect, tabulate, and visualize votes, as with electronic voting systems or modules, and/or rank preferences for others, as in the case of recommendation systems. A preference aggregation tool may also consist of survey/polling and petition software. Examples: eVote/Clerk, PetitionsOnline.com

A *deliberating autonomous agent* refers to an intelligent computer system or component designed to make decisions without the presence of humans. Example: Codex

A Taxonomy of Online Deliberation

From virtual government agencies to collaborative document writing software, from a virtual public-private sphere to a deliberating autonomous agent, the above list of online deliberation types shows that online deliberation includes much more than the instantiation of deliberative democratic ideals.

But how can we better understand these types? Taking its cue from Davies (2009), the following taxonomy categorizes the types listed above into three main groups or levels. The taxonomy allows us to see similarities across deliberative activities that have political and non-political purposes. The taxonomy is summarized as follows:

Level	Description	Examples
Agent	Code for deliberative reasoning tasks of intelligent systems	Deliberating autonomous agents
Applications	Software for deliberative activities used on a variety of platforms	Preference aggregation tool Visualization tool Collaborative writing tool
Systems	A sociotechnical system that coordinates and sustains the overall design, implementation, recruitment, and execution	Virtual meeting space Virtual government debate hall Virtual government-citizen space Virtual civil society Online news media space Online public-private sphere

Table 1. A taxonomy of online deliberation

At the agent level, online deliberation can be understood within a set of tasks executed in an intelligent system. This type of online deliberation involves an agent involved in some form of reasoning, communicating, negotiating, and/or transferring information. It involves interactions that occur within a computer or computer network as well as between computer(s) and user(s).

At the applications level, online deliberation can be understood as a computer program. Important features of this form of online deliberation include: the goals of deliberation, the methods (e.g., moderated/unmoderated discussion, presentation of information, categorization of discussion, voting, ranking), the platform or platforms on which the software operates, the way or modality in which users experience deliberation, the setting in which the software is used, the user populations, and the legal context of software distribution (e.g., proprietary, open source, or free).

At the systems level, online deliberation can be understood as a sociotechnical system that is coordinated or managed by a government institution, news outlet, civil society organization, corporation, educational body, or other institution (or set of institutions). Apart from the question of who manages such a project or endeavor, this level of online deliberation entails choices about the goals of deliberation, the software used to achieve those goals, the platforms that host the online deliberation experience, the modality of the user experience, the way in which participants are recruited, the types of participants being targeted, the context and scale of the user experience, the evaluation of deliberative goals, and the economics and managerial style of the deliberative endeavor.

By describing the systems level in sociotechnical terms, I am not suggesting that social values are absent at the other two levels. By contrast, as the work of social constructionists suggests, technologies have values (Winner 1986). Even with the modeling of deliberative reasoning in autonomous agents, it is plausible that developers encode their own, historically situated understanding of deliberation. However, such values may not come into play as much as they do in the case of software or social-technical systems for online deliberation. Thus, it is important to highlight the human or social element prominently in the description of the systems level.

5   The Future of a Diverse Field

Technologies that enhance deliberation and the social systems that support them are constantly evolving. Today, from the agent to the applications to the systems level, the field of online deliberation features an incredible diversity. Online deliberation can happen inside of software, through software, or in a sociotechnical setting. This last category, in particular, is ripe with variety: online deliberation projects occur in governmental, corporate, educational, civil society, consumer, and other contexts.

The taxonomy presented in this chapter provides us with a glimpse into how deep online deliberation runs. Far from being obscure, forms and practices of online deliberation are part of many of our everyday uses of digital technologies. For example, an autonomous agent operating inside of a computer or within a software program makes determinations about when to act on incoming available information or when to coordinate with other agents. Although deliberative reasoning is occurring, an ordinary user is typically ignorant of these processes.

But in the process of categorizing the different types of online deliberation, does the taxonomy diminish the place and rich history of online political deliberation? Designed to be as broad and accommodating as possible, the taxonomy subsumes political debate and decision making into a larger set of online deliberation projects. The system level groups projects that relate to democracy and political decision making as well as those that do not. From consulting the broad public about state regulations to brainstorming in small groups in a corporate setting, from learning about argumentation in an online classroom to disseminating information to consumers of news, a multiplicity of online deliberation projects exist.

While some might worry that political deliberation does not stand out in such a simple taxonomy, this type of broad categorization allows us to see how different projects or applications compare or translate across different settings or contexts. Already, an open slate exists for those who want to use software that facilitates one or more aspects of deliberative behavior. Users can apply a program to any context they wish—political or not. A simplified taxonomy makes it easier to explore differences in the success of online deliberation, whether tied to political debate and decision making or not. Thus, the taxonomy makes it possible to contemplate where projects or tools for e-democracy, e-government, or online civil society have influenced online deliberation for other purposes, and vice versa.

As participants in many interdisciplinary endeavors have discovered, diversity can be mobilized to advantage. In describing the interdisciplinary laboratory, RADLAB, which generated early thinking and work on the personal computer, Peter Galison (1999) once explained: 'Laboratories are about coordinating action and belief—not about translation' (157). The same might be said about the field of online deliberation as it moves forward. The field of online deliberation may not depend on translating for one another the different backgrounds of designers, scholars, and practitioners for one another and harmonizing the multifaceted interpretations of deliberation *per se*. Although such translation work might occur, a willingness to coordinate actions among designers, scholars, and practitioners— coordination to develop new and better tools or techniques for virtual discussion, debate, and decision making, to create more and richer research instruments to document and assess different software, experiments, projects, and experiences in the virtual world, and to promulgate best practices—is what will propel online deliberation into the future.

References

Arnstein, S. 1969. A Ladder of Citizen Participation. *Journal of the American Planning Association* 35(4): 216-224.

Baecker, R. M., D. Nastos, I. R. Posner, and K. L. Mawby. 1993. *The User-Centred Iterative Design of Collaborative Writing Software*. Paper presented at INTERACT '93 and CHI '93 Conference on Human Factors in Computing Systems, Amsterdam, The Netherlands, April 24-29, 1993.

Barber, B. 1998. Three Scenarios for the Future of Technology and Democracy. *Political Science Quarterly* 113(4): 573-589.

Barbrook, R. and A. Cameron. 1998. *The Californian Ideology* (full version). Available at http://www.hrc.wmin.ac.uk/theory-californianideology-main.html (last accessed January 16, 2009)

Bessette, J. M. 1981. Deliberative Democracy: The Majority Principle in Republican Government. *How Democratic is the Constitution?* eds. R. Goldwin and W. Shambra, 102-116. Washington, DC: American Enterprise Institute.

Bijker, W. E., T. P. Hughes, and T. J. Pinch, eds. 1987. *The social construction of technological systems: new directions in the sociology and history of technology*. Cambridge, Massachusetts: MIT Press.

Bohman, J. 1998. Survey Article: The Coming Age of Deliberative Democracy. *The Journal of Political Philosophy* 6(4): 400-425.

Bohman, J. and W. Rehg. 1997. Introduction. *Deliberative Democracy: Essays on Reason and Politics*, eds. J. Bohman and W. Rehg, ix-xxx. Cambridge, MA: MIT Press.

Carey, J. W. 1992. Communication as Culture: Essays on Media and Society. New York: Routledge.

Cassell, J. 2001. Embodied Conversational Agents. Representation and Intellgence in User Interfaces. *AI Magazine* 22(4): 67-83.

Cassell, J., M. Ananny, A. Basu, T. Bickmore, P. Chong, D. Mellis, et al. 2000. *Shared Reality: Physical Collaboration with a Virtual Peer*. Paper presented at the Conference on Human Factors in Computing Systems, The Hague, The Netherlands, April 1-6, 2000.

Churchman, C. W. and H. B. Eisenberg. 1969. Deliberation and Judgment. *Human Judgments and Optimality*, eds. M. W. Shelley II and G. L. Bryan, 45-53. New York: John Wiley & Sons.

Cohill, A. M. and A. L. Kavanaugh, eds. 1997. *Community Networks: Lessons from Blacksburg, Virginia*. Boston: Artech House.

Coleman, S. and J. Gøtze. 2001. *Bowling Together: Online Public Engagement in Policy Deliberation*. London: Hansard Society. Available at http://www.bowlingtogether.net/ (last accessed January 11, 2009)

Conklin, E. J. and M. L. Begeman. 1988. GIBIS: A Hypertext Tool for Exploratory Policy Discussion. *Proceedings of Computer-Supported Cooperative Work*, 148-52. New York: ACM.

Dahlstrom, D. B. and B. Shanks. 2009. Software Support for Face-to-Face Parliamentary Procedure. *Online Deliberation: Design, Research, and Practice*, eds. T. Davies and S. P. Gangadharan, 213-220. Stanford, CA: CSLI Publications.

Davies, T. 2009. The Blossoming Field of Online Deliberation. *Online Deliberation: Design, Research, and Practice*, eds. T. Davies and S. P. Gangadharan, 1-19. Stanford, CA: CSLI Publications.

Davis, M. 2009. Email-Embedded Voting with eVote/Clerk. *Online Deliberation: Design, Research, and Practice*, eds. T. Davies and S. P. Gangadharan, 325-327. Stanford, CA: CSLI Publications.

DeSanctis, G. and M. S. Poole. 1994. Capturing the Complexity in Advanced Technology Use: Adaptive Structuration Theory. *Organization Science* 5(2): 121-147.

Dryzek, J. S. 2002. *Deliberative Democracy and Beyond: Liberals, Critics, Contestations*. New York: Oxford University Press.

Easterday, M. W., J. S. Kanarek, and M. Harrell. 2009. Design Requirements of Argument Mapping Software for Teaching Deliberation. *Online Deliberation: Design, Research, and Practice*, eds. T. Davies and S. P. Gangadharan, 317-323. Stanford, CA: CSLI Publications.

Engelbart, D. C. 1962. *Augmenting Human Intellect: A Conceptual Framework*. Menlo Park, CA: Stanford Research Institute. Available at http://www.bootstrap.org/augdocs/friedewald030402/augmentinghumanintellect /1introduction.html (last accessed January 12, 2009)

Engelbart, D. C. 1992. *Toward High Performance Organizations: A Strategic Role for Groupware*. Paper presented at the GroupWare Conference '92, San Jose, California, June 1, 1992. Available at http://www.bootstrap.org/augdocs/augment-132811.htm (last accessed January 12, 2009)

Fishkin, J. S. 1997. *The Voice of the People: Public Opinion and Democracy*. New Haven, CT: Yale University Press.

Fishkin, J. S. 2009. Virtual Public Consultation: Prospects for Internet Deliberative Democracy. *Online Deliberation: Design, Research, and Practice*, eds. T. Davies and S. P. Gangadharan, 23-35. Stanford, CA: CSLI Publications.

Fishkin, J. S. 2003. Introduction. *Debating Deliberative Democracy*, eds. J. S. Fishkin and P. Laslett, 1-6. Oxford: Blackwell Publishing.

Friedland, L. A. 1996. Electronic Democracy and the New Citizenship. *Media, Culture and Society* 18: 185-212.

Froomkin, A. M. 2004. Technologies for Democracy. *Democracy Online: The Prospects for Democratic Renewal Through the Internet*, ed. P. M. Shane, 3-20. New York: Routledge.

Fung, A. and E. O. Wright. 2003. Thinking About Empowered Participatory Governance. *Deepening Democracy: Institutional Innovations in Empowered Participatory Governance*, eds. A. Fung and E. O. Wright, 3-42. New York: Routledge.

Galison, P. 1999. Trading Zone: Coordinating Action and Belief. *The Sciences Studies Reader*, ed. M. Biagioli. 137-160. New York: Routledge.

Gavish, B. and J. H. Gerdes. 1997. Voting Mechanisms and their Implications in a GDSS Environment. *Annals of Operations Research* 71(0): 47-74.

Genesereth, M. R. and N. Nilsson. 1987. *Logical Foundations of Artificial Intelligence*. Los Altos, CA: Morgan Kaufmann Publishers.

Grudin, J. 1994. Computer-Supported Cooperative Work: History and Focus. *Computer* 27(5): 19-26.

Gutmann, A. 1985. Review: Communitarian Critics of Liberalism. *Philosophy and Public Affairs* 14(3): 308-322.

Habermas, J. 1989. *The Structural Transformation of the Public Sphere: An Inquiry into a Category of Bourgeois Society* (T. Burger, Trans.). Boston, MA: MIT Press.

Habermas, J. 1990. *Moral Consciousness and Communicative Action* (C. Lenhardt and S. W. Nicholsen, Trans.). Boston, MA: MIT University Press.

Habermas, J. 1993. *Justification and Application: Remarks on Discourse Ethics* (C. Cronin, Trans.). Boston, MA: Massachusetts Institute of Technology Press.

Habermas, J. 1996. *Between Facts and Norms: Contributions to a Discourse Theory of Law and Democracy* (W. Rehg, Trans.). Cambridge, MA: MIT Press.

Herod, L. D. 2005. Online Curriculum Deliberation by Adult Literacy Stakeholders: A Case Study. Doctoral dissertation. Ontario Institute for Studies in Education of the University of Toronto.

Horn, R. E. 1999. *Visual Language: Global Communication for the 21st Century* (1st ed.). Bainbridge Island, WA: Macrovu.

Johnson, S. M. 1998. The Internet Changes Everything: Revolutionizing Public Participation and Access to Government Information Through the Internet. *Administrative Law Review* 50(2): 277-338.

Jonassen, D., M. Davidson, M. Collins, J. Campbell, and B. B. Haag. 1995. Constructivism and Computer-Mediated Communication in Distance Education. *The American Journal of Distance Education* 9(2): 7-26.

Keen, P. G. W. 1978. *Decision Support Systems: An Organizational Perspective.* Reading, MA: Addison-Wesley.

Kiesler, S., J. Siegel, and T. W. McGuire. 1984. Social Psychological Aspects of Computer-Mediated Communication. *American Psychologist* 39: 1123-1134.

Kollock, P. and M. A. Smith, eds. 1996. *Communities in Cyberspace.* New York: Routledge.

Kraemer, K. L. and J. L. King. 1988. Computer-Based Systems for Cooperative Work and Group Decision Making. *ACM Computing Surveys* 20(2): 115-146.

Love, N. and M. Genesereth. 2005. *Computational Law.* Paper presented at the Proceedings of the 10th International Conference on Artificial Intelligence and Law, Bologna, Italy, June 6-11, 2005.

Negroponte, N. 1995. *Being Digital.* New York: Knopf.

Noveck, B. S. 2008. Wiki-Government: How Open-Source Technology Can Make Government Decision-Making More Expert and More Democratic. *Democracy Journal* Winter(7): 31-42. Available at http://www.democracyjournal.org/article.php?ID=6570 (last accessed January 12, 2009)

Nunamaker, J. F. 1989. *Group Decision Support Systems (GDSS): Present and Future.* Paper presented at the Proceedings of the Twenty Second Annual Hawaii

International Conference on Systems Sciences, Kailua-Kona, HI, January 3-6, 1989.

Nunamaker, J. F., L. M. Applegate, and B. R. Konsynski. 1988. Computer-Aided Deliberation: Model Management and Group Decision Support. *Operations Research* 36(6): 826-848.

Pateman, C. 1970. *Participation and Democratic Theory*. Cambridge: Cambridge University Press.

Pea, R. D. 1993. Practices of Distributed Intelligence and Designs for Education. *Distributed Cognitions: Psychological and Educational Considerations*, ed. G. Salomon, 47-87. New York: Cambridge University Press.

Poole, M. S. and G. DeSanctis 1989. *Use of Group Decision Support Systems as an Appropriation Process*. Paper presented at the Emerging Technologies and Applications Track, Proceedings of the Twenty-Second Annual Hawaii International Conference on Systems Sciences, January 3-6, 1989.

Poster, M. 1995. Cyberdemocracy: The Internet and the Public Sphere. Available at: http://www.humanities.uci.edu/mposter/writings/democ.html (last accessed January 19, 2009).

Power, D. J. 2003. A Brief History of Decision Support Systems DSSResources.COM (World Wide Web, version 2.8, May 31, 2003). Available at http://dssresources.com/history/dsshistoryv28.html (last accessed January 11, 2009)

Price, V. and J. Cappella. 2002. Online Deliberation and Its Influence: The Electronic Dialogue Project in Campaign 2000. *IT & Society* 1(1): 303-329.

Price, V., J. Cappella, Y. Tsfati, and J. Stromer-Galley. 2001. *Citizen Deliberation Online: An Examination of Factors Influencing Who Participates*. Paper presented at the annual meeting of the International Communication Association, Washington, DC, May 2001.

Putnam, R. D. 2000. *Bowling Alone: The Collapse and Revival of American Community*. New York: Simon & Schuster.

Putnam, R. D., R. Leonardi, and R. Nanetti. 1993. *Making Democracy Work: Civic Traditions in Modern Italy*. Princeton: Princeton University Press.

Raynes-Goldie, K. and D. Fono. 2009. Wiki Collaboration Within Political Parties: Benefits and Challenges. *Online Deliberation: Design, Research, and Practice*, eds. T. Davies and S. P. Gangadharan, 203-205. Stanford, CA: CSLI Publications.

Rheingold, H. 1993. *Virtual Communities: Homesteading on the Electronic Frontier*. New York: HarperPerennial.

Ristroph, G. 2009. Debian's Democracy. *Online Deliberation: Design, Research, and Practice*, eds. T. Davies and S. P. Gangadharan, 207-211. Stanford, CA: CSLI Publications.

Ryfe, D. M. 2007. Toward a Sociology of Deliberation. *Journal of Public Deliberation* 3(1): Article 3. Available at http://services.bepress.com/jpd/vol3/iss1/art3/ (last accessed January 17, 2009)

Sandel, M. J. 1982. *Liberalism and the Limits of Justice.* New York: Cambridge University Press.

Sandel, M. J., ed. 1984. *Liberalism and its Critics.* Oxford: B. Blackwell.

Shane, P. M. 2009. Turning GOLD into EPG: Lessons from Low-Tech Democratic Experimentalism for Electronic Rulemaking and Other Ventures in Cyberdemocracy. *Online Deliberation: Design, Research, and Practice,* eds. T. Davies and S. P. Gangadharan, 149-162. Stanford, CA: CSLI Publications.

Shane, P. M., ed. 2004. *Democracy Online: The Prospects for Democratic Renewal Through the Internet.* New York: Routledge.

Siegel, J., V. Dubrovsky, S. Kiesler, and T. W. McGuire. 1986. Group Processes in Computer-Mediated Communication. *Organizational Behavior and Human Decision Processes* 37(2): 157-187.

Straub, D. W., Jr. and R. A. Beauclair. 1988. Current and Future Uses of GDSS Technology: Report on a Recent Empirical Study. *Proceedings of the Twenty-First Annual Hawaii International Conference on Systems Sciences, Kailua-Kona, Hawaii,* 149-58. Los Alamitos, CA: IEEE Computer Society Press.

Sunstein, C. R. 1985. Interest Groups in American Public Law. *Stanford Law Review* 38(29): 29-87.

Sunstein, C. R. 2001. *Republic.com.* Princeton, NJ: Princeton University Press.

Sunstein, C. R. 2006. *Infotopia: How Many Minds Produce Knowledge.* New York: Oxford University Press.

Taylor, C. 1992. Cross-Purposes: The Liberal-Communitarian Debate. *Liberalism and Moral Life,* ed. N. L. Rosenblum, 64-87. Cambridge, MA: Harvard University Press.

Taylor, C. 1994. The Politics of Recognition. *Multiculturalism: Examining the Politics of Recognition,* ed. A. Gutmann, 25-74. Princeton, NJ: Princeton University Press.

Tsagaroursianou, R., D. Tambini, and C. Bryan, eds. 1998. *Cyberdemocracy: Technology, Cities and Civic Networks.* New York: Routledge.

van Gelder, T. 2002. *Enhancing and Augmenting Human Reasoning.* Paper presented at the Cognition, Evolution and Rationality: Cognitive Science for the 21st Century, Oporto, Portugal, September 2002.

Watson, R. T., G. DeSanctis, and M. S. Poole. 1988. Using a GDSS to Facilitate Group Consensus: Some Intended and Unintended Consequences. *MIS Quarterly* 12(3): 463-478.

Weber, M. 1949. Objectivity of Social Science and Social Policy. *The Methodology of Social Sciences,* eds. E. A. Shils and H. A. Finch, 49-112. New York: The Free Press.

Winner, L. 1986. *The Whale and the Reactor.* Chicago: Chicago University Press.

Wooldridge, M. and N. R. Jennings. 1995. Intelligent Agent: Theory and Practice. *Knowledge Engineering Review* 10(2): 115-152.

Appendix A: List of Online Deliberation Projects and Applications

ActionApps, http://actionapps.org, Collaborative web publishing tools for non-profits.

Akiva Corporation, http://www.akiva.com/, Collaborative web publishing tools for corporate and non-profit organizations.

AmericaSpeaks, http://www.americaspeaks.org/, Non-profit organization that coordinates in-person and online citizen forums on political issues in the United States.

Australian Department of Defense, http://www.defence.gov.au/consultation2/index.htm, Australian public consultation to inform the future of the country's defense system.

BaseCamp, http://basecamphq.com/, Collaborative project management software tools.

Beyond Yes, http://consensuspolling.org/, Online polling tool that visualizes the process or movement towards group consensus.

Breaking the Game, http://www.workspace-unlimited.org/breakingthegame/index.htm, Game environment that encourages deliberative problem-solving for political and non-political issues.

ByDesign/eLab*, http://www.bydesign-elab.net, Research and design organization interested in participatory online public spaces.

Canadian Community for Dialogue and Deliberation, http://www.c2d2.ca, Canadian-based organization focused on offline and online dialogue to build a culture of deliberation.

Citizenscape, http://www.citizenscape.wa.gov.au/index.cfm?event=publicTips, Western Australian governmental portal that provides opportunity for information-gathering, public consultation, and civic engagement.

City of Kalix, http://www.votia.com, Government project in Kalix, Sweden, to coordinate offline and online public consultation.

City of Tampere, http://www.tampere.fi, Government project in Tampere, Finland, to coordinate offline and online public consultation.

Civic Action Network, http://www.civicactionnetwork.com, Wiki-book that details strategies for activists in online and offline settings.

CivicEvolution, http://civicevolution.org/, Website that invites users to formulate and present political problems and propose solutions.

Co-Intelligence Institute, http://www.co-intelligence.org/P-groupware.html, Website that aggregates information about social software.

Community People, http://www.communitypeople.net/, British-based company that sets up online consultation, polling, communication, calendar, collaboration and discussion forums, and more.

CommunityWiki, http://www.communitywiki.org/cw/WikiDrama, Experimental wiki to explore, support, and structure debate by requiring participants to adopt characters or archetypes as a more efficient means of arriving at consensus.

Consensus Group, http://www.usemod.com/cgi-bin/mb.pl?ConsensusGroup, Wiki that models different behaviors (e.g., silence) as consensus.

Conversate*, http://www.conversate.org/, Software tool for creating and managing online discussion.

Cooperation Commons, http://www.cooperationcommons.com, Online forum for coordinating collaboration among different disciplines interested in solving social dilemmas.

County of North Jutland, http://www.nordpol.dk/, E-government website and online discussion forum that provides election and political information to and debate among citizens of the council of Northern Jutland, Denmark.

Cybervote, http://www.eucybervote.org, Research project to develop and experiment with internet voting software in Europe.

Daum Deliberative Democracy Project, N/A, Portal website set up for 2004 Korean General Elections.

David Miliband Ministerial Blog*, http://www.davidmiliband.defra.gov.uk, Website for former British minister, David Miliband, that pioneered online dialogue among constituents.

DCLG Forum, http://forum.communities.gov.uk, Main site for online public consultation and dialogue between local politicians and citizens in the United Kingdom.

Debatepedia, http://debatepedia.com, Wiki tool to organize debate on political issues.

Debatepoint, http://www.debatepoint.com/, Software tool that organizes arguments in order to facilitate consensus-making for political and non-political issues.

Debian, http://www.debian.org, Website for coordinating decision-making structures and packaging open source software projects into a single, freely-distributed operating system.

Decisions, http://decisions.gnuvernment.org/, Website that discusses development of (Drupal-integrated) software for group decision-making.

Delib, http://www.delib.co.uk/, Software tools for online dialogue and participation in government and civil society in the United Kingdom.

Deliberative e-Rulemaking Decision Facilitation Project, http://www.deer.albany.edu, A research experiment funded by the National Science Foundation to generate better and more effective public input in federal agency government rulemakings.

Deme, http://www.groupspace.org, http://deme.stanford.edu, Web-based platform being developed at Stanford University to facilitate online deliberation.

Democracies Online, http://dowire.org, Listserv started by Steven Clift to discuss e-democracy and online deliberation.

Demo-net, http://www.demo-net.org, Research network that studies online political participation in Europe.

Denmark National IT and Telecom Agency, http://www.danmarksdebatten.dk, Danish e-government project.

Department for Transport Road Safety Webchat, http://www.dft.gov.uk/roadsaftey/webchat, British e-government site for discussion on transport safety.

Dialogue Circles, http://www.dialoguecircles.com, Company that assists non-profit associations, corporations, and government in developing and implementing online and offline dialogue and consultation.

Digital Dialogues, http://www.digitaldialogues.org.uk/, Research project to study the use of online technologies for public consultation in the United Kingdom.

Digital Document Discourse Environment, http://d3e.sourceforge.net/, Document management tool that helps facilitate collaboration among contributors.

Dito, http://zeno8.ais.fraunhofer.de/zeno/web?rootid=21449&journal=21449, Software tool for content/document management.

Drupal, http://drupal.org/, Content management software developed mainly for and by political activists and community organizers.

Dutch Centre for Political Participation, http://www.publiek-politiek.nl/english, Non-partisan organization that works with governments and non-governmental groups in the Netherlands and elsewhere to encourage debate, citizen participation, and political knowledge.

EGovBlog, http://www.egovblog.com, Blog that aggregates information about worldwide practices in e-government.

e-Liberate, http://clients.rocket51.com/e-Liberate/about/, Software being developed by Computer Professional for Social Responsibility to facilitate online meetings-- either real-time or asynchronous.

Energy Technology Futures, http://www.nrcan.gc.ca/es/etf/, Canadian e-government site for energy technology.

Environmental Protection Agency, http://www.epa.gov, Website for American environmental regulatory agency that has innovated with online public consultation.

Envisioning Governance*, http://beyondvoting.wikia.com/wiki/Envisioning_ Governance, Project to design software for community governance.

e-Petitions, http://petitions.pm.gov.uk/about, British e-government site that allows citizens and civil society organizations to generate and deliver online petitions to the Prime Minister.

European Youth Parliament/FCO Forum, http://www.eyptalk.net, Online forum related to the European Union's Youth Parliament.

eVote/clerk, http://www.deliberate.com/, Software tool that embeds polls into email or other internet-based software.

Extreme Democracy, http://www.extremedemocracy.com, Website/discussion forum for activists interested in new ways of practicing democracy.

Family Courts Forum, http://www.familycourtsforum.net, http://www.ofcf.net, British e-government site for adult and youth discussion of reforming family court system.

Fax Your MP, http://FaxYourMP.com, British e-government site that helps citizens send fax communciations to government officials.

FSA Chief Scientist Blog, http://www.fsascience.net, British e-government blog on food standards.

Games for Change, http://www.gamesforchange.org/, Organization that supports foundations and non-profit organizations interested in using the digital game environment for social change purposes.

Global Peoples Assembly, N/A, Hypothetical online forum for discussion of global issues.

Global Voices, http://www.globalvoicesonline.org, Aggregator site of internationally-focused, citizen-generated blogs.

Green Party of Canada/Living Platform, http://lp.greenparty.ca/tiki-index.php, Wiki for the Canadian Green Party to create its core document on environmental issues.

GroupServer, http://groupserver.org/, Community-oriented collaboration system for managing online discussion.

Group Systems, http://www.groupsystems.com, Software that assists groups in problem identification, problem solving, and consensus formation.

Hansard Society, http://www.democracyforum.org.uk, http://www.publicevidence.net, http://www.hansardsociety.org.uk/eDemocracy.htm, British organization that stimulates interest in and knowledge of democracy and helps research and organize online deliberation and e-government projects.

Hermes, http://www-sop.inria.fr/aid/hermes/table.html, Argumentation system for discussion on the Web.

Human Sciences, http://humansciences.com.au/, Company that assists local Australian government in public consultation.

HTML Gear, http://htmlgear.lycos.com/specs/poll.html, Free polling software.

ICQ, http://www.icq.com, Free instant message/chat tool.

Ideascale, http://www.ideascale.com, Crowdsourcing software tool that facilitates brainstorming, discussion, and decision making.

Ikonboard, http://www.ikonboard.com/, Free forum software.

iLogos, http://www.ilogos.com/en/expertviews/webinars/RFP/, Prototype software for classroom use to visualize processes of argumentation.

Independent Media Center(s), http://www.indymedia.org, Open publishing-based news site with anti-corporate globalization origins.

Information Renaissance*, http://www.info-ren.org, Organization that promoted participation in electronic government by assisting governments and non-profit groups in the United States to use networking technology.

Inteam, http://www.inteam.com, A suite of tools to assist groups in brainstorm, decision making, document creation, file sharing, and general project comunication.

International Teledemocracy Centre, http://www.teledemocracy.org/ourwork/our-work-projects.htm#consultations, http://www.teledemocracy.org, Research organization that studies technology-enabled democratic discussion and decision making.

Iperbole, http://www.comune.bologna.it, E-government website for the city of Bologna, Italy.

IPS Community, http://www.invisionboard.com/, Free forum software.

Issue Congress, N/A, Hypothetical tool for online discussion.

Issue Deliberation Australia, http://www.ida.org.au, Australian-based research organization that studies and conducts offline and online deliberation.

Jurat, http://www.juratcanada.com/, For-profit company that designs and implements tools for engaging groups in stakeholder discussion and decision making.

Kettering Foundation, http://www.kettering.org, Organization that facilitates offline and online deliberation on political issues in the United States.

Knowledge Forum, http://www.knowledgeforum.com, Online conferencing platform for educators.

Law Commission Forum, http://forum.lawcom.gov.uk, Website for public consultation on legal reform in England and Wales.

Limehouse Software, http://www.limehousesoftware.com/, A suite of tools to assist groups in collaborating, meeting, publishing, and creating documents.

Listening to the City Online Dialogues*, http://dialogues.listeningtothecity.org/, Project of the Civic Alliance and Web Lab to conduct online town hall meetings concerning design plans for Ground Zero (New York).

Mailman, http://www.list.org/, Free software to manage electronic discussion lists and e-newsletter lists.

Meatball Wiki, http://www.usemod.com/cgi-bin/mb.pl?MeatballWiki, Wiki that provides information exchange and discussion about tools for online organizing.

medi@komm*, http://zeno.gmd.de, E-government website for the city of Esslingen, Germany.

MeetingWorks, http://meetingworks.com, Meeting software.

MeetUp, http://www.meetup.com, Website based in the United States that helps likeminded individuals meet, share interests, and/or participate in similar causes.

Microsoft Windows NetMeeting, http://www.microsoft.com/downloads/details.aspx?FamilyID=26c9da7c-f778-4422-a6f4-efb8abba021e&displaylang=en, Videoconferencing software that runs on VoIP on versions of Microsoft Windows (from Windows 95 OSR2 to Windows XP).

MSP Resource Portal, http://portals.wi.wur.nl/msp/?Links, Dutch website that aggregates resources for participation and deliberation on issues related primarily to agriculture and water.

National Coalition for Dialogue and Deliberation, http://thataway.org/index.php/?cat=32, Organization that facilitates offline and online deliberation on political issues in the United States.

Neighborhood America, http://www.neighborhoodamerica.com, For-profit company that designs and implements online consultation projects for government and corporate clients.

NetAid, http://www.netaid.org/, Website that centralizes information about fighting global poverty.

NewAssignment.net, http://www.newassignment.net, News site that facilitates collaboration among journalists.

Obiki, http://obiki.org/, Software to create websites and documents for groups. Serves for-profit companies as well as government, educational institutions, and civil society groups.

OhMyNews, http://ohmynews.com, Korean-based citizen-generated news site.

Online Deliberative Polling®, http://cdd.stanford.edu, Social science experiment run by the Center for Deliberative Democracy at Stanford University to study political deliberation.

Online Public Disputes Program*, http://www.publicdisputes.org, Organization that provided technologies and facilitation to mainly government agencies conducting public consultation, convening expert panels, or engaging group decision making.

ONS Small Area Geography Policy Review Blog, http://www.onsgeography.net, British e-government site for discussion on neighborhood statistics.

OpenACS, http://openacs.org/, Open source software tools for building scalable, community web-oriented applications.

OPEN (Seoul Online Procedures ENhancement for Civil Applications)*, http://open.metro.seoul.kr/, A Web-based system established by municipal government in Seoul, Korea, that took advantage of process-tracking software to assist citizen monitoring of corruption-prone applications for permits and approvals.

Open Government Initiative, http://www.whitehouse.gov/open/, Website for citizens to learn about as well as collectively brainstorm, propose, and create federal policy related to open government initiatives.

OpenFlow, http://www.openflow.it/EN/index_html, Free software for workflow or project management.

Open Text Corporation, http://opentext.com, For-profit company that helps clients manage content systems.

OpenSpace, http://www.openspace-online.com, For-profit company that provides technology and facilitation for online meetings and collaboration.

Parliament, N/A, Software tool for managing online meetings according to Robert's Rules of Order.

Participatory Politics Foundation, N/A, Organization which runs OpenCongress, an online tool to track Congressional bills as they move through Congress.

Partnerships Online*, http://www.partnershipsonline.org.uk, Website that contains information for civil society practitioners interested in learning more about and accessing tools for online discussion and facilitation, and participation in electronic government, and more.

Party Funding Review Forum/Webchat, http://forum.partyfundingreview.gov.uk, http://chat.partyfundingreview.gov.uk, British e-government site for discussion on party funding.

Peer to Patent, http://peertopatent.org, Developed by the New York Law School Institute for Information Law and Policy in cooperation with the United States Patent and Trademark Office, an e-government project that enables the public to submit prior art and commentary relevant to the claims of pending patent applications in Computer Architecture, Software, and Information Security (TC2100).

Perlnomic, http://perlnomic.org/, Experimental game in which rules are adjudicated by Perl code.

Phorum, http://www.phorum.org, Open source message board system written in php.

phpBB, http://www.phpbb.com/, Open source software for developing online forums.

phpGroupware, http://www.phpgroupware.org/, Free software that facilitates content management, forums, email, and more.

Planning Portal Forum, http://www.planningportalforum.net, British e-government site that facilitates communities and local governments' online information, dialogue, and decision-making on planning and building.

Plone, http://plone.org/, Open source software for content management.

PoliticalSim, http://www.accuratedemocracy.org/s_sim.htm, Game that enables users to simulate the experience of deliberation in an online environment.

Politalk, http://politalk.org, Non-partisan discussion forum for political issues

Politika Latvia, http://www.policy.lv, Independently-run website that centralizes, organizes, and offers public policy debate in Latvia.

PostNuke, http://www.postnuke.com/, Open source content management tool.

Project PICOLA (Public Informed Citizen Online Assembly), http://caae.phil.cmu.edu/picola/, Software tool that creates multimedia environments for online structured dialogues or meetings.

Public Agenda, http://www.publicagenda.org, Organization that produces information about political issues in the United States.

Public Voice Lab*, http://www.pvl.at/solutions/ediscours/, Website that operated as a free software coop, distributing or alerting (mostly e-government related) software to its members.

QuickTopic, http://www.quicktopic.com/, Online forum/discussion that can be integrated into email and that is used for document collaboration.

Rationale, http://rationale.austhink.com/, Software that diagrams reasoning and argument.

Regulations.gov, http://www.regulations.gov, Website run by the United States government to facilitate public engagement in the rulemaking system.

Samretano 1.0, http://www.sammondano.org/products.html, Open source software tools for non-profit organizations that allow users to vote, rate, categorize, create, and organize collective knowledge.

Scoop, http://scoop.kuro5hin.org/, Software tools that facilitate content management and build bulletin boards and blog capability.

Slashcode, http://www.slashcode.com/, Website that collaboratively manages revisions and development of open source/free software for news posting and discussion.

Source d'Europe*, http://www.info-europe.fr/debat, French-European Union e-government project in early 2000.

Stackoverflow, http://www.stackoverflow.com, Website that allows programmers to collaboratively publish and tag questions and answers to programming questions and rank users that provide answers

Study Circles, http://www.studycircles.org, Organization that facilitates offline and online deliberation on US political issues.

SurveyMonkey, http://www.surveymonkey.com, Tool for designing, implementing, and analyzing online surveys.

Synanim, http://www.synanim.com, A for-profit internet-based service that offers clients enhance their cooperative and leadership capacities.

Tagsonomy, http://www.tagsonomy.com, Blog that talks about issues regarding classification or tagging.

Tana Otsustan Mina *, http://tom.riik.ee/, Estonian e-government project from early 2000.

The Blogora*, http://blogora.wetpaint.com/, A wiki-based discussion platform where users can discuss controversial political issues as well as the design of online dialogue

The Young and Fresh, N/A, Message board for a private corporation.

TikiWiki, http://tikiwiki.org/, Free software tool that enables content management.

Truth Mapping, http://www.truthmapping.com, Website that deconstructs arguments to facilitate reasoning processes, discussion, and rating of social and political issues.

UK Opening Politics, http://www.uk.openingpolitics.org/index.php? title=Deliberative_structure, British-based wiki that allows individuals to edit arguments and opinions of different political issues.

Unchat, http://www.unchat.com, Project that structures face-to-face communication in an on-line environment to enable real-time moderation and collaboration.

USENET, http://groups.google.com/, Decentralized discussion system featuring a variety of topics created in 1979 and now archived on Google.

Vacheland, http://vacheland.playmoa.com/, Simulated game environment created French Agricultural Ministry to teach people, particularly youth, about issues concerning the cattle industry.

Values Exchange, http://www.values-exchange.com, New Zealand-based website that invites visitors to debate on topics of social concern.

Vivarto-Nornorna, http://www.vivarto.com/tiki-index.php?page=Nornorna, Online conferencing software that facilitates group decision-making.

Web Lab*, http://www.weblab.org, Organization started in 1997 to discuss, design, implement, and fund online dialogue projects for non-profit and government groups in the United States.

Wikimocracy, http://www.wikimocracy.com/, Website where a user can weigh in, contribute to, add, delete, and/or modify topics of controversial nature.

Windows Meeting Space, http://www.microsoft.com/windows/downloads/default.aspx, Replacement for Windows NetMeeting, this software allows filesharing and set-up of ad hoc conferences provided that users are running Windows Vista.

Wornex World Director, http://www.demos-project.org, Hamburg-based project of the European Union to develop e-government, facilitate citizen-politician debate.

Wordle, http://www.wordle.com, Free visualization tool for analyzing word frequency of Web pages.

XML Gov, http://xml.gov, Software for virtual government.

Xoops, http://www.xoops.org/, Free software tool for content management.

YackPack, http://www.yackpack.com, A patented, voice-based interface that facilitates group communication

YouthNoise, http://www.youthnoise.org, A website for youth that includes news and information related to youth issues and that includes an online discussion forum for young people.

*No longer operating or site is unavailable.

Name Index

359

Subject Index

accountability, 151, 160, 245, 248-249, 339

administration, administrators (political), 13, 158, 163-164, 168, 177, 338

administration, administrator (system), 74, 76, 157-158, 168, 235, 246, 269, 312, 326

Administrative Procedure Act (APA), 135, 143, 145

adversarial (debate, activity), 108, 113, 152-156

agents (autonomous, deliberative, reactive), 330-331, 334-335, 337, 339, 340-341

AJAX paradigm, 288, 297

anonymity, 14-15, 37, 43, 53, 111, 225, 227, 229-230, 243-249, 327, 332, 339

Antifederalist, 24

argument mapping, argument software, argument visualization, 17, 317-322, 337, 339

asynchronous discussion, 14, 72-73, 75-76, 78, 154, 158, 203, 210, 233, 279, 283, 303-304, 312, 314, 336, 339

Back-office domain, 13, 177-190

biased assimilation, 107

Blacksburg Electronic Village, 124-125, 127

blog(s), blogging, bloggers, blogosphere, weblog(s), 6, 83-84, 95-96, 112-114, 124, 126-127, 136, 181, 193, 195, 349, 351-2, 354, 356-357

Canada, 13-14, 177-190, 203-205

cartographers, critical, 262-263

censor, censorship, 15, 83, 205, 233-241

Citizens First, 124

citizen participation, 13, 71, 125, 134, 158, 171-173, 178, 193, 330, 333-351

citizen relationship management, 163-164

Citizen Space's E-democracy Forum, 234, 240

civic deliberation, 16, 293-301

civic education, 19, 59, 65

civic engagement, 4, 10, 40, 52-54, 159, 195-196, 276, 348

civic space, civic commons, 234, 337

civil society, 153, 178, 294, 296, 338, 340, 342, 350

369